Marketing Techniques for Financial Inclusion and Development

Dhiraj Jain
Symbiosis International University (Deemed), India

Adya Sharma
Symbiosis International University (Deemed), India

A volume in the Advances in Marketing, Customer Relationship Management, and E-Services (AMCRMES) Book Series

IGI Global
DISSEMINATOR OF KNOWLEDGE

Published in the United States of America by
IGI Global
Business Science Reference (an imprint of IGI Global)
701 E. Chocolate Avenue
Hershey PA, USA 17033
Tel: 717-533-8845
Fax: 717-533-8661
E-mail: cust@igi-global.com
Web site: http://www.igi-global.com

Library of Congress Cataloging-in-Publication Data

Names: Jain, Dhiraj, 1971- editor. | Sharma, Adya, 1972- editor.
Title: Marketing techniques for financial inclusion and development / Dhiraj Jain and Adya Sharma, editors.
Description: Hershey : Business Science Reference, [2018] | Includes bibliographical references.
Identifiers: LCCN 2017027621| ISBN 9781522540359 (hardcover) | ISBN 9781522540366 (ebook)
Subjects: LCSH: Finance--India. | Financial literacy--India. | Social integration--India. | Finance--Developing countries. | Financial literacy--Developing countries. | Social integration--Developing countries.
Classification: LCC HG187.I4 M47 2018 | DDC 332.1068/8--dc23 LC record available at https://lccn.loc.gov/2017027621

This book is published in the IGI Global book series Advances in Marketing, Customer Relationship Management, and E-Services (AMCRMES) (ISSN: 2327-5502; eISSN: 2327-5529)

British Cataloguing in Publication Data
A Cataloguing in Publication record for this book is available from the British Library.

Advances in Marketing, Customer Relationship Management, and E-Services (AMCRMES) Book Series

ISSN:2327-5502
EISSN:2327-5529

Editor-in-Chief: Eldon Y. Li, National Chengchi University, Taiwan & California Polytechnic State University, USA

MISSION

Business processes, services, and communications are important factors in the management of good customer relationship, which is the foundation of any well organized business. Technology continues to play a vital role in the organization and automation of business processes for marketing, sales, and customer service. These features aid in the attraction of new clients and maintaining existing relationships.

The Advances in Marketing, Customer Relationship Management, and E-Services (AMCRMES) Book Series addresses success factors for customer relationship management, marketing, and electronic services and its performance outcomes. This collection of reference source covers aspects of consumer behavior and marketing business strategies aiming towards researchers, scholars, and practitioners in the fields of marketing management.

COVERAGE

- Electronic Services
- Relationship marketing
- E-Service Innovation
- Telemarketing
- Social Networking and Marketing
- Data mining and marketing
- Cases on CRM Implementation
- B2B marketing
- Ethical Considerations in E-Marketing
- Customer Relationship Management

IGI Global is currently accepting manuscripts for publication within this series. To submit a proposal for a volume in this series, please contact our Acquisition Editors at Acquisitions@igi-global.com or visit: http://www.igi-global.com/publish/.

The Advances in Marketing, Customer Relationship Management, and E-Services (AMCRMES) Book Series (ISSN 2327-5502) is published by IGI Global, 701 E. Chocolate Avenue, Hershey, PA 17033-1240, USA, www.igi-global.com. This series is composed of titles available for purchase individually; each title is edited to be contextually exclusive from any other title within the series. For pricing and ordering information please visit http://www.igi-global.com/book-series/advances-marketing-customer-relationship-management/37150. Postmaster: Send all address changes to above address.

Titles in this Series

For a list of additional titles in this series, please visit:
https://www.igi-global.com/book-series/advances-marketing-customer-relationship-management/37150

Analyzing Attachment and Consumers' Emotions Emerging Research and Opportunities
Giuseppe Pedeliento (University of Bergamo, Italy)
Business Science Reference • ©2018 • 308pp • H/C (ISBN: 9781522549840) • US $185.00

Building Brand Identity in the Age of Social Media Emerging Research and Opportunities
Amir Ekhlassi (University of Tehran, Iran) Mahdi Niknejhad Moghadam (Sharif University of Technology, Iran) and Amir Mohammad Adibi (University of Tehran, Iran)
Business Science Reference • ©2018 • 189pp • H/C (ISBN: 9781522551430) • US $145.00

Neuromarketing and Big Data Analytics for Strategic Consumer Engagement...
Joana Coutinho de Sousa (Unlimited-Hashtag, Portugal)
Business Science Reference • ©2018 • 200pp • H/C (ISBN: 9781522548348) • US $165.00

Holistic Approaches to Brand Culture and Communication Across Industries
Sabyasachi Dasgupta (O.P. Jindal Global University, India) Santosh Kumar Biswal (Symbiosis International University, India) and M. Anil Ramesh (Siva Sivani Institute of Management, India)
Business Science Reference • ©2018 • 281pp • H/C (ISBN: 9781522531500) • US $225.00

Multi-Platform Advertising Strategies in the Global Marketplace
Kenneth C. C. Yang (The University of Texas at El Paso, USA)
Business Science Reference • ©2018 • 377pp • H/C (ISBN: 9781522531142) • US $205.00

Digital Marketing Strategies for Fashion and Luxury Brands
Wilson Ozuem (University of Gloucestershire, UK) and Yllka Azemi (Indiana University Northwest, USA)
Business Science Reference • ©2018 • 460pp • H/C (ISBN: 9781522526971) • US $210.00

Exploring the Rise of Fandom in Contemporary Consumer Culture
Cheng Lu Wang (University of New Haven, USA)
Business Science Reference • ©2018 • 300pp • H/C (ISBN: 9781522532200) • US $225.00

For an entire list of titles in this series, please visit:
https://www.igi-global.com/book-series/advances-marketing-customer-relationship-management/37150

IGI Global
DISSEMINATOR OF KNOWLEDGE

701 East Chocolate Avenue, Hershey, PA 17033, USA
Tel: 717-533-8845 x100 • Fax: 717-533-8661
E-Mail: cust@igi-global.com • www.igi-global.com

Editorial Advisory Board

List of Reviewers

Table of Contents

Detailed Table of Contents

innovation, and setting up new businesses and the like. One of the latest objectives of present day banks was financial inclusion as efforts taken before had not proved very fruitful. The RBI therefore has introduced the concept of differentiated banks where it intends to issue licenses for specialized banks like small and payment banks, infrastructure banks, and so on so that the banks could develop specialized skills and affect greater financial penetration so that the overall objective of financial inclusion could be met. The guidelines have been issued for the first kind of differentiated banks—small and payment banks—and applications have been invited for the same. Though the RBI has taken a very conservative approach for different kinds of banks to co-exist, it may prove to be a step in the right direction and help in greater financial inclusion.

Customer ownership is a new practice that seeks integration and customer loyalty. In this chapter, the authors try to analyze this hybrid status to deepen ties between the customer and the company. To this end, they developed, initially, a comparative study between the customer and shareholder mutualism to identify the similarities and differences between the two models. Secondly, they tried to analyze the role of the client in creating value by using the stakeholder theory. Finally, they dealt with the possibilities and limitations of the client as shareholder loyalty means.

An inclusive financial system has been the major agenda of the Indian government over the past few years and several steps have been taken in this direction. The main purpose of the study is to assess the effectiveness of financial inclusion initiatives taken by Rajasthan government. A questionnaire was drafted and was sent to people from weaker section of the society who have been the beneficiaries of the financial inclusion initiative of the government. Research methodology adopted for the study includes descriptive statistics and one-way ANOVA was used to test the association/non-association between the variables. The study concluded towards lack of awareness and usage of financial inclusion initiatives, especially internet, mobile banking, and credit card. In terms of experience with financial services, respondents were positive towards interest on loans and help received by banking staff with respect to documentation and identification norms as well as branch timings. However, distance from the bank and the availability of ATM was an issue for them.

In today's switching economy, customers' needs are changing and they are demanding more transparency, higher involvement, and clear communication in day-to-day banking processes. The rationale behind carrying out the present research is to identify the role of customer analytics in the new digital customer journey in terms of enhancing their engagement, loyalty, and satisfaction. The present research emphasizes opportunities that would accrue to financial institutions after demonetization and collecting large amount of demographics, customer transaction, and account-related data. Primary data was collected from 300 customers through a structured questionnaire to know their perceptions about the role of customer analytics and digital technologies to build their confidence and capability to use financial services. This study brings out the customer analytics trends and identifies the reasons due to which banks are struggling to keep pace with the increasing demand of both digital savvy and traditional consumers.

According to the RBI governor, technology-enabled financial information will spread financial literacy in an efficient and secure manner. India needs inclusive growth to pull millions out of poverty and mobile phone penetration can be a good opportunity. Consumers are exposed to a plethora of financial products but the knowledge is either not there or limited to make judicious choices. The successful implementation of financial literacy services would benefit rural people but it is a challenge to all stakeholders today. One-hundred twenty-five people all over India were selected for a survey and results point that rural poor accept mobile technology for banking related information but do not want to adopt the technology. There are various challenges for financial literacy in India discussed in the chapter. Also, opportunities are many for digital literacy and can be achieved if the challenges are overcome. All the stakeholders should put in concerted efforts at all levels to achieve financial inclusion through mobile technology disruption.

This chapter focuses on researching the consumer awareness of people towards financial inclusion by conducting a study on Mahanagar Co Op Bank in Kharghar, Mumbai. The study adopted survey method to approach the respondents through a well-structured questionnaire. Stratum sampling method was used in order to select the sample respondents and collect data from those who are consumers of Mahanagar Co Op Bank Ltd, Kharghar Branch. A sample size of 150 consumers was taken. Following the data search, analysis was done by applying descriptive analytical tools like standard deviation and mean. The researcher used factor analysis, descriptive statistics, and one-way ANOVA in order to find the difference among the variables. SPSS software has been used for conducting the analytical tests. The results indicated an association between demographic variables and awareness and availing of financial inclusion services by the consumers of the bank. However, there was no association between demographic variables and some of the financial inclusion services.

Financial institutions, especially banks, have proved to be a boon for the economic development of a country like India. An attempt has been made in the present chapter to analyze the state of financial inclusion and the role of banking in achieving full financial inclusion in India. The journey of financial inclusion through banking in India has been critically appraised. Some of the important outcomes that can be highlighted are increased banking access of rural population in past few years together with the huge expansion in banking infrastructure in rural areas. Banking in India has been transformed with the introduction of PMJDY, BC Model, etc. Increasing trend has been observed in IMPS and M-Wallet penetration. North-eastern part of the country is still a challenge in the way of financial inclusion. The journey of financial inclusion on the wheels of Indian banking industry is still in search of the ultimate destination, and it will take miles to achieve full financial inclusion.

Preface

INTRODUCTION

Financial inclusion has been one of the most propagated ideologies in countries and significant efforts have been taken to nurture a financially included society. A financially included society would not only help develop a better society but also help in transferring the needed benefits to the end user. Various financial institutions and societies have taking steps in different forms for financial inclusion and have also been marketing their initiatives with varying successes and penetration. The following book has been a sincere effort to understand the Marketing techniques adopted by various financial institutions and societies for promoting financial inclusion initiatives for the development of the society at large.

ORGANIZATION OF THE BOOK

Mr. Varun Rajan in his study tried to study (Chapter 1) how personal banking evolved and how the ulterior motive to a financially included society became the objective of the evolution of personal banking. He looked at Financial Inclusion from a customer's point of view and how various factors helped in brining every individual to the finance and the banking industry. He found that the pace and energy of progress was not abating but rather expanding supported and abetted by mechanical changes in correspondences and data innovation.

Dr. Dhiraj Jain and Mr. Vijay P. Misra in their study (Chapter 2) talked about how the central banks have a major role to play in their financial inclusion initiatives. They talked about the differentiated banks (payment banks and small banks) being set up with a single objective of spearheading financial inclusion and how are their initiatives better marketed and spread across so that the society could make use of those initiatives. They used examples of various countries where these kinds of initiatives have been successful in having a greater financially included society.

Dr. Sara Elouadi, Dr. Rachid Elotmani (Chapter 3) attempted to analyze a new managerial practice using essentially the stakeholder theory and the mutual model, which had several similarities with client shareholding. They deplored the laconic character of the empirical literature as they felt only a few studies had been carried out on the subject of customer ownership and recognition.

K. Sanal Nair and Ms. Saumya Jain (Chapter 4) in their study concluded that the awareness and the usage level of the weaker sections of the society was only towards Loans, debit cards (used as ATM card more often), cash transaction cheques and Kisan Credit Card. The awareness towards the technological means of financial inclusion was severely lacking specially among females on account of their social structure, lack of proper internet facilities as well as slow speed was also adding to the problem. The authors found that the banking staff helped the beneficiaries in following procedures such as documentation and identification norms. The authors further found that proper internet facilities and free wifi-connectivity could further aid in generating awareness and technological usage levels. They concluded that this would not only help in attaining the goal of financial inclusion but also of a cashless economy.

Mr. Yuvraj Sharma (Chapter 5) identified that most of the companies across the world were currently in the early stage of big data planning and execution. Lack of budget, technology dependable partners and absence of unified vision were the main issues facing the industry. The study explored opportunities for financial institutions on customer transactions and account related data. He found that customer analytics and adoption of digital technologies could play an important role in terms of improving customer experience and provide insights about customers. He concluded that in order to provide quick attention to customer needs, maintaining large database and monitoring over services delivered to rural and unbanked areas, new generation analytics could be beneficial for financial institutions in developing nations like India.

Dr. Smriti Pathak and Dr. Shreya Virani (Chapter 6) in their study wanted to find if financial literacy was important for using mobile technology and if people were ready to adopt banking services using mobile phones. They found that adequate measures need to be taken to discuss with the rural people about the importance of financial literacy and security issues regarding their data for banking purposes. It would help to improve inclusive growth. They found that there were various challenges and opportunities for digital literacy in India, but for real inclusion concerted efforts at all levels only could help to achieve financial inclusion. She found that the initiatives aimed at creating an ecosystem to support people for banking services daily.

Dr. Juan Bernardo Amezcua, Dr. Alicia De la Peña, Dr. Arturo Briseño, Dr. Alfredo Sánchez-Aldape, Dr. Juana María Saucedo-Soto and Prof. Alicia Hernández-Bonilla (Chapter 7) in their study concluded that mobile bank services and the use of digital platforms represented a great opportunity for traditional banks to appeal to the youngest segment of the millennials. Selling financial products and services through the digital world allowed to establish affordable prices that could ensure that many of these young adults started using financial instruments properly. Fintech tools could may help to include those young adults not using any financial services or those who were "underbanked" in the formal financial system.

Dr. Deepa Pillai, Dr. Ravi Kumar VV (Chapter 8) through their study gave various recommendations for a stronger financial inclusion. They vouched for collaborations amongst financial service providers, gram panchayats and technology service providers, integration using technology as a tool, customization of financial products, formation of Business Correspondent groups across demographic profiles, standardizing an approach for evaluating financial literacy and identifying the barriers to enable financial choices, creating financial education program life cycles, using gaming technologies on mobile phones for sensitizing the youth to real life situations and making informed financial decisions, creating financial education program life cycle, focusing on enhanced financial learning's at different life stages of an individual rather than one time learning, provisioning of Interactive multilingual voice response based training facility on mobile phones for financial products & wealth management, designing multilingual simulation games parallel to schools and colleges curriculum based on the concept of money, savings and banking. They found that Self Help Groups(SHGs) could act as financial intermediaries at the rural level for marketing of retail bank products such as savings, micro credit, micro insurance, payments and remittances facilities. They finally concluded that the financial inclusion initiatives should be interpreted in a relative dimension, the degree of financial inclusion would differ depending upon the state of economy and the stage of development exposing banks and financial institutions to diverse cliques of challenges for catering to the weaker sections of the economy.

K. Sanal Nair and Ms. Garima Gupta (Chapter 9) had different implications for various stakeholders and helped understanding the level of consumer awareness among the various target groups and associated them to future revenues as well.

Dr. Abhineet Saxena, Dr. Ashish Sharma (Chapter 10) found that the banking industry was definitely a backbone of the Indian economy and talked about the various initiatives taken by the government and stated that there was an urgent need to fast-track the financial inclusion initiatives especially for the rural people with improved and advanced banking. They concluded that the journey of financial inclusion which is on the shoulders of Indian banking industry was still in search of an ultimate destination and would take miles to achieve a fully financially included society.

Ms. Richa Sawhney (Chapter 11) found the areas that required attention of the government and had to be accordingly examined. She concluded that a financial exclusion of MSMEs needs a multi-dimensional approach. Apart from all the other government initiatives, tax laws were playing a significant role in this direction. By using "a carrot and a stick approach" they were maneuvering the informal sector businesses towards the formal economy, where formal sources of finance and credit would become a reality.

Ms. Pooja Sharma (Chapter 12) concluded that it was time that financial inclusion came out of the shadow of charity to became a viable and sustainable business case for banks and financial institutions. Only then could it be viewed with a marketer's lens and made customer-centric! She extracted certain crucial learnings out of her whole study which various stakeholders could adopt.

Mr. Vaibhav Misra Dr. Anubha Vashisht, Ms. Parul Tolani, Dr. Kushendra Mishra (Chapter 13) concluded that the dwelling in slums and factors affecting openings of bank accounts under the Pradhan Mantri Jan Dhan Yojna (PMJDY) had a positive relationship. They found that behavior of the bank employee had a high impact over the customers while opening a bank account under the PMJDY scheme. Other factors had low effect on the slum customers' opening a bank account under the PMJDY scheme as compared to the past experiences of the peer group and behavior of the bank employees, except for the location of the bank. They found that the location of the bank had a minimum effect on the slum customers in opening bank accounts.

Dr. Rahul Vyas and Dr. Nidhi Nalwaya (Chapter 14) in their study concluded that SHGs were a prospective mechanism for self-employment which lead to growth of micro enterprises in any region and the micro credit system worked as an integral part thereof. Micro enterprises contributed significantly to the economic growth, social stability and the resultant financial inclusion of the members. SHGs could help in the growth of micro enterprises and income from micro enterprises could provide for better amenities: be it in the perspective of food, housing, health care or education for families. Micro Enterprises and SHGs were key to Rural socio-economic transformation and expansion of micro enterprises through SHG and micro credit system had led to the financial inclusion of a vast rural population which in turn significantly helped in eradicating poverty.

Acknowledgment

This book would not have been completed without the support of many people who helped make this a reality.

Our sincere thanks to all the authors who contributed with their expertise, knowledge and time. The advice and guidance given by our reviewers was equally valuable in making this book a quality edition. We also acknowledge the extra efforts put by many authors who contributed both as authors and reviewers of some chapters.

Our heartfelt thanks to the IGI Global team who supported and guided us with the book right from the beginning at every stage. Their supervision was instrumental in completing the different phases of this journey.

Our thanks to Symbiosis International University for providing an environment that encourages research and intellectual discussions.

The project would not be complete without the support of our families. Our appreciation, love and thanks to them for being so supportive and understanding.

Last but not the least—Thank you God for your blessings.

Dhiraj Jain
Symbiosis International University (Deemed), India

Adya Sharma
Symbiosis International University (Deemed), India

Chapter 1
Boundless Banking:
The Role of Evolution in Personal Banking for Financial Inclusion in India

Varun Rajan
Symbiosis International University, India

ABSTRACT

This chapter covers the evolution and growth of the personal banking industry (i.e., banking for customers) and its role in leading to financial inclusion. Since the personal banking industry deals with making banking an ease for customers. The chapter will emphasize the various milestones in the personal banking industry that were significant to improve and increase financial inclusion in India. Personal banking has come a long way from paper formats to now fully computerized formats and this all has been a boon for all customers in the banking industry in India. The chapter looks at the evolution of regulation, technological innovation, and customer acceptance as modern delivery systems outpaced the old. The research article's emphasis is on how the customer has found it easier to perform personal banking transactions over time.

INTRODUCTION

"The term 'financial inclusion' was used for the first time in April 2005 in the Annual Policy Statement presented by Y.Venugopal Reddy,the then Governor, Reserve Bank of India."Financial Inclusion is the process of making financial services available to all easily and Personal Banking has a major role in this process. This is because, as the name suggests "Personal" Banking helps in catering to each and

DOI: 10.4018/978-1-5225-4035-9.ch001

every individual in the country which will help in Financial Inclusion. Financial Inclusion will eventually lead to the growth and development of the country.

Later on, this concept gained ground and came to be widely used in India and abroad. While recognizing the concerns in regard to the banking practices that tend to exclude rather than attract vast sections of population, banks were urged to review their existing practices to align them with the objective of financial inclusion. Even though this term was first used in April 2005 Personal Banking has provided a base for implementing Financial Inclusion. Personal Banking has evolved significantly especially over the four decades. Personal Banking has offered various services to the consumers which were not available earlier which has made finance and banking very affordable, secure and safe. If Personal Banking had not evolved at such a rapid pace it would be difficult to implement Financial Inclusion that easily.

Like any human generational change, personal banking too has embraced change over the last four decades. While banking regulators gave the initial impetus, information technology (IT) and the communications revolution in India spurred the growth of personal banking sector to its present incarnation. The paper will look to cover these various stages which are a compilation of events that made personal banking a friendly and time-saving process to help encourage Financial Inclusion. Presented here are the milestones that helped the personal banking sector to where it is today.

- **The Passbook Period (Paper Formats):** This includes the initial stage of banking when it was a very slow and tedious process. But this was still important to help the banking industry to reach where it is currently.
- **The Transisition Into Technology:** Since there was a need for improving the flow of money and speed of transactions this stage will cover the steps taken for the purpose of the same
- **Cash Cache:** These are the various services and features of the personal banking industry which are major attractors helping in Financial Inclusion. The paper will also cover a lot of marketing strategies used by banks here in the various services they provided . Eg: ATM, MICR, CTS, Debit and Credit Cards
- **Wonderful Web:** This is the process of using the internet
- The Future to Financial Inclusion

All these stages will be covered in a way to show their importance and role in Financial Inclusion. The paper will also show various marketing strategies employed by Financial Institutions, Regulatory Bodies in the various stages to encourage Financial Inclusion. The Marketing strategies which were used by the above mentioned are very significant to help to enroll each and every individual possible

The paper will also cover recent trends in Marketing Strategies for Financial Inclusion in the Personal Banking Industry to show the importance and significance of each marketing strategies in the various stages of Marketing.

The Passbook Period (Paper Formats)

This is the initial phase of banking in India and this is the way all banking processes were conducted at that time. It was very different from the current banking industry. The Banking industry has moved on a lot from this to where it is now thanks to institutions, rise of technology, and efforts for Financial Inclusion through marketing.

Individual saving money was a dull procedure then. Take, for instance, pulling back cash from a bank. In any case, one needed to remain in a line with either a check or withdrawal slip. When you achieved the leader of the line, the agent at the bank would discover your record, physically enter the exchange, put the withdrawal instrument on that page and pass on the record to a senior director. You, thus, would get a numbered token, which was to be submitted at the clerk counter. In the mean time, the senior administrator would check your mark and pass on the withdrawal instrument to the clerk. Your token would then be called by the clerk and you would in the long run get your cash. For your very own record, every one of the exchanges were recorded in a Passbook.

The entire procedure had many imperfections. Your record could as of now be being used since it had more than 100 different records. Staff overseeing counters would regularly disappear. Passbooks were frequently taken and kept by the bank and must be gathered later after updation. To top it everything, it could take an hour to get your cash, and possibly more toward the start of the month, when pay rates were credited. Also, mind you, you could just bank at the branch where you had opened your record and not at some other branch of a similar bank.

The exchange of cash was similarly tedious. In the event that one issued a check, it could take 3-5 days before it got credited into the beneficiary's record in a similar city. For outstation checks, it could take 7-10 days or more for the cash to reach. What's more, top of it, a few banks set a charge for issuing outstation checks. Be that as it may, change was around the bend.The pace of money exchanges was moderate and repetitive and along these lines there was a requirement for better devices in individual managing an account to build the fulfillment of bank clients.

Financial Inclusion

- There was minimal financial inclusion due to the above flaws mentioned but at least it was a start.
- Even though the process was slow and tedious at least there was a particular infrastructure set up for the same.

- This infrastructure just had to be developed framed and moulded to reach where it is now.

The Transition Into Technology

Clearly, there was a squeezing need to expand the speed of cash stream for individual managing an account clients. What's more, the stimulus originated from the Reserve Bank of India.

In 1984, the nation's national bank set up the Committee on Mechanization in the Banking Industry. Its proposals included:

- Banks should set up service branches at centres where they have more than 10 branches. The service branch so set up would exclusively be devoted to clearing operations of the bank at that particular centre.
- Banks to be in readiness for the introduction of MICR Clearing at the four metropolitan cities by assessing their requirements for encoders, adopting standardised cheque forms and reorganising work procedures where necessary, and training staff down to the branch level (Rangarajan, 1984).

According to information available on

In the first phase of computerisation spanning the five years ending 1989, banks in India had installed 4776 ALPMs (Advanced Ledger Posting Machines) at the branch level, 233 mini computers at the Regional/Controlling office levels and trained over 2000 programmers/systems personnel and over 12000 Data Entry Terminal Operators. The Reserve Bank too had embarked upon an ambitious program to bring about state-of-the-art technology in the clearing process and had introduced MICR clearing at 4 centres and computerized clearing settlement at 9 centres. (Kannan, n.d.)

Based on this success, yet another committee was set up by the Reserve Bank of India, the Committee on Computerisation in Banks, in 1989. Its recommendations included:

- Computerisation of the settlement operations in the clearing houses managed by Reserve Bank of India at Bhubaneshwar, Guwahati, Jaipur, Patna and Thiruvananthapuram.
- Operationalisation of MICR technology and the National Clearing of inter-city cheques at the four metropolitan cities.

- Introduction of one-way collection of cheques drawn on the 4 metros received from Ahmedabad, Bangalore, Nagpur and Hyderabad.
- Framing of Uniform Regulations and Rules of Clearing Houses.
- Branch level computerisation and the establishment of connectivity between branches.
- Improvements in customer service - introduction of on-line banking.
- Standardisation and rigorous security features to ensure an efficient and risk free transfer of funds electronically.
- Setting up a network of Automated Teller Machines (ATMs) in Mumbai. ATMs to be strategically located at airports, railway stations, hospitals, important commercial centres, as well as bank branches, to be used by the customers to perform a variety of functions such as deposits, withdrawals, balance enquiries, statement of accounts etc., at any point of time during the day.
- Introduction of a single 'All Bank' credit card and advocated the need for its widespread acceptance by merchant establishments and usage by customers to reduce the load on cash and cheque transactions. Rangurarajan, 1989)

Looking back, three basic terms in the suggestions set the pace for individual managing an account to be more quick and forward-looking – web based saving money, ATMs and Mastercard.

Another obstacle were the managing an account unions who felt undermined by the robotization of banks. In any case, after extended arrangements, the Indian Banks Association (IBA) speaking to bank administrations and the exchange unions touched base at a settlement in 1993. It proclaimed a noteworthy achievement in the presentation of automated applications and advancement of correspondence systems in Banks.

At the end of the day, the RBI recognized the way that the passbook framework is a moderate and repetitive process. They issue proposals to utilize new innovation for advantage of bank clients.

Cash Cache

Automated Teller Machines

The introduction of ATMs in the early 1990s marked a major change for the personal banking industry. While foreign banks and private banks were first of the block (due to the restrictions on the number of branches imposed on them), they were soon followed by the public sector banks.

At first, ATMs were popular as cash dispersing machines. With the aid of bank-issued ATM Cards, one could only withdraw money from ATMs of banks where one had a banking relationship. For example, State Bank of India (SBI) customers could only take out money from SBI ATMs. However, as networking evolved banks came interconnected and inter-bank use of the ATM became the norm (with the restriction of free withdrawals from your non-bank ATMs).

The number of ATM installations in India has seen an explosive and exponential growth in India. The compounded average growth rate (CARG) was 29% in the period 2005-2010 and expected to be 34% in the period 2010-2016. In sheer numbers, it meant that the installation of base of 16,750 in 2005 increased to 60,153 in 2010 and was expected to touch nearly 175,000 in 2015. (Hota, 2013)

While dispensing cash was the first function of the ATM, technological revolutions would enable to perform various other tasks. However, from the personal banking perspective, the introduction of the ATM represented a cataclysmic change. It brought personal banking out of the branch and nearer to the customer.

Financial Inclusion ATMs

Money being an overwhelming method for executing in India, ATMs introduced in remote areas can guarantee that the holders of the PMJDY records can pull back the endowments credited into their records, through the ATMs. Banks can likewise empower video-teller benefits on the ATMs for monetary training or understanding client questions. From the banks' point of view, in the short and center term, however the ATM channel is a successful channel to benefit the clients going under budgetary consideration, setting up and running ATMs doesn't come modest and is not bother free. Control insufficiency, terrible streets, poor system network, absence of satisfactory supply of ATM fit cash notes, peace issues and so on makes it exceptionally troublesome for banks to run their ATM channel ideally. Outsourcing of these exercises by banks to ATM Managed Service Providers (MSPs, for example, FIS, who are currently dealing with a substantial number of ATMs in India, has diminished the operational bothers and cost for banks and aided in the extension of ATMs in the remote corners of the nation. Notwithstanding, the foundation and operational issues listed above, keep on being a reason for worry for the MSPs.

While exchanges through the versatile and web have the potential and have as of now began making little commitments to the 'less money economy' targets of the Government and the RBI, the significance of ATMs can't be de-underscored, even in the medium term. ATMs can actually, make accessible the fuel for quickening the budgetary consideration handle. This needs support from the strategy producers in the Government and RBI as far as extra financing being made accessible for ATM arrangements, clear controls on interoperability of stores and money preparing, change in the influence, street and system foundation and so forth. The Committee on Medium Term Path for Financial Inclusion set up by RBI has prescribed the utilization of the Rs.2000 crore Financial Inclusion Fund overseen by NABARD, for conveying ATMs in the semi-urban and rustic regions. In the event that actualized, it would most likely give a noteworthy lift to monetary incorporation. The Government ought to likewise consistently move all installments of sponsorships and concedes straightforwardly to the records of the recipients. This will boost banks to send more ATMs. However, in the event that the above does not occur in the close here and now, entire money related incorporation by 2020 might be a far off dream. (Financial Inclusion Labs, 2016)

Marketing Strategies for ATMs

Budgetary organizations that don't use their ATMs as showcasing channels chance missing chances to alleviate the quickening decrease of direct ATM income and gainfulness. Consider the income openings introduced by supplanting the "Please hold up" screen with promoting messages.

Things being what they are, in what manner can ATMs be transformed into devotion and showcasing vehicles that can improve client connections? Different promoting strategies can be connected that may help transform the ATM into a benefit focus. Cases include:

- **Customization:** Through exchange personalization choices, clients can preset their inclinations for the sorts of exchanges they need to perform and the data they need to get, which prompts sentiments of customized connections and faithfulness.
- **Mark Fortification:** ATM screen illustrations and informing can be made reliable with the money related foundation's other promoting channels, strengthening messages with every ATM exchange.
- **Strategically Pitch Open Doors:** One-to-one focused on informing by means of an ATM can bring about higher reaction rates than from other advertising channels. Also, monetary establishments have the chance to strategically pitch to non-clients who utilize the money related foundation's ATMs.
- **Client Information:** Marketing projects can be refined much further to target clients in view of client data and particular reactions (i.e., client information) caught at the ATM.
- **Fetched Investment Funds:** ATM advertising efforts can be more affordable to make and circulate than showcasing through customary direct channels.
- **Publicizing:** Some budgetary establishments have banded together with neighborhood dealers to send ATMs in their areas, offering coupons and different motivations to drive ATM movement and increment shipper ticket sizes.

Example: Advertising by *Kotak Mahindra Bank* – Kona Kona Kotak for ATMs implying that they have set up ATMs in each corner of the country.

Personal Banking becomes easier for cash withdrawals with the advent of ATMs. All the features and functions provided by the banks during this period were all helpful for bank users. It made life for bank users easier as they could do all these functions from anywhere at anytime (ATM Market Place, 2010)

Credit Cards

Personal Banking brought another jump with the presentation of charge cards. Despite the fact that they were presented in the mid 1980s, it wasn't till 10 years after the fact that their fascination began meeting their potential. On the off chance that you met some budgetary conditions, banks would issue you a Mastercard with a recommended restrain. The banks had tie-ups with charge card organizations like Visa, Mastercard and Diners, for instance, to present to you the administration.

At to start with, Mastercards were restricted to withdrawal of money and for shopping at retail locations. Installments could be made later to charge card organizations at settled dates or later dates at a rate of intrigue. This proclaimed the 'purchase now, pay later' culture among bank clients. All the more essentially, individual saving money now brought the idea of here and now credits into its ambit.

It is fundamentally here and now unsecured credits which is exceptionally useful for a few people who require cash dire. This is for individuals who might need to purchase something who might not have money at that specific time or have not gotten their compensation, installment yet.

Marketing Strategies Used by Banks for Credit Cards

- Offer to previous platinum card clients
- Leave no client with practically nothing
- Secured Cards
- Offering credit-based items to customers, for example, credit protection or credit observing
- Contracts with Hotels, Restaurants and different dealers for extraordinary offers.
- Dissemination of Card Readers to little retailers, Groceries, Luxury great shops having lasting.
- Clients could utilize their current card as opposed to applying for and convey another card. (Merkle Inc., 2017; Subrashanka, 2014)

Debit Card

Many Indian customers shun the idea of debt. Enter the Debit Card. It signaled the movement away from the cash-based economy to an easier system for purchases. Essentially, a debit card allows you to withdraw cash or purchase goods or services by directly debiting your bank account. Not only did it keep spending habits in check but more importantly it got rid of the need to keep large piles of cash in your wallet. It is estimated that by 2017, debit cards will constitute nearly 90% of all card usage in India. (Wizbowski, 2014)

People do not like to keep a lot of cash in hand because it is not secure. Debit card users can swipe for any product or service they want to buy at anytime. The money will directly be deducted from the bank account.

Wonderful Web

The Bank Comes Home

Putting money on the Internet has upset individual managing an account as it conveyed the bank to your home. There is no need of holding up in lines or acclimating to bank hours any more, you can get to your financial balance online at whatever time you need. It helps one to keep a tab on their cash even once a day. By watching out for your assets one generally realizes what is happening in your record.

Account Information is one of the capacities given by web based managing an account. This gives a rundown of your financial balances. It likewise permits simple following of past exchanges. One can likewise enquire about their record adjusts and exchange cash starting with one record then onto the next if necessary. This is additionally helpful to check their bank account and furthermore to pay of credits if necessary. This data is accessible at whatever time online which is an aid to all record holders. Individuals can likewise request an E-proclamation which incorporates all exchanges which have happened amid a specific timeframe.

Paying for Services Online

With banks and clients associated, the following intelligent stride was to finish the triangle with specialist co-ops to make life simpler for clients. On account of the Internet, a wide assortment of service bills and intermittent installments can now additionally be made straightforwardly with a push of a catch.

By utilizing the "Pay Bills" office, purchasers can pay every one of their bills from their PC. This spares time and furthermore head out cost to various specialist organizations. In addition, it fills in as a connection between the specialist organizations and the purchasers and advantages them two. Phone Bills, Electricity Bills, Internet/Landline Charges are a couple of normal cases that can all be paid on the web. A standing guideline can likewise be made to pay these bills at a specific date on every month. Protection Premium and charge card bills can likewise be paid straightforwardly to the particular insurance agencies or banks. (CIBC, n.d.; Shodhganga, n.d.).

ECS

ECS is an electronic mode of payment / receipt for transactions that are repetitive and periodic in nature. ECS is used by institutions for making bulk payment of amounts towards distribution of dividend, interest, salary, pension, etc., or for bulk collection of amounts towards telephone / electricity / water dues, cess / tax collections, loan installment repayments, periodic investments in mutual funds, insurance premium etc. Essentially, ECS facilitates bulk transfer of monies from one bank account to many bank accounts or vice versa.

- **ECS Credit:** ECS Credit is utilized by associations as an apparatus to pay workers or financial specialists having their ledgers in various areas. It was presented by RBI and enables client to specifically get their compensation, benefits, profit and enthusiasm into their financial balance. The ECS credit installments can be started by any individual who needs to make a great deal of installments to recipients. The client needs to give subtle elements of the recipients and the exchange sum, date when it must be finished. This is known as the credit-push office and is partitioned in parts of the year like quarterly half yearly or month to month.
- **ECS Debit:** ECS Debit is utilized by an association for raising charges to countless (for example, shoppers of utility administrations, borrowers, financial specialists in common supports and so forth. It is valuable for installment of phone, power charge water bills, cess/assess accumulations, advance portion reimbursements, occasional interests in shared assets, protection premium and so forth., It can be utilized by any individual who needs to get or gather enormous sums from an expansive number of individuals. It deals with programmed charge to client accounts on due dates. Clients don't have to monitor when they have to pay their bills. It additionally spares time and cash. It is known as charge – push –facility or many to one and installment can be effectively made through foundations either corporate or government (Rajan, 2008; RBI, 2012).

NEFT and RTGS

National Electronic Fund Transfer (NEFT) and Real Time Gross Settlement (RTGS) allow individuals, companies and firms to transfer funds from one bank to another. You can check the RBI website for a list of NEFT and RTGS-enabled branches of your bank. These facilities can only be used for transferring money within the country. To opt for these, you need to fill a form providing your or the beneficiary's details — name, bank branch where the account is held, the Indian Financial System Code, a unique code for identifying the branch, and the account number and type. You have to submit a cheque while opting for this facility. You can also transfer funds through net banking. These are third-party transfers and the option is available under the same header on your net banking home page. (Gupte, 2011)

Financial Inclusion for Digital Payments

National Payments Corporation of India (NPCI) has assumed a noteworthy part in forming the money related administrations scene with the usage of numerous installment activities, for example, RuPay, Automatic Clearing House, electronic clearing framework (ECS), Aadhaar-empowered installment frameworks and Immediate Payment System (IMPS).

Managed push from the RBI has been continuously sharpening its rules around BCs, versatile keeping money and exchange security to guarantee that purchaser assurance is not traded off with the expanding range of saving money benefits on the back of innovation. This has enabled banks to alter their plans of action and grow reach to the unserved districts of the nation without bringing undue dangers into the framework. (Reserve Bank of India, n.d; RBI: Scripts: Annual Report Publications, 2014)

Mobility Through Mobile Phones

The advent and rapid growth of mobile phones in India offered another platform for banking services using the Internet medium. Nearly all banking applications on PCs and laptops soon found their way to the mobile phone. In other words, all Internet Innovations were now ported to the smartphone.

According to 2011 figures, a mere 7 percent of Indian customers used Internet banking. Mobile banking has also been on a low-volume high-growth trajectory - the user base in 2013 was 22 million, up 74 percent over the previous year, though transaction value grew 228.9 percent over the same period. (Mallya, 2014)

Moreover, mobile banking increases the depth and breadth for personal banking services. Especially in rural areas where the number of phones easily outnumber computing devices.

The mobile platform helps more consumers to enter as one can bank from anywhere as well as everyone has smartphones and an internet network with the emergence of 3G and 2G.

Financial Inclusion in Mobile Banking

These days, more than 60 percent of the populace is in control of a cell phone. This incorporates a huge segment of the provincial populace. Individuals have begun understanding the esteem, accommodation and simplicity of owning a cell phone. Versatile saving money has proved to be useful in view of next to zero framework cost to the bank and no extra venture from clients. So this might be a helpful channel where the vast majority of the populace is unbanked. Cell Phone, a Personal Device, which expands security however Second Factor Authentication, may likewise be included. On contrasting portable managing an account and branch saving money and web saving money versatile, portable keeping money could be most available with least cost of administrations

Mobile Banking can improve your clients' accommodation:

- Sparing time and cost: every minute of every day access to record movement anyplace
- Enhancing control: subsidize exchanges, online bill installment and redid alarms for low adjusts
- Expanding security: push notices and alarms to anticipate extortion

Enhance Your Mobile Banking Strategy

Utilizing portable managing and account methodologies, banks have a staggering chance to build the quantity of relationship touch-focuses they have with their clients. Versatile keeping money reveals interesting chances to:

- Present new saving money items
- Increment strategically pitch and up-offer
- Trigger customized associations with clients

The devices are accessible today to create new income streams by means of versatile and to interface with qualified and checked clients and prospects so you can make in-the-minute offers on their terms.

We can see the exponential growth in mobile banking transactions from FY 2012 TO FY 2016 in mobile transactions from a value of 1800 Rs crore and volume of 26 million to value of 103000 Rs Crore and volume of 172 millions(Live Mint, 2015)

The Future of Financial Inclusion

While data innovation and correspondences innovation will keep on driving client cordiality and convenience of individual managing an account administrations, new gadgets would make new stages for the conveyance of these administrations. While the PC and tablet enabled clients to work out of their home, the versatile helped them in betting moving. Different developments are additionally making progress.

Take for instance, biometric ATMs. Presented only two or three years back, it is making quick advances in provincial regions, where lack of education is high. Villagers can now utilize their thumbprint rather than a PIN number to get to their financial balances. Add this to the Prime Minister Narendra Modi's drive to grow the profundity of financial balances to achieve each Indian and additionally the Aadhar Card's biometric database, individual managing an account is balanced for a jump in provincial India.

However another breakthrough in individual keeping money is being crossed with the presentation of the Digital Mobile Wallet. It is basically a cell phone that enables a person to effectively subscribe to and peruse through many administrations, including installment cards, offers, vouchers, steadfastness projects, tickets and different things they require in their day by day lives. The wallet will likewise have the capacity to dispatch an application from a retailer, bank, transport administrator or another specialist co-op.

The following stop lies with Artificial Intelligence (AI). Take, the savvy for instance. Include voice acknowledgment offices. So later on, you can talk into your watch and say "Exchange Rs. 50,000 to mother". The AI in your watch will make an interpretation of the message into an individual cash exchange benefit and execute the request. A couple of minutes after the fact, a message from mother, "Thanks child". A long ways from the time you live in or your folks lived in.

CONCLUSION

At the end of the day it is a mix of various factors like the marketing strategies in the personal banking industry, the role of regulatory bodies in enhancing Financial Inclusion and their steps in making a platform for Personal Banking, the global rise of technology without which all this would not be possible. The paper is looking at Financial Inclusion from a customer point of view and how the various factors mentioned above have helped involving each and every individual in the finance and banking industry.

From passbooks to passwords, individual saving money has made some amazing progress in current reformist India. In any case, the pace and energy of progress is not abating but rather expanding step by step, supported and abetted by mechanical changes in correspondences and data innovation. Which at last for the individual keeping money will just outcome in more client decision and client enchant

REFERENCES

ATM Market Place. (2010, June 28). *ATM Market Place: Articles*. Retrieved from ATM Market Place: https://www.atmmarketplace.com/articles/changing-atm-strategies-to-increase-revenue-opportunities/

CIBC. (n.d.). *CIBC Advice Centre*. Retrieved from CIBCC: https://www.cibc.com/ca/student-life/banking-101/intro-to-banking/benefit-online-bnkng.html

Financial Inclusion Labs. (2016, April). *Financial Inclusion Labs*. Retrieved from Financial Inclusion Labs: http://www.fisfilab.com/2016/04/atms-as-access-enablers-to-financial-inclusion/

Gupte, M. (2011). *Articles: Business Standard*. Retrieved from Business Standard: http://www.business-standard.com/article/pf/what-are-neft-and-rtgs-111053100076_1.html

Hota, J. (2013). *Publications: Researchgate*. Retrieved from Researchgate: http://www.researchgate.net/publication/235436177_Growth_of_ATM_Industry_in_India

Kannan, R. (n.d.). *E-Banking: Kannan Personal*. Retrieved from Kannan Personal: http://kannanpersonal.com/inbank2/e-banking/rbi-role.html

Live Mint. (2015, September 21). *Live Mint: Money*. Retrieved from Live MINT: http://www.livemint.com/Money/5f8BrGcfJG8mO6Iwdz6TCN/Newage-banking-increases-the-ambit-of-financial-inclusion.html

Mallya, A. (2014). *Finacle: Infosys*. Retrieved from Infosys: http://www.infosysblogs.com/finacle/2014/10/the_evolution_of_banking_chann.html

Merkle Inc. (2017). *Merkle Inc: Industry Solutions: Financial Services*. Retrieved from Merkle Inc: https://www.merkleinc.com/industry-solutions/financial-services/payments-and-credit-card-marketing

Rajan, P. (2008). Payments in India Going the E-way. Bangalore: Celent.com.

Rajan. (1984). *Publications: Reserve Bank of India*. Retrieved from Reserve Bank of India: http://www.rbi.org.in/scripts/PublicationsView.aspx?id=162

Rangarajan. (1989). *Publications: Reserve Bank of India*. Retrieved from Reserve Bank of India: http://www.rbi.org.in/scripts/PublicationsView.aspx?id=162

RBI. (2012). *FAQS: RBI*. Retrieved from Reserve Bank of India: http://www.rbi.org.in/commonman/english/scripts/FAQs.aspx?Id=205

RBI: Scripts: Annual Report Publications. (2014, August 21). Retrieved from Rbi: https://www.rbi.org.in/Scripts/AnnualReportPublications.aspx?Id=1127

Reserve Bank of India. (n.d.). *RBI: Scripts*. Retrieved from RBI.ORD: https://rbi.org.in/scripts/bs_viewcontent.aspx?Id=2598

Shodhganga. (n.d.). *Inflibnet: Shodhganga*. Retrieved from Shodhganga: http://shodhganga.inflibnet.ac.in/bitstream/10603/2031/13/13_chapter%204.pdf

Shyam, M. (2013). *Finacle: Solutions: Thought Papers: Documents: Infosys*. Retrieved from Infosys: http://www.infosys.com/finacle/solutions/thought-papers/Documents/Evolution-of-cheques-and-paper-based-clearing-in-India.pdf

Simplydecoded. (2012, 11 3). *Business and Economics: SimplyDecoded*. Retrieved from Simply Decoded: http://www.simplydecoded.com/2012/11/03/what-is-micr/

Subrashanka. (2014, February 4). *slideshare*. Retrieved from https://www.slideshare.net/bobsubhrasankha/marketing-credit-card

Wizbowski, R. (2014, March 21). *Articles: Datacardedge*. Retrieved from Datacardedge: http://datacardedge.com/articles/debit-cards-emerging-growth-opportunities-banks-india/

Chapter 2
Payment Banks and Small Finance Banks:
A Route to Better Financial Inclusion?

Dhiraj Jain
Symbiosis International University (Deemed), India

Vijay Prakash Misra
Symbiosis International University (Deemed), India

ABSTRACT

Banking in India has taken various forms and has undergone severeral reforms as and when the markets needed. Because of the growing need, the banks today not only strive for greater profits but also have various social targets like the priority sector lending, setting up various branches in the rural areas, extending loans, encouraging innovation, and setting up new businesses and the like. One of the latest objectives of present day banks was financial inclusion as efforts taken before had not proved very fruitful. The RBI therefore has introduced the concept of differentiated banks where it intends to issue licenses for specialized banks like small and payment banks, infrastructure banks, and so on so that the banks could develop specialized skills and affect greater financial penetration so that the overall objective of financial inclusion could be met. The guidelines have been issued for the first kind of differentiated banks—small and payment banks—and applications have been invited for the same. Though the RBI has taken a very conservative approach for different kinds of banks to co-exist, it may prove to be a step in the right direction and help in greater financial inclusion.

DOI: 10.4018/978-1-5225-4035-9.ch002

INTRODUCTION

Banks have evolved over a period of time. They have moved from catering industrialists, big businessmen and persons of high net worth to the masses living at the bottom of the pyramid. The expansion of the bank branches brought the masses under the banking fold. In 2014, the new government at the centre in a major initiative launched the Pradhan Mantri Jan Dhan Yojna (PMJDY) under which around 30.97 crore accounts (as on 3rd January 2018) have been opened (PMJDY, 2018).

When viewed from a different perspective banks are moving towards being lifestyle choices rather than payments processors. Historically they were chosen on the basis of their vicinity to the customers' homes. It didn't matter what they charged or how they priced, as all banks provided similar services. Branding was never a matter of consideration. But over the years, as the banks retrenched and sent their people packing their bags out of the branches to do things for themselves, they have become even less differentiated. Now, most folks are picking their banks for the same reason as in its physically local (over 60% of new account openers still make the decision based on the branch being near) but, once opened, they never want to go there again. Soon, as the dynamics of the role of the branch shift became less important, customers stopped opening accounts due to the proximity of the branch and move towards lifestyle choices. How does the bank reflect one's personality, needs and goals? Do they share common ethics and values? Do they fit in their lifestyle and outlook?

The Reserve Bank of India (RBI) in the recent times has also introduced innovation-friendly regulations and has been trying to bring as many people as possible under the ambit of financial inclusion which has today become one of the most sought for objectives of the Indian banking system as a significant value is seen at the bottom of the pyramid. The latest in this initiative was the issuing of licenses to Payments banks and Small finance banks taking a step forward in promoting niche banking in the country thus providing a framework for a variety of organizations with a sturdy distribution muscle to provide financial services at scale in India.

Existent Banking Structure and Efforts for Financial Inclusion

There have been four different phases in which the banks evolved. These phases brought in major structural changes in the banking structure and objective. Banks started moving form just the customers at the higher end to the ones at the lower end of the pyramid. There were a number of events triggering these changes. These trigger events, phases and the major changes have been depicted in Figure 1.

The existing structure of the Indian banking industry is also given in the flow chart in Figure 2.

Figure 1. Evolution of Indian banking industry

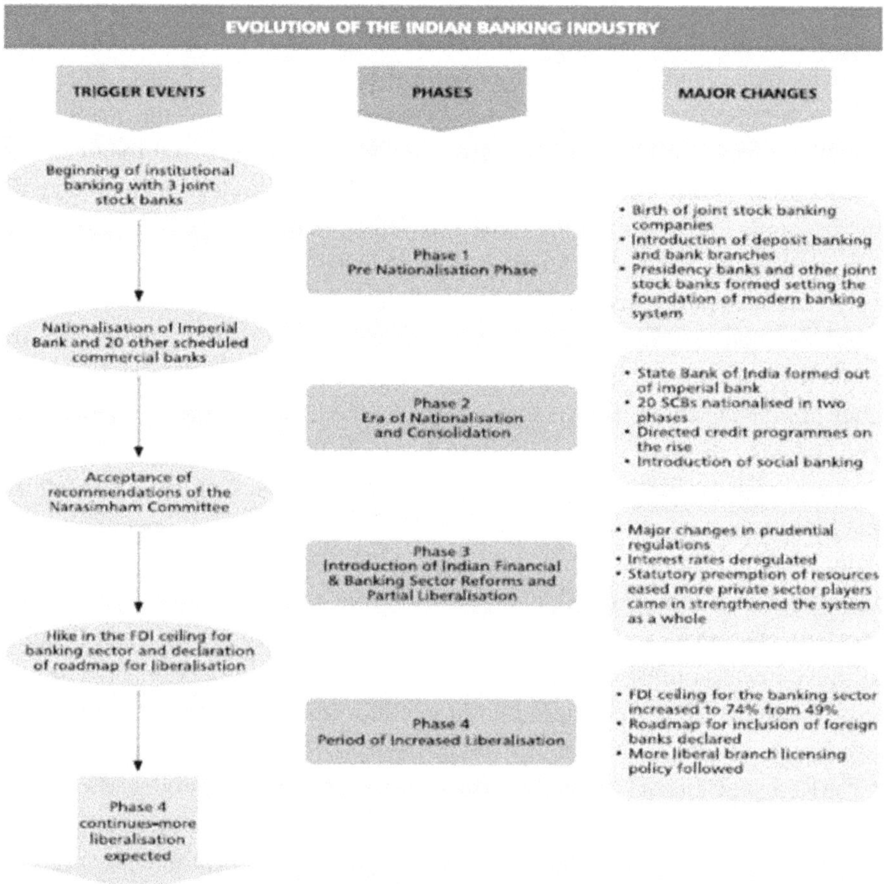

Source: D&B Industry Research Service

The growth of banking business to the GDP ratios in the past and its projected business for the next 10 years is given in Figure 3 and Figure 4.

Though the size of the economy enlarged, number of triggers enabled and domestic savings expanded in multiples, the coverage of the banking and financial sectors have been inadequate. Only 40% of the adults have formal bank accounts (Gandhi, 2015). Many of the villages of the country are still unbanked. The Jan Dhan Yojana though has increased the financial penetration the increased inclusion is yet to be attained. Relations between financial structures and the economic growth have to date remained in- conclusive. Depending upon the emerging structure and the needs of the economy, the country's banking system has to evolve and remain competitive to cater to the emerging needs of the society. Banking on the poor could

Figure 2. Existing structure of Indian banking industry

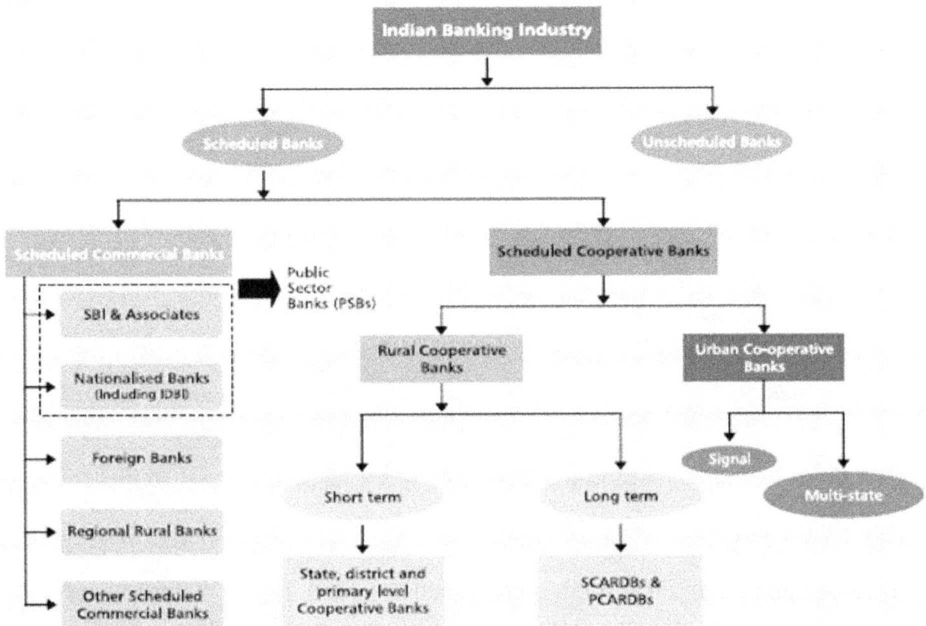

Source: D&B Industry Research Service

Figure 3. Banking business/GDP ratio
Source: (DEPR, 2013)

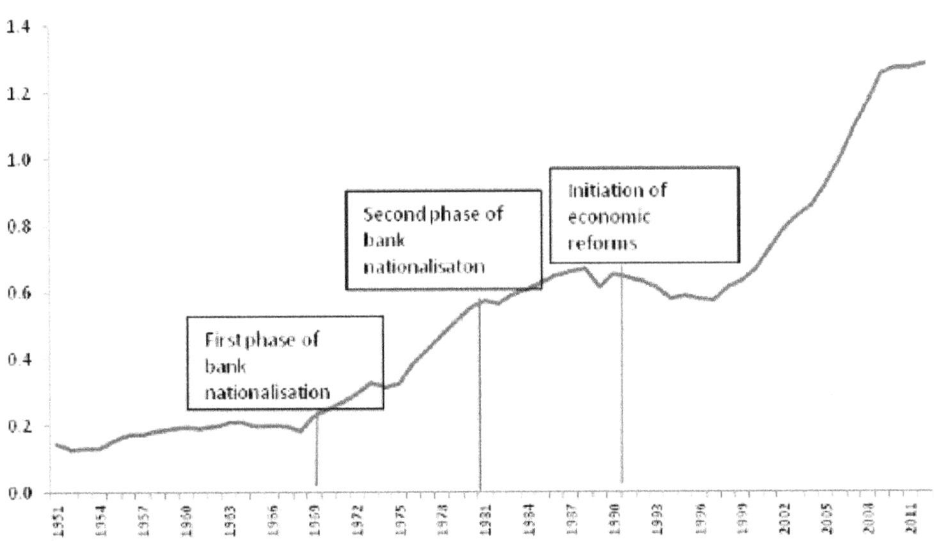

Figure 4. Projection of banking business
Source: (DEPR, 2013)

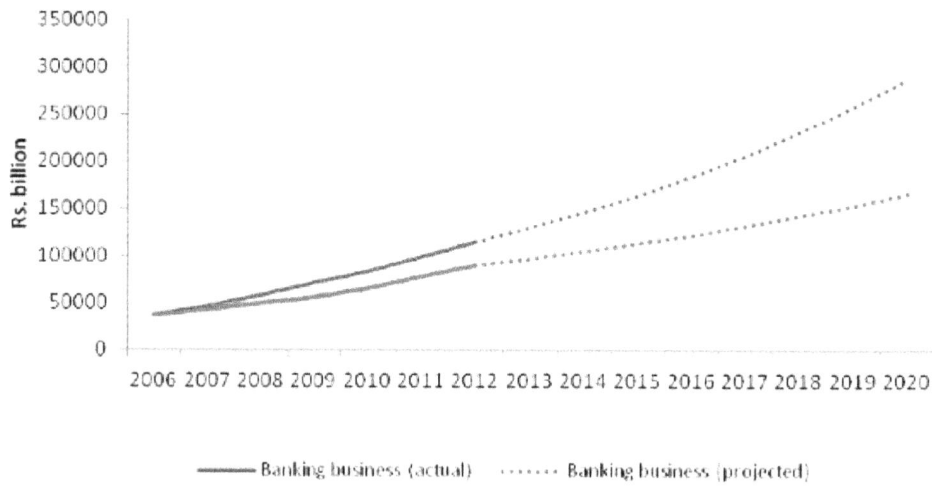

be a viable option in India as there is an immense potential lying at the bottom of the pyramid. There is an enormous unmet potential lying in the rural areas for financial institutions. If financial institutions could successfully tap this potential, it would be a win-win situation for institutions and the country at large (Krishnan, 2014) .

The New Banking Structure

Practitioners and researchers have started visualizing the next generation banking models like multi-channel banks, socially engaging banks, financial and non-financial digital eco-system banks and finally the differentiated banking structure that has started emerging in the form of Payment Banks and Small Banks. RBI, had been issuing only a single class of banking licence for both domestic and foreign banks and all of them enjoyed equal access to the payment and the settlement system and were provided a similar deposit insurance cover (Jain, 2014b). These commercial banks that had been set up have a significant role to play in the economic development of the country. But as the changing objectives of financial inclusion were not being met by the existing licensing structure, the RBI has proposed to reorient the banking system with distinct tiers of banking institutions in one of its discussion paper titled "Banking Structure in India – The way forward". The *first tier* would consist of three to four large Indian banks with domestic and international presence along with branches of foreign banks in India; the *second tier* likely to comprise several mid-sized banking institutions including niche banks with an economy-wide presence capable of offering a broad range of banking products and services to the domestic economy such as investment banking, wholesale banking and funding large infrastructure projects, the *third tier* encompassing old private sector banks, Regional Rural Banks (RRBs), and multi state Urban Cooperative Banks and the *fourth tier* embracing many small privately owned local banks and cooperative banks, which would specifically cater to the credit requirements of small borrowers in the unorganized sector in unbanked and under banked areas. The details of all the four tiers and their role and structure is depicted in the table given below:-

In short, the reoriented structure would be dynamic, with the emergence of well capitalized specially focused banks, which would be prudently regulated and rigorously supervised. The task of restructuring the Indian banking system is a complex exercise and poses a number of challenges and would require wading through several cumbersome and conflicting processes and execution of set plans for action.

But in spite of all the developments that have taken place, a sizeable section of the population particularly the vulnerable groups like the weaker sections and the lower income groups continue to remain excluded from even the most basic opportunities and services provided by the financial sector or could be called financially excluded. Around 40% of the country still remains unbanked (Gandhi, 2015). In order to include such a population financially, this initiative of inclusion should not be seen as a social responsibility of the government and the various stakeholders but as an

Table 1. Indicative re-orientation of banking structure in India

Indicative Re-Orientation of Banking Structure in India		
First Tier **International Banks**	i. Three or four very large banks ii. Foreign Banks in India	• Possible mergers of Associate Banks with SBI. • Voluntary merger of a few large Public Sector Banks having significant overseas presence. • Organic and in-organic growth of one or two large Private Sector Banks.
Second Tier **National Banks**	i. Public Sector Banks, ii. New Private Sector Banks, iii. Subsidiaries of Foreign Banks incorporated in India, iv. Specialized banks	• Voluntary merger of banks both in the Public and Private Sector. • Encourage foreign banks to have subsidiary mode of presence in India. • Grant differentiated licences for specialized banks.
Third Tier **Regional Banks**	i. Old Private Sector Banks, ii. Regional Rural Banks, iii. Multi-State Urban Cooperative Banks	To carry forward the process of consolidation of the Regional Rural Banks and the conversion of a few well managed, financially sound Multi-State Urban Cooperative Banks into commercial banks
Fourth Tier **Local Banks**	i. Local Area Banks (LABs)/ small banks, Single-State Urban Cooperative Banks (UCBs), State Cooperative Banks (SCBs), District Central Cooperative Banks	• Well managed and financially sound UCBs would have opportunities to convert into commercial banks • Well managed and financially sound LABs/small banks would have opportunities to expand their area of operations. • Rural cooperatives to be made financially sound to serve the local needs.

Source: (Kainth, 2014)

opportunity – a viable business proposition providing the poor with opportunities to build savings; make investments and get credit. The financial services to be included would cover the entire range of services like savings, loans, insurance, credit, payments, etc. (Jain, 2014a).

In 2005, the annual policy statement of the RBI recognized the concerns regarding banking practices that excluded rather than attract vast sections of the population and urged banks to review their existing practices to align them with the overall objective of financial inclusion. Banks were advised to provide non-frill accounts with nil or very low minimum balances as well as charges that would make such accounts accessible to vast sections of the population. They were advised to give wider publicity for these measures so that the needy population could be better financially included.

Initiative Towards Priority Sector Lending and Financial Inclusion

Time and again the RBI has also introduced structural changes first in order to build the Banking structure and then to get the country financially included. One of the key objectives of bank nationalization in 1969 and 1980 was to spread the banking habit through opening branches in hitherto un-banked areas (Gandhi, Differentiated Banks: Design Challenges, 2015). The Government has introduced various reforms and changes which has led to better and included banking. The following tables give the time line of the various structural changes and the initiatives taken by the banks for increased priority sector lending.

Need for Niche Banking

After the structural changes and the initiatives adopted for higher priority sector lending, there was felt a need for niche banking or specialized banking services as all the banks were exposed to similar regulation but were not operating in the same segment of the business and they hence felt the need to be regulated separately so that they could utilize their resources optimally. The impetus to license 'niche banks' also arises out of the need to spread financial inclusion in the country, considering that almost 40 per cent of the population does not have access to formal banking, this becomes a priority (Narasimhan, 2014). Under such a glut, the existing businesses and need for banking services started expanding and different services that were being provided by the banks turned into their core business and those respective banks started specializing themselves in those fields. Various such factors also led to payments growing from just a service to core business. The factors responsible for the same are as follows:

Table 2. Time line for structural changes in Indian banking framework for financial inclusion

Year	Event	Significance
1949	Nationalization of RBI	
1952	State Financial Corporations Act, 1951 came into effect	Enabled state governments to establish Financial corporations for meeting the credit needs of medium and small scale industries.
1964	Unit Trust of India established Commenced operations in July 1964.	extend facilities for an equity type investment to small investors
1965	Credit Regulation introduced to align the growth of bank credit with Plan requirements. Credit Authorisation Scheme (CAS).	Initiation of priority sector lending
1966	Operations of co-operative banking system brought under the regulatory ambit of the RBI	
1969	14 major Indian Scheduled Commercial Banks with deposits of over Rs 50 crores nationalised and Lead Bank Scheme introduced	To serve better the needs of development of the economy in conformity with national policy objectives (priority sector lending). Envisaged an area approach to banking to meet the credit gaps in the economy.
1971	Credit Guarantee Corporation of India Ltd. established	To facilitate bank lending to the priority sectors.
1975	Regional Rural Banks were set up	To provide credit to rural people in the context of the 20 Point Programme. These were expected to "combine the rural touch and local feel, ...with the modern business organisation...".
1979	Rural Planning and Credit Cell set up in the Reserve Bank of India	To ensure proper implementation of the multi-agency approach to credit in rural areas.
1980	Six private sector banks nationalised	"...in order further control the heights of the economy, to meet progressively, and serve better, the needs of the development of the economy and to promote the welfare of the people in conformity with the policy of the State..."
1982	National Bank for Agriculture and Rural Development (NABARD) established	For providing credit for the promotion of agriculture, small scale industries, cottage and village industries, handicrafts, and other rural crafts for promoting integrated rural development and securing rural prosperity
1990	Agriculture and Rural Debt Relief Scheme, 1990	providing debt relief up to Rs 10,000 to small borrowers banks
1996	Guidelines for setting up local area banks in the private sector	To promote rural savings and enhance credit facility
2001	Kissan Credit Cards introduced.	To enhance financial inclusion
2001	RBI issues guidelines for internet banking	Heralding in a new era in banking.

Source – Compiled from RBI Data

Table 3. Initiatives for priority sector lending

Year	Event and Its Significance
1968	National Credit Council Meeting which emphasised on increased involvement of commercial banks in the financing of priority sectors
1980	Chief Executive Officers of public sector banks, agreed to aim at raising the proportion of their advances to priority sector to 40 percent by March 1985
2005	Internal Working Group of the RBI (C. S. Murthy) made recommendation regarding Priority Sector Lending
2007	Guidelines for Priority Sector Lending revised
2011	RBI set Committee to re-examine the existing classification and suggest revised guidelines with regard to Priority Sector lending (M V Nair)
2014	Internal Working Group set up in to revisit the existing priority sector lending guidelines

Source – Compiled from RBI Data

- **Significant Rise in Retail Payments:** Though banks have been traditionally dominating payments, pre-paid instruments (PPIs) or mobile wallets, money transfer agents, post offices started cropping up with various options for shopping and bill payments, online purchases and funds transfers.
- **Varied Channels for Payments:** Traditional cheque payments, Demand Drafts today are barely used unless specified as NEFT, RTGS, ECS (Debit), Debit cards are spelling convenience and Immediate Payment Service (IMPS), mobile banking, mobile wallets are catering to 24X7 funds transfer needs directly from one's mobile phone. Yet, cash is used quite frequently by migrant laborers to remit money back home.
- **Un-Banked Areas Exist Despite Financial Inclusion Initiatives Taken by the RBI:** Jan Dhan Yojana was launched to boost Financial Inclusion since RBI mandated the Financial Inclusion Plan for banks through the Business Correspondent (BC) Model that saw only a modest success because of various challenges such as low viability, low connectivity to remote areas, inactive accounts and lack of motivation with low agent remunerations. Thus, RBI's Payments bank guidelines focused on remittances and payments but with widespread network of access points.
- **Deposits, Remittances but no Direct Loans or Credit Cards:** Payments banks could accept demand deposits subject to a cap of Rs 100,000 per customer and provide payments and remittance services through various channels like internet, branches, business correspondents (BC) and mobile banking (Bandyopadhyay, 2016). These banks cannot offer credit facilities directly but can choose to act as a BC of another bank for credit and other services.

Payment Banks/ Small Finance *Banks: Role*

The RBI recently introduced innovation-friendly regulations, in the form of licensing of Payments Banks and Small Finance banks taking a step forward in promoting differentiated banking in the country thus providing a framework for a variety of organizations with a strong distribution muscle to provide financial services at scale in India. It is felt that these banks would bring in more money into the system and spread the reach of banking to rural areas as it is a step in the direction of enabling the last-mile connectivity to the consumers. Differentiated banking licences allow for the creation of a variety of small banks that target a specific region or population (Briefing, 2014).

The objectives of payments banks would be to provide small savings and payment remittance services to migrant labour workforce and low income households while that of small finance banks would be to ensure financial inclusion and supply of credit to small businesses and farmers through high-technology and low cost operations (Mehra, 2016). The focus would be to reach the end of the tunnel by enabling technology based services at minimal costs, enabling the poor masses to engage in financial transactions. If Kenya's M-PESA and Somaliland's Telesom ZAAD – are any of the models to go by it could be expected that these niche banks in India would also succeed, as they have been successful in enabling financial inclusion in both the countries and more so in the poorer areas.

Structural Framework for Payment and Small Finance Banks

A comparative chart of the structural framework for the differentiated banks (Payment and Small banks) is given:

Possible Benefits of Payment Banks and Small Banks

The comparative chart of the possible benefits that the payment banks and small banks could give for better financial inclusion is as follows:

Global Success of Specially Structured Financial Inclusion Payment Models

M-Pesa in Kenya

M-PESA, a small-value electronic payment and store of value system accessible from ordinary mobile phones has been the key in opening the door to formal financial services for Kenya's poor. It succeeded because of the exceptionally high cost of sending money by other conventional methods. Other benefits include the regulator's

Table 4. Structural framework for differential banks

Criteria	Payment Banks	Small Finance Banks
Objective	Provide small savings account and payment/ remittance services to migrant labour workforce and low income households	Financial inclusion and supply of credit to small business units and farmers through high-technology and low-cost operations
Initial Capital	100 crores	100 crores
Time Frame to Start Operations	18 months	18 months
Minimum Promoters Contribution	40% (for first 5 years)	40% (will be brought down to 26% in 12 years)
Foreign Holding	Up to 74% of paid-up capital on par with private banks	Up to 74% of paid-up capital on par with private banks

Source: Compiled by the authors from various sources

Table 5. Comparison of benefits between differential banks

Payment Banks	Small Finance Banks
Must maintain CRR, minimum 75% of demand deposits should be in government bonds of up to one year maturity and maximum 25% in current and fixed deposits with other scheduled commercial banks for operational purposes and liquidity management.	Must extend 75% of its Adjusted Net Bank Credit (ANBC) to sectors eligible for classification as priority sector lending by the RBI. Maximum loan size would be 10% of the capital funds to single borrower, and a maximum of 15% to a group
Can accept demand deposits, issue debit cards and offer internet banking, set up branches, ATMs, BCs	Take small deposits and disburse loans; 25% of its branches must be set up only in unbanked areas.
Can accept remittances to be sent to or receive remittances including cross border remittance transactions and utility bill payments	Capital adequacy ratio should be 15% of risk weighted assets, Tier-I should be 7.5%
Allowed to distribute mutual fund products, insurance products and pension products	Can distribute mutual funds, insurance products and other simple third-party financial products but with RBI Approval
Can hold maximum balance of Rs 100000/- per individual customer	At least 50% of loan portfolio should constitute loans and advances of up to Rs. 2500000/-
Cannot accept NRI deposits	Cannot lend to big corporates and groups
Cannot issue credit card	Cannot open branches with prior RBI approval for first five years
Not allowed to set up subsidiaries to undertake non-banking financial services activities	It cannot set up subsidiaries to undertake non-banking financial services activities
Activities of the promoters should not be mingled with the working of payment banks (financial or non-financial)	Cannot be a BC of any other bank

Source: Compiled by the authors from various sources

initial decision to allow the scheme to proceed on an experimental basis, without formal approval, a clear and effective marketing campaign ("Send money home") and the post-election violence in the country in early 2008 which made some Kenyans regarded M-PESA as a safer place to store their money than the banks, which were entangled in ethnic disputes. The payment system demonstrated the value of leveraging mobile technology to extend financial services to large segments of the unbanked poor people and showed the importance of designing usage-based rather than float-based revenue models for reaching poor customers with financial services and revealed the need for a low-cost transactional platform that enabled low-income customers to meet a range of payment needs (Radcliffe, 2010).

Telesom ZAAD: Somaliland

Somaliland does not have any formal banking infrastructure and no internationally recognised banks operate there. Telesom recognised the negative impact of the lack of formal financial services on the country's economy and thus Telesom ZAAD came to the picture. The objective of the company was to bring financial inclusion to the country and drove the company to offer free services to their customers. Telesom ZAAD succeeded in convincing users to keep money in their e-wallets by building an ecosystem of salary payers and merchants. Telesom has created a new model for mobile money whereby customers are encouraged to keep money in the system rather than cashing it out (McGrath, 2013).

EcoCash: Zimbabwe

EcoCash a part of Econet Services, an independent company set up in 2012 by Zimbabwe's largest mobile network operator, Econet Wireless was able to start fast as it had an effective operational strategy and an unusually large investment in mobile money. In 18 months, 2.3 million Zimbabweans had registered for EcoCash mobile money accounts, outnumbering all of Zimbabwe's traditional bank accounts combined. Their goal was to become the dominant payment infrastructure in Zimbabwe by making it the primary way people pay for goods and services – from sweets to school fees. The success of EcoCash was due to five key strategies - finding the pain point, taking a long-term view, keeping mobile money separate, starting with a simple product and embracing the financial ecosystem (Levin, 2013). The opportunity that EcoCash saw in Zimbabwe at the outset of hyperinflation and loss of trust with the banks was to - bring payment services to the informal economy, replace cash in the retail environment to solve the "change problem" and Bridge the formal and informal economies.

Orange Money and MTN: Ivory Coast

In Ivory Coast, mobile money is a fairly recent and quickly growing phenomenon. With mobile penetration rates as high as 92%, there is significant potential for mobile money to play a key role in Ivory Coast's financial inclusion strategy. *Orange* sharpened the company's focus on mobile money by starting a separate business unit Orange Money, which proved to be an essential ingredient for success in other mobile money markets. Orange also strengthened Orange Money's brand image by partnering with established companies like the national water and electricity utilities to administer bill payments. It also invested in building a network of ATMs, which allowed customers to access cash at any time without the assistance of a mobile money agent, further reinforcing the image of Orange Money as a reliable and a secure service. The external factor driving the adoption of mobile money was the country's return to civil peace and economic recovery in 2012.

At the same time *MTN* focused on consolidating its distribution network, developing stronger recruitment criteria for agents, managing agent performance more closely, and increasing support for agent liquidity. Very quickly, and without changing the commission structure, agent profitability multiplied fourfold. In the course of only a few months, agents became more motivated and provided better service to customers at the point of sale. With over 95% of its agent's active on a 30-day basis, MTN Côte d'Ivoire now has one of the highest agent activity rates in the world (Pénicaud, 2014).

MTN: Uganda

Though there are over 30 banks in Uganda, the banking penetration rate is no more than 10%. The traditional banking model involves taking branches to various locations, an option that is not compatible with poor countries such as Uganda. In these circumstances the advent of mobile money provided everyone with the opportunity to access financial inclusion which also presented an opportunity for the company to provide banking services using mobiles. The go-to-market strategy was designed to ensure rapid uptake of the services. However, even the highest hopes of the partners were exceeded by the response. It was testament to the robust Fudamo platform that MTN was able to continue to sign up new customers onto the system, completely relying on the integrity of the Fundamo solution (Fundamo). In just over a year MTN Uganda registered 1 million Mobile Money service users - 16% of its subscriber base. MTN Uganda continues to be one of the most successful Mobile Money deployments globally to date.

A recent World Bank report said: "Mobile money has the potential to become a game changer for the economy. There is evidence that mobile money transfers to rural areas have a productive impact by enabling just-in-time payments for farm labour or to procure agricultural inputs. The poor also benefit from mobile money as it permits transfer payments in a low-cost environment and in a way that safeguards their cash and reduces insecurity."

Zoona: Zambia

When M-Pesa, the preeminent mobile money service in Africa, was beginning to thrive in Kenya in 2008, Zoona's founders were inspired to set up a mobile money transfer service beginning in Zambia that could help to overcome the above challenges and stimulate economic growth. Zoona held a vision of a 'cashless Africa', in pursuit of which, the company aimed to support small businesses by allowing entrepreneurs to transact through their mobile money product, providing them with the necessary capital and giving them tools to manage their businesses. The lessons learnt were to - get the right staff and processes in place early on, always focus on the set customers and ensure that partnerships are based on common interest and don't deviate from the vision (McNally, 2014). The results - The first of these is the number of Zoona entrepreneurs (customers/agents facilitating the service) currently standing at over 650 - and the number of unique end users who transact at least once every 90 days, of which there are currently over 600,000 and finally the Combined monthly average volume is over $25,000,000.

Challenges for Success of Payment Banks and Small Banks

The various challenges that the upcoming differentiated banks would face are as follows:

- Stiff competition from the existing infrastructure of BCAs and the already present and growing banks in the country.
- The cost of digital transaction will have to be as low as possible so that it encourages the masses to undertake non-cash transactions.
- How will the existing market accept the new structure and be able to transfer benefits to the ones at the end of the tunnel or will it be just used for faster payment services to a pizza consumer is a matter to be seen
- There is a complete possibility of banks collaborating with the existing banking structure and new models or new loop holes emerging thus posing further regulatory challenges.
- The challenge of overdependence on technology will always remain.

- Unregulated virtual currencies like bitcoins would also pose a challenge or an obstruction as they are similar in many respects and increasingly becoming popular.

Viability of Payments Banks and Small Finance Banks

Low cost delivery, cost effective cash out capability, robust compliance with regulatory standards would be the key for the viability of these differentiated banks.

Viability of Payment Banks

Since credit is not directly allowed, tie-ups with banks or functioning as BCs would allow a payment bank to acquire credit products. The various measures that could be adopted to make the banks viable are

- A Multi-distribution format through multiple channels for cost effective management and sharing services with tie-ups with banks or alliances would prove good. The banks may not invest in traditional brick and mortar branches and ATMs at all locations.
- They could have a combinational product offering of m-wallet + savings account + payments service for product pricing as per the usage, robust remittance options and PMJDY products such as savings account, pension, insurance, Demat, etc.
- Cash will play a major role and cash withdrawals should be there over PoS machines at more retail outlets. Card less cash withdrawals would also reduce card management costs and therefore help in the viability of payment banks.
- Various upcoming payment options such as USSD, IMPS, IVR payments will further increase payment penetration
- Strong analytics, simple GUI for early customer adoption, customer awareness and optimal customer service are critical for cost management and helps to make initiatives viable.
- They could have IT systems that foresee compatibility with NPCI's unified architecture; RBI's Bharat Bill Payments Systems and have appropriate tools to gather insights for efficient functioning.

Viability of Small Finance Banks

- India is already overbanked but is highly underserved and so there could be a huge opportunity lying ahead if the business model is concentrating towards the enhancement of services. There have been cases of success and failure across the world. In US, the small finance banks are called as community banks and only a few are doing well and hold less than 15% of the country's total banking assets. Similar banks in Nigeria and Tanzania have not significantly increased financial inclusion and in Philippines and Ghana such banks needed intensive, subsidized upgrading to survive. Small regional banks have been existent in India for long but have had limited impact.

- Competition would be fierce as these small finance banks would not only compete with the new entrants, they would also compete with the existing banking structure who are becoming more technology savvy and are acquiring national ambitions.
- Not all the allocated of small finance banks have exposure in banking and finance.
- They can provide credit only up to 10% of the capital funds to an individual and a maximum of 15% to a group thereby rendering the risk exposure of banks.

CONCLUSION

The Road Ahead

The RBI has taken an innovative step to fulfill its objectives of enhanced financial inclusion by allowing for the establishment of the payment and small finance banks. Though having no experience in this area, taking a decision with the help of successful examples and the discussion that it carried out is highly commendable. The establishment of differentiated banks would coexist with the existing banking structure and give a great challenge to the existing services provided by the conventional banking structure. The establishment of the new structure would lead to the consolidation of various services and have the potential to disruptively challenge the existing dynamics in the banking space. It would lead to greater technological innovations which could prove to be highly disruptive. The regulator also acknowledges the role of innovations in enhancing affordability, interoperability, inclusivity and security. But the insight is very clear. There would be other kinds of differentiated banks also that would come up thereby breaking down various banking services into their core businesses. The establishment and the utilization of the existing infrastructure for services specialization would be the key for the survival.

The various examples and experience of other countries have proved that it is possible but how will the Indian consumer take this new banking structure is a matter to be seen. The head of Motorola once said that it was very difficult to do business in India as Indian consumers were different. Warren Buffet, the world famous investor

Table 6. Comparison between the different types of banks

Criteria	Universal Bank	Payment Banks	Small Finance Banks
Eligibility	Companies private / public sectors and NBFCs will be eligible to set up a bank through a wholly-owned non-operative financial holding company (NOFHC), successful track record of 10 years	Prepaid payment Instrument issuers, individuals/professionals, NBFCs, corporate business correspondents, mobile telephone companies, super-market chains, real sector cooperatives owned and controlled by residents, and public sector entities	Resident individuals/ professionals with 10 years' experience in banking/ finance, companies and societies owned and controlled by residents, existing NBFCs/ microfinance institutions/local area banks
Capital Requirement	500 crore. Listing within three years of starting business	100 crore	100 crore
Scope of Activity	Accept deposits and carry out lending activities without limitations in the area of operations. 40% per cent of their lending should be towards the priority sector	Accept deposits of up to Rs 1 lakh a customer and issue debit cards, payments and remittance services; distribute insurance and mutual fund products. Payments banks can also serve as a business correspondent of another bank	Basic banking activities of accepting deposits and lending to the unserved and underserved sections
Promoters Contribution	NOFHC and the bank will not have any exposure to the promoter group. The bank will not invest in equity / debt capital instruments of any financial entities held by the NOFHC	Initial contribution 40% of the paid-up equity capital for the first 5 years from the start of its business	Initially 40% and needs to be gradually brought down to 26% within 12 years from the start of operations.
Foreign Shareholding		According to FDI policy (49% automatic route, 74% approval route)	According to FDI policy (49% automatic route, 74% approval route)
Other Conditions		Fully networked and technology-driven from the beginning and it should also have a high powered customer grievances cell to handle complaints	Required to extend 75% of adjusted net bank credit to the priority sector, at least 50% of its loan portfolio should comprise loans and advances of up to Rs 25 lakh

Source: Compiled by the authors

when asked about investing in India once said that he was not able to understand the Indian business environment and the Indian consumer. Rama Bijapurkar, a famous strategist had written a book on the Indian consumer titled "We are like this only" trying to explain and characterise the Indian consumer behaviour. The successful experience faced in the other countries may or may not be replicable in India. It completely depends upon how the Indian consumer adapts to the new kind of service provision. The objective of the government is surely the person sitting at the end of the tunnel.

REFERENCES

Bandyopadhyay, T. (2016, April 11). *Why banking in India will never be the same again*. Retrieved from http://www.livemint.com/Opinion/VXJOMNx2O5xbi2nXIr8nPJ / Why-banking-in-India-will-never-be-the-same-again.html

Briefing, I. (2014, June 17). *Reserve Bank of India to Offer Differentiated Banking Licenses*. Delhi: National Capital Region.

DEPR. (2013). *Banking Structure in India - The Way Forward (Discussion Paper)*. Reserve Bank of India, Department of Banking Operations and Development (DBOD) and Department of Economic and Policy Research (DEPR). Mumbai: Reserve Bank of India. Retrieved from https://rbidocs.rbi.org.in/rdocs/PublicationReport/Pdfs/DPBS27082013_F.pdf

Fundamo. (n.d.). *MTN Uganda Achieves One of The Most Remarkable Mobile Money Growth Rates Working With Fundamo*. Fundamo. Retrieved from http://docplayer.net/7800095-Mtn-uganda-achieves-one-of-the-most-remarkable-mobile-money-growth-rates-working-with-fundamo-case-study-mtn-uganda.html

Gandhi, R. (2015, April 20). Differentiated Banks: Design Challenges. *Differentiated Banks: Design Challenges*. Kumbakonam, Tamil Nadu, India: Reserve Bank of India. Retrieved from https://rbi.org.in/scripts/BS_SpeechesView.aspx?Id=954

Gandhi, R. (2015). Dy. Governor, RBI in the V. Narayan Memorial Lecture. *Differentiated banks: Design Challenges*. Retrieved from https://www.rbi.org.in/Scripts/BS_SpeechesView.aspx?Id=954

Jain, D. (2014a). Differentiated banking - Is India really prepared? *Journal of Indian Institute of Banking and Finance*, *85*(4), 27–32.

Jain, D. D. (2014b). Differentiated Bank Licences: Emergence of a New Bank Structure. *Pacific Business Review International*, *6*(12), 144–145.

Kainth, G. S. (2014). *Differentiated Banking in India: A Long Way to Go*. Amritsar: Guru Arjan Dev Institute of Development Studies. Retrieved from http://www.academia.edu/8126893/differentiated_banking_in_india_a_long_way_to_go

Krishnan, D. R. (2014). Differentiated banks and Financial Inlcusion. *20th Thinkers and Writers Forum*.

Levin, P. (2013). *Big ambition meets effective execution: How EcoCash is Altering Zimbabwe's Financial Landscape*. London: GSMA. Retrieved from https://www.gsma.com /mobilefordevelopment/wp-content/uploads/2013/07/EcoCash-Zimbabwe.pdf

McGrath, C. P. (2013). *Innovative Inclusion: How Telesom ZAAD Brought Mobile Money to Somaliland.* London: GSMA. Retrieved from https://www.gsma.com/mobilefordevelopment /wp-content/uploads/2013/07/Telesom-Somaliland.pdf

McNally, P. (2014). *Case study: Zoona.* London: GSMA. Retrieved from https://www.gsma.com/mobilefordevelopment/wp-content/uploads/2016/02/Case_Study_-Zoona.pdf

Mehra, P. (2016, March 29). *All you need to know about payment banks*. Retrieved from http://www.thehindu.com/business/all-you-need-to-know-about-payment-banks/article 7561353.ece

Narasimhan, C. R. (2014, July 27). *Differentiated banks: Has their time come?* Retrieved from http://www.thehindu.com/opinion/columns/C_R_L__Narasimhan/differentiated-banks-has-their-time-come/article6252844.ece

Pénicaud, C. (2014). *Mobile Money in Côte d'Ivoire: A Turnaround Story.* London: GSMA. Retrieved from https://www.gsma.com/mobilefordevelopment/wp-content/uploads/2014/05/ MMU_Cote_dIvoire_Turnaround_Story.pdf

PMJDY. (2018, January 3). *Pradhan Mantri Jan Dhan Yojana (PMJDY).* Retrieved from PMJDY - Progress Report: https://pmjdy.gov.in/account

Radcliffe, I. M. (2010). *Mobile Payments go Viral: M-PESA in Kenya.* World Bank. Retrieved from http://siteresources.worldbank.org/AFRICAEXT/Resources/258643-1271798012256/M-PESA_Kenya.pdf

Chapter 3
Customer Shareholding as a Radical Approach to a Sustainable and Profitable Relationship

Sara Elouadi
La Faculté des Sciences Juridiques Economiques et Sociales Ain Sebaâ, Morocco

Rachid Elotmani
ISCAE, Morocco

ABSTRACT

Customer ownership is a new practice that seeks integration and customer loyalty. In this chapter, the authors try to analyze this hybrid status to deepen ties between the customer and the company. To this end, they developed, initially, a comparative study between the customer and shareholder mutualism to identify the similarities and differences between the two models. Secondly, they tried to analyze the role of the client in creating value by using the stakeholder theory. Finally, they dealt with the possibilities and limitations of the client as shareholder loyalty means.

INTRODUCTION

In France, the banking sector is experiencing strong competition, accentuated by the entry into force since 6 February 2017 of the new Macron law providing for free banking mobility for customers. Indeed, it is now up to the new receiving bank to fulfill all administrative burdens. The client only has to sign a mobility mandate to his new bank and provide him with the bank account details in his origin bank. The new bank then take over all the transactions necessary to inform all its users

DOI: 10.4018/978-1-5225-4035-9.ch003

of withdrawals and recurring transfers. A maximum of 12 working days is set to carry out all of these steps.

In addition, the proliferation of online banks does not address the interests of conventional banks. The competition is fierce among the following players: ING Direct is a subsidiary of the Dutch bank ING, and is a leading player with 920,000 customers.

Immediately thereafter, Boursorama, a subsidiary of Société Générale, was ranked second.

Also, we can find other competitors such as the on line bank of “Crédit Mutuel Arkéa”, “Fortuneo” and “BforBank” which belongs to “Crédit Agricole”.

In the same race, we also find Hello Bank subsidiary of BNP Paribas, or the Monabanq online bank of the Crédit Mutuel group.

Customers prefer online banks to what they blame traditional banks, such as the low rates charged by online banks and even the free offer of certain services, such as the bank card offered free of charge by 4 banks among those already mentioned.

And because the bank employees are accused of being more of a salesperson than an advisor. Indeed, customers criticize the relationships and exchanges they have with their banks, which are motivated by benefits and lack of transparency.

Moreover, the experience of certain African countries shows that banking is not an imperative for trade and economic operations, indeed, African countries have a real alternative. In fact,, the transfer of money between individuals and payments by simple sms is practically unknown in Europe, but it is very widespread in developing countries and particularly in Africa, shows a map published by the Quartz information site.

According to the GSM Association data, 242 operators, in 89 countries, offer this kind of service. For example, it was used by 44% of Tanzanians in 2013, while only 13% of them have a bank account.

For all the aforementioned reasons, the banking sector suffers from a back of progress and the rise of alternative circuits. This state generates widespread discontent with current practices and raises awareness of the importance of good governance, respecting the human and the environment. Now, inevitably, good governance is the recognition and integration of the client, in order to humanize and moralize the process of creation and sharing of value.

The measure we propose for this purpose is hybridization in order to give the client more power and operationalization of the latter .Indeed, and in accordance with pluralistic partnership governance, the company must integrate all its stakeholders into the value creating process and break with the shareholder dictatorship that attaches importance to the shareholders of the company and financial results.

We therefore believe that a greater involvement of consumers in the company’s system taking the form of equity participation and thus committing them in the long term would be capable to satisfying a dual objective. First, the client will have empowerment to act in order to extinguish the greedy supremacy of the shareholders and the second, constitutes the loyalty of the customer through the strengthening of the bond established with the company.

Our work aims to develop the theoretical concept of an embryonic research current. Client shareholding is a hybrid option that has existed for a long time, particularly in mutualist societies (banks and insurance companies, among others); Recently, the firms have undertaken, timidly moreover, to consider it as an instrument of customer loyalty.

CUSTOMER SHAREHOLDING AND THE COOPERATIVE MODEL

Client shareholding is an aimed device at integrating the client into the capital in order to take advantage of the synergies associated with this grouping. The customer thus enjoys a hybrid status, he is both a customer and a shareholder of the same company. This status has several similarities with the cooperative model, and we suggest exploring the similarities and dissimilarities between the two models.

Mutualism comes from the Latin "mutuus" meaning "reciprocity", it is defined as an interaction presenting benefits for both protagonists.

The cooperative configuration is an organizational form that is distinguished by the application of a number of principles that Defourny, Laville and Cattani, (2005) explain as the purpose of services to members or the community rather than profit, autonomy of management, free accession, democratic control by the members, the primacy of people and the social purpose over capital in the distribution of surpluses.

Moreover, the cooperative model is distinguished by its democratic functioning which grants one vote to each person regardless of the share of the capital held. Also, profit sharing is intended for all employees whether or not they are associated with the capital.

According to Mauléon and Saulquin (2009), the foundations of mutualism are still very present today for those who claim to belong to the sector of the social economy. The principles of cooperative and mutualist governance are as follows:

- Solidarity
- The promotion of the individual
- Free collective initiative.
- Democracy.
- The fair distribution of bénéfits.
- The total or partial indivisibility of own funds.
- Independence from government

The atomization of the power of each member who emanates from the principle, one vote per man, leads to the reduction of the individual influence that characterizes the capitalist system.

The mutual banks are not listed on the financial market, which puts them free from any threat of external takeover. The financial compensation granted to the members is lower than the dividends received by the shareholders.

There are several points of resemblance between the statutes of client ownership and the partnership. Indeed, both statuses are characterized by the consumption of the products and services of the companies in which the two players hold shares of capital. In addition, this superior status of ownership provides benefits such as access to information, political participation, and the collection of interest and dividends.

In addition, the two profiles benefit from privileged treatment by receiving commercial advantages and services at reduced prices.

However, there are several dissimilarities between the two statutes, the absolute and equal voting rights granted to all members in mutualism, whatever the shares held.

Conversely, the vote right in the system of client shareholding is proportional to the securities held.Also, listing on a financial market induces fluctuations in terms of risk and compensation and creates a possible volatility behavior of the shareholders. On the other hand, the mutualist system enjoys great stability and loyalty among the members. Similarly, the shares do not give a right to the net assets, in the event of liquidation, unlike the stocks, the members can only claim the nominal repayment of the units invested.

Furthermore, we believe that the main difference between client shareholding and membership is the asymmetry of the statutes. Indeed, the member is a customer who has made the choice of joint ownership. On the other hand, the customer shareholder relationship is reached according to two different configurations. The first is that of the loyal customer who has chosen to cross the cape of the property in order to become a client shareholder. The second configuration is that of the individual shareholder who has chosen to consume the products of the same company.

CONSUMER SHAREHOLDING AND VALUE CREATION

Theoretical Analysis

The stakeholder theory recognizes the permeability between different stakeholder groups and asserts the existence of a plurality of identities and status within the same groups. As such, Martinet (1984) discerns the internal stakeholders of external stakeholders while recognizing the existence of a third category called "ubiquist" stakeholders to describe the parties enjoying plural status.

In the same way, (Gibson, 2000) mentions the possibility for the same stakeholder to belong to several groups. Similarly, Cazal (2011) states that the boundaries between the different groups are now "highly porous" and these groups are partially "superimposable or even substitutable".

The best example of successful hybridisation is that of employee share ownership, the financial participation of employees can be considered as an irreplaceable measure, aimed at increasing the employees income while intensifying their link with the company.

According to the work of Elouadi (2014), the hybridity of the status of the employee shareholder leads to an increase in the partnership value according to the model of Brandenburger and Stuart (1996) and Charreaux and Desbrières (1998). This increase is due to lower opportunity costs borne by the stakeholders. Employee share ownership then constitutes a double contract binding the employee to his company. This relationship of trust encourages the emergence of positive attitudes towards the organizationElouadiorganization Elouadi (2015), which are an operationalization of trust.

In this regard, Couteret (1997) emphasizes the productive aspect of trust and the role of positive behaviors in strengthening constructive exchange, "mutual trust is based on the observation of mutual positive behaviors, engenders new behaviors that build confidence. "(Couteret 1997: 168).

The customer shareholding then constitutes a confidence mark in the company. Lemoine and Onnée (2000, 2003) explain, in this respect, that the most loyal customers of the company develop a strong propensity to be shareholders. And conversely, shareholders customers are often "over-consumers" products of their companies.

Moreover, the hybrid status of the client shareholder gives it a poetical power that can counter the management entrenchment that is materialized by the actions of appropriation of rents and the increase of managers personal wealth to the detriment of other stakeholders.

In this respect, Richez-Battesti (2006) argues that the presence and human owner-users investment in the various decision-making and management bodies helps to limit financial risk-taking and to reduce agency costs linked to asymmetries inherent in the relationship between managers and owners and owners-clients, to better satisfy the needs of consumers in symbiosis with the local economic and social fabrics.

Similarly, Onnée (2004) emphasizes the positive role played by individual shareholders in sociocognitive governance, which can enrich value creation by suggesting new ideas and the contribution to the resolution of sociocognitive conflicts

The study carried out by Duran (2012) confirms the presence of client shareholders in France and highlights its positive impact on customer loyalty and involvement. The study also clarifies that customer shareholding is formed from an individual shareholder, initiated to the financial markets.

Customer shareholding is an inclusive managerial practice, likely to involve the client and instill an inventive dynamism within the company.

In the context of the insurance market and the banking market, the customer will maintain the relationship with its provider and reinforce its conviction to perpetuate this relationship, as long as the shareholder value will induce an overall profit derived from the exchange with its supplier superior to which it could obtain from other competitors

This could be particularly plausible in markets where the perceived quality of service is relatively equivalent and where the volatility of customers is potentially significant. Here, shareholder value will be a factor of differentiation and loyalty, all the more so as the identification or evaluation of the contribution of the shareholder value to the overall benefit of the exchange is relatively easy.

The establishment and encouragement of customer shareholding creates, from an agency perspective, a lack of conflicts of interest between shareholders and customers because the two statutes are grouped into one. Long-term interests are not compromised by the "short-term" vision imposed by shareholders whose sole objective is to maximize their shareholder value. As a result, performance appraisal incorporates extra-financial criteria, taking into account the value created for all stakeholders.

In this respect, the work of Jaeger, Ory and Gurtner (2006) highlights the decline in agency conflicts in French cooperative banks.

Indeed, client shareholders are overcustomers of the products of their companies and constitute ambassadors, in addition, these proprietary clients are an invaluable source of enrichment and creativity. As such, Cova (2008) explains that creative customers have certain characteristics, such as, for example, the lasting implication for a product or brand or the pleasure of communicating their ideas.

The current client, by acquiring the status of individual shareholder reinforces his sense of belonging to the company; This leads him to more fidelity, thus generating more volume and margin for the latter.

As for the individual shareholder, by becoming a current customer, he intensifies his relationship with the company and develops his loyalty on a dual level, as a provider of funds and as a consumer; Resulting in better performance for the company (figure 1).

In this context, such as that of the insurance market and that of the mutual banks, for example, the client will maintain the relationship with his provider and will reinforce his conviction to perpetuate this relationship, as long as the shareholder value will induce an overall profit, Exchange with its supplier superior to that it could obtain from other competitors.

Figure 1. The bipolarity of the client shareholder status and its effects on value

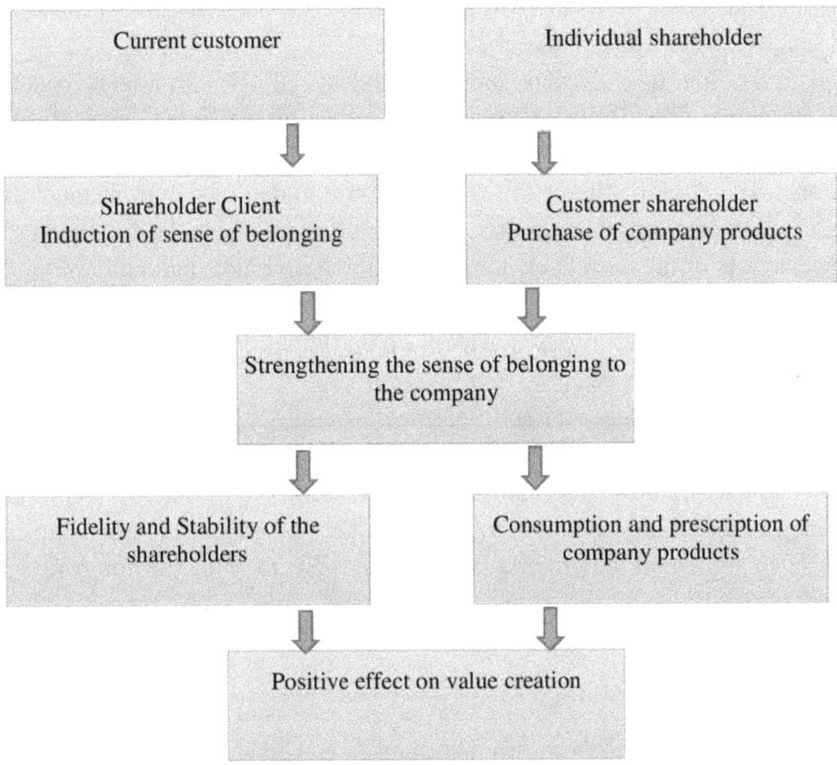

This could be particularly plausible in markets where the perceived quality of services is relatively equivalent and where the volatility of customers is potentially significant. Here, shareholder value will be a factor of differentiation and loyalty. especially since the identification or evaluation of the contribution of shareholder value to the overall benefit of the exchange is relatively easy.

This situation can be conventionally expressed by the following relation:

Overall profit taken from the exchange by the customer (BGE) = Profit from the exchange / core of the product (central supply) + perceived value of the supplier's loyalty program + perceived shareholder value. The result of this formula is higher than the BGE that can be obtained from direct competitors.

However, the growing involvement of consumers in corporate social responsibility issues prompts us to take this into account and rephrase the previous phrase as follows:

Overall profit taken from customer exchange (BGE) = Profit from exchange / product core + perceived value of supplier's loyalty program + perceived shareholder value + perceived quality and level of supplier's social responsibility. The result must be greater than the BGE that can be obtained from the direct competitors.

Considering the corporate social responsibility factor leads one to assume that customer loyalty could be acquired to some extent, even in a situation of deterioration of the specific economic gains of the customer.

And according to Prahalad and Ramaswany (2004), strategies based on crowdsourcing and cooperative networks are interesting in that they allow the client to be involved in the process of creating partnership value. We summarize the effects of customer shareholding in the following diagram. Indeed,the improvement of the results of a company and consequently of its value results from the combined effect of the behaviors of the current customers and the individual shareholders.

Michie (2012) says that customers and local communities are more committed to their organizations, by the use of a diversified participation that extends ownership to customers and employees .

Padmashantini, Gengeswari and Sharmeela-Banu (2013) argue that the use of membership loyalty program may lead to more commitment and customer retention.

In the same way, Bolton, Kannan and Bramlett (2000) argue that loyalty programs represent an opportunity to build "longer, stronger and deeper" relationships with clients. They argue that the programs allow customers to value the company vis-à-vis the competition.

Empirical Analysis

Empirical works focusing on customer share ownership are very scarce. To our knowledge, the only company to have launched a customer shareholding transaction is T-Mobile, a subsidiary of Germany's Deutsche Telekom, which announced on its website: "For us, you are more than just a customer, so we offer you a stake in the company". This unprecedented marketing initiative has been part of T-Mobile's customer-friendly approach for the past three years. T-Mobile's marketing director told Reuters: "These offers will be expensive, but we consider them a very good investment. In addition to offering these shares to their 12 million customers, the company plans to reward sponsors of new subscribers with free shares".

At the launch date, 6 june 2016, of this major customer shareholding operation the action of T-Mobile was worth 43 dollars.

The comparative graph of subscriber growth among mobile operators (figure 2) shows strong growth in T-mobile subscribers compared to other competitors in the fourth quarter of the year 2016. According to the experts, these performances are the fruit of the company's creative marketing strategy.

Shares of T-Mobile are among the largest market capitalisations of the American market.

Figure 2. Postpaid subscriber year-over-year growth (4q16)

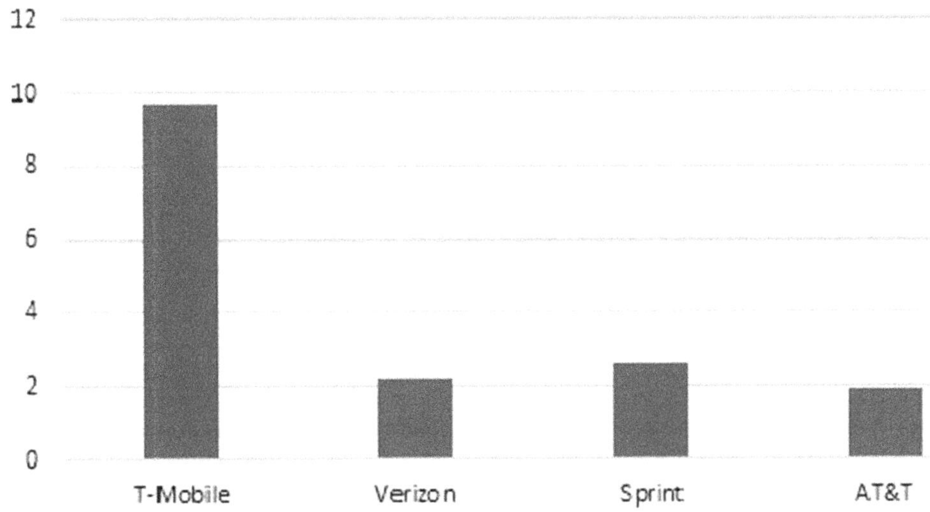

The following graph shows the history of TMUS over a period of 18 months from June 2016, when the customer shareholding was launched. The figure 3 shows a considerable increase after the last quarter of 2016.

Otherwise, Muhia (2014) conducted a study on variables that influence client retention BEEP program (Bright Enriched Empowerment Program), a non-governmental microfinance organization in Kenya. The variables tested are accessibility to financial services, customer service recovery, credit recovery, and customer shareholding.

Figure 3. T-Mobile US, INC. Common Stock Historical Stock Prices

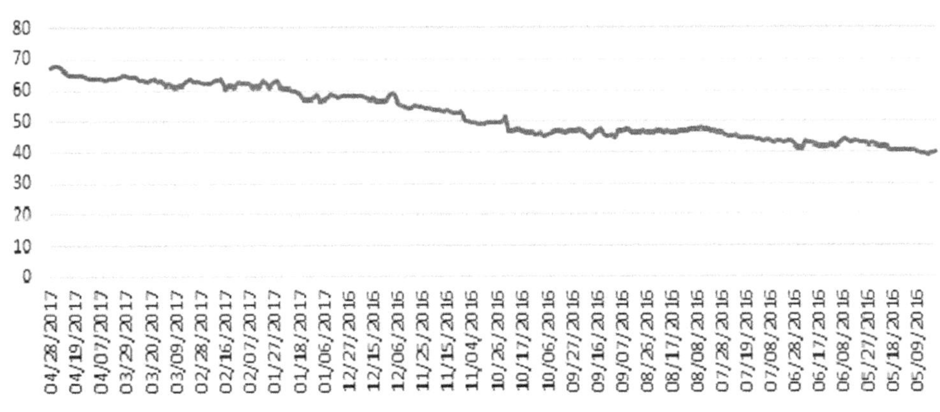

Table 1. Relationships between the variables-Pearson correlation

	Customer shareholding	Credit recovery	Customer service recovery	Accessibility of financial services	Customer retention
Customer shareholding	1				
Credit recovery	.260**	1			
Customer service recovery	.309**	.341**	1		
Accessibility of financial services	.281**	.267**	.357**	1	
Customer retention	.331**	.297**	.352**	.339**	1

(Source: Muha 2014, p. 64)

The research used a cross-sectional methodology based on the administration of questionnaires for Nairobi-based clients served by BEEP.

The dependent variable was customer retention, while the independent variables were affordability, customer service recovery, credit recovery, and customer shareholding.

Empirical results indicate that customer shareholding has had a significant and positive relationship with client retention in the Nairobi County PEEP (table 1) .

According to the study, the positive relationship is explained by the appel of high bonus payments (table 2) and increased participation in decisions.

Table 2. The appeal of bonus payments

Count

		Length of Membership in the BEEP			
		Below 2 Years	2 - 5 Years	Over 5 Years	Total
Most people in my group are attracted to this institution by the good bonus payments.	Strongly disagree	5	16	19	40
	Disagree	1	18	17	36
	Somehow Disagree	1	11	17	29
	Somehow Agree	7	24	24	55
	Agree	19	52	37	108
	Strongly Agree	8	28	33	69
Total		41	149	147	337

(Source: Muha, 2014, p. 59)

CONCLUSION

The integration of the customer shareholder into the process of creating value begins with the recognition of its existence and the adoption of targeted financial communication. As such, Léger (2008) uses the term "financial marketing" to describe informational efforts directed at employee shareholders in order to promote the financial image of the company. These efforts can materialize through interactions with investors through the creation of communication support including websites. The same author summarizes the objectives of the website "informing and seducing, explaining and convincing, attracting and retaining investors". Lemoine and Onnée (2003) suggests the following mechanisms for better integration of individual shareholders: shareholder clubs, advisory committees, information services, monetary and non-monetary advantages.

Similarly, the work of Lemoine and Onnée (2000) emphasizes the need to adopt an integrative management with respect to customers in order to push them to share ownership.

The practice of customer shareholding is still little known by companies, but we think there is a beginning of early interest of its positive effect on the value. For example, during the last communication of 2 November 2017, sent by the company Seb to its French shareholders, there is an explicit presentation of Seb products offered at preferential prices. This shows the awareness of the effect on the value of converting shareholders into loyal consumers.

In this work, we have attempted to analyze this new managerial practice using, essentially, stakeholder theory and the mutual model, which has several similarities with client shareholding. We deplore, however, the laconic character of empirical literature, to our knowledge very few studies have been carried out on the subject of customer ownership and recognition of this hybrid status.

REFERENCES

Bolton, R. N., Kannan, P. K., & Bramlett, M. D. (2000). Implications of Loyalty Program Membership and Service Experiences for Customer Retention and Value. *Journal of the Academy of Marketing Science*, *28*(1), 95–108. doi:10.1177/0092070300281009

Brandenburger, A. M., & Stuart, J. H. Jr. (1996). Value-based business strategy. *Journal of Economics & Management Strategy*, *5*(1), 5–24. doi:10.1111/j.1430-9134.1996.00005.x

Cazal, D. (2011). RSE et théorie des parties prenantes: les impasses du contrat. *Revue de la Régulation,* (9). Retrieved from http://regulation.revues.org

Charreaux, G., & Desbrières, P. (1998). Gouvernance des entreprises: Valeur partenariale contre valeur actionnariale. *Finance Contrôle Stratégie*, *1*(2), 57–88.

Couteret, P. (1997). L'impact de la confiance interpersonnelle sur l'implication organisationnelle: le cas de l'adjoint au dirigeant de petite entreprise. *Actes du 8ème congrès de l'AGRH*, 163-177.

Couteret, P. (1999). La pertinence du concept de confiance Dans la transition entre contrôle du manager et autonomie du subordonné: le cas des petites entreprises. *Actes du 10ème congrès de l'AGRH*, Lyon, France.

Cova, B. (2008). *CONSUMER MADE quand le consommateur devient producteur. In Décisions Marketing n°50* (pp. 19–27). Avril-juin.

Debord, G. (1992). *La société du spectacle (1967)* (p. 83). Paris: Gallimard.

Defourny, J., Laville, J.-L., & Cattani, A.-D. (2005). *Dictionnaire de l'autre économie*. Paris: Desclee de Brouwer.

Duran, N. (2012). *L'actionnaire individuel client: étude du cas français*. Toulon: Université de Toulon.

Elouadi, S. (2014). *Analyse des effets induits par l'actionnariat salarié sur la création de valeur partenariale des entreprises du SBF 250*. Thèse de doctorat. Université du Sud.

Elouadi, S. (2015). Les effets attitudinaux de l'actionnariat salarié: une étude empirique dans le contexte des entreprises françaises du SBF 250. *Question (s) de management*, (3), 11-24.

Elouadi, S. (2016). To increase the development of human capital through employee ownership: an empirical analysis in the context of French companies in the SBF 250. *Memorias, 14*(26).

Gibson, K. (2000). The Moral Basis of Stakeholder Theory. *Journal of Business Ethics*, *26*(3), 245–257. doi:10.1023/A:1006110106408

Helfer, J.-P. (2005). Et si le marketing était éthique par définition? In La responsabilité sociale de l'entreprise. Mélanges en l'honneur du Professeur Roland Pérez. EMS.

Léger, J. H. (2008). *La communication financière (2nd ed.)*. Paris: Dunod.

Lemoine, J. F., & Onnée, S. (2000), Le statut d'actionnaire-client: faisons le point, *5ème congrès mondial de l'ASAC-IFSAM*, Canada, Montréal: juillet.

Lemoine, J. F., & Onnée, S. (2003). Vers une analyse des enjeux et des pratiques de la gestion de la relation avec l'actionnaire individuel. Décisions Marketing, 31, 25-37.

Martinet, A.-C. (1984). *Management Stratégique, Organisation et Politique*. Paris: Mc Graw Hill.

Mauléon, F., & Saulquin, J. (2009). Une approche comparative de la RSE par le statut juridique. Le cas des banques coopératives et des actions solidaires en France. *Management & Avenir*, *23*(3), 105–122. doi:10.3917/mav.023.0105

Michie, J. (2012). *Mutual advantage? The future implications of mutualism for employment relations*. University of Oxford.

Muhia, p. G. (2014). *Factors influencing microfinance customer retention: The case of bright enriched empowerment programme in Nairobi county, Kenya.* University of Nairobi Research Archive.

Onnée, S. (2004). *L'intégration des actionnaires individuels lors d'une fusion transeuropéenne: enjeux socioculturels et pratiques de gestion*. Congrès CIDEGEF.

Ory, J. N., Jaeger, M., & Gurtner, E. (2006). La banque à forme coopérative peut-elle soutenir durablement la compétition avec la banque SA? *Finance-Contrôle-Stratégie*, *9*(2), 121–157.

Padmashantini, P., Gengeswari, K., & Sharmeela-Banu, S. A. (2013). Investigation on the Customer retention practices at a major retailer in Malaysia. *Interdisciplinary Journal of Research in Business.*, *2*(Issue. 10), 40–50.

Perez, R. (2002). L'actionnaire socialement responsable. *Revue Française de Gestion*, *141*, 131-151.

Prahalad, C. K., & Ramaswamy, V. (2004). Co-creation experiences: The next practice in value creation. *Journal of Interactive Marketing*, *18*(3), 5–14. doi:10.1002/dir.20015

Richez-Battesti, N. (2006). Gouvernance coopérative et reconquête du sociétariat: une aventure inachevée? Le cas des banques coopératives en France. *XXIIème Conférence Internationale de recherche coopérative*.

Chapter 4
Effectiveness of Financial Inclusion Initiatives:
A Case Study of Rajasthan State

K. Sanal Nair
Samsidh Mount Litera Zee School, India

Saumya Jain
Cognus Technology, India

ABSTRACT

An inclusive financial system has been the major agenda of the Indian government over the past few years and several steps have been taken in this direction. The main purpose of the study is to assess the effectiveness of financial inclusion initiatives taken by Rajasthan government. A questionnaire was drafted and was sent to people from weaker section of the society who have been the beneficiaries of the financial inclusion initiative of the government. Research methodology adopted for the study includes descriptive statistics and one-way ANOVA was used to test the association/non-association between the variables. The study concluded towards lack of awareness and usage of financial inclusion initiatives, especially internet, mobile banking, and credit card. In terms of experience with financial services, respondents were positive towards interest on loans and help received by banking staff with respect to documentation and identification norms as well as branch timings. However, distance from the bank and the availability of ATM was an issue for them.

DOI: 10.4018/978-1-5225-4035-9.ch004

INTRODUCTION

Financial inclusion is a situation by which everyone has an access to the entire collection of quality financial services that are provided at affordable cost, in a convenient way and with respect and dignity. This area has long been neglected by the government but now it is one of the top priorities of government as the exclusion of disadvantaged and low-income segments of society from financial services inhibits the economic growth. Moreover, financial inclusion is a also a crucial means by which poverty can be reduced (Kumbhar, 2011). Having a proper access to financial instruments may allow poor people to invest in a variety of physical assets as well as education. This may further bring a reduction in income inequality and contribute towards economic growth (Gwalani, 2014). To ensure towards the concept of financial inclusion, the Indian government as well as Reserve bank of India has taken concerted efforts for the same and it has been regarded as one of the important national objective of the nation. Some of the major efforts are inclusive of nationalisation of banks, zero balance accounts, Pradhan Mantri Jan Dhan Yojana, direct cash transfer schemes among others (Goyal, 2016). The fundamental objective is to reach that section of the Indian society that has been finically excluded. In this respect, the need is to identify the effectiveness of financial initiatives that have been taken by the government of Rajasthan.

LITERATURE REVIEW

Jain (2016) made an attempt to analyze the awareness level of various financial services available for house hold workers in Jaipur city. It has been concluded that dream of complete financial inclusion cannot be fulfilled until there is a launch of mass awareness drive for educating the masses about availability and usage of these services. Bank is further required to introduce need based product offerings so that unbanked people can be financially included.

Dixit and Ghosh (2013) concluded towards a huge variation in the state of financial inclusion for different states in India. Kerala, Maharashtra and Karnataka have shown higher inclusion rate while Gujarat, Manipur, Rajasthan. Assam, Bihar, UP and MP are poor on the grounds of financial inclusion. The issue is in terms of geographical and demographic reach, followed by lack of financial literacy and awareness level about using the financial products.

Neha Sharma (2017) has revealed that financial inclusion in Rajasthan state is 75.3 percent and the state has a poverty rate of 64.2 percent. Hence as per the low, medium and high classification of extent of financial exclusion in Indian states, Rajasthan lies in low index of financial inclusion.

Majundar (2013) carried out a study on Hooghly district of West Bengal so as to conclude that scheme related to financial inclusion has not been successful for scheduled castes, scheduled tribes, Other Backward Classes and the ones who are less educated. It was further revealed that this scheme is ill targeted as the benefits are reaped by higher sections of society.

Gwalani (2014) has concluded that efforts have been taken by the Indian government for financial inclusion but seeing the nature of diversified nature of the country the need is to focus on basics and customize models as per need so as to accelerate the process of economic growth.

Kumar (2013) has concluded that there is a presence of positive and valuable change in financial inclusion on account of technological up gradations. He further recommended towards the need to have adequate provisions in place so that poor people do not drift away from banking.

Goyal (2016) made an attempt to investigate the present state of PMJDY in India so as to conclude that accounts opened in rural area on account of PMJDY is higher as compared to urban banking area. Study further depicted that there was an opening of 60% accounts in PMJDY that were mobilized into deposit of 24939.22 crores while the rest of 40 percent were opened with zero balance as on September 30, 2015. The state wise scenario further depicts that highest number of accounts were opened in UP in urban as well as rural areas due to highest rate of population. RBI reports further reveal that with the introduction of business facilitators as well as correspondents, opening of ATM and bank branches has led to coverage of rural areas as well (Mohanty, 2015).

Pokhriyal (2011) carried out a study on microfinance and financial inclusion in India so as to conclude that rural areas as well as the rural people are still deprived and discriminated with respect to financial inclusion. There is a presence of diminishing branch network in rural area which signifies that much importance has not been given here. Moreover, major proportion of banking facilities has been inclined towards Southern and Northern regions of the nation. This is thus going against the objective of creating more inclusive financial growth for rural people.

Mukherjee (2012) critically examined the role and efficacy of the commercial banks in Jharkhand state with respect to their responsibility towards promotion of financial inclusion. The author concluded that the primary responsibility of ensuring financial inclusion in India lies with the commercial banks that are adhering with the guidelines of RBI. But due to the huge size and diversity of population the commercial banks have been taking the assistance of various social and financial entities like co-operative banks, regional rural banks (RRBs), self-help groups (SHGs), joint liability groups, and other non-banking finance companies (NBFCs) to fulfill the goal of financial inclusion.

Shah (2015) carried out a study on financial inclusion practices going on within Indian nations so as to reach at a conclusion that addressing of financial exclusion is only possible when banking industry takes holistic approach in terms of creating awareness towards financial products and providing advice on money management, savings and credit schemes. The committee formed by RBI further believes that there is a need to unite financial policies with structural reforms where the government has main role to play in order to deliver financial inclusion in a stable manner (Mohanty, 2015).

Ancona (2014) has concluded from the study on Udaipur district in Rajasthan that several problems have made the state financially excluded which are in form of tremendous burden on females for household work, In addition, low literacy and education levels along with lack of exposure to financial education have led to continued financial exclusion within the state.

Morgan (2014) revealed that financial stability can be attained in developing economies when there is an increase in share of lending to small and medium sized enterprises (SMEs), followed by reducing non-performing loans (NPLs) and the probability of default by financial institutions. The study further recommended that policy measures should be tank for increasing financial inclusion, at least by SMEs so as to attain the side-benefit of contributing to financial stability as well.

Park (2015) has concluded that areas such as per capita income; demographic characteristics and rule of law is significantly impacting financial inclusion in developing Asia. It has also been noted by the author that financial inclusion significantly reduces poverty followed by lowering of income inequality. The author has further recommended that provisions for retirement pensions; and stronger rule of law, including enforcement of financial contracts and financial regulatory oversight is likely to enhance financial inclusion.

Kumbhar (2011) made an attempt to study the Scope and Problems in India with respect to financial inclusion through m-banking services so as to conclude that mobile telephone service has shown a tremendous growth in the last five years and this has provided an opportunity for financial inclusion. However, because of various problems in m-banking system this is not widely accepted by Indian bank customers. Hence the need here is to improve m-banking service including network coverage and security in m-banking.

Mir (2014) has concluded that banks have maintained a compliance with respect to RBI norms in terms of opening new bank branches, offering no frills account, Kinas credit card, simplifying KYC norms, but still efforts are needed to put financial inclusion into rapid progress. A lot has been done but a lot more is required to be attained. Hence the bankers are needed to keep on reforming their plans and ensure that the poor are not left to the clutches of informal sources of finance. Banks within Jammu and Kashmir are required to open more branches within rural areas and create awareness about banking services by telling them about the benefits of the banking services. Dixit and Ghosh (2013) recommended towards the need of stakeholder coordination (banks, government, NGOs) so as to achieve the aim of financial inclusion. States should further develop customized solutions based on the experiences of their peers across the nations. Majumdar (2013) recommended that proactive steps should be taken by banking officials, panchayat as well as district administration so as to aid in overall success of mission.

Research Gap

After having an extensive review of literature, it was observed that though there was a vast literature on financial inclusion as well as its effectiveness in India. But very few studies have focused on its effectiveness within Rajasthan state of India.

Objectives Framed for the Study

The present study tries to understand the Effectiveness of financial inclusion initiatives by government in Rajasthan.

Hypothesis

See Table 1 for hypotheses.

RESEARCH METHODOLOGY

The study has undergone quantitative nature where primary data collection was done by usage of structured questionnaire method, in order to study the effectiveness of financial inclusion initiatives within Rajasthan State. Data collection was done from 200 individuals who were from weaker section of the society and were eligible for

Table 1. Hypotheses frame for the study

H_{01}	There is no significant influence of gender on awareness of financial services
H_{02}	There is no significant influence of education on awareness of financial services
H_{03}	There is no significant influence of gender on usage of financial services
H_{04}	There is no significant influence of education on usage of financial services
H_{05}	There is no significant influence of gender on experience with financial services
H_{06}	There is no significant influence of education on experience with financial services

financial inclusion initiative given by government. Convenience sampling method was adopted as undertaking the technique has helped to collect information based on ease and comfort. A total of 300 questionnaires were distributed among the respondents and only 200 questionnaires were completely filled and thus used for the study. All items use a 5-point Likert scale, with 5 = strongly agree and 1 = strongly disagree. Study has undergone quantitative test such as descriptive statistics, cross tabulation and ANOVA test in order to find out influence between the variables.

Data Analysis and Interpretation

Interpretation

Most of the respondents were male (70%) and the rest were female (30%). Majority of them were educated till primary school (43.5%) while the rest were divided into being illiterate (21.5%), secondary school pass out (19.5%) and graduate (15.5%). The occupation of the majority respondents was of job (39%) while labour class, farmer

Table 2. Demographic profile

		Frequency	Percent
Gender	Male	140	70
	Female	60	30
	Total	200	100.0
Occupation	Farmer	54	27
	Job	78	39
	Own business	46	23
	Labour	22	11
	Total	200	100.0
Educational Qualification	Illiterate	43	21.5
	Primary school	87	43.5
	Secondary school	39	19.5
	Graduate	31	15.5
	Total	200	100.0
Income	Below Rs. 12000	10	5.0
	Rs. 12000 to Rs. 30000	73	36.5
	Rs. 30000 to Rs. 60000	97	48.5
	Above 60000	20	10.0
	Total	200	100.0

Table 3. Descriptive statistics on awareness of financial services

	Mean	Std. Deviation
Loans	3.97	1.173
Internet Banking	1.91	.287
Mobile Banking	1.91	.294
Credit Cards	1.91	.287
Debit Cards	3.96	1.179
Cash Transaction	4.35	.699
Cheque Book	3.97	1.171
Insurance	3.97	1.173
Kisan CC	3.95	1.189

and those having own business formed a percentage of 11, 27 and 23 respectively. Majority of them (48.5%) had Rs 30000 to Rs 60000 as income. 36.5% had Rs. 12000 to Rs. 30000 as annual income while the rest earned either below 12000 (5%) or above 60000 (10%).

Interpretation

As per the results drawn from arithmetic mean it can be interpreted that the respondents have awareness towards Cash transaction (4.35) followed by Cheque book (3.97) and insurance (3.97). This shows that respondents had some awareness about financial inclusion services provided by the bank. However standard deviation value indicates that majority of respondents are aware about the concept of financial inclusion. Responses vary around consumer awareness towards Kisan Credit Card (1.189) followed by Debit card (1.179) and Loans (1.173) and insurance (1.173).

Interpretation

As per the results drawn from arithmetic mean it can be interpreted that the respondents have been using Cash transaction (2.43) followed by Cheque book (2.19). In addition the respondents also use financial services such as insurance (2.14) and Kisan credit card (2.14). This shows that respondents having been using some of the financial inclusion services provided by the bank. However, the standard deviation value indicates that majority of the respondents have been using financial inclusion services. Responses vary around the usage of Debit cards (0.783) followed by loans (0.779).

Table 4. Descriptive statistics on usage of financial services

	Mean	Std. Deviation
Loans	2.13	.779
Internet Banking	1.09	.372
Mobile Banking	1.08	.346
Credit Cards	1.08	.346
Debit Cards	2.13	.783
Cash Transaction	2.43	.726
Cheque Book	2.19	.716
Insurance	2.14	.737
Kisan CC	2.14	.737

Table 5. Descriptive statistics on experience with financial services

	Mean	Std. Deviation
Bank Employees 'Attitude	2.69	1.254
Bank's Interest in your Problem	2.69	1.250
Reasonable Interest on Loan	3.49	1.156
Branch Timings	3.45	1.259
Bank Charges	2.72	1.076
Banking Procedures	3.47	1.169
Availability of ATM	2.26	1.140
Maximum Interest on Savings	2.95	1.023

Interpretation

As per the results from arithmetic mean an interpretation can be drawn that respondents have positive experience with interest on loan by bank (3.49) followed by banking procedures such as documentation and identification (3.47) as well as branch timings (3.45). This shows that respondents have a positive experience towards financial inclusion services provided by the bank. However, the standard deviation value indicates that majority of the respondents have positive response towards usage of financial inclusion services. Responses vary around branch timings (1.259) followed by Bank employees 'attitude (1.254).

ANNOVA Tables

Interpretation

It has been interpreted from the ANNOVA table that null hypothesis was rejected in case of cash transaction. This is as the significant value is lower than .05%. This indicates the presence of significant influence of gender on awareness of financial services. It was however accepted in rest of the cases as significant value is greater than .05%. This shows that there is an absence of any significant influence of gender on awareness of financial services. The analysis shows that in majority of variables like insurance, Kisan CC, cheque book, debit and credit card, mobile and net banking consumers have same perception while the perception is different in case of cash transaction. Thus, it can be said that there is absence of significant association between gender and awareness of consumers towards financial inclusion.

Interpretation

It has been interpreted from the ANNOVA table that null hypothesis was rejected in case of internet banking, mobile banking and credit cards. This is as the significant value is lower than .05%. This indicates the presence of significant influence of education on awareness of financial services. It was however accepted in rest of the cases as significant value is greater than .05%. This shows that there is an absence of any significant influence of education on awareness of financial services. The analysis shows that in majority of variables like insurance, Kisan CC, cash transaction, Cheque book users have same perception while the perception is different in case of debit and credit card, mobile and net banking. Thus, it can be said that there is absence of significant association between education and awareness of consumers towards financial inclusion.

Interpretation

It has been interpreted from the ANNOVA table that null hypothesis was rejected in case of Cheque book as the significant value is lower than .05%. This indicates the presence of significant influence of gender on usage of financial services. It was however accepted in rest of the cases as significant value is greater than .05%. This shows that there is an absence of any significant influence of gender on usage of financial services. The analysis shows that in majority of variables like insurance, Kisan CC, debit and credit card, mobile and net banking and cash transaction users have same perception while the perception is different in case of cheque book. Thus,

Table 6. H_{01}: There is no significant influence of gender on awareness of financial services

		Sum of Squares	df	Mean Square	F	Sig.
Loans	Between Groups	.420	1	.420	.304	.582
	Within Groups	273.400	198	1.381		
	Total	273.820	199			
Internet Banking	Between Groups	.009	1	.009	.104	.748
	Within Groups	16.371	198	.083		
	Total	16.380	199			
Mobile Banking	Between Groups	.002	1	.002	.025	.875
	Within Groups	17.193	198	.087		
	Total	17.195	199			
Credit Cards	Between Groups	.009	1	.009	.104	.748
	Within Groups	16.371	198	.083		
	Total	16.380	199			
Debit Cards	Between Groups	.259	1	.259	.186	.667
	Within Groups	276.336	198	1.396		
	Total	276.595	199			
Cash Transaction	Between Groups	2.059	1	2.059	4.286	.040
	Within Groups	95.136	198	.480		
	Total	97.195	199			
Cheque Book	Between Groups	.362	1	.362	.263	.608
	Within Groups	272.393	198	1.376		
	Total	272.755	199			
Insurance	Between Groups	.420	1	.420	.304	.582
	Within Groups	273.400	198	1.381		
	Total	273.820	199			
Kisan CC	Between Groups	.214	1	.214	.151	.698
	Within Groups	281.286	198	1.421		
	Total	281.500	199			

Table 7. H_{02}: There is no significant influence of education on awareness of financial services

		Sum of Squares	df	Mean Square	F	Sig.
Loans	Between Groups	3.095	3	1.032	.747	.525
	Within Groups	270.725	196	1.381		
	Total	273.820	199			
Internet Banking	Between Groups	.912	3	.304	3.853	.010
	Within Groups	15.468	196	.079		
	Total	16.380	199			
Mobile Banking	Between Groups	.797	3	.266	3.176	.025
	Within Groups	16.398	196	.084		
	Total	17.195	199			
Credit Cards	Between Groups	.912	3	.304	3.853	.010
	Within Groups	15.468	196	.079		
	Total	16.380	199			
Debit Cards	Between Groups	3.525	3	1.175	.843	.472
	Within Groups	273.070	196	1.393		
	Total	276.595	199			
Cash Transaction	Between Groups	2.108	3	.703	1.448	.230
	Within Groups	95.087	196	.485		
	Total	97.195	199			
Cheque Book	Between Groups	3.225	3	1.075	.782	.505
	Within Groups	269.530	196	1.375		
	Total	272.755	199			
Insurance	Between Groups	3.095	3	1.032	.747	.525
	Within Groups	270.725	196	1.381		
	Total	273.820	199			
Kisan CC	Between Groups	3.694	3	1.231	.869	.458
	Within Groups	277.806	196	1.417		
	Total	281.500	199			

Table 8. H_{03}: There is no significant influence of gender on usage of financial services

		Sum of Squares	df	Mean Square	F	Sig.
Loans	Between Groups	1.234	1	1.234	2.047	.154
	Within Groups	119.386	198	.603		
	Total	120.620	199			
Internet Banking	Between Groups	.029	1	.029	.207	.649
	Within Groups	27.526	198	.139		
	Total	27.555	199			
Mobile Banking	Between Groups	.006	1	.006	.049	.824
	Within Groups	23.869	198	.121		
	Total	23.875	199			
Credit Cards	Between Groups	.006	1	.006	.049	.824
	Within Groups	23.869	198	.121		
	Total	23.875	199			
Debit Cards	Between Groups	1.339	1	1.339	2.200	.140
	Within Groups	120.536	198	.609		
	Total	121.875	199			
Cash Transaction	Between Groups	.034	1	.034	.065	.800
	Within Groups	104.986	198	.530		
	Total	105.020	199			
Cheque Book	Between Groups	4.086	1	4.086	8.249	.005
	Within Groups	98.069	198	.495		
	Total	102.155	199			
Insurance	Between Groups	.137	1	.137	.252	.617
	Within Groups	107.943	198	.545		
	Total	108.080	199			
Kisan CC	Between Groups	.137	1	.137	.252	.617
	Within Groups	107.943	198	.545		
	Total	108.080	199			

it can be said that there is absence of significant association of gender on usage of financial services.

Interpretation

It has been interpreted from the ANNOVA table that null hypothesis was accepted in all of the cases as significant value is greater than .05%. This shows that there is an absence of any significant influence of education on usage of financial services. The analysis shows that all the users of financial inclusion services have same perception. Thus, it can be said that there is absence of significant association of education on usage of financial services.

Interpretation

As per the ANNOVA table an interpretation can be drawn that null hypothesis was accepted in all the cases as significant value is greater than .05%. This shows the absence of significant influence of gender on experience with financial services. The analysis shows that users had same kind of perception towards the financial inclusion services offered by the banks. Thus, it can be said that there is absence of significant association of gender on experience with financial services.

Interpretation

The ANNOVA tables have led to the conclusion that null hypothesis was rejected in case of branch timings, charges as well as availability of ATM. This is as the significant value is lower than .05%. This indicates the presence of significant influence of education on experience with financial services. It was however accepted in rest of the cases as significant value is greater than .05%. This shows that there is an absence of significant influence of education on experience with financial services. The analysis shows that consumers held same perception with respect to variables like bank employees 'attitude, interest in the issues, reasonable interest on loan, banking procedures and maximum interest on savings.

Table 9. H_{04}: There is no significant influence of education on usage of financial services

		Sum of Squares	df	Mean Square	F	Sig.
Loans	Between Groups	3.783	3	1.261	2.115	.100
	Within Groups	116.837	196	.596		
	Total	120.620	199			
Internet Banking	Between Groups	.778	3	.259	1.898	.131
	Within Groups	26.777	196	.137		
	Total	27.555	199			
Mobile Banking	Between Groups	.638	3	.213	1.794	.150
	Within Groups	23.237	196	.119		
	Total	23.875	199			
Credit Cards	Between Groups	.638	3	.213	1.794	.150
	Within Groups	23.237	196	.119		
	Total	23.875	199			
Debit Cards	Between Groups	3.682	3	1.227	2.035	.110
	Within Groups	118.193	196	.603		
	Total	121.875	199			
Cash Transaction	Between Groups	.029	3	.010	.018	.997
	Within Groups	104.991	196	.536		
	Total	105.020	199			
Cheque Book	Between Groups	.964	3	.321	.622	.601
	Within Groups	101.191	196	.516		
	Total	102.155	199			
Insurance	Between Groups	.195	3	.065	.118	.949
	Within Groups	107.885	196	.550		
	Total	108.080	199			
Kisan CC	Between Groups	.195	3	.065	.118	.949
	Within Groups	107.885	196	.550		
	Total	108.080	199			

Table 10. H_{04}: There is no significant influence of gender on experience with financial services

		Sum of Squares	df	Mean Square	F	Sig.
Bank Employees'Attitude	Between Groups	.000	1	.000	.000	.990
	Within Groups	313.155	198	1.582		
	Total	313.155	199			
Bank's Interest in Your Problem	Between Groups	.004	1	.004	.002	.961
	Within Groups	310.776	198	1.570		
	Total	310.780	199			
Reasonable Interest on Loan	Between Groups	2.429	1	2.429	1.825	.178
	Within Groups	263.526	198	1.331		
	Total	265.955	199			
Branch Timings	Between Groups	0.000	1	0.000	0.000	1.000
	Within Groups	315.500	198	1.593		
	Total	315.500	199			
Bank Charges	Between Groups	2.777	1	2.777	2.417	.122
	Within Groups	227.543	198	1.149		
	Total	230.320	199			
Banking Procedures	Between Groups	.801	1	.801	.585	.445
	Within Groups	271.019	198	1.369		
	Total	271.820	199			
Availability of ATM	Between Groups	.747	1	.747	.574	.450
	Within Groups	257.733	198	1.302		
	Total	258.480	199			
Maximum Interest on Savings	Between Groups	.259	1	.259	.247	.620
	Within Groups	208.136	198	1.051		
	Total	208.395	199			

CONCLUSION

From the above report it can be concluded that awareness and usage level of weaker sections of society is only towards Loans, debit cards (used as ATM card more often), cash transaction cheques and Kisan Credit Card. Majority of them are not aware of and hence do not use technological means of financial inclusion such as internet, mobile banking and credit card. This is majorly true for females on account of the social structure that is present in the state where they are restricted to household

Table 11. H_{04}: There is no significant influence of education on experience with financial services

		Sum of Squares	df	Mean Square	F	Sig.
Bank Employees'Attitude	Between Groups	.458	3	.153	.096	.962
	Within Groups	312.697	196	1.595		
	Total	313.155	199			
Bank's Interest in Your Problem	Between Groups	.428	3	.143	.090	.965
	Within Groups	310.352	196	1.583		
	Total	310.780	199			
Reasonable Interest on Loan	Between Groups	6.056	3	2.019	1.522	.210
	Within Groups	259.899	196	1.326		
	Total	265.955	199			
Branch Timings	Between Groups	22.908	3	7.636	5.115	.002
	Within Groups	292.592	196	1.493		
	Total	315.500	199			
Bank Charges	Between Groups	19.250	3	6.417	5.959	.001
	Within Groups	211.070	196	1.077		
	Total	230.320	199			
Banking Procedures	Between Groups	1.346	3	.449	.325	.807
	Within Groups	270.474	196	1.380		
	Total	271.820	199			
Availability of ATM	Between Groups	17.138	3	5.713	4.639	.004
	Within Groups	241.342	196	1.231		
	Total	258.480	199			
Maximum Interest on Savings	Between Groups	2.325	3	.775	.737	.531
	Within Groups	206.070	196	1.051		
	Total	208.395	199			

chores and do not get a chance to get awareness of financial initiatives. Lack of proper internet facility in the villages as well slow speed is further aiding to the issue. However people from rural areas are more aware of the financial initiatives as they want to get an advantage of the same. Moreover they often get a chance to interact with panchayat officials who play a major role in their overall awareness. In terms of experience with financial services, the respondents have been found to have a positive interest towards loans as they find it to be reasonable enough. They also get the help of banking staff with respect to procedures such as documentation and identification norms. The branch timings of bank has also been found suitable however distance from the bank is a major issue for them. This is especially true for people living in rural areas as branches are very less in comparison to city. Same applies to the availability of ATM whose number is not so widespread. It is thus recommended to the government that financial inclusion of the masses is only possible when people get more educated towards the financial services. This should be followed by increasing the number of bank branches and ATM outlets both in villages and cities. The provision of proper internet facilities and free wifi will further aid in generating the awareness level as well as usage of services like internet and mobile banking. This will not only help in attaining the goal of financial inclusion but also of cashless economy.

REFERENCES

Dixit, R., & Ghosh, M. (2013). Financial Inclusion For Inclusive Growth Of India - A Study. *International Journal Of Business Management & Research, 3*(1), 147–156.

Goyal, M. A. (2016). Pradhan Mantri Jan Dhan Yojana: A Step Towards Financial Inclusion. *Pacific Business Review International, 8*(9).

Gwalani, H. A., & Parkhi, S. (2014). Financial Inclusion–Building A Success Model In The Indian Context. *Procedia: Social and Behavioral Sciences, 133*, 372–378. doi:10.1016/j.sbspro.2014.04.203

Jain, M. R. (2016). A Study of Financial Inclusion of Household Workers in Jaipur. *Sumedha Journal of Management, 5*(2), 94.

Kumar, N. D. (2013). Current Situation of Financial Inclusion in India and Its future vision. *International Journal of Management and Social Sciences Research*, *2*(8).

Kumbhar, V. (2011). *Financial Inclusion Through M-Banking Services: Scope And Problems In India*. Academic Press.

Majumdar, C. A. (2013). Financial Inclusion In Hooghly. *Economic and Political Weekly*, *48*(21), 55–60.

Mir, S. B. (2014). A Study On The Effectiveness Of The Financial Inclusion Program In Jammu And Kashmir: Initiatives By The Major Banks. *Global Journal Of Finance And Management*, *6*(3), 281–286.

Mohanty, D. (2015). *Report OfThethe Committee on Medium-term Path on Financial Inclusion*. RBI.

Morgan, P. A. (2014). *Financial Stability And Financial Inclusion*. Academic Press.

Mukherjee, A. A. (2012). *Financial Inclusion Of The Poor And Marginalised In Jharkhand: Analysis Of The Existing Model*. Academic Press.

Neha Sharma, R. G. (2017). Financial Inclusion Initiatives In Rajasthan: An Overview. *Inspira-Journal of Commerce, Economics & Computer Science*, *3*(1), 156–160.

Park, C. A. (2015). *Financial Inclusion*. Poverty, And Income Inequality In Developing Asia.

Pokhriyal, A., & Ghildiyal, V. (2011). Progress of Microfinance and Financial Inclusion "A Critical Analysis of SHG-Bank Linkage Program in India". *International Journal of Economics and Finance*, *3*(2), 255. doi:10.5539/ijef.v3n2p255

Shah, P., & Dubhashi, M. (2015). Review Paper on Financial Inclusion-The Means of Inclusive Growth. *Chanakya International Journal of Business Research*, *1*(1), 37–48. doi:10.15410/cijbr/2015/v1i1/61403

Chapter 5
How Customer Analytics and Digital Technologies Drive Banks to Understand Consumer Awareness Towards Financial Inclusion

Yuvraj Sharma
SLK Global Solutions Pvt. Ltd., India

ABSTRACT

In today's switching economy, customers' needs are changing and they are demanding more transparency, higher involvement, and clear communication in day-to-day banking processes. The rationale behind carrying out the present research is to identify the role of customer analytics in the new digital customer journey in terms of enhancing their engagement, loyalty, and satisfaction. The present research emphasizes opportunities that would accrue to financial institutions after demonetization and collecting large amount of demographics, customer transaction, and account-related data. Primary data was collected from 300 customers through a structured questionnaire to know their perceptions about the role of customer analytics and digital technologies to build their confidence and capability to use financial services. This study brings out the customer analytics trends and identifies the reasons due to which banks are struggling to keep pace with the increasing demand of both digital savvy and traditional consumers.

DOI: 10.4018/978-1-5225-4035-9.ch005

INTRODUCTION

In this time of heightened expectations world, it is essential for financial institutions to meet desires of customers by delivering superior experience to them. In the context of delivering sustained customer experience, banks are going beyond traditional customer services. However, financial institutions in developing countries like India are facing challenges to keep pace with their customers. The main aim of the present chapter is to be identified the role of customer analytics and adoption of digital technologies to enhance consumer experience and getting insights into customer's data. This chapter provides detail about impact of use of customer analytics and digital technologies on various financial inclusion related activities such that customer insights, risk management, improve payment frond-ends, establish strong integration, framing policies and focus on high value activities. Researcher explored different challenges including change in polices, legacy control environment, absence of centralize data management system, lack of clarity on technology implementation and reacting too slowly to the needs of today's 'non-stop customers which are main hurdle in the path of adoption new technologies in banks. However, to overcome these gaps, the present Indian government is more concentrating on adoption of modern methods including mobile payment and online banking to reach wide audience. By using this, financial institutions would be able to enhance customer experience, manage enterprise risks, profiling of customers and established customized communications with people in a proper manner. On the other side, consumer account and transaction related data generated after demonetization decision taken by Modi's government could be beneficial for financial institutions in framing polices and taps untargeted consumers. Furthermore, respondents views have been incorporated the study to identify opportunities generate for financial institutions after using analytics and producing large amount of data. It can be said that customer analytics and digital technologies can be useful in term of overcome financial inclusion gaps such that improving financial services for the poor, strengthening fraud detection and simplifying activation processes.

BACKGROUND

The term financial inclusion could be understood in term of appropriateness of financial services and products and their reach to all income groups at affordable cost. Customer analytics term is a combination of processes and technologies that provides opportunity to organizations to get insight customers data and understands their needs (PWC, 2014). According to Analytics India Industry report (2017), financial institutions and small and medium business verticals in India are focused on adoption of Big data to enhance interaction with their customers and mange large volume of data effectively. SAP has emerged as a dominant player after the recent GST move in country and it is playing huge role in SME marketplace to improve efficiency and cut operational costs. This study presents the boom of customer analytics in various sectors in India including Finance & Banking, E-commerce, Retail & CPG, Telecom, Travel & hospitality and Parma& healthcare. Furthermore, study finding explored that 37% or $756 Million revenue generates in India is coming from Finance & Banking sector (Analytics India Magazine, 2017). Customer analytics techniques such that social media analysis, credit analysis, sentimental analysis, customer profitability and life time value can help banks to better understand customer experience and monitoring over strategies. On the other hand, digital technologies including mobile and internet banking could help to connect with large population. Customer analytics is a wide topic and researcher has been concentrated mainly on role of analytics and digital techniques and their impact on financial inclusion. Major area of study is focused on needs of customer analytics and adoption of digital technologies and their impact on customer experience, data collection & management and customer insights based on their behaviour. Furthermore, chapter provide information about how new data practices could be helpful for financial institutions to serve customers who are poor and have lack formal identification documents to open bank account. Researcher has tried to find relationship between use of analytics and its future implication on financial inclusion. It is tried to identify that how by using customer analytics in operations, banks could be able to overcome financial inclusion gaps like improving financial services for the poor, strengthening fraud detection and simplifying activation processes. Primary data has been collected from respondents to identify role of customer analytics and digital adoption and their future implications on financial inclusion. Apart from that, challenges faced by financial institutions in reaching unbanked and under-banked customers have been discussed in study.

OBJECTIVES OF THE RESEARCH

- To examine the impact of Customer analytics and digital technologies adoption on financial institutions
- To identify challenges faced by institutions in reaching unbanked and under-banked customers in developing nations like India
- To explore association between Customer analytics and digital adoption in banks and overcome financial inclusion gaps

REVIEW OF LITERATURE

What Is Customer Analytics and Why Should Banks Focus on It?

According to Infosys report (2012) the primary goal of analytics is to collect and manage information about customers and timely deliver products and services chosen by them. There are several challenges including transforming raw data into structured information and deeper insights based of huge amount of data associated with the implementation of analytics in banking process. Analytics can be applied on customer's historical and real time data. A broad classification of analytics could be done on the basis of internal customers (bank branch staff, and selling agents) and external customers (regulatory bodies and research firm). The purpose of customer analytics is to analysis of customer relationship with banks and assessing life time profitability from them (Infosys, 2012). The main key results of analytics are segmentation, cross selling and attrition analysis. Srivastava and Gopalkrishnan (2015) studied that marketing analytics would be useful for banks in terms of targeting specific customer segment and lead sales opportunities. Furthermore, it is explored that, many banks are using Fraud analytics for the purpose of fighting against fraud and managing data privacy across the world. Predictive analytics is also using by many banks in order to predict the future of their business and understand customer buying behaviour and spend pattern Srivastava and Gopalkrishnan (2015).

According to IBM executive report (2012), different types of customer analytics techniques including Predictive modelling, data visualization, segmentation and information management, Artificial Intelligence and Machine Learning have been used by financial institutions across the world. Segmentation and developing digital delivery systems techniques could be helpful for banks to specifically target underserved customers and reduced cost and barriers. Predictive modelling technique are using by financial institutions to decrease attrition by accurately predicting customer's demands and better execution of right proactive campaigns to retain them. Information management is used by financial organisations to enhance customer loyalty, increase response rate and deliver highly relevant offers and messages to them within stipulated time. Data visualisation are implementing by many companies to give a clear picture about customer life cycle including usage of services, collection recovery and understand customer behavior in more appropriate manner (IBM executive report, 2012).

In addition, Big data technologies including Machine learning, Regression analysis, social network analysis, classification tree analysis, sentiment analysis, genetic algorithm and association rule learning are currently using in industry to create business value. These analytics techniques can be helpful for financial institutions to create culture of innovation and manage large amount of data including history of customers, geography, measure customers trust in the banking industry. In the context of understanding customers' buying habits and lifestyle preferences, analytics would be beneficial for banks (Carrie, 2017). On the other side, after using mobile and online banking services, people would be able to access information anywhere at any time.

How Financial Institutions Can Benefit From Analytics and Adoption of Digital Technologies

Rao and Budde (2015) explored that implementation of digital technologies and analytics would open up the door to deeper understanding of customers needs and reducing the risk of fraud. In order to predict probability of happen an event and deliver services to right set of people, it could be helpful for banks. In the context of carrying out customer acquisition and engagement strategies, analytics can help financial institutions (Rao & Budde, 2015).

Wright et al. (2013) described that urban people have easy and universal access to get financial services as compared to low-income group. There are several factors behind that such that social-dynamics, literacy levels and absence of collection of demographics details. These are responsible behind creating unbalance situation between urban and rural people in term of getting services. Moreover, rapid technological innovations and analytics could be helped to overcome these financial inclusion gaps (Wright et al., 2013). Deb (2014) explored that banking firms are using advanced data analytics in order to target underserved customers in emerging markets and extending their credit limits. It was identified that for expanding the boundaries of financial inclusion, credit-scoring consumers via data analytic helpful for financial institutions. The other major impact of advanced analytics on non-traditional data sources could be seen in form of expanding the boundaries of financial inclusion and overcome gap between rural and urban people. Deb has given example of Cignifi that had taken pre-paid mobile call record data to determine credit scores and provide effectively services. Its major advantage could be seen on delivering cheaper and better credit to underserved consumers (Deb, 2014). In addition, Gupta (2014) also supported the study done by Deb. Scholar identified Furthermore, scholar explored uses of advance analytics in simplifying various operations such that improving mobile money services, making activation processes fast, providing key inputs into product design and strengthening fraud detection etc. Other impact of analytics could be seen on enhancing marketing effectiveness and solve current problems in digital financial services in a significant manner (Gupta, 2014).

Krause (2016) explored financial inclusion term that could be defined in term of managing appropriate financial services and products in a responsible manner. Different types of financial services including credit, insurance, saving payment are available to all income group customers at affordable price. However, along with several advantages of digital technological and analytics, researcher has defined different risks such that fraud and mis-selling, privacy and data-management associate with the adoption of analytics and digital technologies (Krause, 2016).

Customer Analytics and Digital Technologies and Their Impact on Financial Institutions

Bokman and his colleagues (2014) have conducted survey of 400 top managers of large international companies to identify relationship between the use of customer analytics and corporate performance. It was found that enhanced marketing earnings, generating above-average profits and gained higher ROI than competitors were major benefits gained after adoption of analytics. After implementing analytics, financial firms were able to emphasize on their strategic key performance indicators including customers acquired, retained and enhanced their loyalty and increase satisfaction towards services offered to them (Bokman et al.,2014). In addition, advanced analytics techniques including R, Python and SAS, Spotfire, Hive, Tableau, and Hadoop could be beneficial for banks to maintain large amount of data and understand customer life-cycle management in an effective manner. As per the survey report of PWC (2015), digital technologies and advance level analytics interface with banks have undergone a huge transformation towards improving processes and driving value. Furthermore, report disclosed about major reasons behind adopting new technologies in various business operations such that reduce cost of operations, strengthen delivery channels, scale up business and understand trends by better connecting with their customers etc. This report further discloses that to better understand the consumer attitudes towards financial inclusion, customer analytics could be helpful for organisations. In the context of discovering new revenue streams, penetrate rural areas, tapping the unbanked population of developing nations like India, digital technologies and social media platforms could be beneficial for financial sector. Social, Mobile, Analytics and Cloud (SMAC) have become so essential and taken mind bending leaps over the last decade. In addition, PWC survey report explored that in India 16% of the banks were actually allocating funds towards adoption of digital technology and innovation (PWC, 2014). From the result of survey, it has been observed that analytics not only help banks to deal with the tech-savvy customers but also deal with traditional customers who wants personalised approach in getting services and products. It is identified that with the rise of digital and social media, majority of the banks have started to perform their operations using analytics solutions to arrive at key business decisions. Marketing analytics, customer acquisition, credit risk, up-sell, cross-sell, and segmentation and churn prediction are major areas in which analytics could be beneficial for banks. Apart from that, digital technologies can help financial institutions to identify trends, establishing a better pricing structure and improving customer's experience. By directly interacting with traditional and digital savvy customers, banks could be able to understand their awareness and preferences about product and services in a more effective way. Along with this, it is found that most of the banks were using mature digital payment platforms likes national electronic clearing service (NECS), real-time gross settlement (RTGS), ATM and nation electronic fund transfer (NEFT). These techniques are producing large amount of transaction related data that could be helpful for banks for getting insights and delivery of services in remote areas. Along with this, strategies enabled by customer analytics techniques Predictive modelling and data visualisation can help banks to enhance customer experience management and improve their experience.

Major Challenges Faced by Financial Institutions to Reach Unbanked And Under-Banked Customers

In digital era, major banks in developing nations like India and Brazil are emphasizing on using analytics and digital technologies to improve customer's satisfaction level. But due to some reasons they are failing to gain real advantages from it. It is identified that lack of smart customer-segmentation, absence of a robust mechanism for customer grievance, presence of inconsistency to deliver personalised services across multiple channels and inadequate training to staff are major causes behind reaching unbanked and under-banked customers in developing nations like India (PWC, 2014). According to Corrigan and Battista (2015), income gaps between India's states, rise in inequality, a growing urban-rural divide and gender gaps in labour force participation and wages are major hurdle in path of successful implementation of tapping unbanked and under-banked customers. Other story of major issues is that 400 million people of the world are live in developing nations and they are still disconnected from the financial system. Only 55% of men and 37% of female customers have bank accounts. Besides that, other digital facts including 82% people who have not access of Internet, and only 5.5% population have mobile broadband showed that India is still far behind other countries in developing Asia in term of use of digital technologies in banking sector. However, positive changes came after pro-business, pro-growth, and anti-corruption momentum initiated by Modi government (Corrigan & Battista, 2015). According to World Bank Index Survey, only 35% Indian adults had access to a formal bank account. On the other side, presence of only 1, 15, 082 bank branch network and 1, 60,055 ATM network are not enough to capture unbanked and under-banked customers in rural areas (Financial Inclusion Summit, 2016). The low level of financial literacy about digital banking services, inadequacy of the banking infrastructure and presence of limited number of financial services players are the main hindrances to financial inclusion in developing country like India. Nevertheless, initiated taken by government like Pradhan Mantri Jan-Dhan Yojana (PMJDY) scheme could be helpful for banking sector to deliver financial services to the vast sections of the disadvantaged and low-income groups.

Opportunities Generate for Financial Institutions After Adoption of Analytics and Digital Platform

Set-Up Unique Identity Infrastructure

Lack of documentation to establish an individual identity and absence of accurate information are major challenges facing by financial institutions. In addition, many people have not basic identity documentation like an electricity bill, a proof of address and a birth certificate etc. In the absence of identity documentation unbanked and under-banked customers are unable to access financial services and resources. In order to address this issue and overcome financial inclusion, 'Aadhaar' issued by the Unique Identification Authority of India (UIDAI) could be helpful for financial institutions. According to Financial Inclusion Summit report (2016), in the context of converting raw data into meaning information, customer analytics could be helpful for banks. Demographic and biometric data of over half a billion residents, MongoDB database could be helpful for institutions. This large capture data could help banks to meet know-your-customer (KYC) rules and maintain online-biometric authentication of an individual (Financial Inclusion Summit, 2016). Besides that, data generated from mobile and online applications could be helpful for banks to tap un-targeted areas.

Huge Amount of Customer Data Collection and Management

In the new era, the banking sector has an opportunity to improve customer engagement strategy by effective utilisation of data and information. Analytics along with digital technologies are using to improve provisioning of financial services. There are different ways through which massive amount of data will be gathered like mobile phones, online banking, and linking 'Aadhaar' with bank customers account. Mobile money networks and online banking would help customers to easy Cash-In Cash-Out options so that customers would be able to deposit, transfer, and access their financial assets within stipulated time. Transaction related data produced by above methods could be helpful for financial institutions to tap un-targeted market and strengthening fraud detection (Gupta, 2014). Rana Kapoor, CEO of Yes bank welcome Modi government's decision to demonetize currency. Further, he described the impact of bold and revolutionary decisions on several fronts which include improve monetary transmission, structural moderation in currency, reach to large unbanked population in the country (Kapoor, 2016).

After demonetization, government emphasizes on linking 'Aadhaar' with bank customers account. Through initiated this move, people will motivate to provide their identity related information to banks and use of digital technologies to carry out their daily transaction online. Along with this, several other opportunities such that facilitate entry for poor and underprivileged residents into banking system and increase transparency in overall banking process. In the context of a creating a unified payment infrastructure and direct distribution of subsidies to beneficiary account, digital technologies could play crucial role. Through collecting and managing massive customer data, financial institutions would be able to remove barriers related to provide benefits of financial services to financially excluded segments in more effective manner (Cognizant report, 2015). Customer analytics and digital technologies could be helpful for financial institutions in term of strengthening back-end administrative processes; identifying loan defaulter and monitoring over services deliver to rural and unbanked areas people in an effective manner. Through digital modernization and analytics, banking sector would be able to create a superior customer experience and balance key customer values like loyalty, satisfaction and retention etc. With help of analytics and getting deeper insights into large amount of customer transaction and account related data, financial institutions would be able to better understand customer's needs.

Accelerating the Growth of Digital Transaction and Financial Inclusion

The adoption of electronic payment methods including mobile-money, electronic rupee and digital payment are helping banks to reach wide population. After the demonetization move and cash crunch, digital payment through e-wallet such that Oxigen, Paytm and MobiKwik etc. have increased 63 lakh from 17 lakh as on December'2016. In addition, high growth rate up 503% at 16 lakh daily transactions was marked through RuPay Cards (Rs 236 crores in monetary term). Through promoting digital transactions, transparency will increase and money will directly come into the system (Dovall, 2016). The other major impact of this decision could be seen in future on various activities such that improve monetary transmission, structural moderation in currency and reach to large unbanked population in the country. The major impact of setting up a cashless economy could be seen on creating better welfare financial inclusion schemes, enhance transparency, increase tax base and add to tax revenues and restrain the creation of black money. Along with digital technology, right product mix can help banks to meet consumer's needs and aspirations. As per the Wright et al. (2013) report, more than 700 million people in India had UIDAI which is based on finger-print and iris recognition technologies. On the other side, presence of varieties of technology options Mobile Apps, SMS, Mobile ATM and Voice IVR could be useful for banks to increase awareness among under-bank customers. However, there are several challenges including limited usage of Aadhaar number (KYC Proof) by some authorities, lack of Inter-bank Interoperability and poor infrastructure can affect the financial inclusion overcome goal of government and institutions (Wright et al.,2013). But now the situations are changes and present Indian government is concentrating towards make UIDAI compulsory to provide financial and subsidies related advantages to needed people. This step will help banks to reach unbanked and under-banked customers in India. Peppers and Rogers (2016) explored that absence of proper information about local enables, demographics, quality and cost of existing alternatives can create negative impact on consumers trust. Through understanding customer perceptions and considering different factors including reliability, convenience, transaction cost and increasing awareness among under-bank and rural customers towards advanced services/ facilities, financial institutions could be able to overcome financial gaps. However, in the absence of education, empowerment and increasing people awareness, banks would be unable to fill financial inclusions gaps and achieve future set of objectives (Peppers & Rogers, 2016). Gambetta, García-Benau and Zorio-Grima (2016) were provided information about various sources from where government and financial institutions can collect data. The major sources of customer data collections are market research, proprietary data (management/ IT data from firms) and third party research and statistics firms (García-Benau & Zorio-Grima, 2016).

RESEARCH METHODOLOGY

A survey of respondents from different educational qualifications and designations would be taken. For this purpose, survey was created online and link sent to the respondents in India. Secondary data was collected to investigate the latest digital trends and their role in financial inclusion. A total of 800 questionnaires were administered and after filtration we ended with 300 questionnaires completely filled in all respect. Primary data was collected from 300 customers through a structured questionnaire to know their perceptions about role of customer analytics and digital techniques. The first section of the study defined demographic profile of the respondents and their perceptions about use of analytics and digital technologies in banking sector. The second section tried to understand respondents views about opportunities generate after producing large amount of transactions and account related data and its relationship with financial inclusion. The third section evaluates impact of analytics and digital platform to fill financial inclusions gaps. One Way ANOVA and Chi-Square have been used to understand the association between customer analytics, digital technology adoption and financial inclusion in developing nations like India.

Data Analysis and Interpretation

Findings

On the basis of table, it can be said that most of the respondents participated in survey were male (73.0%) and they belong to 21-30 years (64.0%) age group.

Findings

Table 2 describes that 62.67% customers were aware about use of digital technologies in banking operations. In addition, most of the customers 60.67% were generally preferred Modern type of services in their day to day business operations. Higher usage of digital technologies in day to day bank operations by less than 1 year time period indicates that after demonetization and government moves, customers have motivated towards use of digital technologies to carry out their banking operations.

Table 1. Demographic profile of respondents

Demographic Profile		Frequency	Percent
Age (in Years)	< 20 years	32	10.70%
	21- 30 years	192	64.00%
	31- 50 years	54	18.00%
	> 50 years	22	7.30%
	Total	300	100.00%
Gender	Male	219	73.00%
	Female	81	27.00%
	Total	300	100.00%

Table 2. Awareness of customers and digital technologies usage pattern

		Frequency	Percentage
Awareness About Use of Digital Technologies in Banking Operations	Yes	188	62.67%
	No	112	37.33%
	Total	300	100.00%
Type of Banking Services Preferred	Modern	182	60.67%
	Traditional	118	39.33%
	Total	300	100.00%
Since How Long Have You Been Using Digital Technologies in day to day Bank Operations	Less than 1 year	148	49.30%
	1-3 years	82	27.03%
	4-10 years	24	8.00%
	More than 10 years	25	8.30%
	None	21	7.00%
	Total	300	100.00%

Table 3. Online transactions usually carried by various age groups

Age of Respondents	Online Transactions Usually Carried Out Monthly After Demonetization				
	1-5 Times	**5-10 Times**	**More Than 10 Times**	**None**	**Total**
<20	27	10	6	0	49
21-30	140	20	2	30	192
31-50	4	23	21	1	49
>50	0	10	5	1	16
Total	171	63	34	32	300

Findings

Table 3 explores that impact of demonetization decision taken by Indian government and their impact on various age groups. Most of the customers (140) who belong to 21-30 year age group were highly motivated to carry online transaction monthly. However, lack of awareness were seen in 31-50 and >50 age groups customers towards use of digital technologies and carried out their transaction online. The negative perceptions of customers indicates that banks should target >31 age group customers by increasing awareness among them towards utilization of digital technologies.

Findings

From Table 4, it is clear that most of the respondents who participated in survey was aware about used of digital technologies and customers analytics in banking operations. They were hoping that after implementing these banks would be able to meet their need in better way.

From the secondary research and interacting with respondents, it is observed that there are several positive impacts of customer analytics and digital technologies adoption by financial institutions to overcome financial inclusion gaps. In the present study, researcher has considered two major future financial inclusion implications including Customer insights and Customer experience management of customer analytics and digital adoption within financial institutions. Chi-Square was applied to identify significant association between two variables and testing of hypothesis.

- **H01:** There is a significant association between Customer analytics and digital adoption in banks and Customer Insights.

Table 5 explored that there is a significant difference between the customer analytics & digital techniques and their implication on getting customer insights. The probability of the chi-square test statistic (Chi-Square=6.218) was p=0.013, less than the alpha level of significance of 0.05.

Phi nonparametric correlation coefficient value 0.144 shows positive relationship between customer analytics and Customer Insights.

- **H02:** There is a significant association between customer analytics and digital techniques and Customer experience management.

Table 7 described that there is a significant association between the customer analytics and digital techniques and their implication on Customer experience

Table 4. Awareness and hope of positive change after use of digital technologies and Customer analytics in banking services

		Do You Hope Positive Change After Using Digital Technologies and Customer Analytics in Banking Functions		
		No	Yes	Total
Awareness About Use of Digital Technologies and Customers Analytics in Banking Operations	No	20	9	29
	Yes	113	158	271
	Total	133	167	300

Table 5. Association between customer analytics and customer insights

	Value	df	Asymp. Sig. (2-Sided)	Exact Sig. (2-Sided)	Exact Sig. (1-Sided)
Pearson Chi-Square	6.218a	1	.013		
Continuity Correction	5.280	1	.022		
Likelihood Ratio	6.307	1	.012		
Fisher's Exact Test				.018	.011
Linear-by-Linear Association	6.197	1	.013		
N of Valid Cases	300				

Table 6. Symmetric measures

Symmetric Measures		Value	Approx. Sig.
Nominal by Nominal	Phi	.144	.013
	Cramer's V	.144	.013
N of Valid Cases		300	

Table 7. Association between customer analytics and customer experience

	Value	df	Asymp. Sig. (2-Sided)	Exact Sig. (2-Sided)	Exact Sig. (1-Sided)
Pearson Chi-Square	13.066a	1	.000		
Continuity Correction	11.651	1	.001		
Likelihood Ratio	12.663	1	.000		
Fisher's Exact Test				.000	.000
Linear-by-Linear Association	13.022	1	.000		
N of Valid Cases	300				

management. The probability of the chi-square test statistic (Chi-Square=13.066) was p=0.000, less than the alpha level of significance of 0.05.

Phi nonparametric correlation coefficient value 0.209 shows positive relationship between customer analytics and Customer experience management.

- **H03:** There is no significant difference between respondents' views about Customer analytics adoption and opportunities generated for financial institutions.

Table 8. Symmetric measures

Symmetric Measures		Value	Approx. Sig.
Nominal by Nominal	Phi	.209	.000
	Cramer's V	.209	.000
N of Valid Cases		300	

Table 9. Opportunities generated after large data producing

Opportunities Generated for Financial Institutions After Demonetization		Sum of Squares	df	Mean Square	F	Sig.
Maintaining Strong Know Your Customers (KYC) Database	Between Groups	2.443	1	2.443	13.660	.000
	Within Groups	53.303	298	.179		
	Total	55.747	299			
Increased Transparency in Overall Banking Process	Between Groups	.701	1	.701	3.869	.050
	Within Groups	54.019	298	.181		
	Total	54.720	299			
Strengthening Back-End Administrative Processes	Between Groups	1.608	1	1.608	8.768	.003
	Within Groups	54.642	298	.183		
	Total	56.250	299			
Monitoring Over Services Deliver to Rural and Unbanked Areas	Between Groups	.003	1	.003	.014	.907
	Within Groups	58.664	298	.197		
	Total	58.667	299			
Creating a Superior Customer Experience	Between Groups	.048	1	.048	.200	.655
	Within Groups	71.099	298	.239		
	Total	71.147	299			
Identifying Fraud and Loan Defaulter Easily	Between Groups	1.361	1	1.361	6.622	.011
	Within Groups	61.236	298	.205		
	Total	62.597	299			

Findings

The null hypothesis was rejected in cases of maintain strong KYC, strengthening back-end administrative processes and identify Fraud and loan defaulter easily. It can be said that there is a statistically significant difference between age of customers and opportunities generated for financial institutions after demonetization and managing large database. It is identified that through managing large database management and linking UIDAI with bank accounts banks would be able to grasp opportunity and overcome financial inclusions gaps in a significant manner. If bank accounts will integrate with personal identity of system then government and financial institutions would be able to frame appropriate policies for under-bank customers. It will also help them to deliver appropriateness of financial services and products to all income groups at affordable cost.

CONCLUSION

Management Implications

It is identified that most of companies across the world are currently in early stage of big data planning and execution phase. Lack of budget, lack of technology dependable partners and absence of unified vision are main issues facing by industry. The study explored opportunities generate for financial institutions after collecting large amount of customer transactions and account related data. From the analysis, it is found that customer analytics and adoption of digital technologies could play an important role in term of improving customer experience and provide insights about customers. In order to provide quick attention to customer needs, maintaining large database and monitoring over services deliver to rural and unbanked areas, new generation analytics could be beneficial for financial institutions in developing nations like India.

Along with this, it is observed that through linking the Unique Identification Authority of India (UIDAI) and other identify proof related documents with bank account; banks would be able to tap unbanked and under-banked customers. It was found that higher used of digital technologies in online transaction and other activities less than 1 year time period indicates that, customers have motivated towards use of digital technologies after demonetization and government move. It is considered that through adopting digital technologies and customer analytics in banking operations, financial institutions would be able to provide quick attention to their customer needs and increased transparency in overall banking processes in a significant manner. The following study tried to know customer preference about use of digital technologies and customer analytics in banking operations and their positive impact on various day to day functions. From the responses of respondents, it can be said that monitoring over services deliver to rural and unbanked areas, strengthening back-end administrative processes and identified fraud and loan defaulter easily would be main opportunities that would be generated after adoption of analytics and digital technologies. Apart from that, building centralise system and maintaining large amount of customer information, banks would be able to increase transparency and provide financial services advantages to needed people like direct subsidy advantage to needed people within stipulated time. However, without tacking challenges such that low level of financial literacy about digital banking services, inadequacy of the banking infrastructure and presence of limited number of financial services, financial institutions would be unable to overcome financial gaps. This study could be helpful for banks and financial institutions to understand the role of customer analytics and digital technologies to enhance consumer's awareness and achieve future set of objectives within stipulated time. It is observed that customer analytics has the capacity to enable financial institutions to manage and get deeper insight into customer transactions and account related data. By doing this, banks and policy makers could be able to improve public faith and confidence in organizations and better execution of policies to reach unbanked and under-banked customers. It is identified that digital platform could be helpful for both government and financial institutions in order to analyze massive amounts of unstructured data and monitor and control over financial frauds and scams kinds of activities.

FUTURE RESEARCH DIRECTIONS

The present study would be helpful for all type of financial institutions, research scholars and students to understand the importance of digital technologies and Customer Analytics to carry out their operations. Customer insights and Customer experience management implications were discussed in the present chapter. However, there are several areas including compliance & risk management, cost containment, cyber threat and increase accuracy of real time information using dynamic machine learning algorithms could play an important role but not considered into present study. Further study on these emerging techniques would be beneficial for researcher to understand analytics role for banks to tap unbanked and under-banked customers in developing nations like India.

Financial services organizations should allocate budget for gathering and managing immense volumes of data assets. Banks should tie up with government agencies to understand 360-degree view of the customer by collecting personal data, browsing history, service and transaction history data. For aligning Customer Analytics with financial inclusions strategies, government and banking institutions should take move towards motivating people to use of digital technologies to carry out financial transaction activities. In addition, privacy policies, security concerns and banking policies could also affect use of digital technology and customer analytics but could not be considered into the current study. Future research could be done to measure the impact of Big Data technologies implementation on people and financial inclusions.

Presently, government of Indian is concentrating on linking of personal identification proof of customers with bank accounts to overcome gap of financial gaps. But in near future, they can take help of Interactive Voice Response (IVR) and call center operators digital technologies to interact with people and aware them about share identity related information with institutions. Further study could be conducted to understand the impact of Big Data on changing the way of sending and receiving money by technology reformation. Apart from this, present study can be further explored by considering various data points such that person's creditworthiness, fraudulent use of biometric data and other personal information and segments of people based on inferences drawn, etc.

REFERENCES

Analytics India Magazine. (2017). *Analytics India Industry Study*. Retrieved from https://analyticsindiamag.com/wp-content/uploads/2017/07/Analytics-India-Industry-Study-2017.pdf

Bokman, A., Fiedler, L., Perrey, J., & Pickersgill, A. (2014). *Five Facts how customer analytics boost corporate performance*. Retrieved from http://www.mckinsey.com/business-functions/marketing-and-sales/our-insights/five-facts-how-customer-analytics-boosts-corporate-performance

Carrie, G. (2017). *Customer analytics and its importance*. Retrieved from https://www.sas.com/en_us/insights/marketing/customer-analytics.html

Cognizant report. (2015). *Digital Banking: Enhancing Customer Experience; Generating Long-Term Loyalty*. Retrieved from https://www.cognizant.com/InsightsWhitepapers/Digital-Banking-Enhancing-Customer-Experience-Generating-Long-Term-Loyalty.pdf

Corrigan, G., & Battista, A. (2015). *19 charts that explain India's economic challenge*. Retrieved from https://www.weforum.org/agenda/2015/11/19-charts-that-explain-indias-economic-challenge/

Deb, A. (2014). *It's Time to Listen to the Voice of the Consumer*. Retrieved from http://www.cgap.org/blog/its-time-listen-voice-consumer

Dovall, A. (2016). *Digital payments soar by up to 300% after demonetisation*. Retrieved from http://timesofindia.indiatimes.com/business/india-business/Digital-payments-soar-by-up-to-300-after-demonetisation/articleshow/55902284.cms

Financial Inclusion Summit. (2016). Retrieved from http://cashlesscatalyst.org/wp-content/uploads/2017/01/Financial-Inclusion-Summit.pdf>. /

Gambetta, N., García-Benau, M. A., & Zorio-Grima, A. (2016). Data analytics in banks' audit: The case of loan loss provisions in Uruguay. *Journal of Business Research, 69*(11), 4793–4797. doi:10.1016/j.jbusres.2016.04.032

Gupta, N. (2014). *How Analytics Drive Innovative Financial Services for the Poor.* Retrieved from http://www.cgap.org/blog/how-analytics-drive-innovative-financial-services-poor

Gupta, N. (2014). *How Analytics Drive Innovative Financial Services for the Poor.* Retrieved from http://www.cgap.org/blog/how-analytics-drive-innovative-financial-services-poor

IBM Executive Report. (2012). *Analytics: The real-world use of big data in financial services.* Retrieved from https://www-935.ibm.com/services/multimedia/Analytics_The_real_world_use_of_big_data_in_Financial_services_Mai_2013.pdf

Infosys. (2012). *Why banks are turning to analytics?* Retrieved from https://www.edgeverve.com/wp-content/uploads/2017/03/why-banks-are-turning-analytics.pdf

Kapoor, R. (2016). *7 Reasons Why Demonetization Is A Masterstroke By Modi.* Retrieved from http://www.huffingtonpost.in/rana-kapoor/7-reasons-why-demonetization-is-a-masterstroke-by-modi/

Krause, S. (2016). *How can we leverage digital technology for financial inclusion?* Retrieved from https://blogs.worldbank.org/psd/psd/how-can-we-leverage-digital-technology-financial-inclusion

Mazer, R., & Kaffenberger, M. (2014). *Simple Messages Help Consumers Understand Big Data.* Retrieved from http://www.cgap.org/blog/simple-messages-help-consumers-understand-big-data

Peppers, D., & Rogers, M. (2016). *Managing Customer Experience and Relationships: A Strategic Framework.* John Wiley & Sons. doi:10.1002/9781119239833

PWC. (2014). *Connecting the dots: Wiring business, technology and operations.* Retrieved from https://www.pwc.in/assets/pdfs/publications/2014/8th-cii-banking-tech-summit-connecting-the-dots.pdf

Rao, Y. V., & Budde, S. R. (2015). Banking technology innovations in India: Enhancing customer value and satisfaction. *Indian Journal of Science and Technology*, *8*(33). doi:10.17485/ijst/2015/v8i33/78280

Srivastava, U., & Gopalkrishnan, S. (2015). Impact of Big Data Analytics on Banking Sector: Learning for Indian Banks. *Procedia Computer Science*, *50*, 643–652. doi:10.1016/j.procs.2015.04.098

Wright, G. A. N., Chhopra, P., Mehta, S., & Shukla, V. (2013). *Financial Inclusion Through Digital Financial Services*. Retrieved from http://www.microsave.net/files/pdf/1367585756_Financial_Inclusion_Through_E_M_Banking.pdf

Chapter 6
Financial Literacy for Financial Inclusion Using Mobile Technology in India

Smriti Ashish Pathak
Symbiosis International University, India

Shreya Virani
Symbiosis International University, India

ABSTRACT

According to the RBI governor, technology-enabled financial information will spread financial literacy in an efficient and secure manner. India needs inclusive growth to pull millions out of poverty and mobile phone penetration can be a good opportunity. Consumers are exposed to a plethora of financial products but the knowledge is either not there or limited to make judicious choices. The successful implementation of financial literacy services would benefit rural people but it is a challenge to all stakeholders today. One-hundred twenty-five people all over India were selected for a survey and results point that rural poor accept mobile technology for banking related information but do not want to adopt the technology. There are various challenges for financial literacy in India discussed in the chapter. Also, opportunities are many for digital literacy and can be achieved if the challenges are overcome. All the stakeholders should put in concerted efforts at all levels to achieve financial inclusion through mobile technology disruption.

DOI: 10.4018/978-1-5225-4035-9.ch006

BACKGROUND

KMPG (KPMG, 2015) said that the 'Digital India' initiative will improve financial inclusion due to technological disruptions. Also people find mobile technology user friendly which has resulted in rising data traffic in the country. The initiative by the present government focuses on digital empowerment and it will positively drive financial literacy.

Microfinance and Mobile phones should join the technology bandwagon to change the face of financial services in India. Developed economies (G20 nations) recognize financial inclusion as a key driver for achieving financial stability. Technological innovations can act as the middlemen between potentially unbanked mobile phone owners. Financial education or literacy is important to deal with the imbalance between adaptability of customers to the technology and using the device for banking related work. Mobile apps tailored for financial education or literacy should be customer specific so that they helping to understand how financial instruments can address their daily financial concerns and provide advice in such manners. The chapter tries to address financial education problem in this evolving landscape and how customers are adopting mobile technology to solve banking related matters. A few terms used in the chapter are financial literacy, mobile technology, stakeholders etc are discussed.

Literacy rate among females in India is low according to a study in IBEF. According to a paper by the New York-based International Commission on Financing Global Education Opportunity nearly 48 percent of the girls in rural India are literate. India is the second-largest telecommunication market and has the third highest number of internet users in the world according to IBEF. The internet connectivity as per the new digital India program aims to digitally empower citizens in remote areas. As part of this plan, the government wants to make mobile connectivity available in more than 40,000 villages by 2018.

India is currently the world's second-largest telecommunications market and has registered strong growth in the past decade and half. The Indian mobile economy is growing rapidly and will contribute substantially to India's Gross Domestic Product (GDP), according to report prepared by GSM Association (GSMA) in collaboration with the Boston Consulting Group (BCG) (Shubhashis, 2009). By the year 1980s people has basic telephone service in India where it was only owned by the top 0.001% of the population. But now after nearly 45 years this luxury has passed down to maximum population due to positive reforms, growth in infrastructure and technology disruption. Now further the growth is happening more rapidly with so many players the market is booming with advanced technology, great mobile devices and affordable services.

The liberal policies of the Government are the key drivers for the growth in mobile and internet users. The policies focus on availability of telecom services at affordable prices to the consumers.

Most of the mobile phone designs are targeted to attract rural consumers and Nokia was the forerunner in early 2000 – 2004. With that the mobile services / apps also started to develop and technology started to disrupt the face of handheld device and the services provided.

In terms of revenue, mobile services market revenue in India according to telecom sector report will be nearly 37 billion US dollars in 2017 according to research firm IDC (VISA, 2016) and may cross 100 billion US dollars by 2020. The Indian market is flooded with variety of mobile devices and as per Ericsson Mobility Report India more consumers are adopting smartphones which will increase internet traffic. More than 100 million devices were sold in 2016 with GSMA technology. With the coming up of 4G at affordable rates the number is sure to rise. Some of the major developments related to the telecom industry boom are:

- Merger of financial services giants like hutch – Vodafone, Airtel and Telenor etc.
- Setting up of manufacturing units like Apple in Bengaluru etc, China in UP for Vivo/ Oppo.
- FDI into telecom has also opened up the market and caused this infrastructure change as well as improved effectiveness and affordability for the rural people.

This has all been possible due to the effective Government Initiatives like reforms, investments in infrastructure building, new apps to connect with people, new models for delivery of services, payment mechanism is relaxed, Unified licensing, Public-Private Partnership (PPP) model. Reserve Bank of India in Jan 2006 allowed banks to employ two categories of intermediaries - Business Correspondents (BCs) and Business Facilitators (BFs) to expand their outreach by carrying out basic transactions on behalf of the bank as agents, interacting and advising people.

As per report by Microsoft, India will be the hottest destination for mobile users, suppliers by 2025 due to the above mentioned reforms similar to the computer revolution. The government also plans to promote 46 technology, Internet of Things (IoT), machine-to-machine communications as well as its Smart Cities initiative which will boost the sector further.

India is a cash-based economy with a large population which is unbanked i.e. they do not have active bank accounts. Secondly literacy among the population is an issue as most of the rural population is illiterate. For such a population doing banking using mobile technology is a challenge. As discussed earlier the growing population of mobile users should adopt this technology for banking for effectiveness and cost.

Universal Payment Interface (UPI) provides secure mobile transactions and due to Aadhaar card mandate more people are likely to come under banking framework. 4G will accelerate this rate of penetration but the financial literacy also needs to penetrate at the same level. But this has opened up a plethora of opportunities for the financial services industry for delivery at low cost. Following are the 6 important pointers for financial inclusion (Express, 2012)

INTRODUCTION

The Reserve Bank of India defines financial inclusion as providing access at an affordable cost to the poorest of the poor. This access to banking services can unfold opportunities for financial services to a large section of unbanked population in India. If these financial services are delivered through digital platforms especially in rural/remote regions at a low cost, it will increase access at high quality and affordable rates as it will reduce transaction costs. Thus mobile technology has a major significance in providing financial services to areas where banks or banking correspondents are not able to reach or provide personal service.

India is a land of vibrant diversity where 18% of the total population on earth sustains on nearly 3% of the total land on the globe. The democratic republic gained independence in 1947 from colonial stagnation and since then is motivated to remove economic backwardness. Economic reforms were brought in around 1991 which have helped to make it an open economy. The reforms have also led India to showcase the vast potential it has. These reforms have had a far-reaching impact and have helped India unleash its enormous growth potential and also to understand its best potential is the growing human resource.

Demonetization has been our biggest teacher and people have realized that the dependency on cash needs to be decreased as digital based financial services become more common. Banks must now spread the costs or investments in technology and adapt the utilisation of existing technology in serving the population. All government and regulatory transactions are also becoming digital which further increases the need and active participation of public to become digitally financial inclusive.

Several macroeconomic factors also indicate that a sustainable digital ecosystem is getting ready on the fact that Indian consumers prefer (or are moving towards) digital technologies. The 'Digital India' initiative, together with a payments infrastructure, is laying the foundation for a digital economy with increasing willingness of people to use the internet. It is also based upon facts that government has planned to provide Wi-Fi services in cities with a population of more than one million, broadband internet access to 250,000 village clusters by 2019, providing digital lockers to all citizens etc(According to a recent speech by our PM Mr. Narendra Modi). Linking of one

Table 1. Pointers for financial inclusion

Technology disruption will bring services to people at low cost.	Electronic payments and Big Data will have an impact.	Regulatory reforms will decrease number of unbanked customers.	Effective communication between stakeholders can create value for customers.	Financial education through applications will lead to financial inclusion	Government has to intervene for effective payment and delivery mechanisms.

number for all 'Aadhar' programme is the biggest disruptor in financial inclusion delivery as it is based on biometrics technology and every financial transaction is now done using 'Aadhar' authentication.

The paper uses Technology Acceptance Mode (TAM) and inter mixes the concepts to measure the interrelation between the identified dependent factors for successful diffusion of mobile banking (Behl, 2016). The fitness of measurement model was also judged to confirm if the model is reliable and valid and the framework is acceptable. The 2016 Report by Trai[1] states that the density of mobile users is increasing in rural area.

The report's data clearly indicates the growing penetration of mobile technology in the rural areas of India and how effective mobile technology can help in financial inclusion. Research is growing in the area to measure usefulness of mobile telephony in enhancing financial inclusion which will in turn lead to growth in various related sectors. In a study cross-national data was studied which concluded positive relation between mobile acceptance and national output by Waverman (2005). In India a study by Kathuria in 2009 shows that mobile penetration in Indian states is associated with a positive and statistically significant improvement in output. Various studies have been done to measure the impact of mobile technology on state income, mobile technology and financial income but all over India no study has been done so far.

Education to rural population about banking services and products is being provided through many apps and videos. Skill building for bottom of the pyramid is also an important step for millions of people. Education institutes have to revamp their delivery mechanism to reach out to the population now using such technology. Banks and other financial institutions installed technology-intensive solutions like a small machine to give token in SBI, Noqueue app at SBI to issue token even before you reach the bank branch anywhere in the city. This has led to increase in revenue, enrich customer experience, minimize cost and balance the risk. But more reforms need to be ingrained to deliver fast track solutions to the consumers. In the model below, consumer awareness and behavior are compared to derive knowledge dissemination for improving financial literacy (Figure 1).

Figure 1. Financial literacy dissemination

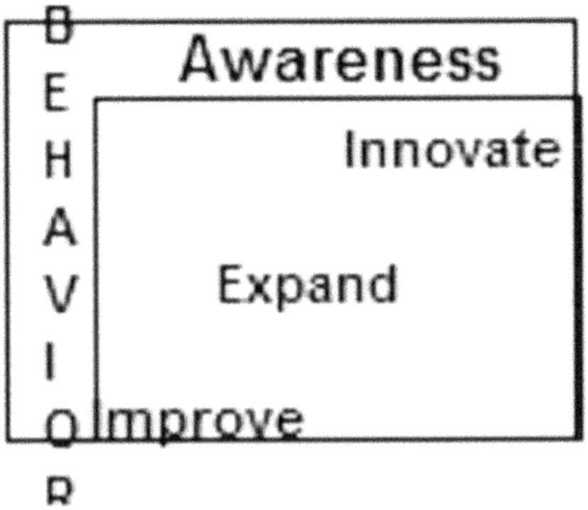

This shift towards internet banking is changing the delivery and payment routes in banks – financial institutions – government etc. With more working population, Indian banks need to implement fast track solutions with business intelligence and analytics to drive their overall profitability. RBI has also encouraged banks to adopt BI to increase transparency and control over the banking business.

Financial literacy is associated with the consumer who understands the products and purchases them or understands how to use / get the financial information using technology. It is mostly based upon knowledge, skills and attitudes. Financial literacy or financial education can broadly be defined as 'providing familiarity with and understanding of financial market products, especially rewards and risks, in order to make informed choices. Viewed from this standpoint, financial education primarily relates to personal finance to enable individuals to take effective action to improve overall well-being and avoid distress in matters that are financial' (RBI). Thus it is more than merely providing information related to money but more related to complexities of financial dealings. It is the capability to know and observe financial security decisions pertaining to self. (Reddy, 2006)

The history of financial literacy is taken from a renowned source as it is very interesting. The snapshot gives outline of the development of mankind into learning the basics of bank communication till date. In a letter to Thomas Jefferson, dated August 23, 1787, John Adams recognized the need for financial literacy: "All the perplexities, confusions, and distresses in America arise, not from defects in their constitution or confederation, not from a want of honor or virtue, so much as from downright ignorance of the nature of coin, credit, and circulation." In 1914, the Smith-Lever Act was passes which was aimed to provide learning experiences for skill development of people including. Slowly financial literacy started to grow and after 1947 in India too he need was felt to educate everyone. Around 1970 many organizations focused attention towards youth education. Dr. Lewis Mandell developed the financial literacy survey (as discussed above) to help organizations involved to spread education. After 2000 with the opening up of global boundaries need for consumer education was felt for finance or banking activities. United Kingdom (UK) started a national strategy on financial capability which was spread widely in various countries. OECD worked on developing similar principles for financial literacy to improve the status of education. Reserve Bank of India launched an initiative in 2007 to establish Financial Literacy and Credit Counselling Centers throughout the country. This initiative was aimed at providing free financial education and counselling to all population. 2008 was declared as the year of financial education by the Indonesian government. The U.S. Congress passed the Dodd-Frank Act, to promote financial education among consumers. State Bank of Pakistan (SBP) launched a national financial literacy program (2010), The Central Bank of Sri Lanka announced financial education initiatives (2011), In Uganda (2011) consumers were trained in financial literacy and Bank of Guam became the first bank in Guam to offer interactive financial literacy games. UK's Department for Education determined that financial education will become compulsory in all schools beginning in September 2014. (Andrianaivo, 2012)

Financial markets have become multifaceted with numerous intermediaries offering numerous services and products. This causes information asymmetry leading to confusion and chaos for the rural people to make good selection. Therefor programmes which focus on spreading financial knowledge are growing in all countries. In India most of the population is in rural areas and a large section of the population still does not have good financial set-up. India has people with diverse social and economic profile staying together and the spread of financial literacy therefore is more difficult.

Many initiatives have been taken by Reserve Bank to teach about bank related concepts but the spread is slow. A project titled 'Project Financial Literacy' aims to teach and spread knowledge related to money, schemes by government for the benefit of the people. The people will also get information related to banking in daily life and general concepts. The information will be in many languages.

Stakeholders embracing the related goals of financial capability and financial inclusion requires a multi-stakeholder framework built around consumers, the financial services industry and government. Financial education is the nexus linking their interests in these common goals. Non-governmental and community-based organizations use it to promote livelihoods and asset building for the poor, integrating it into a range of activities that 8 includes extension services, health education, business-development training, or mentoring. Financial institutions use it to enhance their community profile, increase adoption and use of their products and ultimately, improve performance. Central bankers and regulators embrace financial education to protect consumers from fraud and abuse (Cohen, 2010).

The mobile banking models in India for financial inclusion are: a) Bank led Model – In which all banking services are provided to the customer using simple technology. b) Joint Venture Model – In which Bank collaborates with Telecom operators to provide basic financial services through mobile wallets. c) Third party Model – In which Banks, Telecom operators join hands with third party enterprises to provide banking services.

REVIEW OF LITERATURE

According to the Planning Commission (2009), (RBI, 2018)Financial inclusion refers to universal access to a wide range of financial services at a reasonable cost. The household access to financial services includes access to contingency planning, credit and wealth creation. On the other hand, access to wealth creation includes savings and investment based on household's level of financial literacy and risk perception.

GOI (2008) defines Financial inclusion as the process of ensuring access to financial services and timely and adequate credit where needed by vulnerable groups such as weaker sections and low income groups at an affordable cost (RBI, Bank-wise volumes in mobile transactions, 2017). The meaning of financial inclusion is delivery of financial services to the low income groups especially the excluded sections of the population with the provision of equal opportunities.

A very popular and noteworthy theory to understand adoption of a technological innovation by an individual is the Diffusion of Innovation Theory (DIT) (Sriram, 2016). It was developed by E.M. Rogers in 1962 and originated in communication to explain how, over time, an idea or product gains momentum and diffuses (or spreads) through a specific population or social system. This theory can explain the reasons behind the rate of spread and penetration of any technological innovation.

Technology Acceptance Model (TAM) proposed by Davis comprises two beliefs, the perceived utilities and the perceived ease of application, which determine attitudes to adopt new technologies. Behaviour of the individual toward adoption will be either positive or negative concerning whether the decision is driven by intention or trust.

The unified theory of acceptance and use of technology (UTAUT) is a model formulated by Venkatesh and aims to explain user intentions to use an information system and subsequent usage behaviour (Andrianaivo, Mobile phones, financial inclusion and growth, 2012). It has four core constructs (performance expectancy, effort expectancy, social influence and facilitating conditions) which determine behaviour and in turn are moderated by gender, age, experience, and voluntariness of use. It is argued that by examining the presence of each of these constructs in a "real world" environment.

Abhishek and Abhinav (2016) in the paper used the above mentioned theories to reveal that perception towards usefulness, ease of use or risk aversion plays an important role towards degree of diffusion of mobile banking in rural setup. The result of their paper proposes that banks and financial institutions need to study the degree of perception towards credibility risk before upgrading the technology. The study is done in the area of Rajasthan in India (Kathuria, 2009)

Shubhashis (2009) paper focuses on developing complete solutions and not on restatements of the problem. It tries to define the regulatory framework that encourages greater and universal access to financial services based on a technology platform that allows solutions that are otherwise infeasible. It says that the objective of such technology is not one that earns more revenue from existing market participants but increases the number of participants (Basu, 2013).

KPMG report (KPMG, Customer Adoption of Digital Initiatives, 2016) concludes that banks need to focus on developing compelling products that proliferate active customer adoption. As the unbanked pool reduces over the next few years, due to both physical as well as digital initiatives, the next wave of growth is expected to come by focussing on the underbanked. There is a need for players to adopt a holistic approach on going digital and integrating business strategy with all constituents of their operating model ecosystem to create a remarkable customer experience.

Department of Payment and Settlement Systems (RBI 2016) developed a framework that takes account of the interaction between the demand-side and supply-side payment. It studies to calculate cost of cash limited to certain types of payments. McKinsey found that India could save up to USD 22.4 billion annually by shifting to all electronic government payments. A study by the Fletcher School, Tufts University showed that the RBI and commercial banks face USD 3.5 billion in currency-operations costs annually. Another study by the Institute of Business in the Global Context, the Fletcher School, Tufts University, found that card users in urban India use cash in 73 percent of expenditures compared with only 17 percent by card. (RBI, Role of Financial Education, 2016)

Sriram (2016) in the paper reviewed literature on financial inclusion in the Indian perspective to highlight the awareness level of financial inclusion, digital financial inclusion and barriers confronted to financial access. The vision of the Reserve Bank for the year 2020 is to open more than new 600 million customer accounts. It is expected from the government to encourage the banks to adopt financial inclusion for proper financial assistance using technology to achieve full inclusion.

According to a recent document by Morgan Stanley (2015), India's e-commerce market is set to expand from USD 3 billion in 2013 to more than USD 100 billion by 2020. Of the 354 million Internet users in India in June 2015, over 200 million were first-time users (Internet and Mobile Association of India website). The confluence of these positive factors offers tremendous opportunities for banks and mobile service providers to leverage their strengths and explore the expanding opportunities. (Stanley, n.d.)

Several books, reports and articles were used, of which some of them have been referred below: Deputy Governor of the RBI, K. C.Chakrabarty, in his address titled "The What, Why and How of Financial Literacy" in 2013 talked about issues relating to financial literacy in India. The talk was focused on importance of financial literacy for our people today and the suggestions to improve education at all levels to all people especially backward. (EY, 2015)

"National Strategy for Financial Education" published by the RBI in 2012 traces the origin of financial literacy to 17th century and the need for it. It says that government intervention and policy framing merely will not help in the spread of financial education but the stakeholders too have to play important role. A survey was conducted to find literacy level in all countries in comparison to the population. We lag behind a lot considering that we will have the max working population soon.

PwC is another agency which carries out surveys to understand the need of consumers today. In its 2012 report banking sector is an important growing sector with revolution in technology and services. Payment and deliver mechanisms are also changing. IMF publishes reports every year to state the outlook for every country and world. It has also projected that telecom / internet and mobile will revolutionize delivery and payment of financial products and services. Book by late Dr. APJ also discovers that to be in the top nations India has to develop models for effective banking and educate people regarding the same.

From the research it was evident that the levels of financial literacy in the area were very low. This is something that must be addressed rapidly. RBI and SEBI must come up with fun school / college activities on-line to improve financial literacy for school and college students. Finance or money management in day to day life, importance of saving, banking, etc can be taught to enhace their skill set. In many rural areas the population is too low and this is also a reason for the poor and unbanked to get access beyond.

MAIN FOCUS OF THE CHAPTER

From the above literature it is clear that to achieve financial inclusion enabling financial services using mobile technology is a good option for India. But creating awareness requires designing financial literacy apps based upon mobile phones for spreading banking services which would be acceptable and accessible by the poor individuals or unbanked population. The focus is also to check if financial literacy can help in the growth of financial inclusion and sustainable development. The chapter aims to discuss importance of financial literacy in today's extremely consumer centric scenario for diffusion of mobile services in rural areas. The survey conducted has enabled us to develop a conceptual framework / Model using mobile technology for improving financial inclusion in rural India.

Objectives of the Study

1. To discuss importance of financial literacy for diffusion of mobile banking in rural areas.
2. To develop a conceptual framework / Model using mobile technology for improving financial inclusion in rural India.

Hypothesis

- **H1:** Individual is ready to Adopt Technology for financial literacy.
- **H2:** Individual will use the mobile app for mobile banking.

RESEARCH METHODOLOGY

Data collection was done using a structured questionnaire. Special care was considered regarding the reliability and validity of the questionnaire as the constructs were drawn from existing models. The questionnaire aimed at recording demographic data as well as responses on the items used to measure the constructs. The responses to second part of the questionnaire were recorded using a five point Likert scale with 5 being strongly agree and 1 being strongly disagree. The target audience was selected from different regions in India like Pune, Mumbai, Goa, Kerela, Noida, Ludhiana (17 states) etc. The cities were selected at random and the respondents were selected from nearby villages. The questionnaire was converted in local language so that correct data could be recorded.

ICICI Bank has launched a mobile banking app – Mera iMobile – for rural customers that allows them to access banking services as well as information on agricultural related services. The app is available and is operational in 11 languages. We also took help of this app and bhim app recently initiated by our government. It allows users in rural areas to avail many 35 services on their mobile phones. The services include Kisan Credit Card, Gold Loan, Farm Equipment Loan and loans to Self-Help Groups (SHGs). It also gives crop-wise mandi prices of the area across mandis. "Lime" by Axis Bank is also a similar app, 18 M-Wallet by BSNL, Citi MasterPass are few e-allets providing similar services.

The study recorded 146 complete records out of which 125 respondents with complete information were taken for analysis. SPSS was used for the process of data mining. The fitness of measurement model using Confirmatory Factor Analysis (CFA) is employed to test whether the measures of a constructs are consistent with the researcher's understanding of the nature of that construct. There are two methods of running the CFA namely CFA for individual model and the CFA for pooled measurement model in determining the reliability and validity of the framework. Details of Constructs with their references is given in the table below:

DATA ANALYSIS

A dummy mobile app was run on simple Nokia mobile phone 1280 and 1600 Similar to Bhim[2] App). Data was collected through structured questionnaire. Analysis was done using SPSS Table 3 below shows how the variables are placed. The questionnaire was filled by 63 females and 62 males from all over India. Literacy level among the respondents is 25 Illiterate, 38 who can read but are unable to write, 56 can read and write whereas 6 respondents can read, write as well as converse. Language is mostly local and the mobile app shown to them can be in their convenient language.

Descriptive Statistics was done for the data to find significance between Literacy and if the respondents are ready to adapt or adopt banking transactions using mobile application. The Pearson Correlation shows that only 35% approx. respondents are ready for adapting remaining still want to go to the bank for any banking transactions. During the interview respondents stated that personal interaction in banks make them

Table 2. Details of constructs / variables defined in SPSS

Label	Values	Type	Measure
Name	None	String	Nominal
Gender	{1, Male}...	Numeric	Nominal
Village	None	String	Nominal
Age	{1, 20 to 30}...	Numeric	Nominal
Literacy	{0, Illiterate "No read & Write'}...	Numeric	Nominal
User	{N, No}...	String	Nominal
Awareness	{N, No}...	String	Nominal
Frequency of use	{0, Do Not Use}...	Numeric	Scale
Ready to Adapt	{0, Not sure}...	Numeric	Scale
Rate the app	{1, Not Satisfied}...	Numeric	Scale

Source: Variables defined as in SPSS

Table 3. Detailed analysis of data collected

1	Gender	Male 62 Female 63
2	Literacy	M F Total Illiterate (1) 13 12 25 Can read Not write (2) 12 26 38 Can read & Write (3) 32 24 56 Can read, write n talk (4) 5 1 06
3	Use Mobile App for Banking	Male 37 (Yes) 60% approx 25 (No) 40% approx. Female 50 (Yes) 79% approx. 13 (No) 21% approx
4	Awareness about Bank Operations using Mobile App	Male 37 (Yes) 60% approx 25 (No) 40% approx. Female 50 (Yes) 79% approx. 13 (No) 21% approx.
5	Frequency of Doing Financial Transactions using Mobile App	Male Do Not Use (0) 4 Very Less Use (1) 12 Moderate Use (2) 28 Lot of Times (3) 18 Female Do Not Use (0) 2 Very Less Use (1) 8 Moderate Use (2) 25 Lot of Times (3) 28

felt comfortable and builds the trust for money related matters (financial matters). SPSS Results are shown below in Table 4.

The test for degree of freedom was also passed which can be inferred from the table 4. The correlation between literacy and rating the application was also computed shown in table 4. All the values are found to be greater than the acceptable norm.

SOLUTIONS AND RECOMMENDATIONS

The developed model was accepted by the respondents and therefore is found to be valid. The first Hypothesis (H1: Individual is ready to Adopt Technology for financial literacy) has given positive result as respondents want to use technology for learning the new schemes. But second Hypothesis (H2: Individual will use the mobile app for mobile banking) has proved of no significance or negative as most of the respondents still feel comfortable going to the bank for transactions. . The study was aimed to build a reliable and valid framework for “Readiness for adopting technology” based on the inputs collected from various respondents. The perception of an individual is usually split into “Ease of Use” and “Usefulness”.

Table 4. Descriptive statistics and correlation using SPSS

Descriptive Statistics

	Mean	Std. Deviation	N
Ready to Adapt	1.55	.745	125
Literacy	2.34	.853	125

Correlations

		Ready to Adapt	Literacy
Pearson Correlation	Ready to Adapt	1.000	.346
	Literacy	.346	1.000
Sig. (1-tailed)	Ready to Adapt	.	.000
	Literacy	.000	.
N	Ready to Adapt	125	125
	Literacy	125	125

Model Summary

Model	R	R Square	Adjusted R Square	Std. Error of the Estimate
1	.346[a]	.120	.112	.702

All the stakeholders together should join hands to integrate elements of Technology, government regulation and public private enterprise to provide easy and low cost telecom / mobile enabled services to the unbanked or rural poor. This will ensure spread and increase trust of consumers towards banking products and services using mobile technology. Inclusive and efficient financial markets will drive the growth and improve economic collaboration which will lead to reduction in cost and ease of delivery and payment mechanisms.

People do not fully appreciate the need for bank and loans via formal sector are more useful than the informal sector. Government and Reserve Bank of India have been making continuous efforts to increase financial inclusion, new methods to educate people regarding financial services. Financial illiteracy and low awareness is also resulted in low penetration of financial services. More benefits should be given to banks operating in the rural India, awareness can be created by BCs or Sarpanch of the village, One person can be trained per village and he/she can educate the rest of the people. Preference should be given to a physical branch as the rural people trust the branch more than technology. The existing network of post offices can be transformed as advice or training centres. Schemes should be different for different area and people. Financial literacy should be included in school education needs to be given importance in schools, and student small saving programs, wso that the students will be aware. Regular audits by the government will help to improve the conditions in remote area.

FUTURE RESEARCH DIRECTIONS

Research can be done to understand why and how unbanked population can be made literate, education models and ways to reach can be found. Also schemes which they would benefit from should be thought of. Technology can be more simplified, infrastructure should be good in remote area to help in penetration. In this competitive environment large intermediaries which have strong base will merge / acquire small institutions to strengthen the base and smaller companies lack economies of scale. But these institutions have to keep in mind that the potential lies at the bottom of the pyramid. Methods of keeping track of the payments made directly to the accounts should be mandated and mechanisms should be strong. A strong system of digital identity has to be made leak proof to avoid identity theft.

To address the problem of implementation of technology all the barriers should be removed, improve the computer/digital literacy among rural unbanked people. RBI and Government have to take measures to ensure that the implementation of digital technology is good and is in the concern of people which will help to create a friendly environment for growth and sustainability. To become a developed nation financial inclusion should be complete and digital technology can help in doing so if implemented in an efficient way.

CONCLUSION

India will soon have the largest population in the working age group which will bring technological revolution. Therefor the need and importance of spreading digital literacy and financial literacy is significant as the demand for all the other related factors will rise. The chapter wanted to find to find if financial literacy is important for using mobile technology and if people are ready to adopt banking services using mobile. More measures should be taken to discuss with rural people about the importance of financial literacy and security issues regarding their data for banking purpose. It will help to improve inclusive growth as the present study discusses the acceptance of digital literacy around the globe. There are various challenges and opportunities for digital literacy in India, but for real inclusion concerted efforts at all levels may help to achieve financial inclusion.

The initiatives aim at creating an ecosystem to support people for banking services daily. People usually look at four important points for banking - - payment, credit, insurance and investment. Indian people are savers and investors but only 40% plan investment whereas 60% do not invest and the money does not enter the financial system. Financial literacy is the backbone of a strong financial system. Financial literacy and financial education should be on the agendas of educators, businesses, government agencies, policy makers, NGOs and the issues should be dealt with policy reforms at the national level. Thus, it is important to achieve highest possible financial literacy in the country as its benefits are not restricted to an individual or family, but to the society and the macro economy as a whole.

REFERENCES

Andrianaivo, M. a. (2012). Mobile phones, financial inclusion and growth. *Review of Economics and Institutions*, 30.

Basu. (2013). Policy Reforms in Foreign Investment. *FSI*, 5.

Behl, A. (2016). Analyzing the Barriers towards. *Indian Journal of Science and Technology*, 15.

Express, F. (2012, March). Rupee Exchange Depreciation: Impact Analysis. *Financial Express*, p. 3.

EY. (2015). *Mobile money: The next wave of growth.* EY.

Kathuria, R. M. (2009). *An econometric analysis of the impact of mobile.* Vodafone Policy Paper.

Khokhar, A. S. (2016). *Digital Literacy: How Prepared Is India to Embrace It?* Academic Press.

KPMG. (2015). Digital India. *KPMG*, 36.

KPMG. (2016). *Customer Adoption of Digital Initiatives*. KPMG.

RBI. (2016). *Role of Financial Education*. RBI.

RBI. (2017). *Bank-wise volumes in mobile transactions*. RBI.

RBI. (2018). *Payment systems in India: Vision 2018*. RBI.

Reddy, D. Y. (2006). *The Role of Financial Education: The Indian Case*. OECD.

Shubhashis. (2009). How Can Technology Facilitate Financial Inclusion in India? *Review of Market Integration*, 23.

Singh, A. (2016). Digital Literacy: How Prepared Is India to Embrace It? *International Journal of Digital Literacy*, 7.

Sriram, D. N. (2016). Financial Inclusion in India: A Review. *Review of Management*, 17.

Stanley, M. (n.d.). *Get ready for India's internet boom. Morgan Stanley.*

VISA. (2016). *Accelerating The Growth of Digital Payments in India' Department of Payment and Settlement System*. Visa.

KEY TERMS AND DEFINITIONS

Aadhar: Is a 12-digit unique identification number issued by the Indian government to every individual resident of India. The Unique Identification Authority of India (UDAI) functions under the Planning Commission of India.

BC & BF: Business correspondent is nothing but a bank-in-person that is authorized to collect small ticket deposits and extend small credit on behalf of the banks. Bank facilitators operate a number of channels through which they deliver financial services.

BCG: Boston Consulting Group (BCG) is an American worldwide management consulting firm.

Bhim: Bharat Interface for Money is a mobile app developed by National Payments Corporation of India (NPCI), based on the unified payment interface (UPI).

GDP: Is one of the primary indicators used to gauge the health of a country's economy. It represents the total dollar value of all goods and services produced over a specific time period.

Goerdeler: Is a professional service company and one of the big four auditors.

GSM: Global system for mobile communication is a digital mobile telephony system that is widely used. It uses a variation of time division multiple access (TDMA) and is the most widely used of the three digital wireless telephony technologies (TDMA, GSM, and CDMA).

GSMA: The GSM Association is a trade group that represents network operators that use GSM technology for their networks. The GSMA also counts a number of manufacturers and suppliers that provide the GSM technology as associate members.

IBEF: Is a trust established by the Department of Commerce, Ministry of Commerce and Industry, Government of India.

KPMG: Was formed in 1987 with the merger of Peat Marwick International (PMI) and Klynveld Main.

PPP: Is a contractual arrangement between a public agency (state or local) and a private sector entity. Through this agreement, the skills and assets of each sector (public and private) are shared in delivering a service or facility for the use of the general public.

RBI: Central Bank of India established on April 1, 1935 in accordance with the provisions of the act.

SPSS: The software name originally stood for Statistical Package for the Social Sciences (SPSS), reflecting the original market which is used by researchers to do statistical analysis in many fields.

UPI: Unified Payments Interface (UPI) is a payment system launched by National Payments Corporation of India and regulated by the Reserve Bank of India.

ENDNOTES

1 See http://www.trai.gov.in/sites/default/files/Indicator_Reports_Dec_16_07042017.pdf

2 See http://www.npci.org.in/documents/BHIM-User-Manual.pdf

Chapter 7
Financing Millennials in Developing Economies:
Banking Strategies for Undergraduate Students

Bernardo Amezcua
Universidad Autonoma de Coahuila, Mexico

Alicia De la Peña
Universidad Autonoma de Coahuila, Mexico

Arturo Briseño
Universidad Autonoma de Tamaulipas, Mexico

Alfredo Sánchez-Aldape
Universidad Autonoma de Tamaulipas, Mexico

Juana María Saucedo-Soto
Universidad Autonoma de Coahuila, Mexico

Alicia Hernández-Bonilla
Universidad Autonoma de Coahuila, Mexico

ABSTRACT

Young millennials (i.e., 18 to 24 years old) are not a primary market for the traditional banking system, especially in emerging economies. Despite the fact that almost 30% of college students have partial jobs, economic resources are limited and access to finance seems utopic. Banking services throughout the world but especially in growing economies do not fully serve students because of their lack of resources. Whether to pay for college studies or clothing, dinner or a weekend vacation, young millennials do not expect to receive banking credit from the big bank brands. In fact, this market segment is served by the retail industry with their own credit programs and financial services. In this chapter, the authors explore how young millennials

DOI: 10.4018/978-1-5225-4035-9.ch007

have access to savings and credit, their spending behavior, their attitudes towards traditional sources of finance, and their financial inclusion and literacy. They also conducted an empirical exploratory study among college students in Mexico to hear firsthand how they managed their finances.

INTRODUCTION

What do millennials want? Are they dreaming of travel and adventure, or do they want to buy their first apartment and start a life of their own? How do they manage their money? Are they saving for a rainy day? Do they have a piggy bank or a formal savings account?

An exploratory study conducted among undergraduate students in a public school in Mexico showed us that young middle class millennials are full of dreams and out of money.

In this study, 50 young men and women were asked to build a collage (Coulter & Zaltman, 1995) describing the life they want to have as well as the obstacles interfering with it. The collages were full of magazine clippings on exotic journeys, state-of-the-art electronic devices, fashion clothing, brand-new cars, comfortable homes and university logos. They also included images of piggy banks, sad faces and cracked money icons. They were enthusiastic about getting things in life but recognized that they did not currently have the economic resources to afford them.

Despite the fact that almost 30% of the student participants had at least part-time jobs, their financial resources are limited, and access to finance seems utopic to them. Given students' lack of resources, banking services, throughout the world but especially in growing economies, do not fully serve young people.

For example, only 3 million out of the 11 million young Mexicans in the age range for college studies are currently enrolled, and only 12,000 of these receive financing from private banking institutions (Contreras, 2014). According to a FORBES article, in Mexico only five private credit firms grant financing in a market of 4.8 million potential college students. In fact, from the young people point of view, financing studies from private institutions is expensive and complicated, while other sources of financing (e.g., NGOs and government offices) are insufficient (Contreras, 2014).

Being a priority getting a graduate degree, young millennials do not expect to receive banking credit for smaller things, and the relationship with these institutions seems to be fractured. Millennials are not fond of big bank brands, as they do not feel they are part of the present finance system (Jabbour, 2016).

However, this not happening solely in Mexico. According to a Goldman Sachs report (2017) millennials characteristics are similar across economies. There are not really any differences between millennials from developed and emerging economies. Young people from emerging economies (86% of the world's millennials) crave for digitalization, leisure/experience and premium brands. Millennials from Brazil,

South Africa, China, India or any other emerging market show similar expending and saving habits representing opportunities for the traditional and also innovative industries (Goldman-Sachs, 2017). Millennials across economies, also face similar barriers to enter the traditional banking system, where financial institutions do not pay attention to this market segment.

In this chapter, we focus on the younger segment of millennials (i.e., men and women between 17 and 24 years old), who are the appropriate age to become college students in growing economies but are not a primary target for banks, even though they might become a profitable market segment. Financial exclusion towards young millennials evident, even when they possess some limited economic resources, the lack of formal credit history drift them away from the bank system and throw them into the new digital and mobile financial industry delivered by commercial firms (Goldman-Sachs, 2017).

We develop four sections to address this topic: (a) Millennials' sources of finance, (b) Millennials' spending behavior, (c) Millennials' attitudes towards traditional sources of finance, and (d) Millennials' financial inclusion and literacy. We also conducted an empirical exploratory study among college students in Mexico to hear firsthand how they manage their finances. The obtained data is presented as a case study for further comprehension.

Millennials' Sources of Finance

In a globalized context, especially in developing economies, there are great economic and social challenges. The effects of these challenges translate into the search for better productivity levels and a higher dependency on adequate information for the new generations (Banco Base, 2016). Recent studies dealing with generational differences can be found in many areas, such as employment, education, and consumption, allowing for a better understanding of the behavior and attitudes of the newer generations of consumers. For this reason, leaders from private and public organizations require information about the lifestyles and consumption habits of this growing segment (Goldman-Sachs, 2017).

The millennial generation (i.e., individuals born between the years 1980 and 2000) (Strauss & Howe, 1991), have lived in a period of constant changes in a globalized context, which has generated a peculiar behavior in the management of their personal finances. This generation is expected to transform the economy by finding new ways to manage personal finances. It is expected that millennials will allocate their financial resources differently, have new prioritization criteria, and have higher expectations compared with previous generations. However, millennials' decision-making has severe implications for their own financial security and their standard of living. Financial education is crucial to allow millennials to integrate with the traditional bank system. A person with adequate financial literacy is better prepared in comparison with those who lack such knowledge and capabilities (García, Griffoni, López, & Mejía, 2013).

Millennials are the newest customer segment in the banking sector, where firms must attract and retain them using innovative solutions and empathy. This is highly important since most millennials use non-banking strategies to satisfy their financial needs. The challenge here is for the traditional banking system to adapt to the changing preferences of the new generation. The banking sector has identified millennials as an opportunity to generate an online banking culture and increase the number of users (BBVA Innovation Center, 2015). Especially for emerging economies, where millennials face harsher economic challenges, mobile bank services seems to be the right path to approach this next to be very profitable segment.

Even though millennials are open to other, more innovative financial alternatives and are receptive to financial products offered by firms such as Google, Apple, Amazon, and Paypal (Molina, 2016), they show a natural rejection to saving. As a result, traditional banking must consider the renovation and diversification of their processes to attract and retain millennials. For example, the Spanish bank Santander has recently offered their youngest segment a proposal that fits their needs, facilitating their use of banking services with less bureaucratic process (La Vanguardia, 2017).

Recent research shows that some millennials have proven to manage their money in a balanced way and to be conservative in acquiring debt (Goldman-Sachs, 2017). In addition, these studies reveal that the more common financial demands among millennials are: a) 24-hour loans with no collateral, b) student loans to complete their professional education, c) entrepreneurial loans to start or grow small to medium businesses) and, d) credit cards.

Young millennials are economically active, but, how are they currently spending their money?

Expenditure Patterns of Millennials

Individuals make decisions all the time, and many of those decisions are related to how they use money to meet their daily needs. Economic theory suggests that individuals should treat their resources as limited and make specific plans for their expenses (Fernbach, Kan, & Lynch, 2015). But not all individuals think alike, and thus they make different decisions, specifically when it comes to their financial well-being (Lynch et al., 2010). In fact, consumers are not really rational, and in most cases they make their shopping decisions based in simple heuristics (e.g., known brand, promotional price, package, etc.), which might lead them to mindlessly buy products they do not need, thus spending their money in a careless way (Norman, 2010; Kardes, Posavac, & Cronley, 2004; Chaiken, 1980).

Of particular interest is the study of the millennial generation. It is expected that by 2020 millennials will account for one in three adults in the World, and by 2025 they will account for three quarters of working-age people. They represent the consumer market of the future, and they are currently forming their lifelong shopping preferences and habits (Catalyst, 2015). Millennials distinguish themselves from older generations by their spending habits, values and brand preferences. According to a Goldman-Sachs study conducted in 2016, the millennial generation in the US represents an attractive market segment. Larger than the generation X and baby boomer cohorts, millennials have grown up in an era of rapid change that has lead them to set priorities differently than previous generations.

Due to their lower employment level and their smaller income, younger millennials (18 to 24 years old) have less money to spend, while older millennials (25 to 34 years old) dedicate a growing portion of their income to pay for student loans (Goldman-Sachs, 2017). As a result, their behavior patterns have changed, as have their priorities. The percentage of young people who are married and living on their own has decreased almost 40% since 1968 (Goldman-Sachs, 2017). Their milestones are different than those of their parents; owning a house or car, getting married or having a child are not on the top of their lists of priorities, and therefore they live with their parents for longer periods, which leaves them with reduced financial responsibilities and spare money to spend on themselves.

At the same time, their values and interests are also different. Millennials value their time, seek flexible jobs, care for the environment, show concern for political issues (e.g., war and terrorism), seek balance between work and their personal lives,

Figure 1. College Students' income ranges for expenses (in USD)

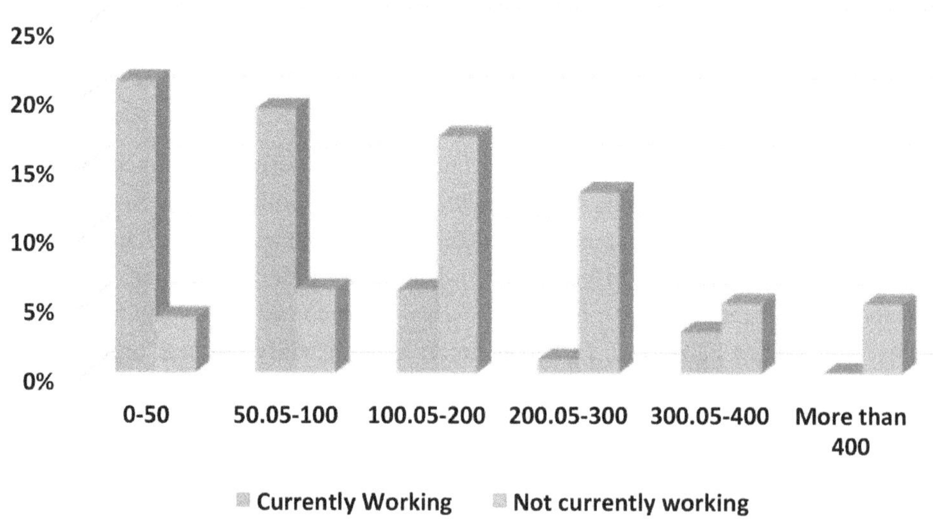

are technologically savvy, check for promotions on their smartphones, and prefer paying for experiences (e.g., beer festivals, themed runs, adventure trips) than for material things (Barton, Koslow, & Beauchamp, 2014; Deloitte, 2017). Millennials are wary of traditional financial institutions; they value success, happiness, curiosity and passion and are considered the most marketing-savvy generation (Maccaro, 2015).

More than previous generations, millennials love to buy smartphones and video games, but for those expensive items they prefer rentals instead of ownership (Goldman-Sachs, 2017). Millennials are engaging in access-based consumption (i.e., transactions that can be market-mediated, but where no transfer of ownership takes place) (Bardhi & Eckhardt, 2012). They prefer to download music instead of buying CDs, watch TV online, use Uber instead of owning a car, stay at AirBnB properties when they travel and use streaming services without property issues in what now is called sharing economy and collaborative consumption—a form of alternative modes of acquisition and consumption of goods based not on individual ownership but on organized sharing and exchange (Belk, 2014; Scaraboto, 2015).

This consumption practice enables millennials to live a more sustainable lifestyle that is consistent with their values. By leasing or selling the things they no longer use to others, they avoid hoarding and make some additional income; moreover, when they need items for a one-off experience (e.g., a mountain bike for just one trip), they have access to the item temporarily and avoid the costs of buying a new product (Phillip, Ozanne, & Ballantine, 2015). In addition, when leasing or selling their belongings to other people, millennials are not only able to reduce their personal consumption but also feel that they are being altruistic and helping people who may not be able to afford to buy those items (Albinsson & Perera, 2012; Phillip et al., 2015).

Being part of the sharing economy does not mean that millennials do not care about value. They still look for quality with the aid of technology, which means that they have the power to make accurate comparisons among brands and retailers, as well as price and financial terms. Thus, more than ever, delivering maximum convenience at the lowest cost is essential (Goldman-Sachs, 2017). With their smartphones, they can search, share, appraise, and shop with just a click. The best value is essential for millennials, but they look for good quality at an affordable price. Being tech-savvy allows them to join digital reward programs, enabling them to save money and earn points and rewards from their everyday purchases (Logsdon, 2016).

According to GFK (2016), 41% of younger millennials subscribe to the motto "Enjoy life today, worry about savings and investments later," while 36% of older millennials share the same idea. However, this does not mean that millennials are careless. We have to acknowledge that decisions like saving money or buying on the spur of the moment involve trade-offs, rewards, or costs in the near future versus the distant future, which implies that young adults are not really paying attention to the outcomes of their actions, and some of them might prefer to indulge in the present instead of saving money for the future (Hershfield et al., 2011; Thaler & Sunstein, 2009).

All these previous characteristics defining millennials are present across borders. No matter they lived in a developed or emerging economy, characteristics remain the same (Goldman-Sachs, 2017). However, some emerging economies such as Brazil, India, China, South Africa, Nigeria and Mexico still have high poverty rates (PwC, 2017).

Millennials' Saving Behavior

Given that retirement is an event that seems to be in the distant future, young millennials prefer to indulge in the present and use their resources on small guilty pleasures (e.g., a good cappuccino, a tasty pizza, etc.) or on experiences (e.g., adventure trips, concerts, etc.) that allow them to create memories, bond with friends and family members, connect with the community through charity and volunteer activities, and broadcast on social media to overcome their FOMO (fear of missing out) (Albinsson & Perera, 2012; Eventbrite, 2016).

Millennials have a big desire for luxury, novelty and variety. They tend to be early technology adopters; 84% of them love exposure to different cultures (including music and food), and 47% are willing to pay more for a brand that understands multicultural needs. Regarding music, they prefer a good set of wireless headphones that allows them to listen to their music anywhere and at any time. In general, they demand from brands an acute understanding of how they think, act and solve problems in order to buy their products and services (Harris, 2017).

At the same time, they are looking for ways to save money by engaging in behaviors such as comparing prices, using coupons, seeking sales and cooking and eating at home instead of eating out. They have not abandoned their favorite brands, but they buy in smaller quantities, shop across channels to take advantage of discount channels, and lease and rent articles in order to pay less for items they will use only a couple of times (Magni, Martínez & Motiwala, 2016).

Young millennials' consumption behavior seems to be in conflict with the traditional bank system. With 33% of millennials believing they do not need a bank at all, and 73% excited with the idea of receiving financial offerings from Amazon, Google or Paypal (MDI, 2014) is it possible for banks to engage this new market segment?

Millennials' Attitudes Toward Traditional Sources of Finance

Older millennials are already part of the bank system (Jabbour, 2016). At least in development economies, where educated young consumers with stable jobs are paying for their school debts while thinking about buying a car or home or starting their own business (Jabbour, 2016), banks are part of the picture. This group of millennials, who have already graduated from school and are economically active, are fully incorporated in the traditional banking system.

Younger millennials face a different story. Not having a full-time job or being dependent on their parents' income makes them an unattractive segment for banks. However, banks should not ignore this group of youngsters, as they will become the clients of tomorrow. Even before they graduate, they represent a profitable market in growing economies, since many young people work and study simultaneously. College students, especially those from public schools, work part-time and sometimes full-time to cover their education expenses as well as to afford their preferred lifestyle.

Banks need to pay attention to the next generation of consumers as they feel left aside from banks. Traditional bank strategies do not target younger generations. Banks need to anticipate what young millennials need in terms of credit, investment and money disposition. Young millennials, or those between 18 and 24 years old, are active consumers looking for state-of-the-art gadgets, apparel, dining and recreational activities (Goldman-Sachs, 2017).

Millennials' spending behavior can be inferred from their posts and comments on social media. With more of 75% of 18- to 29-year-old millennials being heavy social media users, outpacing older subjects (Pew Research Report, 2010), their buying and spending behavior can be observed and tracked. They text frequently and share videos related to their everyday activities.

Although 33% of millennials classify themselves as short-term spenders looking for a way to survive (Aviva, 2017), banks have to stop thinking that millennials are irresponsible with money and recognize that actually they are very good at saving money. According to recent research, 40% of millennials keep some savings in banks, and 60% of them are long-term savers thinking about their professional growth, future retirement or their children's' education (Bumeran, 2017).

Even older millennials (i.e., those who are already banking consumers) are expecting financial institutions to move further into the digital or mobile services era. Banking millennials will look for convenience regardless of whether it is provided by a recognized or a small firm as long they use technology (e.g., apps and platforms) (Pew Research Report, 2010). For instance, Jaboour (2016) reports that 18- to 25-year-olds use digital and community banks twice as often compared to older millennials. However, they also report that young millennials have problems with receiving personalized financial advice through digital devices, indicating banks need to work with these technologically savvy but financially illiterate young consumers.

Although young millennials are highly optimistic that they will earn enough in the future to fulfill all their needs and wishes (Pew Research Center, 2010), they feel that they are of no interest to banks. It seems that commercial institutions are more aware and interested in their finances compared to the traditional financial system.

Different financial strategies are being deployed by commercial institutions to serve young millennials' financial needs in growing economies. These new alternatives are not at odds with the banking system; rather, most of the time a joint effort is needed between the store, the bank and even some intermediaries (Lee & Kwoon, 2002).

Below, we analyze some of the new financial initiatives that are taking place in emerging economies and that can constitute a profitable way for banks to target young millennials. These financial initiatives are evidence from Mexico, however are based on the suggested strategies for growing business in most emerging markets (Bourlier & Gomez, 2017).

Retailers are making remarkable efforts to attract young consumers and establish long term relationships with them. Rapid growth and loyal consumers are easily attained through financial aid.

For example, C & A, a Dutch apparel store for young people with a presence in more than 22 European countries and success in emerging economies like Brazil, China and Mexico, has targeted college students as their primary market. They approach young millennials by offering financial aid through different options.

C & A offers a complimentary store card with consumers' first purchase. This welcome card is not a debit or credit card, but it grants consumers a 15% discount on their next purchase in the store. This welcome card promotes repeat purchases and helps young consumers to get used to using store cards while showing deference and support for newly independent consumers who are now taking responsibility for their buying behavior.

C & A also offers consumers complementary money cards, delivered at some promotional events throughout the year and are intended for full or partial payment of future purchases. Consumers may add up different promotions and manage their "credit" for multiple purchases. This card functions like a training credit card, helping young people to learn how to deal with savings and credit. Similarly, the FashionGift card can be bought at any time inside the store and, in addition to its primary gift-giving function, can be managed like a non-expiring debit card. Consumers can deposit extra money into their FashionGift card, which can be used in multiple future purchases. Consumers can consult their balance online or in store, where they can also recharge the card with extra cash.

Finally, C & A offers a bank credit card to customers age 18 and older with minor requirements: filling out the request form, presenting an ID and a proof of income or a credit card from some other store or bank. C & A makes an exception for college students; instead of requiring them to present proof of income or another credit card, it offers them the store credit card just by presenting a student ID or grading report card.

With these types of financial strategies, retailers are not only trusting young millennials but actively engaging with these active consumers and educating them in the credit system. Stores are even replacing banks and ATMs as a source of cash.

A similar story can be seen in convenience stores, as they help non-banking consumers and businesses to come closer. With online purchasing being more frequent than ever and with young millennials as the more likely online shoppers, new and more creative paying systems are required. For example, the biggest convenience store chain in Mexico, with more than 15,000 units in the country and with a presence in several Latin-American countries, is increasing its financial services.

Oxxo has proven successful as an intermediary between Mexican immigrants in USA and their families in Mexico. With Oxxo Envíos, immigrants working in the USA can send money to their families. Oxxo may cash out up to 50 USD dollars a day, depositing bigger amounts to a bank-Oxxo credit card obtained with minimum requirements that can also be used as a payment method in all Oxxo stores and VISA affiliates.

Having primarily young millennials in mind, Oxxo has developed the Oxxo Pay, a financial solution to promote commerce online. An alliance between Oxxo and a software company allows unbanked consumers, especially young people, to access more efficient forms of payment. Oxxo understands that in Mexico, as in other emerging economies, there is a gap between young buyers and businesses that must be resolved with urgency. Oxxo Pay allows consumers to make real-time payments quickly and easily. There is no need for bank intermediation. Businesses that wish to integrate the Oxxo Pay system can register free online, with no system charges for single transaction. Unbanked consumers also benefit by not needing to print any barcode; they just have to present a 14-digit code sent to their smart phones. With this new strategy, Oxxo is replacing the banking system in providing innovative financial services that are more attractive for this market segment.

Even payment intermediaries like PayPal continue innovating to serve young millennials. Partnering with mobile phone companies, PayPal is providing new ways of shopping and paying for services in a secure way. An example is the Pagamobil payment platform by TELCEL/America Móvil, the leading mobile phone company in Mexico and Latin America. Young millennials are now able to make payments and recharge their mobile phone credit just by using the Pagamobil app without having to leave home, school or the office. Through this app, consumers may opt to be charged to PayPal or directly to a debit or credit card. The linked credit card may be their own or a third person's. With prepaid plastic cards being the reason for mobile phone companies' great success in Latin America and Eastern Europe (Dhanani, 2015), it was a natural step to target unbanked consumers, even those in rural areas. Not having to present any printed form at a point of sale and not having to use ATMs has opened millions of new possibilities for mobile companies and banks.

For example, streaming services for young consumers like Spotify, Google Play, and Netflix, which used to sell prepaid plastic cards at stores, now can be paid from home, providing young consumers with the possibility of enjoying music, films and videos with constant use from anywhere. According to the music Biz/LOOP study, young millennials are eager to use and pay for premium streaming services that allow personalization and offline use (Music Biz/LOPP, 2016). Although young millennials are not necessarily paying for the premium streaming services they use (due to free trials, bundle programs or using someone else's account), they are willing to do so.

However, young millennials are not only in need of financial aid for recreational or private consumption purposes. There also an important sector of young millennials looking for credit to start their own businesses when jobs are otherwise scarce.

Millennials as Entrepreneurs

According to data published by the Mexican government, almost 30 million young adults in the 18- to 30-year-old cohort have a very remote possibility of getting a remunerated job. Moreover, of those who can get a job, 85% earn less than 300 USD per month (Torreblanca, 2016). To counter this lack of job opportunities, the Mexican government has created some financial programs to encourage entrepreneurship among young millennials. The Crédito Joven program is aimed at men and women from 18 to 35 years old who wish to establish a small business through their first credit. This program offers credit from private banks at preferential fixed rates under 10% per year (Crédito Joven, 2017). Young entrepreneurs may finance up to 80% of the project value. To initiate the credit solicitation, millennial entrepreneurs must join and complete an incubator program, with no need for previous experience in the business or a proven financial plan. Incubator coaches lead them through the planning process until they are ready to ask the bank for the money.

Young entrepreneurs soliciting credit do not need to provide employment history or proof of income, nor do they need to own warranty properties. However, once they have completed their incubation program, applicants need to demonstrate a clear credit history and an endorsement and need to contribute the remaining 20%.

Recognized multinational bank brands participate along with the Government in this program that allow young millennials to be banked.

Despite a few examples of banks supporting entrepreneurs, a different kind of financial companies are taking the lead. Fintech companies are firms that operate in financial markets with a strong technology support, modifying traditional banking for entrepreneurs. These firms generally concentrate on a single service, allowing them to be agile, efficient, low cost, and emotionally linked to the consumer. Fintech offer millennials with more innovative alternatives than those of traditional banks. Molina (2016) highlights some of the characteristics offered by Fintech:

1. **Crowdfunding:** Collective financing in which participants with monetary surplus are willing to assist financially with specific projects in return for equity.
2. **Crowdlending:** Collective financing in which participants with monetary surplus and are willing to assist financially with specific projects in return for a monthly payment.
3. **Rob-Advisor:** Digital platforms that provide financial assistance to potential investors in real time.

Although young millennials represent a profitable market segment for traditional banks, they are currently underserved. Banks must find a way to serve young millennials beyond the use of modern technology. Financial education may be that path.

Millennials' Financial Inclusion and Literacy

Financial literacy and financial inclusion are highly related topics. Knowledge about managing personal finances and how to use the right financial products is crucial for the access to savings and debt in an appropriate way. In the same way, the availability and access to financial products creates more knowledge about its use and the risks involved. As a result, different studies around the world argue for increasing financial literacy to improve financial inclusion (Atkinson & Messy, 2012; Lusardi & Mitchell, 2014). In the case of millennials, both financial literacy and financial inclusion are important aspects that need to be addressed. For example, Malcolm (2012) argues that millennials struggle with balancing their finances. He reports that young adults in the US have an average debt of $45,000 US dollars, which is very high for a young adult. Brown, van der Klaauw, Wen, and Zafar (2013) argue that a solution to this problem is appropriate financial education for the young. In their findings, a better financial education can reduce adverse outcomes such as negative accounts on credit reports or higher debt.

While developed countries have problems with financial inclusion and literacy for the youngest generation, developing countries have issues of their own. Kefela (2010) argues that financial literacy is crucial for promoting access to finance in emerging economies. He argues that, in order to increase financial inclusion, it is necessary to increase people's knowledge about how to manage their money.

Poverty in these countries should not be an excuse for stopping financial education or market penetration.

These arguments highlight the importance of financial literacy and financial inclusion. However, and despite the advancements in the literature, there are still few studies that includes both financial inclusion and literacy for young adults in developing countries. For this reason, this section will look for a deeper understanding of the role and impact of millennials in a developing economy such as Mexico in terms of financial literacy and inclusion.

Financial Literacy

The millennial generation (i.e., people born between 1980-2000) has faced an interesting financial context during the last couple of decades. International events such as the dotcom bubble, 9/11, the subprime mortgage crisis, and national events including devaluations and the unstable political climate have created a generation aware of the interconnected financial world. These events have shaped the way individuals, especially the younger generations, perceive financial and economic consequences. However, there are still strong concerns regarding the extent of the financial knowledge of the millennial generation and how these individuals make financial decisions (Hastings, Madrian, & Kimmyhorn, 2013).

Financial literacy is conceptualized as the ability of a person to understand and use financial concepts (Servon & Kaestner, 2008). As a result, financial literacy involves not only one's degree of understanding of basic finances but also the application of that knowledge to the individual's financial decisions.

During the last couple of decades, financial literacy has been a worldwide effort, pushed by international organizations such as the Organization for Economic Co-operation and Development (OECD) and the World Bank (WB). The focus of these efforts has been primarily to reduce poverty and to increase financial best practices. For example, the OECD, with its PISA test, measures secondary education students' knowledge on specific areas, one of which is financial literacy. In their study, which includes a sample of OECD members, they find that socio-economically advanced students perform better on financial literacy in comparison with other groups. Also, persevering and problem-solving traits are related with higher levels of financial literacy, with no gender differences (OECD, 2014).

Improving financial literacy is more complex than it might appear. The design and implementation of programs to increase financial literacy depend not only on delivering contents but also on considering the context and psychological traits of individuals. Fernandes, Lynch, and Netemeyer (2013) conducted a meta-analysis of the relationship between financial education and financial behavior. In general, their findings are not very encouraging. In their study, there is a weak relationship between financial education and how individuals improve their financial decision making, especially in the lower-income segments. They suggest that future studies need to consider more psychological traits to really understand financial behavior and create narrower, specific programs to improve financial literacy.

In the case of Mexico, there have been attempts to develop programs, identify main factors, and assess the level of financial literacy in both the young and adult segments. In general, as in many developing countries, Mexico has a low average financial literacy (Amezcua, Arroyo, & Espinosa, 2014). Mexico is among those countries that are in the process of establishing but have not yet implemented a national strategy for financial literacy. Although important, the government role is not sufficient for a national strategy on financial education. To increase the probability of success, the participation of different actors is required. In the case of Mexico, so far the national strategy involves both financial and education institutions (Grifoni & Messy, 2012).

In the meantime, millennials in Mexico are learning (or not learning) in a social context (i.e., families and friends), and they may not be very motivated to acquire financial knowledge. In a study of voluntary financial education programs, Bruhn, Lara, and Mckenzie (2013) found that Mexicans might not be very interested in financial education just for the sake of learning. In their experiment, they found that participants were marginally interested only when financial educational programs included a payment, but even in that case the benefits of the information learned had short-term effects. Another factor affecting how Mexicans might respond to financial information is how it is presented. In their study, Hastings and Tejeda (2008) found that participants reacted better if fees were presented in pesos rather than in annual interest rates. This implies that Mexicans could have low mathematical skills to deal with basic arithmetic operations, thus impeding financial evaluations.

These studies suggest some of the challenges facing financial education in a developing country such as Mexico. However, an additional issue is converting financial education programs for millennial audiences. A common mistake for financial education is to pretend that there are no differences between millennials and other groups (McCormick, 2008). Millennials have unique characteristics. As a group, they are already bigger than the baby boomer generation (i.e., individuals born between 1946–1964). In general, the millennial generation is more racially diverse, digitally native, educated (25% with college degrees), and multitasking (DeVaney, 2015; Sandeen, 2008). There are few studies on millennials and money management. For example, Cudmore, Patton, Ng, and McClure (2010) highlight that millennials fear investing because they lack knowledge on where and how to begin their financial efforts. Also, they argue that millennials are more attached to popular brands and, as a result, are more willing to invest in firms such as Nike or Starbucks.

Another study measuring financial literacy in younger audiences was carried out by Sohnm, Joo, Grable, Lee, and Kim (2012). Their work found two factors that positively influence financial literacy in adolescents: having a bank account and using social media as a socialization agent. Interestingly, they also found a positive relationship between financial literacy and allowances. There is higher financial literacy when adolescents received mid-range monthly allowances in comparison with the highest group. This suggest a U-shaped relationship between financial literacy and money management (i.e., lower or higher levels of money do not provide the same impact on adolescents to increase their financial knowledge).

With these results we can conclude that different generational groups require different strategies in financial education. There is no general recipe that can be used to increase the financial literacy of all groups. However, there are specific actions that can be implemented to improve knowledge and its application specifically among younger users. The context, at both the individual and regional levels, plays a crucial role in getting financial content to millennials and, more importantly, in guaranteeing that this content produces real effects on financial behavior.

Financial Inclusion

Financial inclusion, defined as "the use of formal accounts" (Allen, Demirguc-Kunt, Klapper, & Martínez, 2012, p. 2), is a crucial indicator for an economy. Higher access of individuals to a formal financial system in a country is associated with higher access to financial products that create opportunities for economic development. According to the Global Financial Inclusion Index, around 50% of people in the total world population have a bank account. The index measures 148 economies in terms of savings, borrowing, payments, and risk management (Demirguc-Kunt & Klapper, 2012).

There are several reasons why financial inclusion should be promoted, especially for millennials. According to the Center for Financial Inclusion, there are several benefits to implementing strategies to increase access to formal accounts. First, financial inclusion increases economic transactions, helping individuals to improve economic activities by making use of a secure financial platform. In the case of millennials, their entrepreneurial activities can benefit from the use of formal accounts. Second, financial inclusion facilitates day-to-day operations for both business and households, especially for the lower income segment. Financial accounts and products grant individuals liquidity in the short term. In the case of millennials, this is true especially in the use of online banking. Finally, financial inclusion helps to improve quality of life by granting access to basic services such as health, education, and food while at the same time protecting against vulnerabilities such as illness and unemployment CFI (2009).

Financial inclusion can be increased mainly through two sources: the banking sector and the government. In the former, inclusion of financial services can be accomplished by lowering financial fees, offering free accounts, decreasing required documentation in applying for financial products, or increasing the bank's geographic penetration. In the latter, inclusion can be accomplished by creating institutions and policies that push the financial sector to increase its financial coverage.

In the case of Mexico, the government has made attempts to move in this direction. In 2011, the Mexican government created the CONAIF (Consejo Nacional de Inclusión Financiera), an institution that deals with information gathering, determination of long- and short-term inclusion objectives, and suggestions on financial inclusion policies. There have also been other attempts by the government to achieve financial inclusion, such as Oportunidades, a federal program that provides financial support for the lowest income segment. With this program, the Mexican government incentivizes the use of bank accounts.

Despite these attempts by the government, financial inclusion remains underserved in Mexico. One of the main reasons for this is the highly concentrated banking sector, with 80% of the market occupied by the six largest players (CGAP, 2010). To get a clearer picture of financial penetration in in Mexico, Table 1 presents some of the main financial inclusion indicators in the country. According to data from the World Bank, only 39.1% of the population over 15 years of age had a bank account in 2014. In the case of millennials, 39.4% own a bank account. Interestingly, the millennial generation is the second largest group, just after the richest segment (45.9%). Also, young adults borrow the second largest amount from financial institutions (11.7%), again following only the richest segment. This information clarifies the importance of the millennial segment in Mexico for financial services.

Comparing Mexico with other developing economies is important to grasp a clearer picture of the need for financial inclusion. For example, as it is shown in Table 1, in comparison with the Latin American Region, Mexico scores above in the majority of the indicators. Clear exceptions are accounts own by the richest (45.9%) and those by male users (39.4). As a result, Mexico can be seen as a good case study for best practices on financial inclusion in comparison with its Latin American counterparts. However, other developing countries are performing better in some indicators than Latin American countries. For example, in the case of use of accounts, China, India, and South Africa outperformed Latin American countries with a 20-30 points above in most account indicators. Interestingly, the gap between the accounts and the money borrowed is greater in these countries in comparison with the Latin American countries. The indicators on financial credits are less advanced in developing economies such as China, India, and South Africa. In comparison Mexico, performs relatively well, which allows for an interesting case study for financial inclusion strategies.

Table 1. Financial Inclusion indicators across emerging countries

Developing Economies Financial Inclusion Indicators (in Percentage)	Mexico				Latin America	China	India	South Africa
	2011	2012	2013	2014	2014			
Account (% age 15+)	27.4	..	..	39.1	39.0	78.9	53.0	70.3
Account, female (% age 15+)	22.0	..	..	38.9	34.8	76.4	42.6	68.8
Account, income, poorest 40% (% age 15+)	11.9	..	..	29.3	24.1	72.0	43.7	56.5
Account, income, richest 60% (% age 15+)	37.8	..	..	45.9	49.5	83.6	58.6	77.3
Account, male (% age 15+)	33.2	..	..	39.4	44.0	81.4	62.0	68.8
Account, young adults (% ages 15-34)	28.7	..	..	39.4	26.1	74.2	43.0	51.0
ATMs per 100,000 adults	43.4	47.0	46.9	48.5	..	..	..	
Borrowed from a financial institution in the past year (% age 15+)	7.6	..	..	10.4	7.9	9.6	6.4	12.1
Borrowed from a financial institution in the past year, female (% age 15+)	6.7	..	..	9.3	7.4	8.7	4.9	11.4
Borrowed from a financial institution in the past year, income, poorest 40% (% age 15+)	5.3	..	..	6.5	5.6	5.9	4.9	4.9
Borrowed from a financial institution in the past year, income, richest 60% (% age 15+)	9.1	..	..	13.1	9.5	12.0	7.3	17.5
Borrowed from a financial institution in the past year, male (% age 15+)	8.5	..	..	11.6	8.3	10.4	7.8	12.8
Borrowed from a financial institution in the past year, young adults (% ages 15-34)	5.7	..	..	11.7	3.0	6.0	4.2	4.4
Branches per 100,000 adults	14.1	14.9	14.9	14.7	..	..	..	..

(World Bank, 2017)

In addition, Table 2 presents information on financial penetration in Mexico. For example, in terms of households, 26% of families have a credit account, while 37% have a savings account. An important aspect to increase financial inclusion is the cost involved in financial products. In terms of affordability, Mexico has a very high cost of credit services and very low real annual return for savings. This aspect is important, since such a situation results in less incentive for the users of financial services. Also, there is a relatively low minimum investment and relatively high fees for savings accounts considering the returns that individuals get in return. Finally, in terms of convenience, on average, opening a credit account requires almost 15 days and around four pieces of documentation.

Table 2. Financial penetration in Mexico

Dimension of Inclusion	Credit Account	Savings Account	Payments
Penetration of households that use service	26	37	
Affordability			
Costs to use service	53% to 75% Total Annual Cost (CAT)	(-)3.5% to (-)2.8% real annual return	
Minimum requirements		$12 to $45 opening amount	
Fees of the service		$4 to $5.78	0.4 ATM
Convenience			
Days to complete transaction	14.8		
Documents required	4.4	2.6	

(CFI, 2009)

As a result, financial inclusion still represents a great challenge in Mexico. High interest rates, complicated banking procedures, and a highly concentrated industry are factors that limit the access of both the millennial and adult generations to financial services. The importance of the younger segment is crucial for both the banking sector and governmental institutions. They represent a natural segment to concentrate their efforts to increase access to financial products and, as a result, promote the economic development of a developing country.

To gain a complete picture of how young millennials in emerging markets behave in terms of spending and savings and to explore how immersed they are in the banking system, a survey was conducted among middle-class students.

Proposed Banking Strategies for Targeting Young Millennials

While banking services are evolving rapidly to maintain their current customers, they still have room to improve and attract the younger segment. It has been observed that millennials have market access and purchasing power. They are also interested in using different credit formats to acquire goods and services; however, in order to attract them to the traditional banks, marketing and advertising strategies need to change. While only 39% of millennials have a bank account (Sohnm et al., 2012), 75% have a mobile phone. This makes them a good target for mobile-payment businesses, as well as for the development of mobile technology that favors a saving behavior, like Acorns, an app that allows users to save spare change by rounding up each purchase to the next full dollar amount.

Changing millennials' attitudes towards banks might be hard. However, the CAN approach can be creatively used to guide young people to select the best banking options that are offered in the market (Wansink, 2015). The CAN approach stands for *convenient* to select, *attractive* to use, and *normal* (or typical) behavior among a group of people. There are several ways of implementing this approach.

Since Millennials love their mobility, a *convenient* service should allow them to use their smartphone or tablet devices to pay bills, transfer money and check deposits (Verdone, 2015). A *convenient* bank should have enough branches and ATMs to withdraw money easily. To make it *attractive*, a reward program should be designed to give back exactly what the user wants or needs (e.g., liquid cash to use in other purchases, credit for riding Uber, concert tickets, etc.); to lower or eliminate fees; to make transactions more transparent; to ensure consumer privacy and safety; and to ensure access to banking accounts from every device, including gaming systems (Schaus, 2016).

Finally, to make the use of banking services a normal behavior, banks should try to reach young customers through spokespersons and channels they trust. Why not use Pinterest or Instagram, where users show their dreams and aspirations, instead of more traditional advertising? Moreover, banks can use insights from behavioral economics and create tools based on social norms that allow individuals to compare their financial behavior with similar others, such as the website created by the Bank of America to help individuals acquire better money habits.

CONCLUSION

Millennials represent a large group with great impact from the social and political point of view and with very specific economic peculiarities. Young millennials, especially those from emerging economies, face lack of opportunities to acquire bank services in the traditional way mainly because the absence of formal credit history and low salaries. In consequence they do not really know how the bank system works.

One of the main characteristics of millennials around the globe is that they like to spend. Of concern is the fact that they do not like (or can´t) saving, they spend big, they tend to go into debt and they do not plan for their future. When possible, they acquire financial products (mostly debit and credit cards) to preserve a certain lifestyle without having the corresponding income. Many young millennials fail to understand what a financial instrument is and its potential risks, which sometimes lead them to making bad financial choices. Millennials consider their credit line as an extension of their salary, even though this is not real. Following this path, they cannot expect a bright financial future. A lack of financial education is evident and represents an opportunity for the banking system to approach this new cohort of consumers.

Millennials face great difficulties such as economic uncertainty, in accordance with which they need to be more aware of their finances in order to better select and manage financial products. This is important because sometimes they make decisions about savings, debt and investments that are not beneficial to them and may affect their personal or family stability. Thus, it is important for them to learn how to benefit from these bank/retail store products without facing large debts or inappropriate costs.

It is observed that there are some factors, such as age, whether or not they live with their parents and their degree of personal growth, that influence them to act responsibly towards their finances.

However, many young millennial still use few or no financial instruments. This segment of young consumers usually pay cash, use informal loans (not from banks or stores), do not use credit cards, and do not like personal loans.

They feel that their income is insufficient and that, because of this, they are unable to save. All these variables taken together reflect this generation's financial illiteracy, which represents an opportunity for banks to fill in this gap gaining over competitive retail stores that are currently serving this market.

Smartphones represent an essential part of the life of these young people, as well as the use of electronic apps. It can be said that they are fully identified with social digital networks.

Mobile bank services and the use of digital platforms represent a great opportunity for traditional banks to appeal to the youngest segment of millennials. Selling financial products and services through the digital world allows to stablish affordable prices that will ensure that many of these young adults start using financial instruments properly. Fintech tools may help to include those young adults not using any financial services or those who are "underbanked" in the formal financial system.

Managerial Implications

To help individuals achieve a good degree of financial literacy it is important to implement different programs to provide knowledge and skills that allow them to manage their personal resources effectively. It seems that millennials need to learn how to make a budget, how to use a credit card and how to save their money. We propose that the same technological tools that individuals are using daily to communicate, study and have fun, can be used to help them acquire the basic skills and with the use of smartphones and apps help the individual to track their income and expense, and establish routine behaviors which might lead to a lifestyle that promotes saving activities.

We found that young millennials are not aware of the importance of planning, making budgets and saving for retirement; therefore marketing strategies should be designed to promote the importance of a wise financial management, and provide incentives to start saving from an early age.

There are several apps that have been designed to help individuals reach their monetary goals in a fun and easy way, like Acorns (acorns.com).

Countries like India had implemented technology based biometric identification program as a way to include those young people that not have the necessary documents to open a bank account. In a similar situation, banks may start to grant credits based on the digital payment made by young millennials instead of requiring a formal credit history.

In a similar way, Uber Mexico launched a new credit card in hand with the British Barclays bank and Visa, for young millennials. The new credit card will operate as a digital card in a first phase and a physical card in a second phase, when millennials get used to it. This card is based on a loyalty program that will redeem points for every purchase with Uber, Uber Eats, Airbnb, airlines, hotels, and other products and services' providers. Uber expects this card to become the way millennials cover their everyday spending habits. The new credit card was designed based on the lifestyle of Uber young users, with no annual fee or foreign transaction fees.

Digital platforms may thrive and create opportunities across the traditional and the new financial institutions. Banks must gain customers from stores who offers easy credit at high rates to young millennials. Through education, these new generation may find in the traditional banking system an ally to conquer their dreams of leisure, traveling and owning high tech products.

Limitations and Further Research

This chapter aims to shed some light in young millennials as they are left out by the traditional banking system. However, the information within may be enriched if complemented with evidence from other emerging economies. Although we deliver some data from other Latin American and Asian emerging markets, it would bring a better picture, if we discuss specific financial instruments used in these countries. Assessing specific financial instruments from other emerging countries that encourage financial inclusion represent a venue of future research.

REFERENCES

Albinsson, P. A., & Yasanthi Perera, B. (2012). Alternative marketplaces in the 21st century: Building community through sharing events. *Journal of Consumer Behaviour, 11*(4), 303–315. doi:10.1002/cb.1389

Allen, F., Demirgüç-Kunt, A., Klapper, L. F., & Martinez Peria, M. S. (2012). The foundations of financial inclusion: Understanding ownership and use of formal accounts. *Policy Research Working Paper*, 6290.

Amezcua, E. L., Arroyo M. G., & Espinosa F. (2015). Contexto de la educación financiera en México. *Ciencia Administrativa*, (1), 21-30.

Atkinson, A., & Messy, F. A. (2012). Measuring financial literacy. *OCDE Working Papers on Finance, Insurance, and Private Pensions,* (15). OECD Publishing. doi:10.1787/5k9csfs90fr4-en

Aviva. (2017). *UK: Generation regret: Over a third of millennials who went to university regret doing so as they struggle with debts and squeezed finances.* Retrieved May 5, 2017, from http://www.aviva.com/media/news/item/uk-generation-regret-over-a-third-of-millennials-who-went-to-university-regret-doing-so-as-they-struggle-with-debts-and-squeezed-finances-17653/

Banco Base. (2016, September 8). *¿Cómo administran los millennials sus finanzas personales?* Retrieved May 7, 2017, from http://blog.bancobase.com/como-administran-los-millennials-sus-finanzas-personales

Bardhi, F., & Eckhardt, G. M. (2012). Access-based consumption: The case of car sharing. *The Journal of Consumer Research, 39*(4), 881–898. doi:10.1086/666376

Barton, C., Koslow, L., & Beauchamp, C. (2014). *The reciprocity principle: How millennials are changing the face of marketing forever.* Boston Consulting Group. Retrieved May 6, 2017, from https://www.bcgperspectives.com/content/articles/marketing_center_consumer_customer_insight_how_millennials_changing_marketing_forever/?chapter=5#chapter5

BBVA Innovation Center. (2015, June 25). *Los millenials un desafio para la banca.* Retrieved May 7, 2017, from http://www.centrodeinnovacionbbva.com/noticias/los-millennials-un-desafio-para-la-banca

Belk, R. (2014). You are what you can access: Sharing and collaborative consumption online. *Journal of Business Research, 67*(8), 1595–1600. doi:10.1016/j.jbusres.2013.10.001

Better Money Habits. (n.d.). Retrieved May 2017 from https://bettermoneyhabits.bankofamerica.com/en/saving-budgeting/spending-tool

Bourlier, A., & Gomez, G. (2017). Strategies for Expanding into Emerging Markets with e-commerce. *Euromonitor International*. Retrieved on November 09 2017 from http://unctad.org/meetings/en/Contribution/dtl-eWeek2017c08-euromonitor_en.pdf

Brown, M., Grigsby, J., van der Klaauw, W., Wen, J., & Zafar, B. (2016). Financial education and the debt behavior of the young. *Review of Financial Studies*, *29*(9), 2490–2522. doi:10.1093/rfs/hhw006

Bruhn, M., Lara Ibarra, G., & McKenzie, D. J. (2013). *Why is voluntary financial education so unpopular? Experimental evidence from Mexico*. World Bank. doi: 10.1596/1813-9450-6439

Bumeran. (2017). *Los Millennials y sus hábitos financieros*. Retrieved May 5, 2017, from http://www.bumeran.com.mx/

Catalyst. (2015). *Catalyst quick take: Generations in the workplace*. New York: Catalyst. Retrieved May 6, 2017, from http://www.catalyst.org/knowledge/generations-demographic-trends-population-and-workforce

CFI. (2009). *Financial Inclusion: What's the Vision?* Retrieved from http://www.centerforfinancialinclusion.org/publications-a-resources/browse-publications/216-financial-inclusion-whats-the-vision

CGAP. (2010). *Update on Branchless Banking Policy and Regulation in Mexico*. Retrieved from https://www.cgap.org/sites/default/files/CGAP-Regulation-of-Branchless-Banking-in-Mexico-Jan-2010.pdf

Chaiken, S. (1980). Heuristic versus systematic information processing and the use of source versus message cues in persuasion. *Journal of Personality and Social Psychology*, *39*(5), 752–766. doi:10.1037/0022-3514.39.5.752

Comparaguru.com. (2016, September 8). *5 tipos ideales de crédito para millennials*. Retrieved May 7, 2017, from https://www.comparaguru.com/blog/5-tipos-ideales-de-credito-para-millennials

Contreras, L. (2014, July 17). *Créditos, una opción costosa para estudiar*. Retrieved from http://www.forbes.com.mx/creditos-una-opcion-costosa-para-estudiar/#gs.gWKiLME

Coulter, R. H., & Zaltman, G. (1995). Seeing the voice of the customer: Metaphor-based advertising research. *Journal of Advertising Research*, *35*(4), 35–51.

Crédito Joven. (2017). *Para iniciar tu negocio*. Retrieved April 25, 2017, from http://www.creditojoven.gob.mx/portalcj/content/iniciar-tu-negocio.html

Cudmore, B. A., Patton, J., Ng, K., & McClure, C. (2010). The millennials and money management. *Journal of Management and Marketing Research*, *4*(1), 1–28.

Deloitte. (2017). *The Deloitte Millennial Survey 2017*. Retrieved May 6, 2017, from https://www2.deloitte.com/global/en/pages/about-deloitte/articles/millennialsurvey.html

Demirgüç-Kunt, A., & Klapper, L. F. (2012). Measuring financial inclusion: The global findex database. *Policy Research Working Paper*, 6025.

DeVaney, S. A. (2015). Understanding the Millennial generation. *Journal of Financial Service Professionals*, *69*(6), 11–14.

Dhanani, S. (2015, March 5). How prepaid and mobile are driving commerce in emerging markets. *Digital Transactional Processing Industry Solutions Insights*. Retrieved May 7, 2017, from http://cartaworldwide.com/news-insights/how-prepaid-and-mobile-are-driving-commerce-in-emerging-markets/

Eventbrite. (2016). *Millennials: Fueling the experience economy*. Retrieved May 6, 2017, from https://www.eventbrite.com/blog/academy/millennials-fueling-experience- economy/?Email=&InferredCountry=United+States&UTM_Source__c=&UTM_campaign__c=&Ref_Code__c=&UTM_Content__c=&UTM_Medium__c=&UTM_Term__c=&FirstName=&LastName=&Company=&Phone=&avg_ticket_price__c=&formid=1044&munchkinId=269-CEG-133

Fernandes, D., Lynch, J. G. Jr, & Netemeyer, R. G. (2014). Financial literacy, financial education, and downstream financial behaviors. *Management Science*, *60*(8), 1861–1883. doi:10.1287/mnsc.2013.1849

Fernbach, P. M., Kan, C., & Lynch, J. G. Jr. (2015). Squeezed: Coping with constraint through efficiency and prioritization. *The Journal of Consumer Research*, *41*(5), 1204–1227. doi:10.1086/679118

García, N., Grifoni, A., López, J. C., & Mejía, D. (2013). *N° 12. La educación financiera en América Latina y el Caribe*. Situación actual y perspectivas.

GFK. (2016). *Enjoy life today, worry about savings and investments later*. Retrieved May 31, 2016, from http://www.gfk.com/global-studies/global-studies-enjoy-life/

Goldman-Sachs. (2017). *Millennials coming of age*. Retrieved from http://www.goldmansachs.com/our-thinking/pages/millennials/

Harris. (2017). *Harris Poll: Millennials increasingly dictating health of America's top brands*. Retrieved May 6, 2017, from http://www.theharrispoll.com/business/Millennials-Dictating-Health-of-Brands.html

Hastings, J. S., Madrian, B. C., & Skimmyhorn, W. L. (2013). Financial literacy, financial education, and economic outcomes. *Annual Review of Economics*, *5*(1), 347–373. doi:10.1146/annurev-economics-082312-125807 PMID:23991248

Hastings, J. S., & Tejeda-Ashton, L. (2008). *Financial literacy, information, and demand elasticity: Survey and experimental evidence from Mexico (No. w14538)*. National Bureau of Economic Research. doi:10.3386/w14538

Hershfield, H. E., Goldstein, D. G., Sharpe, W. F., Fox, J., Yeykelis, L., Carstensen, L. L., & Bailenson, J. N. (2011). Increasing saving behavior through age-progressed renderings of the future self. *Journal of Marketing Research, 48*(SPL), S23-S37.

Jabbour, A. (2016, July 6). *Banks need to adapt to millennials, not vice versa*. Retrieved from https://www.americanbanker.com/opinion/banks-need-to-adapt-to-millennials-not-vice-versa

Kardes, F. R., Posavac, S. S., & Cronley, M. L. (2004). Consumer inference: A review of processes, bases, and judgment contexts. *Journal of Consumer Psychology*, *14*(3), 230–256. doi:10.120715327663jcp1403_6

Kefela, G. T. (2010). Promoting access to finance by empowering consumers: Financial literacy in developing countries. *Educational Research Review*, *5*(5), 205.

La Vanguardia. (2017, April). *Santander lanza '1, 2, 3 Smart', la cuenta para millennials*. Retrieved May 7, 2017, from http://www.lavanguardia.com/economia/20170417/421773258411/santander-1-2-3-smart-cuenta-millennial-jovenes.html

Lavin, M. (2014, October 28). *Los millenials y la nueva banca*. Retrieved May 7, 2017, from https://www.forbes.com.mx/los-millenials-y-la-nueva-banca/

Lee, J., & Kwon, K. N. (2002). Consumers' use of credit cards: Store credit card usage as an alternative payment and financing medium. *The Journal of Consumer Affairs*, *36*(2), 239–262. doi:10.1111/j.1745-6606.2002.tb00432.x

Logsdon, B. (2016). *Little-known millennial loyalty trends: Marketing insights*. Retrieved May 6, 2017, from https://www.ama.org/publications/MarketingInsights/Pages/millenials-driven-by-loyalty-rewards.aspx

Lusardi, A., & Mitchell, O. S. (2014). The economic importance of financial literacy: Theory and evidence. *Journal of Economic Literature*, *52*(1), 5–44. doi:10.1257/jel.52.1.5 PMID:28579637

Lynch, J. G. Jr, Netemeyer, R. G., Spiller, S. A., & Zammit, A. (2010). A generalizable scale of propensity to plan: The long and the short of planning for time and for money. *The Journal of Consumer Research, 37*(1), 108–128. doi:10.1086/649907

Maccaro, C. (2015). *Why finance brands need to inspire & empower millennials now*. Retrieved April 16, 2017, from https://www.ama.org/resources/Best-Practices/Pages/-Empower-Millennials.aspx

Magni, M., Martínez, A., & Motiwala, R. (2016). *Saving, scrimping, and... splurging?* McKinsey & Company Report. Retrieved March 8, 2017, from http://www.mckinsey.com/industries/consumer-packaged-goods/our-insights/saving-scrimping-and-splurging-new-insights-into-consumer-behavior?cid=other-eml-ttn-mip-mck-oth-1612

Malcolm, H. (2012). Millennials struggle with financial literacy. *USA Today*.

McCormick, M. H. (2009). The effectiveness of youth financial education: A review of the literature. *Journal of Financial Counseling and Planning, 20*(1), 70–83.

MDI. (2014). *Millennial Disruption Index*. Retrieved April 20, 2017, from: http://www.millennialdisruptionindex.com/

Molina, D. I. (2016). *Fintech: Lo que la tecnología hace por las finanzas*. Profit Editorial.

Music Biz/LOOP. (2016, July 12). *Millennials turn from radio to embrace streaming*. Retrieved May 7, 2017, from https://musicbiz.org/news/music-bizloop-study-millennials-turn-radio-embrace-streaming/

Norman, A. S. (2010). Importance of financial education in making informed decision on spending. *Journal of Economics and International Finance, 2*(10), 199–207.

OECD. (2005). *Recommendation on principles and good practices for financial education and awareness*. Directorate for Financial and Enterprise Affairs. Retrieved from http://www.oecd.org/finance/financial-education/35108560.pdf

Pew Research Center. (2010). *Millennials, a portrait of generation next: Confident. Connected. Open to change*. Retrieved April 25, 2017, from http://www.pewsocialtrends.org/files/2010/10/millennials-confident-connected-open-to-change.pdf

Philip, H. E., Ozanne, L. K., & Ballantine, P. W. (2015). Examining temporary disposition and acquisition in peer-to-peer renting. *Journal of Marketing Management, 31*(11-12), 1310–1332. doi:10.1080/0267257X.2015.1013490

PwC. (2017). *Los mercados emergentes siguen carentes de sistemas financieros aptos para el propósito*. PwC. Retrieved November 9, 2017 from https://www.pwc.com/ia/es/prensa/pdfs/pwc-project-blue.pdf

Sandeen, C. (2008). Boomers, Xers, and Millennials: Who are they and what do they really want from continuing higher education? *Continuing Higher Education Review*, *72*, 11–31.

Scaraboto, D. (2015). Selling, sharing, and everything in between: The hybrid economies of collaborative networks. *The Journal of Consumer Research*, *42*(1), 152–176. doi:10.1093/jcr/ucv004

Schaus, P. (2016). *What millennials want from their bank*. ABA Bank Marketing. Retrieved May 2017 from http://ababankmarketing.com/insights/what-millennials-want-from-their-bank/

Servon, L. J., & Kaestner, R. (2008). Consumer financial literacy and the impact of online banking on the financial behavior of lower-income bank customers. *The Journal of Consumer Affairs*, *42*(2), 271–305. doi:10.1111/j.1745-6606.2008.00108.x

Sohn, S. H., Joo, S. H., Grable, J. E., Lee, S., & Kim, M. (2012). Adolescents' financial literacy: The role of financial socialization agents, financial experiences, and money attitudes in shaping financial literacy among South Korean youth. *Journal of Adolescence*, *35*(4), 969–980. doi:10.1016/j.adolescence.2012.02.002 PMID:22418452

Strauss, W., & Howe, N. (1991). Generations: The history of America's future, 1584 to 2069. New York: Academic Press.

Thaler, R., & Sunstein, C. (2009). *Nudge: Improving decisions about health, wealth, and happiness*. New York, NY: Penguin.

Torreblanca, E. (2016, July 22). *Créditos blandos a jóvenes mexicanos*. Retrieved April 25, 2017, from http://www.elfinanciero.com.mx/opinion/creditos-blandos-a-jovenes-mexicanos.html

Verdone, M. (2015). How to be hip: Big banks can market to millennials. *Advertising Age*. Retrieved May 2017 from http://adage.com/article/cmo-strategy/hip-ways-banks-market-millennials/299176/

Wansink, B. (2015). Change their choice! Changing behavior using the CAN approach and activism research. *Psychology and Marketing*, *32*(5), 486–500. doi:10.1002/mar.20794

APPENDIX

AN EMPIRICAL EXPLORATION OF YOUNG MILLENNIALS' FINANCES:A CASE STUDY

According to the literary review carried out in which the context of financial inclusion in the banking system for young millennials is described, a field investigation was carried out in the Marketing School of a Public University North East Mexico. The goal for this field study is to better understand how undergraduate students of a public school manage their finances and the use of financial apps. An instrument was applied to 100 students between March and April 2017. We got a 50/50 female/male participation with ages ranging from 18 to 26 years old.

The information is divided into two blocks, the first has to do with millennials' habits and spending behavior and the second block with their finances.

Block 1: Millennials Habits and Spending Behavior

76% of local students live with their parents and only 12% rent a room or a house.

96% of students go out to dinner on average 4 times a month; 90% like to go to the movies 3 times a month, and 76% buy clothes once or twice a month. They watch movies on streaming services almost 7 time a month, buy or rent music from streaming services at a similar rate, and go dancing and drinking at least once a month.

Regarding whether they prefer to buy or rent (streaming service) music or movies, the results show:

Millennials from this public university prepay for streaming music and movies services, usually Netflix and Spotify.

62% uses the Uber transport service, from which 48% pay in cash and 14% with their own bank credit card.

Table 3. Buying vs. renting

CONCEPT	Neither %	Always Buy %	Both %	Always Rent %
Music	24	25	13	28
Movies	18	22	6	43
Videogames	42	31	9	13

Block 2: Millennials' Finances

Only 50% of students have a job. Of those who do not currently have a job, 27% have had one paid full or partial job in the last year. Although working, students earn small salaries. 17% earn between 105 and 210 USD a month 13% earn up to 315 USD, and a very small percentage (5%) earn more than 421 USD monthly.

26% of students do not save at all, Table 4, shows saving amounts for men and women. As shown, men save the most.

Regarding the financial instruments that young people have and use, the percentage is low, as shown in Table 5, most of them have store credit cards, since most apparel stores for young low income consumers has offered credit as a marketing strategy to acquire new customers, even though they charge higher interest rates than bank does.

28% of young people have debts averaging 143 USD, most of them are men buying cars.

Regarding the use of financial apps, they mostly use it to check their credit balance (40%), to quote or plan some activities (17%), to save (9%) and, to plan their payments (8%).

Table 4. Saving habits

Amount	Male %	Female %
10 USD	4.2	11.5
16 USD	10.4	7.7
26 USD	10.4	9.6
42 USD	2.1	5.8
25 USD	10.4	17.3
105 USD	10.4	0
157 USD	8.3	1.9
263 USD	2.1	1.9

Table 5. Financial instruments

Financial Instrument	I Don'T Have Any %	I Have My Own %
Bank debit card	40	48
Bank credit card	70	14
Store credit card (apparel or department store)	64	24
Store account to make/receive payments	86	10
Other, specify	96	3

Only 13% use Paypal or some other intermediary payment system.

With this information at hand, what recommendations would you make to financial institutions to attract and keep young millennials as loyal customers? Provide a marketing approach to assure financial inclusion.

Chapter 8
Challenges Faced by Banks for Financial Inclusion:
Growth and Viability in the Indian Context

Deepa Pillai
Symbiosis International University, India

Ravi Kumar V. V.
Symbiosis International University, India

ABSTRACT

The banking system in India significantly differs from that of other Asian nations due to unique geographic, social, and economic spread. In India, financially excluded sections largely comprise of marginal farmers, slum dwellers, migrants, women, self-employed, and senior citizens. There have been many formidable challenges in financial inclusion for bridging the gap between the demand and supply side. The chapter deliberates the challenges faced by banks for financial inclusion in context of infrastructure and institutional credit, risk perception, illiteracy, compliances, financial awareness, products, and services. Barriers to financial services expansion and product and service delivery in rural markets will be reviewed, and the primary focus will be on challenges with respect to marketing and delivery of financial services in rural areas. Reaching out to the excluded sections through financial literacy campaigns, and in the process marketing, the banks and their schemes would be an important step towards financial inclusion.

DOI: 10.4018/978-1-5225-4035-9.ch008

INTRODUCTION

Banking sector in India had been instrumental in bringing about growth and prosperity of the economy since 1969; tremendous changes have taken place in the banking industry. The banks have shed their traditional functions and have been innovating, improving and coming out with new types of the services however there exists a large segment outside the formal banking sector. The banking industry worldwide has been showing steady progress since 2002, the growth in the worldwide banking industry is attributed to the surge in the retail-banking sector in the Asia Pacific region.

The changing paradigm of financial service industry in a global scenario has converged banking, insurance and capital market products with new business strategies interventions for delivering value to the customer and creation of revenue margins to the banks Retail banking has paved ways for customer centricity encompassing multiple product offerings, enormous geographical coverage, acquisition of large customer base, cross selling of financial products and stringent risk management practices. Cost effective alternate channels of service delivery with technological interventions has redefined the conventional banking business model with enhanced product portfolio to increase the customers' wallet. All these advancements have increased complexity of business and new threats to the financial sector nonetheless financial exclusion still remains a debatable topic amongst policy holders and financial institutions.

Despite of growth in the financial sector a sizeable section of the population, particularly the vulnerable groups, categorized as weaker sections and low income groups, continue to remain excluded from even the most basic opportunities and services provided by the financial sector. A recurring phenomenon in financial exclusion is lack of institutional finance leading to income disparity but also resulting in slower economic growth. The absence of formalized institutional finance increases the dependency on the informal financial sector by the secluded groups restraining the financial decision making capability of the poor from making rationale choice of their savings and investments. This situation also leads to these excluded sections approaching money lenders for their financing needs and getting exploited in various forms.

Exposure to financial services empowers the poor in investing their savings into productive assets whereby generating returns helping in reducing vulnerability of income and facilitating them to be in the mainstream of the economy and economic development process thus rural outreach of financial services thus becomes imperative in a growing economy like India. Report of committee for medium term path on financial inclusion (2015) indicates that an eco-system comprising multiple models should be encouraged fostering partnerships amongst national full-service banks, regional banks of various types, NBFCs, semi-formal financial institutions, as well as the newly-licensed payments banks and small finance banks for promoting financial inclusion.

RATIONALE OF THE STUDY

Evidences demonstrate that financial access varies extensively across the nations though expanding access to financial services still remains an important challenge thus it is apparent that there is much role for polices to do around the world for financial inclusion. Study by Handoo (2010) enumerates that RBI has been proactive in ushering enabling environment for expediting financial inclusion across India through various bank led models nonetheless reaching out to a 400 million plus households who are financially excluded at pace with profitability for banks it becomes the single most challenge faced by the stakeholders particularly banks and delivery channels

Financial development go together with economic development which ultimately can be accomplished through broader partaking of the all the sections of the population into the mainstream of the financial sector. Wider access to financial services results into steering of savings into fruitful investment instruments whereby distributing economic opportunity uniformly across all the households. Financial inclusion thus broadens the resource base of the financial system and encourages expansion of markets and competition of the firm.

PREAMBLE OF INDIAN BANKING SECTOR

Since 1969, tremendous changes have taken place in the banking industry. The banks have shed their traditional functions and have been innovating, improving and coming out with new types of services to cater to the emerging needs of their customers. Commercial banks which were of public character have undergone numerous changes since the economic reforms in terms of its outreach, efficiency and financial soundness.

In India, prior to nationalization, banking services was restricted mainly to the urban areas and neglected in the rural and semi-urban areas. Large industries and big business houses enjoyed major portion of the credit facilities. Agriculture, small-scale industries and exports received little or no attention. After the nationalization the breadth and scope of Indian banking sector expanded and was remarkably successful at achieving mass participation. Between 1969 and 1980, the number of private branches grew more quickly than public banks, and on April 1, 1980, they accounted for approximately 17.5 percent of bank branches in India. In April, 1980 the government undertook a second round of nationalization, placing under government control the six private banks whose nationwide deposits were above Rs. 2 billion, or a further 8 percent of bank branches, leaving approximately 10 percent of bank branches in private hands.

During the post-independence era government of India initiated measures to play an active role in the economic life of the nation and industrial policy resolution adopted by the government in 1948 envisaged a mixed economy which resulted in greater involvement of the state in different segments of the economy including banking and finance. Following the Nationalization Act of 1969, the 14 largest public banks were nationalized which raised the Public Sector Banks' (PSB) share of deposits from 31% to 86%. The two main objectives of the nationalizations were rapid branch expansion and the channeling of credit in line with the priorities of the five-year plans. The second wave of nationalizations occurred because control over the banking system became increasingly more important as a means to ensure priority sector lending, reach the poor through a widening branch network and to fund rising public deficits. In addition to the nationalization of banks, the priority sector lending targets were raised to 40%. However, the policies that were supposed to promote a more equal distribution of funds, also led to inefficiencies in the Indian banking system.

Liberalization of the economy in 1990 followed by the government's pronouncement for privatization of banks has culminated to banking sector reforms based on the recommendations of the Narashimham Committee. Globalization has made way for the entry of foreign banks in India, these banks with their advanced technology and varied product range posed a major challenge for the Indian banks which compelled them for innovations in their banking business practices, a sea change has taken place in the banking environment since the initiation of reform process in 1992-93. In the light of sweeping changes that have taken place in banking policies and practices during the last eleven years of reform period, it is thought appropriate to evaluate the impact of reform measures on the efficiency, profitability and overall growth.

The banking system in India is significantly different from that of other Asian nations because of the country's unique geographic, social, and economic characteristics. Mohan (2008) address excerpts make a reference of literature relating to different types of innovation which has been adopted by the Indian Banks such as business model innovation, marketing innovation, product design innovation, product pricing innovation and innovation in business practices.

MAIN FOCUS OF THE CHAPTER

Definition of Financial Inclusion

Financial inclusion is one such initiative that was featured in 2005 when RBI in its annual policy statement of 2005-06 while recognizing the concerns in regard to the banking practices to attract vast deprived sections of the population, urged banks to review their existing practices to align them with the objective of financial inclusion. The focus of Union Budget since 2010 onwards till date has been on the implementation and achieving higher aim of financial inclusion. The objective of financial inclusion is to extend the scope of activities of the organized financial system to include within its ambit people with low incomes which can be concluded as: delivery of banking and financial services at an affordable cost to the people who do not have access to financial services to the people pertaining to low income groups. The goal of financial inclusion appears to be within the reach but achieving it depends on innovation from across the different sectors of the economy (McKinsey, 2010). Innovations in the banking sector especially in products, services and service delivery channels have been a persistent process however the fact which underlies is as to how many of these innovations have helped the banks to achieve the agenda of financial inclusion and fulfill the purpose of these innovations in the sector.

Financial inclusion helps in the empowerment of the underprivileged, poor and women of the society with the mission of making them self-sufficient and well informed to take better financial decisions. Financial inclusion is a multidimensional concept which incorporates all initiatives both supply and demand sides, within the financial sector. It includes delivery of appropriate and quality financing which is both accessible and affordable to the low-income and other vulnerable households. Over the decades financial sector policies in India have been long driven by the objective of increasing financial inclusion, but the goal of universal inclusion is still a distant dream. The strategy for achieving financial inclusion majorly relied on the Regional rural banks, bank branches and government sponsored institutions however there is a change required in the mindset of all the stakeholders for figuring out the effective ways of achieving financial inclusion. Understanding the concept of financial inclusion is a prerequisite, there prevail varied definitions of financial inclusion defined by different stakeholders:

The Committee on Financial inclusion headed by Dr. C. Rangarajan defined financial inclusion as "The process of ensuring access to financial services and timely and adequate credit where needed by vulnerable groups such as weaker sections and low-income groups at an affordable cost." The definition does not encompass delivery of financial services for all at all cost, however it means that the delivery of financial services and products at affordable costs to the excluded sections of the population and lower income groups.

GOI (2008) financial inclusion as the process of ensuring access to financial services and timely and adequate credit where needed by vulnerable groups such as weaker sections and low-income groups at an affordable cost. The definition is inclusive of the delivery of financial services to the low-income groups particularly, the excluded sections of the population with the provision of equal opportunities. The foremost objective anticipated was the access of financial services for better standard of living and income

Planning commission (2009) financial inclusion refers to universal access to a wide range of financial services at a reasonable cost. These include not only banking products but also other financial services such as insurance and equity products. Financial inclusion is not only about credit, but involves providing a wide range of financial services, including saving accounts, insurance, and remittance products.

Subbarao (2009) financial inclusion can be defined as the freedom of financial security equipped with knowledge that helps to make effective choices of financial instruments and informed investment decision making. Financial inclusion is important because it is considered as an important condition for sustaining growth.

According to World Bank (2013), financial inclusion means that individuals and businesses have access to useful and affordable financial products and services that meet their needs transactions, payments, savings, credit and insurance – delivered in a responsible and sustainable way. The definition points on the accessibility to a transaction account is a first step toward broader financial inclusion since it allows people to store money, and send and receive payments further a transaction account serves as a gateway to other financial services.

As per OECD, Financial Inclusion is the process of ensuring access to appropriate financial products and services needed by vulnerable groups such as weaker sections and low-income groups at an affordable cost in a fair and transparent by mainstream Institutional players. The twin objective of this definition was financial literacy and accessibility to credit thus narrowing down the gap between the demand and supply side.

Banking Association of South Africa defines financial inclusion as access and usage of a broad range of affordable, quality financial services and products, in a manner convenient to the financially excluded, unbanked and under-banked, in an appropriate but simple and dignified manner with the requisite consideration to client protection. Accessibility should be accompanied by usage which should be supported through the financial education of clients.

Contrary to the definition of financial inclusion, European Commission definition on financial exclusion states that "Financial exclusion is a process whereby people encounter difficulties in accessing or using financial services and products in the mainstream market that are appropriate to their needs and enable them to lead a normal social life in the society to which they belong.

Chakraborty (2009) study enumerates the use of technology in expanding the banking outreach. Technological innovation would be an enabler for broader reach for consumer banking and financial services, but will also enhance its capacity for continued and inclusive growth.

Ramesh and Sahai (2007) study highlights the micro image of financial exclusion. They argued that basic banking account should not be considered as a luxury but a fundamental right to every citizen. The scheme of no-frills saving account is only a necessity but may not be a sufficient condition for financial inclusion of the poor.

All the reported definitions of financial inclusion refer on the accessibility of financial services. The definitions basically narrate the ability of firms and households to use financial products and services given particular constraints of time and distance. The pertinent measures include the proximity of access points, the variety of access channels such as Automated Teller Machines, Point of Sale networks, agent banking, internet banking and mobile banking etc. also the socio-economic barriers restraining such use. Other important aspect limiting the scope for access to financial services can be the pricing and other terms and conditions of financial products and services and also the opportunity cost involved for availing financial services.

Dimensions of Financial Inclusion

Measurement of financial inclusion evaluates the extent of availability, accessibility and usage of financial services by the households. Sarma (2008) enumerates on five factors that account for the lack of financial exclusion: Access exclusion due to demographic characteristics; Condition exclusion; Price exclusion due to non-affordability of financial services; Marketing exclusion on account of non-attractiveness of conducting business within the society amongst varied groups and Self exclusion due to psychological barriers. The study incorporates these five factors for studying the level of social exclusion and the reasons for being financially excluded. Studying the demand and supply side of financial services also the channels of service delivery mechanism is necessary as it will help in assessing the extent of coverage of financial services and the reasons for lack of financial inclusion.

Lack of financial inclusion always prove costly to the society and households, as far as households are concerned financial exclusion may force them to borrow smaller amount from informal banking sector at higher rate of interest as these informal markets are outside the purview of regulatory norms any discontentment between lender and borrowers cannot be settled legally and may result in suicide attempts by borrowers or threats by the lenders result of such practices would affect the society by increasing poverty, unethical practices and greater risk of exploitation of households. Implications of financial exclusion results firstly for affordable loans leave people to opt for higher interest credit, secondly lack of savings and insurance makes families vulnerable to financial crisis and lastly lack of bank accounts deprive them from availing government benefits and subsidies. Alliance for Financial Inclusion emphasizes on the three aspects of financial inclusion accessibility, usage and quality explained as:

The gaps in access, use, and quality of savings accounts in financial institutions, and in the availability of credit and insurance products among different segments of the economy are still large (World Bank, 2014; Demirguc & Kunt, 2015 et al.). Since financial inclusion is a multidimensional concept, its macroeconomic effects depend on its nature as greater access of financial services to businesses and households lead to higher growth of the economy conversely financial stability risks increases if access to credit is expanded without proper supervision.

Why Financial Inclusion?

1. Financial Inclusion has the ability to generate positive externalities: it results into increased savings rate, investments spurring the processes of economic growth and development.
2. The economic objective of financial inclusion aims at impartial growth amongst all sections of the society leading to reduction of disparities in income, savings and investments.
3. It inculcates the habit of saving money, especially amongst the lower income group who has been constantly living under the shadow of financial constraint,

Table 1. Dimensions of financial inclusion

S.No	Dimensions	Measurable
1	Accessibility	Availability and Proximity of Financial Services: - Branch penetration - Credit penetration - Deposit penetration - Affordability - Opportunity cost: loss of daily wages
2	Usage	Actual usage of financial products and services - Frequency of Usage - Regularity of Usage - Duration of usage
3	Quality	Customized or tailor made products and services - Demographic analysis - Segmentation of markets

Source: Adapted from Alliance for Financial Inclusion Financial Inclusion Data Working Group (2011).

mainly because of assured income, absence of savings, and unfamiliarity with financial products making them a vulnerable section.

4. Eradication of poverty is the major prime objective of financial inclusion schemes through narrowing down the gap between the weaker sections of the society and the sources of their livelihood as means of income and potential for availing credit from formal institutions. Previous studies have shown rural branch expansion program appreciably lowered rural poverty, and enlarged nonagricultural employment.
5. Presence of banking services and products aims to provide a critical tool to inculcate the savings habit for the underprivileged bringing them under the umbrella of formal credit who are otherwise reliant on informal channels of credit like family, friends and moneylenders.
6. Availability of timely, adequate and transparent credit from formal banking channels will allow the entrepreneurial spirit of the masses to increase outputs and prosperity in the countryside.
7. Formal remittance facilities to the low income and unbanked populace will increase limiting the growth of informal channels.
8. Adequate banking facilities will ensure distribution of government benefits and subsidies through direct benefit transfers to the beneficiaries' bank accounts rather than subsidized products and cash payments.

Policies Supporting Financial Inclusion: Measures Taken by RBI and Government of India

The basis of Reserve Bank of India financial inclusion agenda was providing universal access to banking services and improving the forms of credit delivery for the weaker sections of the population. The policy interventions undertaken by RBI for the promotion of financial inclusions programs comprised of multiple approaches such as:

Strategic Approach

1. **Financial Inclusion Plan:** All Scheduled commercial banks (SCBs) were advised to drawn up their strategic financial inclusion plans as a part of their business strategy based on their competitive advantage. These plans were to be implemented over a block of three years these plans included opening of brick and mortar branches in rural areas, employing business correspondents, opening of Basic Savings Bank Deposit accounts (BSBDAs) including through BC-ICT, issuance of Kisan Credit Cards (KCC) and General Credit Cards (GCC) and micro insurance products aimed at the financially excluded

segments. The plan also encompassed opening of 25% of branches by SCBs in Tier 5 and Tier 6 areas.

2. **Priority Sector Lending:** Priority sectors refers to those sectors of the economy like agriculture, small enterprises and housing which, though viable and creditworthy, may not get timely and adequate credit. The priority sector lending policy of the Reserve Bank envisages that banks extend credit to the priority sector as part of their normal business operations and not as a part of corporate social responsibility. In order to render transparency, the pricing of all credit under the scheme has been made free.
3. **Swabhimaan Scheme:** The Swabhimaan campaign addressed Banks to provide banking facilities to habitations having a population in excess of 2000 (as per 2001 census) by March 2012. The banks identified approximately 74000 habitations across the country having a population of over 2000 for providing banking facilities. Nearly 74351 villages with population excess of 2000 have been covered under the banking facilities through diverse service delivery channels.

Bank Led Approach

1. Business Correspondent RBI permitted the use of intermediaries for providing banking services to the financially excluded sections through the use of business correspondents (BCs) which indorsed banking facilities at doorstep thus resolving the issue of last mile reach. Business correspondent model initiated the idea of "branchless banking", the basic aim was on leveraging technology for reducing the per transaction value of the financial transaction at rural level due to low ticket size. The BC model was projected as non-profitable as it required strong technology enabled backend support for multi-channel interfaces especially mobile based interfacing.
2. Self Help Groups In India, Self Help Group is one of the cost-effective mechanism for rendering financial services to the financially excluded which has been successful in meeting their financial needs of the rural poor women but also building voluntary collective groups for mutual benefit. In the year 1991-92 NABARD started the SHG Linkage program was the real take off point for the SHG movement in India. In 1993, the Reserve Bank of India (RBI) allowed SHGs to open saving accounts in banks and avail the banking services and it was the major boost to the movement. Bank offers the structure, accounting services and support to the group to manage their deposits and lending. However, SHGs face challenges in terms of constrained financial resources due to their lower saving capacities, lack of marketable skills amongst group members, multiple membership and inadequate outreach.

3. No-Frill Accounts In November 2005 RBI advised banks to make available a basic banking "No-frill Account" with low or nil minimum balances as well as charges to expand the outreach of such accounts to vast sections of the population.

Regulatory Approach

1. **Relaxed KYC Norms:** Recognizing that KYC requirements and documentation may become a deterrent in encouraging weaker sections of the population in opening bank accounts, the KYC norms were relaxed and simplified.
2. Small accounts could be opened with self-certification in the presence of bank officials.
3. Aadhaar, the unique identification number allotted by the Unique Identification Authority of India (UIDAI), Government of India was allowed to be used as one of the eligible documents for meeting KYC requirement for opening a bank account. Branch Authorization Scheme
4. To address the issue of uneven distribution of bank branches, in the year 2009, RBI has permitted domestic scheduled commercial banks to open branches in areas with a population of less than 50,000 without taking authorization, thus deviating from its normal norms, in tier 3 to 6 city, towns, or villages. In the north-eastern states and Sikkim, domestic scheduled commercial banks can open bank branches in rural, semi- urban and urban areas without prior permission from RBI in each case, subject to reporting.
5. **Opening of Branches in Unbanked Rural Centers:** To further step up the opening of branches in rural areas and to improve banking penetration and financial inclusion rapidly, the need for the opening of more bricks and mortar branches, besides the use of Business Correspondents model. Accordingly, banks have been mandated in the monetary policy statement to allocate at least 25% of the total number of branches to be opened during a year to unbanked rural centers.
6. **Direct Benefit Transfer (DBT):** This scheme ensures that money under various developmental schemes reaches beneficiaries directly and without any delay. Banks play a key role in its implementation.

Product and Service Led Approach

1. **Pradhan Mantri Jan Dhan Yojana (PMJDY):** PMJDY is a National Mission for Financial Inclusion to ensure access to financial services, namely, Banking, Savings & Deposit Accounts, Remittance, Credit, Insurance, and Pension in

an affordable manner. Under the scheme bank account can be opened in any bank branch or with the Business Correspondent with a zero balance.

2. **RuPay Card:** It is a new card payment scheme offering a domestic, open-loop, multilateral card payment system which will allow all Indian banks and financial institutions in the country to participate in electronic payments. RuPay symbolizes the capabilities of the banking industry to build a card payment network at much lower and affordable costs. The RuPay Card works on Automated Teller Machines, point of sale terminals, and online purchases and delivers customers with the flexibility of payment options.
3. **Kissan Credit Card (KCC):** In view of the problem of accessibility to short term credit by farmers, the Government of India introduced the Kisan Credit Card (KCC) scheme in the year 1998-99. This scheme has facilitated the availability of credit in time and has simplified the procedure for availing loan from banks to a large extent (Nahatkar et al., 2002). Although KCC has gained popularity over the years however there exists certain concerns with respect to the interest rates, credit limits and flexibility in repayment. Studies have shown that the banks are stipulating minimum land holding criteria for issue of Kisan Credit Cards; as a result, the small and marginal farmers were finding it difficult to obtain the card from banks nevertheless the total number of KCC issued went up from 24.3 million in March 2010 to 46.4 million in September 2016.
4. **Debit and Credit Cards:** A debit card is an electronic card issued by a bank which allows access to customers to their bank account for withdrawal of cash or for making the payment of goods and services. It is known as the plastic money which eliminates the need for customers to visit the bank for cash withdrawal instead they transact with ATM or pay electronically at merchant locations.

Technology Based Approach

Indian has witnessed technology such as mobile and digitization has the game changer for financial inclusion drive. Digital India will boost the infrastructure, technology and outreach.

1. **Unstructured Supplementary Services Data-Based Mobile Banking:** This service offers the facility of mobile banking using Unstructured Supplementary Service Data (USSD) for money transfer, bill payments, balance enquiries, merchant payments on a simple GSM based-mobile phone, without the need to download any application.

2. **IndiaStack:** Application Programming Interfaces (APIs) is being rolled out by the Government in consultation with iSpirit to bridge the digital divide in the country. The incorporation of IndiaStack API will lay the foundations for innovation in the space of digital payments. Implemented under the open-API policy of Digital India, it contains four distinct layers:
    a. **Presence-Less Layer:** Biometric digital identity for e-KYC (Aadhaar)
    b. **Paperless Layer:** Digital records of an individual (e-Sign and Digi Locker)
    c. **Cashless Layer:** Interoperability of payments across bank accounts/ wallets (UPI, IMPS, AEPS)
    d. **Consent Layer:** Security and control
3. The concept of payments banks introduced by RBI is a huge step towards tech-driven financial inclusion.
4. Immediate Payment Services (IMPS)
5. **Mobile Banking:** It is an efficient and cost-effective tool to reach far-flung semi-urban and rural populations. The Jan Dhan–Aadhaar–Mobile (JAM) has created the building blocks for a digital financial infrastructure.

Towards Inclusive Growth

Benchmarking

World Bank Index Survey (2012) states that only 35% of Indian adults had access to a formal bank account and 8% borrowed from a formal financial institution in last 12 months. A comparison of key performance measures with global counterparts is indicative measure of financial deprivation for the year 2013. Table 2 indicate a cross country analysis of parameters relating to financial inclusion.

Table 2. Global benchmarking parameters

Global Benchmarking Parameters	Brazil	India	South Africa
No. of Commercial bank branches per 1,00,000 adults	47	12	10
No. of Commercial bank branches per 1000 Kms	8	35	3
No. of ATMs per 1,00,000 adults	130	13	62
Deposit accounts with commercial banks per 1000 adults	1153	1197	1567
Loan accounts with commercial banks per 1000 adults	2358	147	482

Source: IMF, RBI and KPMG Report, 2013

Accessibility

As per the census of 2011, more than 40 per cent of the Indian population did not have access to banking facilities (Office of the Registrar General & Census Commissioner, 2011). The graph below shows that a large population base is financially excluded both in urban and rural areas. Since low financial growth impedes economic growth, it was imperative for the government to initiate financial inclusion schemes that would alleviate poverty and reduce social inequity. The census report of India 2001 and 2011 depict the trend as shown in Figure: 1.

Figure 1. Percentage of availability of banking services in India
Source: PMJDY, 2018

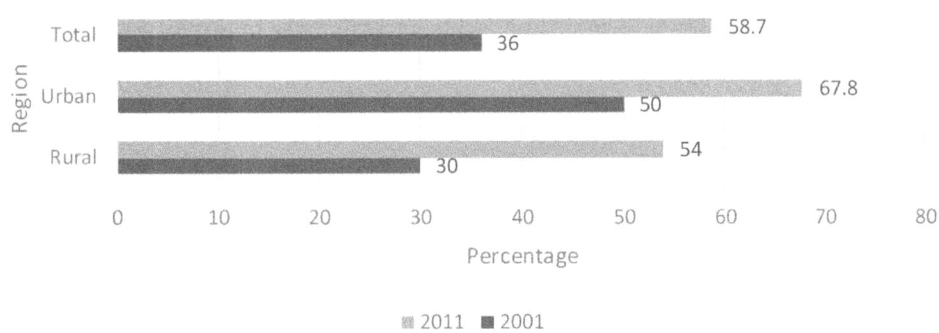

Table 3. Progress of Financial Inclusion Initiatives

Sr. No.	Particulars	Year ended March 2010	Year ended March 2016	Half year ended* September 2016
1	Banking Outlets in Rural locations – Branches	33,378	51,830	52,240
2	Banking Outlets in Rural locations – Branchless mode	34,316	534,477	537,609
3	Banking Outlets in Rural locations -Total	67,694	586,307	589,849
4	Urban Locations covered through BCs	447	102,552	91,039
5	BSBDA-Through branches (No. in million)	60.2	238.2	247.4
6	BSBDA-Through branches (Amt. in ₹ billion)	44.3	474.1	537.9
7	BSBDA-Through BCs (No. in million)	13.3	230.8	247.8
8	BSBDA-Through BCs (Amt. in ₹ billion)	10.7	164.0	181.1
9	BSBDA-Total (No. in million)	73.5	469.0	495.2
10	BSBDA Total (Amt. in ₹ billion)	55.0	638.1	719.0
11	OD facility availed in BSBDAs (No. in million)	0.2	8.0	8.4
12	OD facility availed in BSBDAs (Amt. in ₹ billion)	0.1	14.8	18.1
13	KCCs -Total (No. in million)	24.3	47.3	46.4
14	KCCs -Total (Amt. in ₹ billion)	1,240.1	5,130.7	5,543.4
15	GCC-Total (No. in million)	1.4	11.3	11.5
16	GCC-Total (Amt. in ₹ billion)	35.1	1,493.3	1,613.2
17	ICT-A/Cs-BC- Total number of transactions (in million) *	26.5	826.8	550.6
18	ICT-A/Cs-BC- Total amount of transactions (in ₹ billion) *	6.9	1,686.9	1,199.2

* For the reporting period FY 2009-10/FY 2015-16/Half Year April-September 16.

Source: RBI Annual Report, 2016

Usage

India's financial inclusion agenda has seen a paradigm shift from an emphasis on credit to a more comprehensive approach toward financial services, particularly opening bank accounts and offering basic financial products such as insurance. The big push towards financial inclusion in India has emanated from the Pradhan Mantri Jan Dhan Yojana (PMJDY) in August 2014 and the Jan Dhan Aadhaar Mobile. The deposits under Pradhan Mantri Jan Dhan Yojana (PMJDY) as in November, 2016 was 255.1 million accounts were opened and US$6,971.68 million were deposited. Government initiatives such as MNREGA has enabled in increasing employment generation in the rural areas which has assisted in increasing rural income and is expected to enhance in the near future aided by the recent Jan Dhan Yojana.

These new approaches necessitate an alteration in the existing financial architecture of India's economy as new inclusion drive incorporates multiple stakeholders warranting a robust mechanism for inclusive growth.

The appended table 3 indicates the progress of the various financial inclusion initiatives:

Overall there has been a tremendous change year on year of the numerous initiatives relating to financial inclusion programs. The total number of Basic Savings Bank Deposit Accounts (BSBDAs) increased from 73.5 million in March 2010 to 495.2 million in September 2016.

Figure 2 indicates the financial inclusion status of the households of India. The figure indicates the distribution of banking services between the rural and urban areas of India as per the census report.

Figure 2. Positions of Households availing banking services

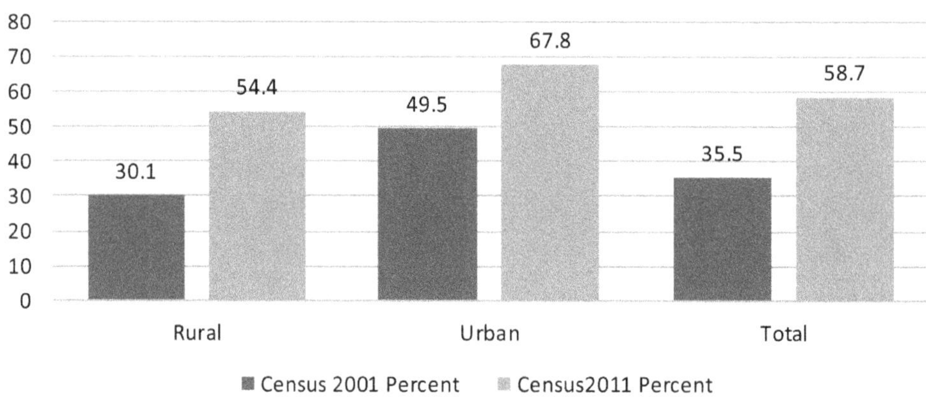

Service Distribution Networks

1. **Bank Branches:** India has shown a drastic increase in the growth of banking delivery channels during the previous five years. Table 4 indicates the number of bank branches of scheduled commercial banks in India distributed population wise.
2. **KYC:** In September 2013, banks were allowed to provide e-KYC services based on Aadhaar thus paving the way for bank accounts to be opened by all and facilitating easy access to banking services. 109 crore Indians can now be digitally authenticated through Aadhaar, thus addressing the first but most cumbersome step to financial access: eKYC.
3. **Deployment of ATMs:** There has been a surge in the rise of offsite ATMs in the year 2014 however a downtrend can be observed in the offsite ATMs in the year 2015.

Table 4. Distribution of bank branches

Bank and Associates	Rural	Semi Urban	Urban	Metropolitan	Total
SBI & Associates	8029	6593	4304	3622	22548
Nationalised Banks	21228	16428	12604	11325	61585
Other Public Sector Banks	377	528	479	378	1762
Private Sector Banks	4302	6457	4521	4698	19978
Foreign Banks	8	12	57	247	324
Regional Rural banks	14613	3748	1071	228	19660

Source: RBI, 2015-2016)

Figure 3. Deployment of ATMs
Source: Trend and Progress, RBI (2016)

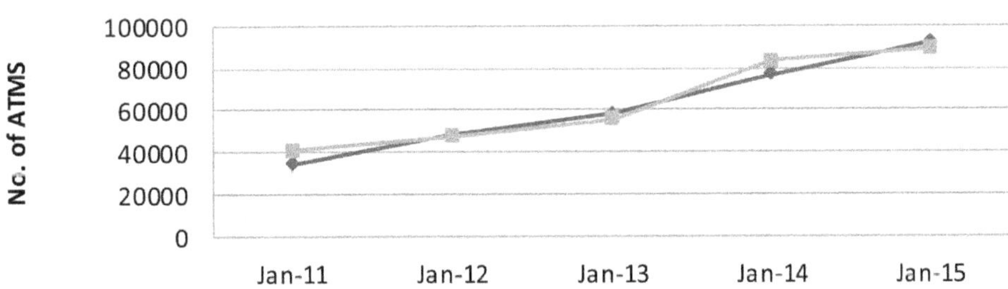

	Mar-11	Mar-12	Mar-13	Mar-14	Mar-15
Onsite ATMs	34377	48141	58254	76676	92191
Offsite ATMs	41268	47545	55760	83379	89061

Products and Services

Pradhan Mantri Jan Dhan Yojana

Pradhan Mantri Jan Dhan Yojana, is an ambitious scheme for comprehensive financial inclusion launched by the Prime Minister of India, Narendra Modi on 28th August, 2014. He had announced this scheme on his first Independence Day speech on 15th August, 2014.The scheme started with a target to provide universal access to banking facilities starting with basic banking accounts with overdraft facility of Rs. 5,000 after six months and RuPay Debit Card with inbuilt accident insurance cover of Rs. 1Lakh and RuPay Kisan card. Table 5 indicates the current status of the scheme for various banks:

Disclaimer: Information is based upon the data as submitted by different banks / SLBCs

Electronic Payment Systems: Representative Data (Updated as on February 09, 2017)

Information technology has given rise to new innovations in the product designing and their delivery in the banking and finance sector. The financial inclusion drives major challenge is catering large numbers with low volumes resulting into higher transaction cost, technology can be leveraged for rendering cost effective banking services to the unbanked segments.

Mobile Banking

Mobile banking transactions have been defined as customers undertaking banking transactions using mobile phones involving debit or credit to their accounts. With the rapid growth in the number of mobile phone subscribers in India, banks in collaboration with telecom companies are seeking to develop an alternate channel

Table 5. Penetration of PMJDY scheme

PMJDY as on 11th January, 2017 [Figures is Crores of Rupees)						
Banks	**Rural**	**Urban**	**No. of RuPay Cards**	**Aadhaar Seeded**	**% Zero Balance Accounts**	**Balance in Accounts**
Public Sector Banks	11.82	9.49	16.82	12.69	25.07	53760.47
Private Sector Banks	0.52	0.35	0.82	0.39	33.68	2518.77
Regional Rural Banks	3.88	0.61	3.36	2.28	20.66	12747.93

Source: PMJDY, 2018

Figure 4. Electronic payment system
Source: RBI

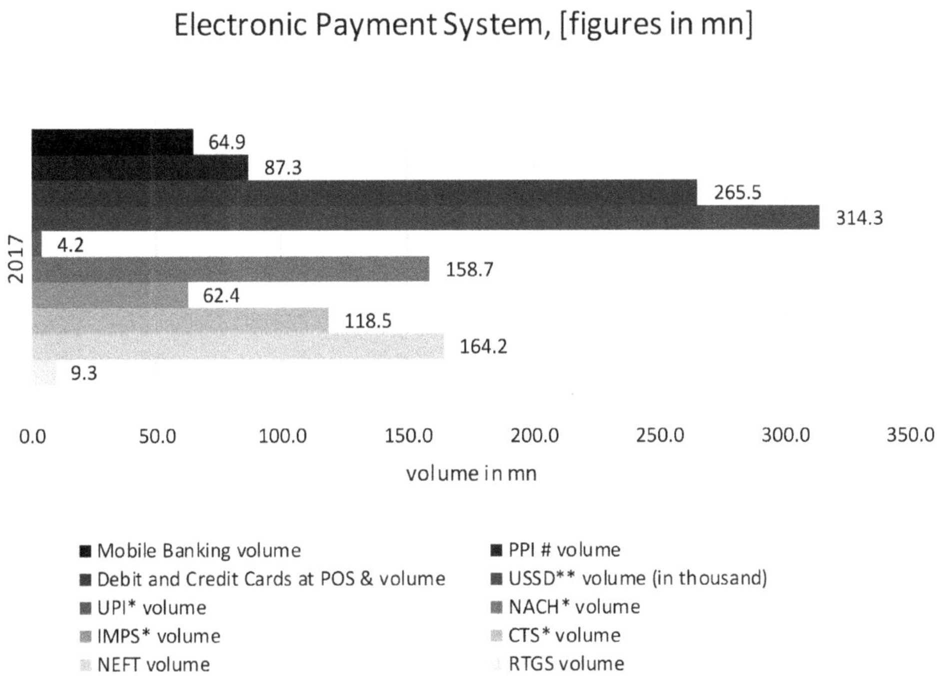

of delivery of banking services. The rise of mobile banking has unlocked a new path for financial institutions to lower the cost to serve their customers, improve their competitive position and increase customer acquisition and loyalty. Mobile banking and banking via non-bank retail outlets have been key drivers of financial inclusion in developing countries, helped by technology and a favorable regulatory environment. Banks to maintain their preferred position with consumers, it is important that they create a strong mobile services presence. Mobile payments are expected to grow exponentially over the next few years (indicated in Figure 5) fueled by strong consumer adoption of smartphones. The World Bank estimates that the cost of reaching customers through mobile banking is around 20% lower than the traditional bank branch cost.

Payment Banks

RBI as a part of its push for financial inclusion, recently granted 'in-principle' licenses for 11 payment banks and 10 small finance banks. The issue of new licenses is a giant step forward for financial inclusion, as they will lead to enhanced use of technology in the banking sector and will result in increased competition. Through

Figure 5. Mobile payment scenario
Source: Global and Regional Mobile Payment Market Forecast, IE Market Research, 2011

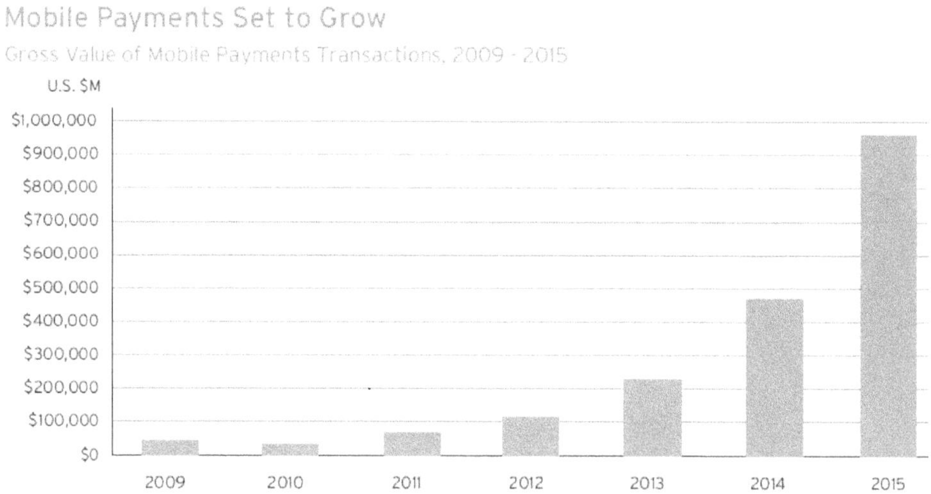

these payment banks, RBI aims to bring the vast unbanked population under digital economy. Use of digital platforms can help consumers spend their money safely and securely, save and build credit profiles for lending opportunities unavailable in the informal banking sector, and participate in a growing online economy.

Small Finance Banks

RBI gave in-principle approval to 10 entities to set up small finance banks. Small finance banks will offer basic banking services, accept deposits and lend to underserved sections of customers, including small business units, small and marginal farmers, micro and small industries, and even entities in the unorganized sector.

Marketing Issues and Concerns in the Rural Market

Financial inclusion has always been in forefront in India as has undergone a strategic shift from credit focus to a holistic approach inclusive of opening of bank accounts, debit cards and micro insurance. Vasantha et al. (2013) indicate financial inclusion as a major driving force for achieving self-sustained inclusive economic growth however achieving cent percent financial inclusion is one of the biggest challenges for the financial sector. There have been many formidable challenges in financial inclusion for bridging the gap between the sections of society that are financially excluded and including them in the ambit of the formal financial systems by providing financial literacy and strengthening credit delivery mechanisms so as to improve the financial economic growth. Despite of noteworthy improvements and initiatives in all areas relating to financial feasibility, productivity, competitiveness and outreach still banking services has not yet covered a measurable section of the population.

Major section of the population in India lives in the rural areas and is engaged in agriculture and allied activities. Commercial banks have been provocative on multiple service delivery channels based on urban and rural geography, yet there exist numerous challenges preventing banks in accomplishing cent percent service infiltration in these sections. In India the financially excluded sections largely comprise of marginal farmers, urban slum dwellers, migrants, women, self-employed and senior citizens.

Liew (2008) study discussed about the poor excluded people of the Pacific Island. They were excluded from both formal and informal financial services. The scholar explained that geographical isolate on demographic dispersion, limited income generating opportunities, financial literacy and traditional socio-economic structures had created formidable challenges for the delivery of financial services in Pacific Island countries, similar is the case for Indian economy.

Report by Crisil indicates that the major challenges for financial inclusion were high cost of delivery, lack of financial awareness, lack of robust technology and inadequate and reliable data, it further stated that there is a need for coordination between the stakeholders, greater consumer understanding and trust. Barriers to financial inclusion can be categorized as income insecurity, socio economic condition, financial illiteracy and technological infrastructure.

The marketing issues associated with rural markets can be categorized as follows.

Geographical Distribution

The Economist (April, 2016) shows that nearly 850 million Indian live in rural areas of which 60% are dependent on agriculture for their livelihood, the median annual wage of a farmer is 19,250 rupees including the implied value of food they consume nonetheless 2008 data shows that rural urban wage gap is 45% which might has increased as of date. World Bank accounts that 260 million people live in poverty and 80% of them live in countryside, accordingly providing banking services to these sections becomes vital for their social upliftment. Indian economy is characterized by diversity in demographics and culture. The changing lifestyle of the Indian folk has paved in way for newer products and services and transition in the banking sector. During the decade there has been a noticeable shift in age groups, earning span, income groups, dependence on urban India and growing share of large cities within urban India.

In India nearly 25% of the population are illiterate and are living below poverty line thus ensuring financial inclusion thus becomes a challenge for the banks.

The major two indicators poverty and illiteracy vary widely across different states of India, rural poverty is extreme which can be attributed to lower farm income, underemployment, lack of sustained livelihood and unemployment thus deposit operations in these sections becomes a major challenge for the banks. The Indian population census, (Office of the Registrar General & Census Commissioner, 2011) is indicative of the rise in the level of population in India since 1991 (Table 6) Further there has been a steady rise in the population of the females, conversely the level of literacy is minimal as against the male population, this makes evident the literacy level of females need to be addressed for social upliftment. Nearly around 33% of the population is excluded from the formal banking ambit which projects a picture of immense potential. However reaching out to the secluded groups becomes a challenge for the banks which can be addressed by identifying channel partners at local levels for increasing the outreach at rural level.

Since poor people do not have much money and often live in meagerly populated areas and have lesser volume of transactions banks have found these potential markets to be non-cost effective (Ivatury, 2006) however opening of 25% branches in rural areas by banks under the new reforms have made ways to newer service channels and products, one such initiative is of business correspondents (BC).

Absence of Customized Product and Services

As the financial inclusion was a social agenda it was not a profit-making business for banks, lack of customer centricity enabled banks in attracting customers for opening bank accounts. However, the frequency of transactions in the accounts happening become negligible thus customer miscue the actual benefits of availing banking services. The business models operated by banks majorly lack flexibility, scalability

Table 6. Population growth in India

S.No	Parameters	Years		
1	**Population (Crores)**	**1991**	**2001**	**2011**
	Total	64.6	102.9	121.1
	Male	43.9	53.2	62.3
	Female	40.7	49.6	58.7
2	**Literacy Rate (%)**			
	Male	64.13	75.26	82.14
	Female	39.29	53.67	65.46
3	**Households Availing Banking Services (%)**	58.7	54.4	67.8

Source: Office of the Registrar General & Census Commissioner. *(2011)*

and convenience attributes. The products are limited and does take cognizance of the specific requirements of the rural folk. The households from rural region are excluded in the eyes of mainstream banks even for deposit products due to lack of assured income further due to lack of high collateral requirements most of them are deprived from credit facilities from the formal banking system. Some of the facts indicate new product initiatives are generally scaled down versions of the existing product range, to enable a successful financial inclusion environment innovation of products for specific needs of the poor becomes vital.

Lack of Robust Technological Infrastructure

The Inter Bank Mobile Payment Service (IMPS) developed by National Payment Corporation of India is an instantaneous 24x7 electronic funds transfer system, irrespective of its tremendous potential of the product, the volumes are low probably because of the reluctance of the telecom companies to offer the common Unstructured Supplementary Service Data (USSD) platform. Similarly, there are less than 15 lakh Point of Sales terminals in India, covering only 6% of all merchant outlets, the intermediation fees and infrastructural costs restrict the small merchants from adopting Point of Sale terminals at local level. Limited number of technology service provides to cover the unbanked areas as well as limited number of service center's for servicing the devices has deterred the banking operations in many rural sections. Lack of availability of trained manpower in the villages for financial counselling and training on technology in the local language erodes the confidence of the rural households. Another factor restricting the use of technology for banking services by the marginalized is security. The security issues may have the potential to undermine public confidence in the use of electronic payment products in case of scams and frauds. Diverse types of technologies may prove counterproductive to be integrated with the existing banking structure and implementation at the operating level especially with the business correspondents.

Operational Challenges

Banks face operational challenges such as obtaining relevant documents for verification while opening of bank accounts. As directed by the regulators banks are required to conduct sufficient identity checks before opening of accounts, these regulations occasionally results in denying access of finance to genuine customers. Rigid regulatory frameworks may hinder the quantity and quality of financial products and services that are accessible by the poor. Banks have a high marketing, advertising and education challenges however there is a growing need for alternative operating models to reach these customers.

Glitches in the Business Correspondent (BC) Model

The study by Laureti (2009) states that the bank's response to BC activities has been fairly slow, which has restricted the growth and sustainability of this model.

The BC model in India has been primarily led by banks, but the players in this model are different from those in the traditional banking models. The BC agents range from unemployed youth to kirana shop owners, microfinance institutions (MFIs), not-for-profit institutions, and other non-bank-related agents. BC Company and its sub-agents open the accounts, perform cash-in/cash-out transactions, and interact with the clients; they are connected to agents, who in turn, connect clients to banks. Most of the time, these clients do not have direct access to banks. The existing model has faced several criticisms and many studies have called the BC model unviable on account of dormant accounts, cost of delivery, and inadequate knowledge about financial products and services, lack of infrastructure facilities and involvement of multiple participants.

Further concerns faced were absence of grievance redressal, consistency of services, risk mitigation, marketing, and feedback. Apprehensions were raised on the remuneration aspect as it did not commensurate with the efforts which weakened the performance of the BC after a particular time also promotion of existing range of banks products by BC ignoring the consumer need and preferences also diluted the efficacy of the system.

Issues Underlying Self Help Group (SHG) Linkage Programs

SHG was a plank for delivering financial services to the poor in a sustainable manner, poor people intended to come together in an informal manner for pooling their savings in their mutual interest. The SHG – Bank Linkage Programme was started as an Action Research Project in 1989 which was the offshoot of a NABARD initiative during 1987 through sanctioning Rs. 10 lakh to MYRADA as seed money assistance for experimenting Credit Management Groups. Planning commission Report (2008) states that the majority of Self-Help Groups [SHGs] are capital scarce, labour surplus by and large bereft of proper knowledge as well as management skill, at the same time it also remains a fact that rural areas do throw ample opportunities for micro enterprises by making use of untapped manpower resources, available raw material of various forms, and existing market channels.

Financial Illiteracy

Table 7 details the level of enrolment rate in the country, it is evident that nearly 50% of the population completes only their Senior Secondary Education and there has been tremendous improvement in the enrolment rate for formal education, similar practice should be adopted to measure the level of financial education at different levels of their formal education period. Financial literacy should start at the primary level and should be evenly distributed throughout the formal education cycle.

The socio demographics have a direct relation with the financial awareness and usage of financial products, figure: indicates the saving rate of the households which shows an insignificant increase year on year which is one of the trigger points for the banks in assessing the causes.

One of the reason for primarily inadequate knowledge about financial products is lower income levels. Ideally banks should ponder on how these lower savings of households can render them assured returns, security and prosperity and targeting the product offerings for smaller savings and identifying alternate income generation opportunities for rural/marginalized individuals.

Table 7. Education level

Enrolment Rate (%)	1950-51	2005-06	2013-14 (Provisional)
Primary Education (I-V)	42.6	109.4	99.3
Upper Primary (VI - VIII)	12.7	71	87.4
Secondary (IX - X)	NA	52.2	73.6
Senior Secondary (XI - XII)	NA	28.5	49.1

Source: Office of the Registrar General & Census Commissioner *(2011)*

Figure 6. Savings rate of households (%)
Source: Office of the Registrar General & Census Commissioner (2011)

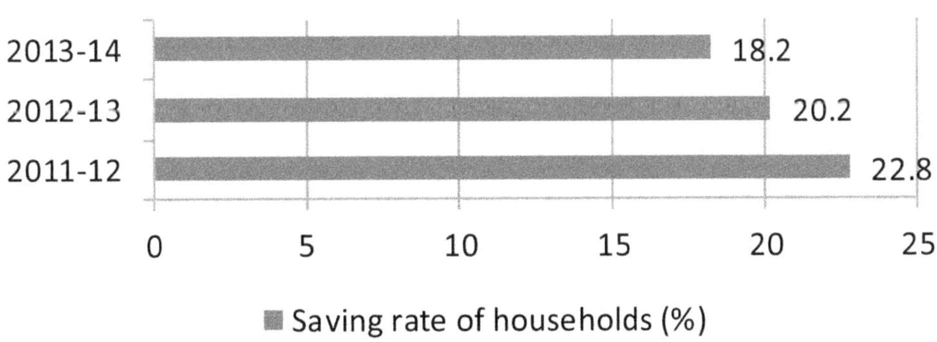

The mean education levels of the households are around 78% taking into consideration the different phases of enrolment nevertheless nearly 22% are still outside the formal education system. Question which needs to be addressed is about financial education, out of these literate (78%) almost 30% will lack awareness about financial products, overall it can be seen that 40% of the population still not have adequate knowledge about financial products and services. The second question which arises is can financial education be imparted using a blanket approach, or should there be a mechanism to assess how effectively financial education can be cascaded to the different strata of the financially excluded nonetheless it is an observed fact that average working age population in India is around 15 to 59 years; increased work span will encourage banks in building customer loyalty, increased customer life cycle through value added products and services backed by effective service delivery channels.

Financial Literacy is one of the biggest components of financial inclusion. It comprises of three elements- financial knowledge, financial attitudes and financial behavior. Standard & Poor's survey indicates that only 24% of Indian adults are financially literate. The subject of financial literacy requires an understanding of the information gap across consumer segments and crafting communication strategies that address the unique needs of specific segments. Besides addressing information gaps, designing products in parlance with the unique characteristics of the target segment such as low financial literacy, cyclical income, minimal collateral, lack of credit history, absence of formal and verifiable identity and illiteracy should be an integral aspect of financial literacy.

Rural Infrastructure

Traditional commercial bank branch could prove to be expensive and too far removed from the local community to be an effective channel for financial services to every single household. The cost of travel to the bank branch along with loss of wages deters bank branch being an effective service delivery channel. Reasons for choosing one provider over another are often related to convenience thus proximity to customers enables the banks in imparting the right service at right place and time however due to branch dispersion, accessibility to right service becomes uncertain.

Mobile banking and ATMs are low cost service delivery channels and most convenient but both run into consumer resistance as they find ATMs to be more complex and inadequate knowledge for mobile based applications on the service provider side many villages in India lack basic infrastructural facilities like roads, electricity, telecommunications and Internet networks which creates operational hurdles for players to enter into these areas further discouraging the rural households to reap the benefits of banking services. Lack of trust in electronic systems as compared to cash amongst the rural or marginalized limits the financial inclusion. Technological barriers for financial inclusion can be concluded as trust and failing networks and connectivity issues and power requirements.

Due to the above cited reasons it becomes a huge challenge for Banks to market their schemes to the financial excluded segments of the society. Illiteracy and financial illiteracy are the two major stumbling blocks to financial inclusion. Whatever marketing efforts the Banks take to reach out to these marginalized sections, it is negated by these two impediments. For increasing literacy levels huge efforts are required at the grass root levels while Banks need to think if they could take up the onus of financial literacy upon themselves. Once the goal of literacy followed by financial illiteracy is achieved, Banks can observe the increased effectiveness of their marketing efforts. Till such time Banks would need to make herculean efforts to market their schemes to this strata of the society. Banks, therefore should keep in mind the challenges as discussed above while designing their marketing techniques. Excellent competences are required at banker's end to establish a balance between the commercial and social considerations.

CONCLUSION

Since four decades of Nationalization of Banks, more than half of the country's population does not have a bank account, does it reflect that banks are not able to cater to the majority section of the society. A combination of encouraging demographics, rising incomes, growing literacy rates, improving infrastructure and economic growth in countryside is providing a compelling need for banking products and services in these areas. Conventional banking solutions are not the answer for profitably capturing the rural opportunity. Banks need to embrace virtualization and the power of cloud computing to reduce the capital expenditures related to building and managing IT infrastructure.

RBI should integrate the financial inclusion policy with the Marketing plans of the banks converting them into a prospect rather than an official compulsion on the banks. Banks should consider financial inclusion as business proposition and not as a regulatory binding.

SOLUTIONS AND RECOMMENDATIONS

- Collaborations amongst financial service providers, gram panchayats and technology service providers will help in enhancing the awareness and usage of mobile banking in these villages. Rendering financial product and service information through automated voice response system in regional/ local language through toll free numbers will help the respondents to be acquainted with the financial products especially for the illiterate segments/ small farmers.

- Customization of financial products is essential based on the demographics of the village population.
- Formation of Business Correspondent groups comprising of people belonging to varied demographic strata from the villages itself. When locals act as Business Correspondents, marketing Bank's products and services becomes easier. Imparting them training on financial services will help a certain extent to map the mindset of the varied households and also to convince them about the banking facilities which will help in enhancing the level of banking outreach in these villages.
- Other critical factor is educating and training of the business correspondents; increase in the frequency of training programs for the Business correspondents in another aspect which may help the banks to gauge the performance of the business correspondents and also will enable these agents to upgrade.
- SHGs can act as financial intermediary at the rural level for marketing of retail bank products such as savings, micro credit, micro insurance, payments and remittances facility. Involvement as business correspondent and financial counselors will enhance their role and will facilitate in overcoming the disadvantages.
- Social development through employment schemes, government grants, health and education scheme, micro insurance and micro credit and financial literacy is essential. Involvement of non-government bodies will help in higher penetration for social development.
- Designing a standard approach for evaluating financial literacy and identifying barriers will assist in solutions that enable financial choice. However other factors such as individual behavioral biases, impulsiveness, external influence and social compulsions may also contribute for poor financial decision making which needs to be taken into consideration by the stakeholders while devising a metric for financial inclusion.
- Creation of financial education program life cycle, focusing on enhanced financial learning's at different life stages of an individual rather than one time learning. Provision of Interactive multilingual voice response based training facility on mobile phones for financial products & wealth management. Designing multilingual simulation games parallel to schools and colleges curriculum based on the concept of money, savings and banking.
- Use of gaming technology on mobile phones sensitizing youth to real life situations and making informed financial decision and Introduction of

Financial gaming zones at employers' premises will facilitate in cascading financial information.

- It has become imperative for retail banks to create a comprehensive mobile strategy that centers on an integrated and seamless multi-channel banking experience.

Financial Inclusion is considered to be the vital objective of many developing nations' research findings indicates direct association between the financial exclusion and the poverty prevailing in developing nations. Financial inclusion initiatives should be interpreted in a relative dimension, the degree of financial inclusion will differ depending upon the state of economy and stage of development exposing banks and financial institutions to diverse cliques of challenges for catering the weaker sections of the economy. Efforts are being made to study the causes of financial exclusion and designing strategies to ensure financial inclusion of the poor and disadvantaged thus banks need to contemplate on strengthening credit delivery mechanism and innovative business practices for improving the financial economic growth of the nation.

FUTURE RESEARCH DIRECTIONS

Achieving financial inclusion in a diverse country like India is a huge challenge and also an opportunity. It therefore offers many opportunities for research. Research could be done in many areas like the effectiveness of the various existing initiatives undertaken in increasing financial inclusion. Research could be undertaken on the satisfaction levels of the beneficiaries of financial inclusion. Research could be done on the impact of the different marketing initiatives of the Banks aimed at the financially excluded segments of the society. Research could also offer new ideas and insights for improving financial inclusion.

REFERENCES

Allen, F., Demirguc-Kunt, A., & Klapper, L. (2012). *The Foundations of Financial Inclusion: Understanding Ownership and Use of Formal Accounts.* World Bank Policy Research Working Paper 6290.

Banking Association South Africa. (2015). *South Africa Annual Review.* Retrieved on May 3, 2017 from http://www.banking.org.za/news-media/publications/reports

Beck, T., Demirguc-Kunt, A., & Levine, R. (2004). *Finance, Inequality and Poverty: Cross-Country Evidence, World Bank Policy Research.* Working Paper 3338, The World Bank. Retrieved from http://documents.worldbank.org/curated/en/824991468778185410/Finance-inequality-and-poverty-cross-country-evidence

Chakraborty, K. C. (2006). Financial Inclusion: Concepts, Issues, And Roadmap. Institute for Development and Research in Banking Technology.

CRISIL. (2015). *Crisil Inclusix, An index to measure India's progress on financial inclusion.* Retrieved on March 16, 2017 from https://www.crisil.com/about-crisil/crisil-inclusix-report.html

Demirguc-Kunt, Klapper, Singer, & Van Oudheusden. (2015). *The Global Findex Database 2014: Measuring Financial Inclusion around the World.* Policy Research Working Paper 7255, World Bank.

Dun and Bradstreet Report. (2008). *Deutche Bank Distribution Going to the Next Level.* Retrieved on May 21, 2017 from http://www.dnb.co.in/FESConfTool/Uploads/Agenda/Distribution%20Agenda.pdf

Handoo, J. (2010). *Financial inclusion in India: Integration of technology, policy and market at the bottom of the pyramid.* Retrieved on April 20, 2017 from http://skoch.in/fir/role%20%financial%20%inclusion%20

Indian Brand Equity Foundation report. (2016). *Indian Banking Industry Analysis.* Retrieved from https://www.ibef.org/industry/banking-presentation

International Monetary Fund. (2016). *IMF Releases the 2016 Financial Access Survey, A Key Tool to Foster Financial Inclusion.* Retrieved on April 12, 2017 from https://www.imf.org/en/News/Articles/2016/10/03/PR16441-IMF-Releases-the-2016-Financial-Access-Survey

International Monetary Fund. (2012). *World Economic Outlook Report: Growth Resuming, Dangers Remain.* International Monetary Fund. Retrieved from http://www.imf.org/external/pubs/ft/weo/2012/01/

Irving Fisher Committee on Central Bank Statistics. (2016). *Measures of Financial Inclusion – A Central Bank Perspective.* Survey conducted by the Irving Fisher Committee on Central Bank Statistics (IFC). Retrieved from https://www.bis.org/ifc/publ/ifc_finan_inclu.pdf

Kapoor, A. (2014, February). Financial inclusion and the future of the Indian economy. *Futures*, *56*, 35–42. doi:10.1016/j.futures.2013.10.007

Khan, S. H. R. (2012). Issues and challenges in financial inclusion – policies, partnerships, processes & products. Deputy Governor of the Reserve Bank of India, at the symposium on "Financial inclusion in Indian Economy", organized by the Indian Institute of Public Administration, Bhubaneswar, India.

Klapper, L., Lusardi, A., & van Oudheusden, P. (n.d.). *Financial Literacy around the World: Insights from the S&P Global Finlit Survey*. Retrieved from http://gflec.org/wp-content/uploads/2015/11/Finlit_paper_16_F2_singles.pdf

KPMG. (2015). *Financial Services: Role of Digital Banking in Furthering Financial Inclusion*. Retrieved from https://www.researchgate.net/profile/.../Digital+banking+in+india4.pdf

Laureti, C. (2009). *Role of Savings in Competitive Microfinance Markets and Feasibility of the Business Correspondent Model in India*. European Microfinance Program.

Liew, L. H., & Wu, H. X. (2008). *The Making of China's Exchange Rate Policy: from plan to WTO entry*. Edward Elgar Publishing.

Miller, Reichelstein, Salas, & Zia. (2014). *Can You Help Someone Become Financially Capable? A Meta-Analysis of the Literature*. World Bank Policy Research Working Paper 6745.

Mohan, R. (2006). *Financial Sector Reforms and Monetary Policy: The Indian Experience*. RBI.

Mohanty, D., Gulati, A., Demirguk-Kunt, A., Hota, A. P., Sukthankar, P., & Udgata, A. (2015). *Report of the Committee on Medium-term Path on Financial Inclusion*. Reserve Bank of India. Retrieved from https://rbidocs.rbi.org.in/rdocs/PublicationReport/Pdfs/FFIRA27F4530706A41A0BC394D01CB4892CC.PDF

National Bank for Agriculture and Rural Development (NABARD). (2012). *Status of Micro Finance in India 2011–12*. National Bank for Agriculture and Rural Development NABARD. Retrieved from http://indiamicrofinance.com/wp-content/uploads/2012/11/Status-of-Microfinance-2011-12.pdf

Office of the Registrar General & Census Commissioner. (2011). *2011 Census Data*. Retrieved from http://www.censusindia.gov.in/2011-Common/CensusData2011.html

Planning Commission. (2011). *Economic Survey 2010-11: Statistical Appendix*. Government of India. Retrieved from http://www.indiabudget.gov.in/es2010-11/estat1.pdf

Pradhan Mantri Jan Dhan Yojana (PMJDY). (2018). *Progress Report*. Retrieved from https://www.pmjdy.gov.in/statewise-statistics

Ramesh, S., & Sahai, P. (2007). *Universal financial inclusion in India: the way forward.* CAB Calling. Retrieved on April 15, 2017 from: http://cab.org.in/CAB%20 Calling%20Content/Financial%20Inclusion%

Reserve Bank of India. (2015-16). *Report on Trends and Progress of Banking in India 2015-2016*. Retrieved on May 20, 2017 from https://rbidocs.rbi.org.in/rdocs/ Publications/PDFs/0FRTP16A120A29D260148E58B484D4A60E381BB.PDF

Resurgent India. (2016). *Financial inclusion summit 2016*. Retrieved from http:// cashlesscatalyst.org/wp-content/uploads/2017/01/Financial-Inclusion-Summit.pdf

Sarma, M. (2008). *Index of Financial Inclusion.* Indian Council for Research on International Economic, Relations Working Paper No. 215, ICRIER.

Sendhilvelan, M., & Karthikeyan, K. (2006). No Frills Account: A Basic Drive for Financial Inclusion. Southern Economist, 45, 13 – 14.

Singh, C. (2016). *Challenges to financial inclusion.* Retrieved on May 1, 2017 from http://www.thehindubusinessline.com/opinion/jan-dhan-yojana-fraud-should-be-curbed/article9169214.ece

Singh, H., & Sekhon, M. K. (2005). Cash-in Benefits of the Kisan Credit Card Scheme: Onus is Upon the Farmer. *Indian Journal of Agricultural Economics, 60*(3), 319–334.

Subbarao, D. (2009). *Duvvuri Subbarao: Financial Inclusion - Challenges and Opportunities*. Reserve Bank of India. Retrieved from https://www.bis.org/review/ r091215b.pdf

The World Bank. (2014). *Global Findex*. Retrieved from http://www.worldbank. org/globalfindex

The World Bank. (2018). *Overview*. Retrieved on May 1, 2017 from http://www. worldbank.org/en/topic/financialinclusion/overview

Thorat, U. (2007). *Usha Thorat: Financial Inclusion - the Indian Experience.* Financial Inclusion Conference 2007. London. BIS Review. Retrieved from https:// www.bis.org/review/r070626f.pdf

Vasantha, S., Varadharaj, V., & Varadharajan, R. (2013). Self Help Group Bank Linkage Model As Catalyst For Financial Inclusion In An Unbanked Rural Area. *Indian Journal of Commerce & Management Studies*, *4*(1).

Chapter 9
Consumer Awareness Towards Financial Inclusion in India:
A Study on Mahanagar Co Op Bank Ltd, Mumbai

Sanal Nair
Samsidh Mount Litera Zee School, India

Garima Gupta
Economic Research India Private Limited, India

ABSTRACT

This chapter focuses on researching the consumer awareness of people towards financial inclusion by conducting a study on Mahanagar Co Op Bank in Kharghar, Mumbai. The study adopted survey method to approach the respondents through a well-structured questionnaire. Stratum sampling method was used in order to select the sample respondents and collect data from those who are consumers of Mahanagar Co Op Bank Ltd, Kharghar Branch. A sample size of 150 consumers was taken. Following the data search, analysis was done by applying descriptive analytical tools like standard deviation and mean. The researcher used factor analysis, descriptive statistics, and one-way ANOVA in order to find the difference among the variables. SPSS software has been used for conducting the analytical tests. The results indicated an association between demographic variables and awareness and availing of financial inclusion services by the consumers of the bank. However, there was no association between demographic variables and some of the financial inclusion services.

DOI: 10.4018/978-1-5225-4035-9.ch009

INTRODUCTION

During the last few decades, the banking industry in India has grown tremendously in volume and complexity. It has also made significant improvements in areas like financial viability and profitability. However, there are still concerns that Indian banks have not been able to include underprivileged sections of the society into fold of basic banking services. The major reason behind this is lack of education, unemployment and poverty. Poverty and exclusion continue to dominate socio-economic and political discourse in India as they have done over the last six decades in the post-independence period. Poverty reduction has been an important goal of development policy since the inception of planning in the country(Bagli & Dutta, 2012).

India, despite being one of the ten fastest growing economies of the world, is home to one –third of poor in the world. Moreover, there is still a major section who are not accessed to products and services offered by the banking sector. In this regards, the Government of India and Reserve Bank of India have been taking concerted efforts to promote financial inclusion. 'Financial inclusion is defined as the process of ensuring access to financial services and timely as well as adequate credit as needed by vulnerable groups such as weaker sections and low-income groups at an affordable cost' (Rangarajan, 2008).

A major step for financial inclusion has been taken since five decades that include nationalization of banks, building a network of scheduled commercial banks, co-operatives and rural banks. These banks aim to help the poorer sections of society so that they can take benefit of banking services at low cost. However, despite of the vigorous efforts taken, the progress is far from satisfactory as there is a large section of population who is not making use of banking services. This is mainly because of their lack of awareness of such banking services introduced by the banks and the Government. There are people who though are aware of facilities like zero balance or minimum balance accounts and various loan options at low interest but still they are unaware of other services like ATM, e-banking and cheaper credit options. Education and income level play a key role in alertness of people towards financial inclusion (Reddy, 2016). Owing to this, it is quite important that poorer sections become aware of such financial services that are beneficial for them so that Government's aim of eradication of poverty can be achieved. Thus, the present study focuses on studying the awareness level of consumers towards financial inclusion in Mahanagar Co Op Bank Ltd, Kharghar Branch in Mumbai.

LITERATURE REVIEW

Definitions

Rajan (2007) broadly defined financial inclusion as a universal access to a wide range of financial services at a reasonable cost. These include not only banking products but also other financial services such as insurance and equity products.

Claessens (2006) has defined financial inclusion as the "availability of supply of financial services at reasonable costs, where reasonable quality and reasonable cost have to be defined relative to some objective standard, with costs reflecting all pecuniary and non-pecuniary costs."

Issues and Challenges in Financial Inclusion

Sharma and Sachedeva (2014) studied financial inclusion in India highlighting its issues and challenges. The paper is based on secondary research and is an attempt to highlight the various initiatives taken by government authorities for eliminating financial exclusion in India. It also focuses on the extent to which the efforts have been successful in this mission. At last, the paper also proposes certain suggestions which can help to meet goal of financial inclusion more efficiently in the country.

Srinivasan (2007) considered that financial exclusion remains a major issue in the unorganized sector. Expansion of services in this area by banks will not be very easy because of the special situation and needs of the sector. The study suggests that though structural solutions are expensive and nevertheless must be pursued but banks should also think of designing a process response to the problem. This can include drawing on the experiences and practices of the traditional lenders to the unorganized sector.

Factors for Financial Inclusion

Nandru, Anand, and Rentala (2016) conducted a study based on secondary data of various states of south India from 2010-2012 through Reserve Bank of India, Hand book of Statistics on the India Economy. The study is based on exploring the factors that have an impact on financial inclusion. The study highlights that size of population, gender ratio, branch penetration and credit to deposit penetration ratio have a significant impact on enhancing financial inclusion programme in south Indian states.

According to Sukaram (2015), efforts for financial inclusion have been recognized as an effective strategy to ensure access to financial services all over the globe.

During the last ten years, countries, both, developed as well as developing have been engaged in efforts ensuring financial inclusion to all and thus enabling access to financial services. Financial access helps the citizens to participate in the economic opportunities and derive the fruits of development which lead them to economic well-being. The paper traces the importance of financial access in the development of financial sector of a country. Financial education or literacy has been identified as a key factor in influencing the demand side of financial inclusion. Financial education to enhance inclusion is explored in detail and the national and international experiences in this regard are documented.

Bhuvana and Vasantha (2016) said that of financial inclusion can be achieved by effective and transparent financial services. In India, government has taken several initiatives to foster financial inclusion. Banks have shown an increase in their extent to reach and provide banking services to people from unreached sections in the society. But World Bank Global Findex Database 2014 has highlighted that, in India, 21% of adults are unbanked and only 53% of adult population possess financial services from a formal financial institution. The paper identifies that financial literacy, high cost, technology, trust, income level, distance and inappropriate products are the factors that determine financial inclusion in rural areas. The study discusses about various innovative delivery channels used to reach the rural people. A conceptual model is also developed to find out the factors that drives the financial inclusion.

Biroch and Pozzebon (2016) adopted a critical stance as a guide for conducting an empirical investigation. The aim of study is to propose a financial education framework, tailored to low-income micro-entrepreneurs, that embraces new information and communication technologies (ICTs) and seeks to improve financial inclusion and social emancipation. The empirical study was conducted in an Amazonian municipality in Brazil where recent access to ICTs has brought about important and varied socioeconomic changes. Results showed that ICT-supported and tailored critical financial education can play a dual role: Firstly, access to financial education might decrease the effects of generative mechanisms on global/ local tensions, triggered by standardized ICT applications. Secondly, such access might increase financial inclusion and social transformation through the integration of guiding principles into financial education programs.

Sarma and Pais (2011) attempted to examine the relationship between financial inclusion and development by empirically identifying country specific factors that are associated with the level of financial inclusion. It finds that levels of human development and financial inclusion in a country move closely with each other. Among socio-economic and infrastructure related factors, income, inequality, literacy, urbanisation and physical infrastructure for connectivity and information are important. Health of the banking sector does not seem to have an unambiguous effect on financial inclusion whereas ownership pattern does seem to matter.

Consumer Awareness

Singh (2016) conducted a research work based on the awareness of working women towards financial inclusion in Satna. The paper focused on working women because they are not aware about all the facilities provided by the banks. Primary data has been collected through questionnaire and respondents were selected from different institutions. It was found that though working women are using banking facilities; still they are not having proper knowledge about other online facilities like online payment of bills, fund transfers, social security schemes and others like online opening of bank accounts and auto renewal of bank deposits.

Meshram and Randad (2015) conducted a study with an aim to measure the level of consumer awareness towards financial inclusion in and around Pune city. The research was carried with the help of primary and secondary data. Questions were framed for the customers and State bank of India gave the permission to have a dialogue with the customers who have availed financial inclusion available at that time in the Banks. Sample size for the study was 100 customers. RBI website, speeches and research papers have been refereed as a secondary source. Researcher found that still a lot needs to be done to increase awareness of people towards inclusion. The results also suggested that low levels of literacy and income are major hurdles in improving consumer awareness towards financial inclusion provided by banks.

Senthikumar, Iyyappan, and Sumbramaniam (2012) carried a study on awareness of electronic banking among people. According to the authors, electronic banking is slowly coming in India. The various governments at the Centre and State level have been strategizing towards achieving total financial inclusion for the citizens of our country. The research paper attempts to study and understand the level of customer awareness of electronic banking with specific reference to the Thanjavur town. The paper is the outcome of a qualitative exploratory research study which covered 770 respondents, after initial screening. The respondents who were bank customers, patronizing one or more banks, were surveyed.

According to Finlayson (2011), The rural sector in India presents a real challenge given its technological backwardness and mass illiteracy as people are still caught in ancient financial systems that were both exploitative and futile. The study explored the intensity of financial inclusion and financial literacy among people. The target groups included unemployed/house wife, agriculturalists, Government employees, Non -Government employees and people engaged in business in Piravom Panchayat in Ernakulam District. Data was collected through primary and secondary sources. Primary data was collected from a sample of 100 respondents belonging to different occupational groups residing in Piravom Panchayat by using a structured questionnaire. The results of the study suggested that though a great change has happened in the last ten years to overcome financial exclusion but there still a lot more to do that include stimulating use of financial services as well as access, ensuring long-term sustainability of current initiatives and tackling new forms of exclusion as they arise.

Annamalai and Vijayarani (2014) examined the financial inclusion services provided by the banks and its awareness of the selected sample of the tribal village people in Dharampuri district vis-à-vis the Government policy. Primary data has been collected directly from the respondents by serving questionnaire. A total number of 639 respondents have been selected as sample through purposive sampling technique basis. The results of study showed that though the scheme of financial inclusion had been implemented among tribal community but still its awareness among tribal people is not satisfactory a they are still not aware of banking services made available for them.

Shukla and Singh (2015) carried a preliminary investigation to understand the nature and extent of financial inclusion using the Banking Correspondent model. The study was carried out in Katni District. The study was carried out using a highly structured questionnaire. The method of quota sampling was used to cover the entire district with 200 as the sample size. Descriptive statistics have been calculated for population variables and chi-square statistic test has been used to find out whether there is any significant difference between male and female with respect to beliefs about money and savings. It can be inferred from the results that vast sections of the population are financially–excluded. It can be said that awareness levels do not necessarily translate into access; it is quite possible that the motivation to be included or self-exclusion may be a limiting factor. Though the level of financial inclusion is average the level of financial illiteracy is high. Financial literacy is prerequisite for achieving the objective of financial inclusion. All financial institutions will have to work in coordination to achieve this aim as it not only insulates households from financial hardships but also generates investment for social development.

Kumar and Anees (2013) carried a study to take into accounts the different dimensions of financial literacy and education in India. This included financial education, its relevance and determinants along with role of regulatory authorities in India. The study concludes that the strategy for improving financial well-being of individuals in India should be focusing the young investors.

Kumar (2014) conducted a study to evaluate the progress of financial inclusion initiatives undertaken in India with respect to branch and credit penetration and financial literacy programs. It attempted to identify some crucial initiatives in reference to financial inclusion initiated by the Government of India Finally, the study depicted that in spite of several measures taken to develop financial inclusion, and a whopping 40 percent of India's population is still devoid of even the plain financial services.

RESEARCH GAP

After having an extensive review of literature, it was observed that though there was a presence of vast literature on awareness of consumers towards financial inclusion but none of the studies were conducted on people visiting a co-operative bank. Moreover, most of the studies were conducted on rural people in different parts of India but none of them were being in a co-operative bank and that too in a metro city.

OBJECTIVES OF THE STUDY

- To study the significant association between demographic variables and awareness of consumers towards financial inclusion services provided by banks.
- To study the significant association between demographic variables and availing of financial inclusion services provided by banks by the consumers.

HYPOTHESES FRAMED FOR THE STUDY

See Table 1 for hypotheses.

Table 1. Hypotheses Framed for the study

H_{01}	There is no significant association between gender and awareness of consumers towards financial inclusion
H_{02}	There is no significant association between education and awareness of consumers towards financial inclusion
H_{03}	There is no significant association between frequency of income and awareness of consumers towards financial inclusion
H_{04}	There is no significant association between gender and availing of financial inclusion services by consumers
H_{05}	There is no significant association between education and availing of financial inclusion services by consumers
H_{06}	There is no significant association between frequency of income and availing of financial inclusion services by consumers

RESEARCH METHODOLOGY

The study adopted survey method so as to approach the respondents through a pre-tested and well structured questionnaire. Stratum sampling method was used in order to select the sample respondents and collect data from those who are consumers of Mahanagar Co Op Bank Ltd, Kharghar Branch. This bank is selected as this is near to a village named as Kopergaun in Navi Mumbai and people carrying small and medium business activities are its customers. The sampling frame for the stratified sampling is the individuals who visit the selected bank. A sample size of 150 consumers was taken who visited the bank on the day of survey. The framework was developed using the variables identified during literature review. It consisted of structured closed ended questions. Following the data search, analysis was done by applying descriptive analysis like standard deviation and mean. Researcher also applied one-way ANOVA in order to find out significant association between the variables. SPSS software has been used for conducting the analytical tests.

DATA ANALYSIS AND INTERPRETATION

Demographics

Among the respondents,73% were males and remaining 27% were females. Majority of them belong to the age group of 30-39 years (44.7%). Majority of them were diploma holders (2.6%) while only 9.2% were secondary passed and post graduated. 45.4% of the respondents were salaried and 18.4% of them were self – employed in non-agriculture field. Majority of them (36.8%) had Rs 2, 00,000-Rs 5, 00,000 as their annual income. 18.4% of them had Rs 10,000- Rs 50,000 as their annual income. 54.6% of the respondents earned monthly while 36.2% had irregular income. 9.2% of them earned daily.

Descriptive Statistics

From the above descriptive statistics table, it can be interpreted that most of the respondents are aware of Pradhan Mantri Jan DhanYojna (4.37) and ATM card services (4.01) as well as cheaper bank loan facility (4.27) drawn from Arithmetic mean value. This shows that consumers of Mahanagar Co-Op Bank are aware of some financial inclusion services provided by the bank. However, the standard deviation value indicates that majority of responses are spread around awareness of consumers towards financial inclusion. Responses vary around awareness of consumers towards internet services (1.612) derived from standard deviation.

Table 2. Demographics of the respondents

		Frequency	Percent
Gender	Male	111	73.0%
	Female	41	27.0%
	Total	152	100.0
Age	20-29 years	42	27.6%
	30-39 years	68	44.7%
	40-49 years	42	27.%
	50 and above	0	0%
	Total	152	100.0
Qualification	Primary	28	18.4%
	Upper primary	41	27.0%
	Secondary	14	9.2%
	Senior secondary	13	8.6%
	Diploma	42	27.6%
	Post graduation	13	9.2%
	Total	152	100.0
Occupation	Self-employed(Agriculture)	14	9.2%
	Labor	14	9.2%
	Self-employed(non-agriculture)	28	18.4%
	Casual labor	14	9.2%
	Salaried	69	45.4%
	Others	13	8.6%
	Total	152	100.00
Annual income	Rs10,000-50,000	28	18.4%
	Rs 50,000-2,00,000	40	26.3%
	Rs 2,00,000-5,00,000	56	36.8%
	Rs More than 10,000	28	18.4%
	Total	152	100.00
Frequency of income	Daily	14	9.2%
	Monthly	83	54.6%
	Irregular	55	36.2%
	Total	152	100

Table 3. Awareness toward financial inclusion

Awareness Toward Financial Inclusion	Mean	Std. Deviation
Zero minimum balance accounts for everyone (no-frills account)	3.72	1.146
ATM card services	4.01	1.042
Credit card facilities	3.46	1.239
Internet banking	3.28	1.612
Mobile banking	3.82	1.204
Cheaper bank loan	4.27	1.145
General Credit Cards (GCC) or Kissan Credit Card (KCC)	3.55	1.167
Electronics Benefits Transfer (EBT)	2.91	1.390
Pradhan Mantri Jan DhanYojna	4.37	.648
Relaxation of KYC (Know Your Customer) guidelines	3.74	1.217
Insurance (motor, heath, crop and cattle insurance)]	3.55	1.504

From the above descriptive statistics table it can be interpreted that respondents avail ATM card services (2.18), cheaper bank loan (2.18) and relaxation of guidelines (2.09) drawn from Arithmetic mean value. This shows that consumers of Mahanagar Co-Op Bank avail some of the financial inclusion services provided by the bank. However, the standard deviation value indicates that majority of responses are spread around availing of financial inclusion services by consumers. Responses vary around availing of Electronics Benefits Transfer (.776) derived from standard deviation.

Table 4. Availing of financial inclusion services

Availing of Financial Inclusion Services	Mean	Std. Deviation
ATM card services	2.18	.577
Credit card facilities	1.55	.500
Internet banking	1.64	.482
Mobile banking	2.00	.737
Cheaper bank loan	2.18	.580
General Credit Cards (GCC) or Kissan Credit Card (KCC)	1.55	.659
Electronics Benefits Transfer (EBT)	1.64	.776
Pradhan Mantri Jan DhanYojna	2.00	.431
Relaxation of KYC (Know Your Customer) guidelines	2.09	.675
Insurance (motor, heath, crop and cattle insurance)	1.73	.754

ANOVA Tables

- **$H_{01:}$** There is no significant association between gender and awareness of consumers towards financial inclusion

From the above ANOVA table it can be interpreted that in majority of the variables null hypothesis gets rejected. This is because significant value is lower than .05%. This means that there is a significant association between gender of respondents and their awareness towards financial inclusion services provided by Mahanagar Co-Op Bank Ltd. But, variable regarding awareness towards ATM card services indicates that null hypothesis gets accepted as the significant value is greater than .05% (.925). This shows that there is no significant association between gender and consumer awareness towards financial inclusion services provided by the bank. The analysis shows that in majority of variables like zero minimum balance, credit card and cheaper bank facilities as well as insurance and Electronics Benefit Transfer (EBT) consumers have a similar perception while only in ATM card services their perception is different. Thus, it can be said that there is a significant association between gender and awareness of consumers towards financial inclusion.

- **H_{02}:** There is no significant association between education and awareness of consumers towards financial inclusion

From the above ANOVA table it can be interpreted that null hypothesis gets rejected in all of the variables. This is because significant value is lower than .05%. This means that there is a significant association between education level of respondents and awareness towards financial inclusion services provided by Mahanagar Co-Op Bank Ltd. It also shows that in all the variables consumers have a similar perception regarding financial inclusion. Thus, this shows that there is a significant association between education level of respondents and awareness towards financial inclusion services.

- **H_{03}:** There is no significant association between frequency of income and awareness of consumers towards financial inclusion

From the above ANOVA table it can be interpreted that null hypothesis gets rejected in all of the variables. This is because significant value is lower than .05%. This means that there is a significant association between frequency of income and awareness towards financial inclusion services provided by Mahanagar Co-Op Bank Ltd. It also shows that in all variables consumers had a similar perception towards financial inclusion. Thus, this shows that there is a significant association between frequency of income and awareness towards financial inclusion.

Table 5.

		Sum of Squares	df	Mean Square	F	Sig.
Zero Minimum Balance Accounts for Everyone (No-Frills Account)	Between Groups	66.648	1	66.648	75.882	.000
	Within Groups	131.746	150	.878		
	Total	198.395	151			
ATM Card Services	Between Groups	.010	1	.010	.009	.925
	Within Groups	163.964	150	1.093		
	Total	163.974	151			
Credit Card Facilities	Between Groups	13.202	1	13.202	9.061	.003
	Within Groups	218.561	150	1.457		
	Total	231.763	151			
Internet Banking	Between Groups	54.321	1	54.321	24.102	.000
	Within Groups	338.073	150	2.254		
	Total	392.395	151			
Mobile Banking	Between Groups	39.632	1	39.632	33.173	.000
	Within Groups	179.210	150	1.195		
	Total	218.842	151			
Cheaper Bank Loan	Between Groups	53.597	1	53.597	55.697	.000
	Within Groups	144.344	150	.962		
	Total	197.941	151			
General Credit Cards (GCC) or Kissan Credit Card (KCC)	Between Groups	44.224	1	44.224	41.087	.000
	Within Groups	161.454	150	1.076		
	Total	205.678	151			
Electronics Benefits Transfer (EBT)	Between Groups	92.034	1	92.034	69.075	.000
	Within Groups	199.855	150	1.332		
	Total	291.888	151			
Pradhan Mantri Jan DhanYojna	Between Groups	28.293	1	28.293	120.995	.000
	Within Groups	35.075	150	.234		
	Total	63.368	151			
Relaxation of KYC (Know Your Customer) Guidelines	Between Groups	109.317	1	109.317	143.641	.000
	Within Groups	114.156	150	.761		
	Total	223.474	151			
Insurance (Motor, Heath, Crop and Cattle Insurance)]	Between Groups	134.200	1	134.200	97.023	.000
	Within Groups	207.477	150	1.383		
	Total	341.678	151			

Table 6.

		Sum of Squares	df	Mean Square	F	Sig.
Zero Minimum Balance Accounts for Everyone (no-Frills Account)	Between Groups	152.183	5	30.437	96.161	.000
	Within Groups	46.211	146	.317		
	Total	198.395	151			
ATM Card Services	Between Groups	135.974	5	27.195	141.801	.000
	Within Groups	28.000	146	.192		
	Total	163.974	151			
Credit Card Facilities	Between Groups	179.918	5	35.984	101.332	.000
	Within Groups	51.846	146	.355		
	Total	231.763	151			
Internet Banking	Between Groups	356.883	5	71.377	293.448	.000
	Within Groups	35.512	146	.243		
	Total	392.395	151			
Mobile Banking	Between Groups	202.509	5	40.502	362.036	.000
	Within Groups	16.333	146	.112		
	Total	218.842	151			
Cheaper Bank Loan	Between Groups	125.721	5	25.144	50.832	.000
	Within Groups	72.220	146	.495		
	Total	197.941	151			
General Credit Cards (GCC) or Kissan Credit Card (KCC)	Between Groups	150.702	5	30.140	80.045	.000
	Within Groups	54.976	146	.377		
	Total	205.678	151			
Electronics Benefits Transfer (EBT)	Between Groups	229.913	5	45.983	108.324	.000
	Within Groups	61.976	146	.424		
	Total	291.888	151			
Pradhan Mantri Jan DhanYojna	Between Groups	47.149	5	9.430	84.882	.000
	Within Groups	16.220	146	.111		
	Total	63.368	151			
Relaxation of KYC (Know Your Customer) Guidelines	Between Groups	179.596	5	35.919	119.517	.000
	Within Groups	43.878	146	.301		
	Total	223.474	151			
Insurance (Motor, Heath, Crop and Cattle Insurance)]	Between Groups	325.458	5	65.092	585.922	.000
	Within Groups	16.220	146	.111		
	Total	341.678	151			

Table 7.

		Sum of Squares	df	Mean Square	F	Sig.
Zero Minimum Balance Accounts for Everyone (no-Frills Account)	Between Groups	47.958	2	23.979	23.750	.000
	Within Groups	150.436	149	1.010		
	Total	198.395	151			
ATM Card Services	Between Groups	79.845	2	39.922	70.706	.000
	Within Groups	84.129	149	.565		
	Total	163.974	151			
Credit Card Facilities	Between Groups	64.781	2	32.391	28.903	.000
	Within Groups	166.982	149	1.121		
	Total	231.763	151			
Internet Banking	Between Groups	171.011	2	85.505	57.548	.000
	Within Groups	221.384	149	1.486		
	Total	392.395	151			
Mobile Banking	Between Groups	74.542	2	37.271	38.485	.000
	Within Groups	144.300	149	.968		
	Total	218.842	151			
Cheaper Bank Loan	Between Groups	28.950	2	14.475	12.763	.000
	Within Groups	168.991	149	1.134		
	Total	197.941	151			
General Credit Cards (GCC) or Kissan Credit Card (KCC)	Between Groups	8.687	2	4.344	3.285	.040
	Within Groups	196.991	149	1.322		
	Total	205.678	151			
Electronics Benefits Transfer (EBT)	Between Groups	35.588	2	17.794	10.345	.000
	Within Groups	256.300	149	1.720		
	Total	291.888	151			
Pradhan Mantri Jan DhanYojna	Between Groups	4.185	2	2.093	5.268	.006
	Within Groups	59.183	149	.397		
	Total	63.368	151			
Relaxation of KYC (Know Your Customer) guidelines	Between Groups	47.209	2	23.604	19.953	.000
	Within Groups	176.265	149	1.183		
	Total	223.474	151			
Insurance (Motor, Heath, Crop and Cattle Insurance)]	Between Groups	36.913	2	18.457	9.023	.000
	Within Groups	304.765	149	2.045		
	Total	341.678	151			

Table 8.

		Sum of Squares	df	Mean Square	F	Sig.
ATM Card Services	Between Groups	1.092	1	1.092	3.334	.070
	Within Groups	49.112	150	.327		
	Total	50.204	151			
Credit Card Facilities	Between Groups	2.944	1	2.944	12.713	.000
	Within Groups	34.734	150	.232		
	Total	37.678	151			
Internet Banking	Between Groups	.023	1	.023	.100	.753
	Within Groups	35.075	150	.234		
	Total	35.099	151			
Mobile Banking	Between Groups	5.644	1	5.644	11.089	.001
	Within Groups	76.356	150	.509		
	Total	82.000	151			
Cheaper Bank Loan	Between Groups	1.905	1	1.905	5.840	.017
	Within Groups	48.937	150	.326		
	Total	50.842	151			
General Credit Cards (GCC) or Kissan Credit Card (KCC)	Between Groups	2.504	1	2.504	5.954	.016
	Within Groups	63.075	150	.421		
	Total	65.579	151			
Electronics Benefits Transfer (EBT)	Between Groups	23.338	1	23.338	51.880	.000
	Within Groups	67.477	150	.450		
	Total	90.816	151			
Pradhan Mantri Jan DhanYojna	Between Groups	6.546	1	6.546	45.770	.000
	Within Groups	21.454	150	.143		
	Total	28.000	151			
Relaxation of KYC (Know Your Customer) guidelines	Between Groups	33.724	1	33.724	144.590	.000
	Within Groups	34.986	150	.233		
	Total	68.711	151			
Insurance (Motor, Heath, Crop and Cattle Insurance)	Between Groups	29.941	1	29.941	80.199	.000
	Within Groups	56.000	150	.373		
	Total	85.941	151			

- **H_{04}:** There is no significant association between gender and availing of financial inclusion services by consumers

From the above ANOVA table it can be interpreted that null hypothesis gets rejected in most of the variables. This is because significant value is lower than .05%. This means that there is a significant association between gender and availing of financial inclusion services provided by Mahanagar Co-Op Bank Ltd. However, variable regarding availing of internet banking indicates that null hypothesis gets accepted as the significant value is greater than .05%. This means that there is no significant association between gender and availing of financial inclusion services given by the bank. The analysis also shows that in most of variables like availing of insurance schemes, Pradhan Mantri Jan DhanYojna and credit card facilities consumers have a similar perception. Thus, it can be said that there is a significant association between gender and availing of financial inclusion services.

- **H_{05}:** There is no significant association between education and availing of financial inclusion services by consumers

From the above ANOVA table it can be interpreted that null hypothesis gets rejected in all of the variables. This is because significant value is lower than .05%. This means that there is a significant association between education of consumers and availing of financial servicesprovided by Mahanagar Co-Op Bank Ltd. It also shows that in all variables consumers had a similar perception towards financial inclusion. Thus, this shows that there is a significant association between education and availing of financial inclusion services.

- **H_{06}:** There is no significant association between frequency of income and availing of financial inclusion services by consumers

From the above ANOVA table it can be interpreted that null hypothesis gets rejected in most of the variables. This is because significant value is lower than .05%. This means that there is a significant association between frequency of income of consumers and availing of financial inclusion services provided by Mahanagar Co-Op Bank Ltd. However, variable regarding availing of Pradhan Mantri Jan DhanYojna indicates that null hypothesis gets accepted as the significant value is greater than .05%. This means that there is no significant association between frequency of income and availing of financial inclusion services given by the bank. The analysis also shows that in most of variables like availing of insurance schemes, ATM card services and credit card facilities consumers have a similar perception. Thus, it can be said that there is a significant association between frequency of income and availing of financial inclusion services.

Table 9.

		Sum of Squares	df	Mean Square	F	Sig.
ATM Card Services	Between Groups	24.993	5	4.999	28.947	.000
	Within Groups	25.211	146	.173		
	Total	50.204	151			
Credit Card Facilities	Between Groups	28.800	5	5.760	94.722	.000
	Within Groups	8.878	146	.061		
	Total	37.678	151			
Internet Banking	Between Groups	25.879	5	5.176	81.964	.000
	Within Groups	9.220	146	.063		
	Total	35.099	151			
Mobile Banking	Between Groups	63.447	5	12.689	99.858	.000
	Within Groups	18.553	146	.127		
	Total	82.000	151			
Cheaper Bank Loan	Between Groups	25.631	5	5.126	29.686	.000
	Within Groups	25.211	146	.173		
	Total	50.842	151			
General Credit Cards (GCC) or Kissan Credit Card (KCC)	Between Groups	49.246	5	9.849	88.039	.000
	Within Groups	16.333	146	.112		
	Total	65.579	151			
Electronics Benefits Transfer (EBT)	Between Groups	81.482	5	16.296	254.924	.000
	Within Groups	9.333	146	.064		
	Total	90.816	151			
Pradhan Mantri Jan DhanYojna	Between Groups	11.667	5	2.333	20.857	.000
	Within Groups	16.333	146	.112		
	Total	28.000	151			
Relaxation of KYC (Know Your Customer) guidelines	Between Groups	24.377	5	4.875	16.056	.000
	Within Groups	44.333	146	.304		
	Total	68.711	151			
Insurance (Motor, Heath, Crop and Cattle Insurance)	Between Groups	76.607	5	15.321	239.672	.000
	Within Groups	9.333	146	.064		
	Total	85.941	151			

Table 10.

		Sum of Squares	df	Mean Square	F	Sig.
ATM Card Services	Between Groups	29.457	2	14.728	105.776	.000
	Within Groups	20.747	149	.139		
	Total	50.204	151			
Credit Card Facilities	Between Groups	15.603	2	7.801	52.657	.000
	Within Groups	22.075	149	.148		
	Total	37.678	151			
Internet Banking	Between Groups	24.662	2	12.331	176.052	.000
	Within Groups	10.436	149	.070		
	Total	35.099	151			
Mobile Banking	Between Groups	47.508	2	23.754	102.611	.000
	Within Groups	34.492	149	.231		
	Total	82.000	151			
Cheaper Bank Loan	Between Groups	4.288	2	2.144	6.862	.001
	Within Groups	46.554	149	.312		
	Total	50.842	151			
General Credit Cards (GCC) or Kissan Credit Card (KCC)	Between Groups	5.617	2	2.808	6.978	.001
	Within Groups	59.962	149	.402		
	Total	65.579	151			
Electronics Benefits Transfer (EBT)	Between Groups	10.106	2	5.053	9.329	.000
	Within Groups	80.709	149	.542		
	Total	90.816	151			
Pradhan Mantri Jan DhanYojna	Between Groups	0.000	2	0.000	0.000	1.000
	Within Groups	28.000	149	.188		
	Total	28.000	151			
Relaxation of KYC (Know Your Customer) guidelines	Between Groups	2.274	2	1.137	2.550	.081
	Within Groups	66.436	149	.446		
	Total	68.711	151			
Insurance (Motor, Heath, Crop and Cattle Insurance)	Between Groups	8.541	2	4.270	8.221	.000
	Within Groups	77.400	149	.519		
	Total	85.941	151			

CONCLUSION

From the recent trends of 2014 provided by IBGC Working Paper, it can be said that only 52 of 17 banks in India issue cards to customers owing the prohibitive costs from 2010. Only 360 million debit cards were issued by the banks against a bankable population of 800 million. Over 92% of transactions through cards are for cash withdrawals at ATMs. This means debit card is used at point of sales for only 8%. This illustrates the need for improve retail payments in India. The present study concludes that though Government of India and Reserve Bank of India are doing commendable work to include financial inclusion in India but still there is a lot to do. Statistics of 2014 show that nearly 268, 000 banking outlets have been set up in villages as on March 13 as against 67,694 banking outlets in March 2010. Nearly 109 million Basic Savings Bank Deposit Accounts (BSBDAs) have been added, taking the total number to 182 million. 3.6 million households have been provided with small entrepreneurial credit by the end of March 2013, of whom 2.25 million were added during the last three years.

From the research it can be concluded that there is an association between demographic variables of gender, education as well as frequency of income of consumers and their awareness towards financial inclusion services provided by Mahanagar Co-Op Bank Ltd. However, the research also concludes that consumers are aware of ATM services irrespective of gender as there is no significant association between them. In addition, it can also be concluded that there is an association between gender, frequency of income and education and availing of financial inclusion services by the consumers of Mahanagar Co-Op Bank Ltd. But, the study also shows that availing of internet banking services and Pradhan Mantri Jan DhanYojna has no association with gender and frequency of income of consumers respectively.

The present research has different implications for various stakeholders. Firstly, the research and its findings would be of great significance to the academicians. It would provide them huge literature related to consumer awareness on financial inclusion and its findings would help them in conducting further research. The paper has practical implications for the policy makers and for the financial sector. Though this research, the extent to which the people having different demographic profile are conversant with banking habits is known. It helps to understand that though people are having awareness of financial inclusion and its benefits but still they do not avail its services owing to various factors like distance from bank and their field of work. The paper helps to raise awareness among policy makers that various sophisticated forms of banking services do not become feasible to be accessed by less educated and lower income group people. Thus, this paper helps in understanding the level of consumer awareness among the target group. The paper has associated future revenues as well. Further study can be conducted on ways in which customer awareness regarding financial inclusion can be raised by banks among people. Further, research can take place on awareness of financial inclusion among other people of other remote areas in and around Mumbai. Also, financial literacy of people can also be studied in various co-operative banks of Mumbai as these are many in number.

REFERENCES

Annamalai, C., & Vijayarani, K. (2014). Awareness of financial inclusion on tribal people in Dharmapuri district. *Asia Pacific Journal of Research*, *1*(17), 56–62.

Bagli, S., & Dutta, P. (2012). A study of financial inclusion in India. *Radix International Journal of Economics & Business Management, 1*(8).

Bhuvana, M., & Vasantha, S. (2016). Drivers of Financial Inclusion to Reach Out Poor. *Arabian Journal of Business and Management Review, 6*(235).

Biroch, R., & Pozzebon, M. (2016). Improving financial inclusion: Towards a critical financial education framework. *Rev. adm. empres., 56*(3).

Claessens, S. (2006). Access to Financial Services: A Review of the Issues and Public Policy Objectives. *The World Bank Research Observer*, *21*(2), 1–34. doi:10.1093/wbro/lkl004

Finlayson, A. (2011). Financialisation, Financial Literacy and Asset-Based Welfare. *British Journal of Politics and International Relations*, *11*(3), 400–421. doi:10.1111/j.1467-856X.2009.00378.x

Joseph, D. (2014). A study on Financial Inclsuion and Financial Literacy. *International Journal of Business and Administration Research Review*, *2*(4), 126–134.

Meshram, P., & Randad, A. (2015). A Survey and Study of an Awareness of Financial Inclusion in an around Pune City, Pune. *International Journal of Engineering Technology, Management and Applied Sciences*, *3*(5), 327–333.

Nandru, P., Anand, B., & Rentala, S. (2016). Exploring the factors impacting financial inclusion: Evidence from South India. *Annual Research Journal of SCMS, Pune*, *4*, 1–15.

Rajan, R. e. (2007). *A Hundred Small Steps: Report of the Committee on Financial Sector Reforms*. SAGE Publications.

Rangarajan, C. (2008). *Report of the Committee on financial inclusion*. Academic Press.

Reddy, J. R. (2016). Financial inclusion: Issues and challenges in India. *Anveshana's Inernational Journal Research in Regional, Law, Social Sciences Journal of Management*, *1*(5), 1–12.

Sarma, M., & Pais, J. (2011). Financial Inclusion and Development. *Journal of International Development*, *23*(5), 613–628. doi:10.1002/jid.1698

Senthikumar, Iyyappan, & Subramaniam. (2012). *Customer awareness on electronic banking in Thanjavur town — An empirical study*. Academic Press.

Sharma, P., & Sachdeva, S. (2014). Financial Inclusion in India - Issues and Challenges. *International Journal of Management and Social Sciences Research*, *3*(6), 41–44.

Shukla, T., & Singh, A. (2015). Financial Inclusion: An Empirical Study of Banking Products. *International Conference on Management and Information Systems*, 17-27.

Singh, S. (2016). A study on financial inclusion awareness among selected working women of Satna (M.P.). *International Journal of Science Techology and Management*, *5*(4), 122–128.

Srinivasan. (2007). Policy Issues and Role of Banking System in Financial Inclusion. *Economic and Political Weekly, 42*(30), 3091-3093+3095.

Sukaram, K. (2015). Financial Access: Inclusion and Literacy. Symbiosis Centre for Management Studies, 3(1), 188-207.

Chapter 10
Journey of Financial Inclusion Driven by Indian Banking Industry

Abhineet Saxena
University of Rajasthan, India

Ashish Sharma
India International School, India

ABSTRACT

Financial institutions, especially banks, have proved to be a boon for the economic development of a country like India. An attempt has been made in the present chapter to analyze the state of financial inclusion and the role of banking in achieving full financial inclusion in India. The journey of financial inclusion through banking in India has been critically appraised. Some of the important outcomes that can be highlighted are increased banking access of rural population in past few years together with the huge expansion in banking infrastructure in rural areas. Banking in India has been transformed with the introduction of PMJDY, BC Model, etc. Increasing trend has been observed in IMPS and M-Wallet penetration. North-eastern part of the country is still a challenge in the way of financial inclusion. The journey of financial inclusion on the wheels of Indian banking industry is still in search of the ultimate destination, and it will take miles to achieve full financial inclusion.

DOI: 10.4018/978-1-5225-4035-9.ch010

INTRODUCTION

Financial Inclusion is one of the major concerns of the banking sector. Financial inclusion drives not only for improving the range, quality and availability of financial services and products but also focuses on the un-served and financially excluded community. Some of the major determinants of financial inclusion are admittance to the affordable banking and financial services, credit, savings, insurance, usage, quality, financial literacy, innovation and diversification.

Central government of India had established a Committee on Financial Inclusion Chaired by Dr C. Rangarajanin (2008) also defines financial inclusion in the same line as the process of ensuring access to financial services and timely and adequate credit where needed by weaker sections and low income groups of Indian society at an affordable cost. Financial inclusion promotes thrift and develops culture of saving and also enables efficient payment mechanism strengthening the various financial institutions across the country which not only benefits the economy but also establish proper infrastructure for efficient payment mechanism and allocation. The empirical evidence shows that countries with large proportion of population excluded from the formal financial system also show higher poverty ratios and higher inequality.

It is also called 'Inclusive Financing'. However, the term financial inclusion was first introduced in India by RBI in its annual policy statement 2005-06. This term was used by RBI in the alignment of the efforts started in 1960s by Indian government along with Indian banking industry to bring majority of India citizens under the banking umbrella. As mentioned by Dr. K.C Chakrabarty in one of his article banking: Key driver for inclusive growth, Financial inclusion in India can be categorized in different phases. 1960-1990 was the initial phase where the whole focus was on channeling of credit to the neglected sectors of the economy. 1990-2005 was the second phase which focused mainly on strengthening the role of financial institution in economic reforms. This was the phase when SHGBLP programmes were encouraged together with kisan credit card promotion in order to enhance the financial support in terms of affordable credit in the rural areas. Since then during the third phase, financial inclusion was considered as one of the major policy measures. In this current phase the focus of financial inclusion is on providing safe facility of saving deposits through 'no frills' account. Similar to the practices regarding financial inclusion in other countries, in India it has been observed that central bank of the country has a vital role to play in. RBI along with the banking sector together with the strong network of NABARD, SIDBI and other development banks have put their hard efforts to achieve the milestone. Henceforward it can be concluded that Financial Inclusion is the way procedure to ensure successful admittance of appropriate financial products and financial services to all sections of the society and especially weaker sections and low-income groups at an affordable cost in a fair and transparent manner by mainstream banking and financial institutions.

SIGNIFICANCE OF FINANCIAL INCLUSION IN INDIAN CONTEXT

Financial Inclusion in developing countries like India is very much essential for sustainable growth and the role of banking industry becomes vital since offering banking services to everyone is a necessary building block for sustainable growth. If everyone has the tolls and resources to better themselves, it would increase individual productivity, growth and economic prosperity. According to the World Bank, around 2 Billion people don't use formal financial services and more than 50% of adults in the poorest households are unbanked.

Though it is a very soothing fact that India boasting economic growth rates are found higher than most developed countries in recent years but regret to mention here that a majority of the country's population still remains unbanked. Financial Inclusion is a relatively new socio-economic concept in India that aims to change this dynamic by providing financial services at affordable costs to the underprivileged, who might not otherwise be aware of or able to afford these services. Existence of small banks like payment banks, small finance banks, Paytm etc was not too encouraging few years ago and due to which lower income group had limited access to financial services and products. This cumbersome financial environment especially in rural and remote areas led to a lot of financial instability. Therefore, believing that financial inclusion may initiate the next revolution of growth and prosperity, Indian government along with the RBI are focusing more on this relevantly new concept of financial inclusion. Policy makers also believe that through this tool the Rural India will get higher excess to banking facilities and with the introduction of recent measures by Indian Government like Pradhan Mantri Jeevan Jyoti Bima Yojana, Pradhan Mantri Suraksha Bima Yojana, Pradhan Mantri Jan-Dhan Yojana (PMJDY), GST, digitalization of economy and direct cash transfers to beneficiary bank accounts instead of physical cash payments the role of banking industry has now become more significant for the achievement of exclusive financial inclusion in the country.

PROMOTION OF FINANCIAL INCLUSION IN INDIA

Achievement of exclusive Financial Inclusion of the unbanked population in India is possible through only strong political will, bureaucratic support and constant persuasion by the RBI and NABARD. It is expected to unleash the hugely untapped potential of the bottom of pyramid section of India economy. In India illiteracy, unemployment and poverty are the biggest hurdles in the way of financial inclusion. Therefore, the Indian government has chosen a unique route along with the increased banking penetration across the country and the turnaround approach for bringing about financial inclusion. Pradhan Mantri Jan-Dhan Yojana, RuPay card, GST and Direct Benefit Transfer scheme proved to be the important weapons on this ground to ensure the exclusive financial inclusion drive in all the states of the country without any discrimination.

Recently honorable Prime Minister Shree Narendra Damodardas Modi tweeted "JAM" (Just Achieving Maximum) which means Maximum value for every rupee spent, Maximum empowerment for the poor and Maximum technology penetration among the masses and ultimately maximum financial inclusion. It reflects from the prime minister's tweet that financial inclusion has become one of the major priorities for the Indian government as it is like a catalyst for inclusive and equitable growth. It is commonly realized that initiatives by government of india like Pradhan Mantri Jan-Dhan Yojana, Aadhar card drive, RuPay card and Digital India have boosted the country's financial inclusion drive.

Importantly Modi Government has realized the potential of mobile as well as digital technology to be game changers vis-à-vis the financial inclusion drive. A number of schemes are implementing through proliferation of mobile technology in rural areas under the policy of downward integration to include rural customers in the organized banking and financial system. RBI's vision for 2020 is to open nearly 600 million new customers' accounts and service them through a variety of channels by leveraging on IT. These would not only improve cash flow to boost the economy, but also help the government facilitate financial inclusion through banks.

HISTORICAL SKETCH OF FINANCIAL INCLUSION AND ROLE OF BANKING IN INDIA

The approach to financial inclusion in developing countries like India is to a certain extent different from the developed countries because of the huge variations in the extent of financial exclusion (Thorat, 2007). The phase-wise financial inclusion and role of banking is presented in Table 1. However, the major thrust has been given to the forth and recent phase.

Table 1.

Phase-1 (1870-1969)	In 1870 the presidency bank of Bengal and bank of madras were found. In total there were eight banks at that time and by the end of 1934 this number reached to 123 (Gangadharan, 2012). during this phase six banks were found with more than 100 cr deposit liability. Inception of RBI was a big feature of this phase followed by banking regulation act. During this phase focus on financial inclusion was very week since priority sector was the major concern in comparison to banking for the government. Banking network was weak and concentrated in major cities only.
Phase-2 (1969-1990)	This phase had witnessed nationalization of Indian commercial banks. The policy of expansion, creation of RRBs, Lead Bank Scheme and NABARD, Credit guarantee schemes and initiation of microfinance etc were the milestones in the financial inclusion path of banking industry in India. This phase has also seen a great increase in the number of rural branches of commercial banks. This phase is also known for the initiatives taken for the individual credit needs of the people of the country and created a path way for financial inclusion of Indian commercial banks. The same is justified with some indicators like rural bank branches, average population per branch, increased bank deposit as % of GDP, rural deposits and rural credit etc.
Phase-3 (1990-2005)	This phase is known for the development of financial inclusion in the country where the expansion of banking services was realized in terms of SHGs formation and their linkage with bank. SHGBLP was launched by NABARD in this phase and the major objective was to offer banking services to the poor at their door step. NABARD introduced the Kisan Credit Card (KCC) scheme in conjunction with co-operative banks, commercial banks and RRBs to smoothen and strengthen the credit delivery system. The KCC scheme increased the farmer's access to credit from institutional sources to enable them financially in a flexible and cost effective manner. It was observed KCC as a vital tool of financial inclusion.
Phase-4 (2005 onwards)	The term 'financial inclusion' was used by RBI for the first time in its Annual Policy Statement, year 2005-06. The emphasis was on including unbanked and underserved people. Committee on Financial Inclusion was established in June 2006 under the chairmanship of Dr. C. Rangarajan to understand the problem of exclusion of rural poor from access to financial services and guidelines were framed to enhance financial inclusion in the country. In year 2007, a High Level Committee on Financial Sector Reform was framed. Rural Co-operative Credit Institutions were revived in this phase. Adoption of Electronic Benefit Transfer (EBT), Swabhiman, Unique Identity Number (UID)/Aadhaar, Direct Cash Transfer (DBT), No Frills Accounts, Simplification/Relaxation on KYC Norms were other key features of this phase which were introduced to achieve 100% Financial Inclusion Drive with the help of State-Level Bankers' Committee (SLBC) conveners. Business Facilitator (BF)/Business Correspondent (BC) Model, Simplified Branch Authorization/ATM Expansion, Opening of Branches in Unbanked Rural Centres, Financial Literacy and Credit Counselling Centres (FLCCs), Microfinance Institutions (MFI)-Bank Linkage Programme and Government initiative like PMJDY, PMJJY, PMJSY etc were the other attractions of this phase for financial inclusion through banks.

Financial Inclusion's Milestones in India

Inclusive access to financial services should be easy, affordable, secure and within the time frame. Different measures and steps were taken in this regard which are presented in Table 2.

Role of FI in Economic Development

The financial system of any country acts as a catalyst in growth of its economy. The conventional channels of financial system collects surplus money with public and then produce this idle fund in distributing it to entrepreneurs, businesses, households and even to the government to run investment projects for the infrastructure development of the country.

This is a fundamental step for economic development process. The role of intermediator by a different financial institution is vital for the mobilization and better allocation of surplus income of common households which is primarily in the idle form. This way this unused and unproductive fund can be used for productive activities in an economy. Another noteworthy role that financial institutions play in an economy is to manage the liquidity so as to meet out the inflationary measures. Simultaneously maintaining enough liquidity push an economy with sustainable growth.

Such financial institutional network also assists the firms and corporate houses to manage the business risks. With the help of strong financial network, business

Table 2. Steps taken to gain inclusive access to financial services in India

Step-I	The concept of 'no-frills' was introduced for low-income people to have saving accounts
Step-II	Banking services were extended by using the services of Business Correspondent (BC)
Step-III	NACH and NFS were launched by NPCI to make retail payments seamless
Step-IV	Guidelines for Prepaid Payment Instruments (PPIs), including mobile wallets, were laid down by RBI
Step-V	IMPS was introduced by NPCI to enable 24 x 7 electronic funds transfer
Step-VI	Aadhaar-Enabled Payment System was launched
Step-VII	RuPay cards were introduced by NPCI as a domestic payment network
Step-VIII	Pradhan Mantri Jan Dhan Yojana (PMJDY) was launched to include more Indians in the banking fold
Step-IX	Licences for Payments Bank and Small Finance Bank were rolled out to enable last-mile reach of financial services
Step-X	Unified Payments Interface was launched by NPCI to allow easy, fast and interoperable P2P payment

houses may improve their portfolio diversification since existence of various financial institutions with all the instruments in their basket as per the needs of the businesses and common people. The backup by financial system provides support against volatile business situations. In the era of globalization external business environment always have a great impact on the economic condition of the country. Therefor the financial system should provide linkages for the different sectors of the economy and the financial inclusion is an emerging concept to achieve the objective of economic growth. Financial inclusion conveys the banking services up to each and every corner of the country while serving not only the privileged but also unbanked and underserved people at an affordable cost. Along with the priority sector, industrialization is must for economic development. Financial inclusion at the first sight not only enhances overall financial intensity of agriculture but also help rural community to get engaged in allied industry. This way exclusive financial inclusion is contributing towards development of rural economy and hence improving economic condition of the country. Financial inclusion is helping in convenient access to financial market, credit market and improving financial literacy across the country where Reserve Bank of India and Government is contributing with full heart with various steps have been initiated to increase banking penetration in the country, nationalization of banks, establishment of RRBs, introduction of SHGBLP, PMJDY, PMJSY Bheem app etc to get easy access of financial markets and their application.

Promoting financial inclusion is proving to be a great success for the country where India has seen remarkable economic growth in past few years and is recognized as one of the most promising economy across the globe. Empowerment and protection of each citizen of the country so that expansion of banking and financial services can produce all the benefits and it is possible only through financial inclusion which is certainly a key driver for economic development at national level and also contributes towards economic empowerment at an individual level.

There are no two opinions in stating that financial inclusion has paved the way for the next revolution of growth and prosperity in India. In the recent times, India as a country is putting all its efforts with banking and finance machinery to advance financial inclusion as a mandate for economic growth of the country. In this line it has been observed that in some of the states

OBJECTIVES OF THE STUDY

The objectives of the present study are:

1. To critically appraise the state of financial inclusion in India.

2. To examine the significance of banking network in compliance of financial inclusion in India.
3. To identify the banking infrastructure gap and thus limitations and challenges of financial inclusion in India.

Identified Parameters of Financial Inclusion

To measure the state of financial inclusion in India researcher has considered some basic indicators such as bank penetration, deposit and credit penetration and business correspondent penetration. Researcher found in various researchers that to access the status of financial inclusion above parameters were used. Researcher found 'CRISIL Inclusix' as one of the most recognized and comprehensive index to measure the status of financial inclusion in the country. Global Findex was the other significant financial inclusion index considered by the researcher for his study.

The present study focuses on trend analysis of data related to Branch and ATM Penetration in Rural as well urban area, Credit Penetration, Deposit Penetration, and Business Correspondent Penetration, Growth of PMJDY scheme, Credit - Deposit Ratio, Deposit per account, and Credit per account, microfinance. Secondary data for the same compiled from various sources i.e annual reports, RBI bulletin, Report on Currency and Finance, Economic Survey, Statistical Abstract, World Development Report. The study period is considered from year 2005 when the term "financial Inclusion" was being introduced for the first time in India. The study is mainly based on secondary data published by RBI, Ministry of finance and NABARD. The research design is exploratory in nature (see Figure 1 and Table 1).

SNAPSHOT OF PROGRESS OF FINANCIAL INCLUSION IN INDIA

A briefing on Progress of Financial Inclusion has been covered as under.

Position of Household's Availing Banking Services in the Country

Interpretation: Figures 2 and 3 demonstrates the Position of household's who avail banking services in India. It is revealed from above graph that only 30.1% of the rural households had banking access in year 2001 whereas it has increased to 54.4% in year 2011. In the case of urban households, it was 67.8% in year 2011 in comparison to 49.5% in year 2001. It implies a constructive growth towards admittance to the banking services. It is observed from the above data that growth in rural areas is on

Figure 1. Dimensions used to measure financial inclusion
Source: Author's compilation

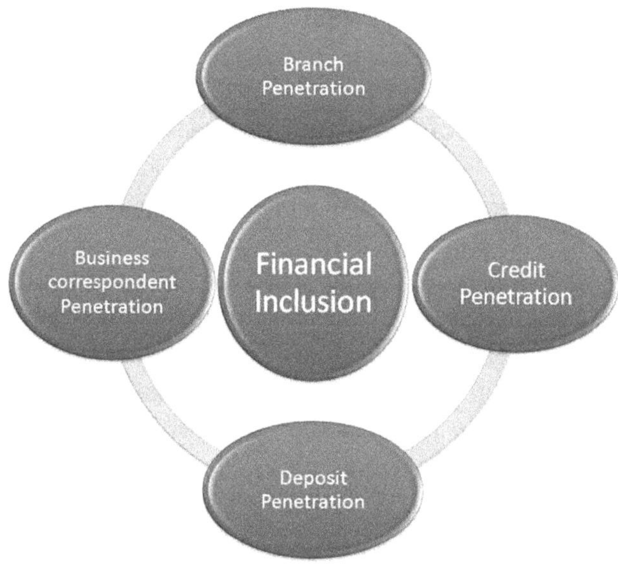

Table 3. Dimensions for measuring financial inclusion

Dimensions	Parameters	Significance
Branch Penetration	Number of bank Branches per one lakh population	Measures the facilities provided by Banks
Business Correspondent penetration	Number of Business Correspondent per one lakh population	Measures the availability of Banking Correspondent in Rural areas for door steps banking
Credit Penetration	Number of loan account per one lakh population	Measures the access of credit facility
Deposit Penetration	Number of Saving account per one lakh population	Measures the access of bank's saving products and services

Source: (Bhuvana & Vasantha, 2016).

higher side as compare to urban areas. Henceforth it can be stated that government and RBI both are focusing on rural penetration so that inclusive growth can be achieved.

Public Sector Bank (PSB) Branches Penetration in India

Public Sector Bank are the backbone of Indian banking since independence and before nationalization of the banks PSUs banks were the only available and approachable

Figure 2. Position of household's availing banking services in the country
(Source: Author's Compilation from website of ministry of finance, financial services division)

	Total Number of households (As per census year 2001)	Number of households availing banking services (As per census year 2001)	Total Number of households (As per census year 2011)	Number of households availing banking services (As per census year 2011)
Rural	138271559	41639949	167826730	91369805
Urban	53692376	26590693	78865937	53444983
Total	191963935	68230642	246692667	144814788

Figure 3. Position of household's availing banking services in the country (%)
(Source: Author's compilation)

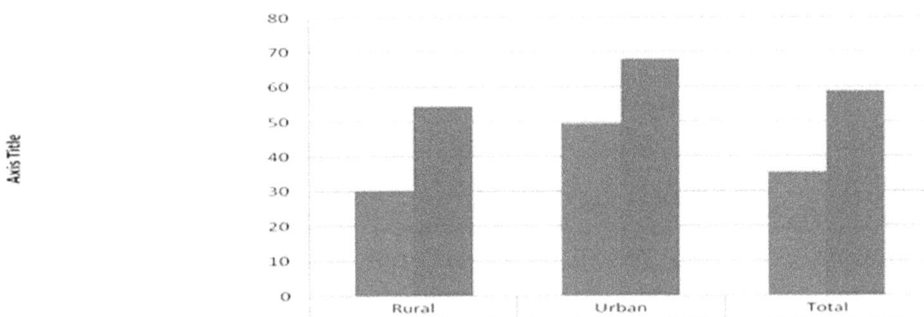

	Rural	Urban	Total
Percent households availing banking services (As per census year 2001)	30.1	49.5	35.5
Percent households availing banking services (As per census year 2011)	54.4	67.8	58.7

option for rural poor. Since Public sector banks have very strong network and infrastructure across the country hence their contribution towards financial inclusion is remarkable. Following is the graphical representation of their penetration during March 2011-15.

Interpretation: Figure 4 reveals the status of Penetration of Public Sector Bank Branches in India. it can be stated from the above graph that during year 2010-2015, penetration of public sector banks has got noteworthy growth in each segment of

Figure 4. Public sector bank branches penetration in India as on March 31
(Source: Author's Compilation from website of ministry of finance, financial services division)

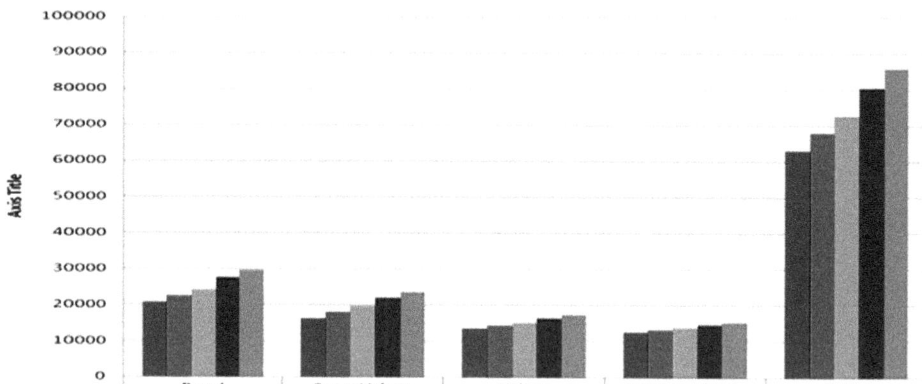

	Rural	Semi Urban	Urban	Metropolitan	Total
2010-11	20658	16217	13450	12612	62937
2011-12	22379	17905	14322	13244	67850
2012-13	24243	19642	15055	13797	72737
2013-14	27547	21952	16319	14644	80462
2014-15	29634	23549	17387	15325	85895

population. In total, Number of branches has been increased by 1.36 times in year 2015 as compared to year 2011.

Scheduled Commercial Bank (SCB) Branches Penetration in India

Scheduled commercial banks include both public and private sector banks. Following is the graphical presentation of penetration of SCBs in India.

Interpretation: Figure 5 reveals the status of Penetration of Scheduled Commercial Bank Branches in India. It can be stated from the above graph that during year 2010-2015, penetration of Scheduled commercial banks has also got remarkable push in each segment of population. It implies the contribution of Private sector banks as well in the financial inclusion. In total, Number of branches has been increased by 1.38 times in year 2015 as compared to year 2011.

Scheduled Commercial and Public Sectors Bank's ATM Penetration in India

ATM also plays an important role in the digital era of banking penetration. Figure 6 shows the growth trend of Onsite and Offsite ATMs establishment in India during 2010-15.

Figure 5. Scheduled commercial bank branches penetration in India as on March 31
(Source: Author's Compilation from website of ministry of finance, financial services division)

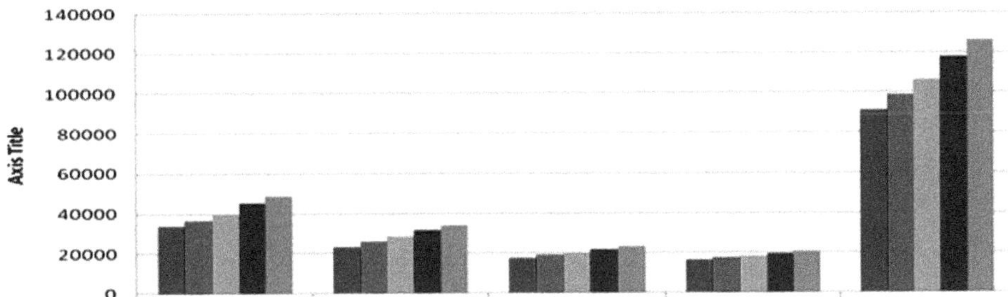

	Rural	Semi Urban	Urban	Metropolitan	Total
2010-11	33923	23089	17629	16255	90896
2011-12	36546	25834	18879	17274	98533
2012-13	39816	28546	19935	18092	106389
2013-14	45293	31530	21532	19275	117630
2014-15	48557	33766	23036	20498	125857

Figure 6. Scheduled Commercial Bank's ATM Penetration in India as on March 31

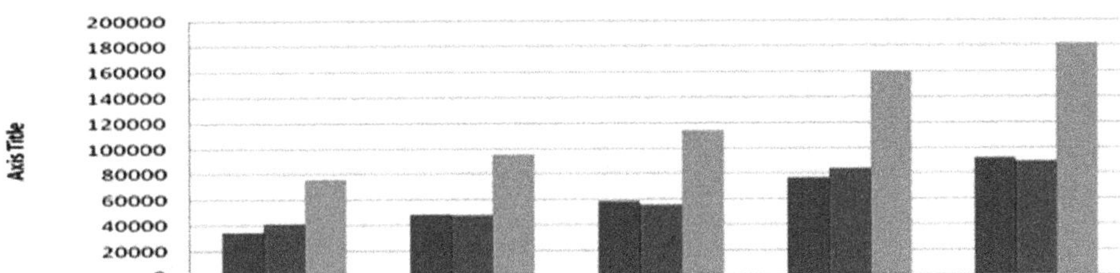

	2010-11	2011-12	2012-13	2013-14	2014-15
Off-Site ATMs	34377	48141	58254	76676	92191
On-Site ATMs	41268	47545	55760	83379	89061
Total ATMS	75645	95686	114014	160055	181252

Interpretation: Figure 7 reveals the status of ATMs Penetration of Scheduled commercial and PSBs in India. It can be stated from the above graph that during year 2010-2015, penetration of ATMs has seen the heights. In total, Number of PSB's ATMs have been increased by 2.61 times whereas in the case of SCBs it was 2.4 times in year 2015 as compared to year 2011.

Trend of Change in All Scheduled Commercial Banks Vis-a-Vis RRBs in India During 2005-2016

Interpretation: Figure 8 demonstrates the trend of change in All Scheduled Commercial Banks along with RRBs across the country for the period of year 2005 to year 2016. It can be stated from it that in year 2004-05 number of total Scheduled Commercial

Figure 7. Public sector ATM penetration in India as on March 31
(Source: Author's Compilation from website of ministry of finance, financial services division)

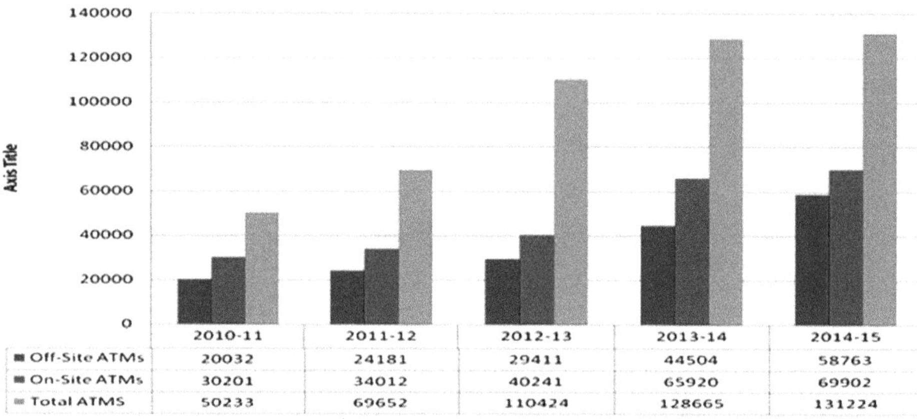

Figure 8. Trend of change in all scheduled commercial banks vis-à-vis RRBs in India during 2005-2016

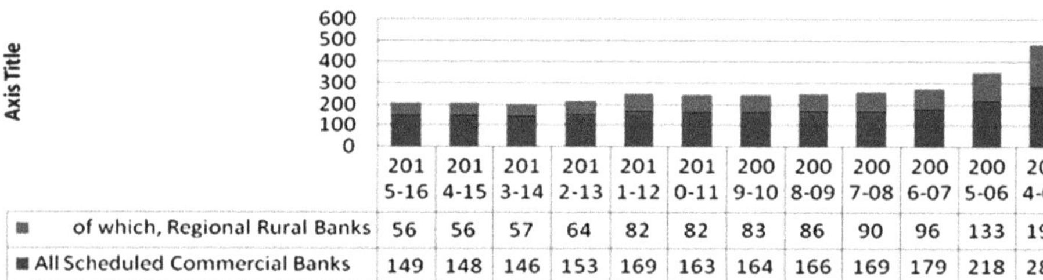

Banks was 284 out of which 196 were RRBs. In comparison to it, at present both of these numbers have been reduced to 149 and 56 respectively in year 2015-16.

Later on Figure 9 demonstrates the proportion of RRBs out of total Scheduled Commercial Banks during the period of year 2005-2016. It can be stated from it that in year 2004-05, RRBs proportion was 69.01% which came down to 37.5%.

Penetration of Reporting Offices of Banks in India During 2005-16

Interpretation: Figure 10 demonstrates number of reporting offices of banks in India during the period of year 2005 to year 2016. It can be stated from it that straight from year 2004-05 till year 2015-16, highest number of reporting offices were opened in rural areas followed by semi-urban areas whereas metropolitan areas were the last preference for the Scheduled Commercial Banks in opening reporting offices.

Figure 9. RRBs proportion (5)
(Source: Author's compilation)

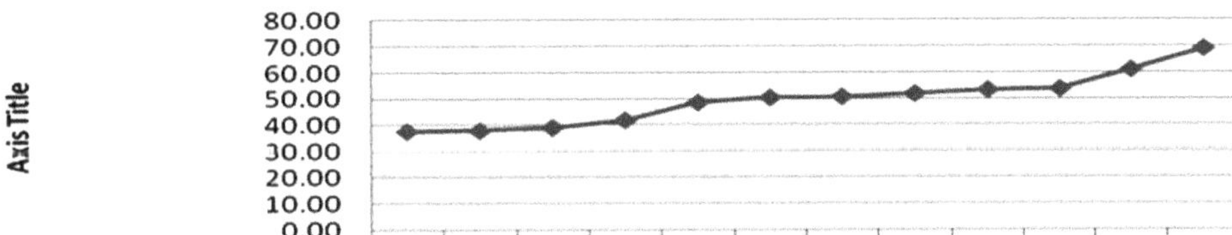

	2015-16	2014-15	2013-14	2012-13	2011-12	2010-11	2009-10	2008-09	2007-08	2006-07	2005-06	2004-05
RRBs Proportion (%)	37.5	37.8	39.0	41.8	48.5	50.3	50.6	51.8	53.2	53.6	61.0	69.0

Figure 10. Number of reporting offices of banks in India during 2005-2016

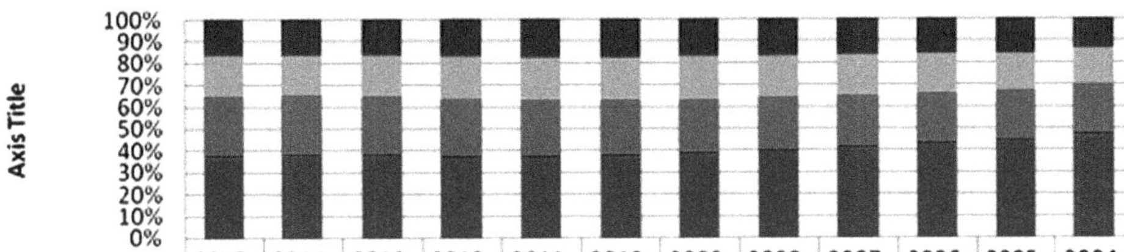

	2015-16	2014-15	2013-14	2012-13	2011-12	2010-11	2009-10	2008-09	2007-08	2006-07	2005-06	2004-05
Metropolitan	22187	20785	19472	18247	17078	15660	14697	13478	12438	11566	10971	9285
Urban	24794	23522	21783	20127	18541	17706	16653	15325	13944	12649	11864	11498
Semi-urban	35704	33523	30926	27822	25076	22419	20358	18764	17212	16035	15274	15375
Rural	49902	48033	43641	38451	35364	33325	32289	31489	30732	30461	30572	31958

Later on Figure 11 demonstrates % change in number of reporting offices of banks in India during the period of year 2005-16. It is revealed from the above graph that since year 2013-14, there is decreasing trend in number of reporting offices of banks across the country. Decrease in number of reporting offices may result in more pressure on individual reporting office with the increase in population and their access to such banking services.

Growth of Bank Deposits in All Population Groups in India During 2005-16

Interpretation: Figure 12 demonstrates the Annual Growth Rates (in %) of Aggregate Deposits (Area wise) during 2005-16. Decreasing trend in aggregate deposits is revealed from the above graph and it was pervasive in each area whether it is rural, semi-urban, urban or metropolitan.

Figure 11. Percent change in number of reporting offices of banks in India during 2005-16
(Source: Author's compilation)

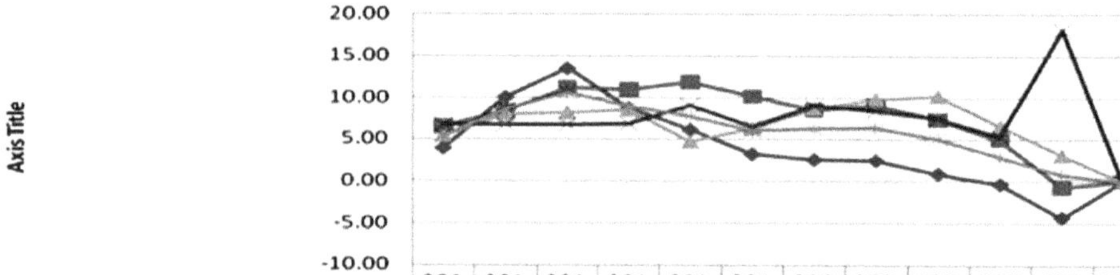

	2015-16	2014-15	2013-14	2012-13	2011-12	2010-11	2009-10	2008-09	2007-08	2006-07	2005-06	2004-05
% Change in Rural	3.89	10.06	13.50	8.73	6.12	3.21	2.54	2.46	0.89	-0.36	-4.34	0.00
% Change in Semi-urban	6.51	8.40	11.16	10.95	11.85	10.12	8.49	9.02	7.34	4.98	-0.66	0.00
% Change in Urban	5.41	7.98	8.23	8.55	4.72	6.32	8.67	9.90	10.24	6.62	3.18	0
% Change in Rural Metropolitan	6.75	6.74	6.71	6.85	9.05	6.55	9.04	8.36	7.54	5.42	18.16	0
% Change in Total No. of Reporting Offices	5.34	8.67	10.68	8.94	7.80	6.09	6.25	6.36	5.11	2.96	0.83	0.00

Figure 12. Annual growth rates (%) of aggregate deposits (area wise) during 2005-2016
(Source: Author's compilation)

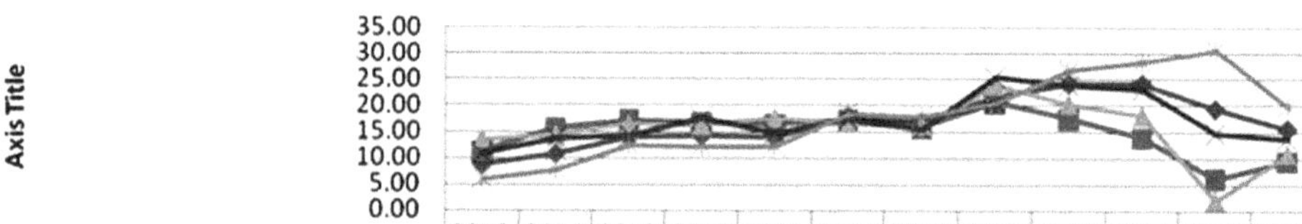

	2015-16	2014-15	2013-14	2012-13	2011-12	2010-11	2009-10	2008-09	2007-08	2006-07	2005-06	2004-05
All Scheduled Commercial Banks Total Aggregate Deposits	8.60	10.7	13.9	14.2	13.8	17.9	16.9	21.9	24.2	24.2	19.4	15.6
Rural	11.2	15.7	17.1	16.7	16.4	17.3	15.9	20.6	17.4	13.9	6.1	9.4
Semi-urban	13.5	14.4	16.5	16.3	17.6	16.7	16.2	23.9	20.3	18.1	2	10.8
Urban	10.8	13.7	14.3	17.5	14.7	17.4	15.4	25.4	23.8	23.1	14.7	13.7
Metropolitan	5.9	7.7	12.4	12.1	12.1	18.5	17.8	20.5	26.6	28.2	30.6	19.8

Growth of Bank Deposits in All Bank Groups in India During 2005-16

Interpretation: Figure 13 demonstrates the Annual Growth Rates (in %) of Aggregate Deposits (Bank GroupWise) during 2005-16. Decreasing trend in aggregate deposits is revealed from the above graph and it was pervasive in each area whether it is SBI group of banks, nationalized banks, foreign banks, RRBs or private sector banks.

Figure 13. Annual Growth Rates (%) of aggregate deposits (bank group wise) during 2005-16
(Source: Author's compilation)

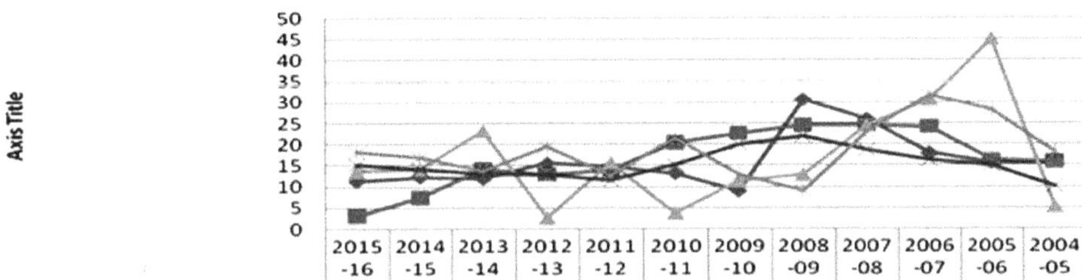

	2015-16	2014-15	2013-14	2012-13	2011-12	2010-11	2009-10	2008-09	2007-08	2006-07	2005-06	2004-05
SBI AND ITS ASSOCIATES	11.3	12.2	11.9	15.5	14.8	13.1	8.9	30.5	25.9	17.9	15.5	15.7
NATIONALISED BANKS	3.1	7.5	14.1	12.9	13.8	20.4	22.6	24.5	24.4	24.1	16.2	15.9
FOREIGN BANKS	13.5	14.1	23.1	2.6	15.5	3.7	11.3	12.7	24.4	30.5	44.9	5.2
REGIONAL RURAL BANKS	15.2	14.1	13	12.8	11.6	15.1	20	21.9	18.6	16.2	15	10
PRIVATE SECTOR BANKS	18.1	16.8	13.7	19.5	12.6	21.4	12.8	8.9	22.9	31.5	28.1	18.2

Nationalized banks have shown the highest downfall in this regard followed by foreign banks.

Trend of Banks Deposit in Commercial Banks of Northern Region During 2005-16

Interpretation: Figures 14 and 15 demonstrate Trend of Banks Deposit in commercial banks of Northern Region during 2005-16. It is very clear from the above graph that in Northern region, metropolitan areas have got the highest bank deposits followed

Figure 14. Trends of banks deposit in commercial banks of northern region during 2005-16

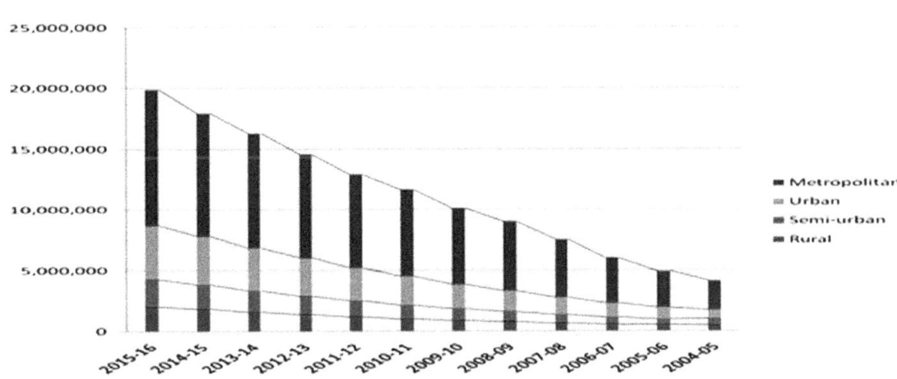

Figure 15. Percent change of banks deposit in commercial banks of northern region during 2005-2016
(Source: Author's Compilation from RBI data Bank)

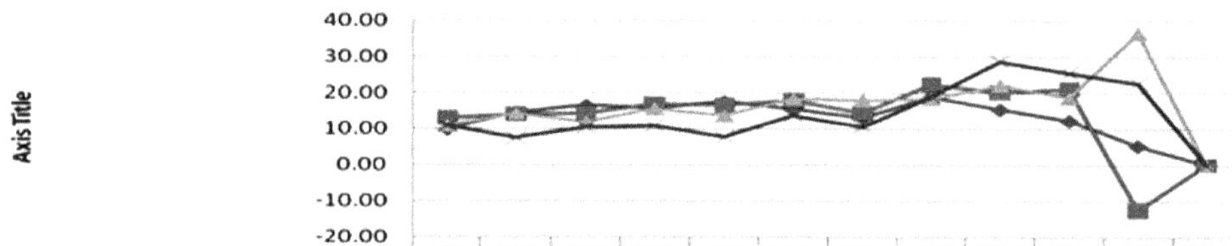

	2015-16	2014-15	2013-14	2012-13	2011-12	2010-11	2009-10	2008-09	2007-08	2006-07	2005-06	2004-05
% Change in Rural Deposits	9.71	14.59	16.49	15.67	17.54	15.44	13.18	18.94	15.53	12.40	5.33	0
% Change in Semi-urban Deposits	13.03	14.04	14.40	16.96	16.65	17.90	14.54	22.42	20.32	21.08	-12.4	0
% Change in Urban Deposits	10.84	14.13	11.98	15.66	13.61	18.40	17.93	18.56	22.11	18.70	36.63	0.00
% Change in Metropolitan Deposits	10.81	7.36	10.41	10.90	7.64	13.76	10.58	19.19	28.91	25.66	22.85	0

by urban areas. Rural areas exist with minimum bank deposits which is definitely a matter of concern since it may be taken as a challenge for financial inclusion.

Trend of Banks Deposit in Commercial Banks of Northern Eastern Region During 2005-16

Interpretation: Figures 17 and 18 demonstrate % change of Banks Deposit in commercial banks of Northern Eastern Region During 2005-16. It is very clear from the above graph that in Northern Eastern region, urban deposits had the highest variation whereas percentage change in rural deposits was found minimum.

Figure 16. Trend of banks deposit in commercial banks of northern eastern region during 2015

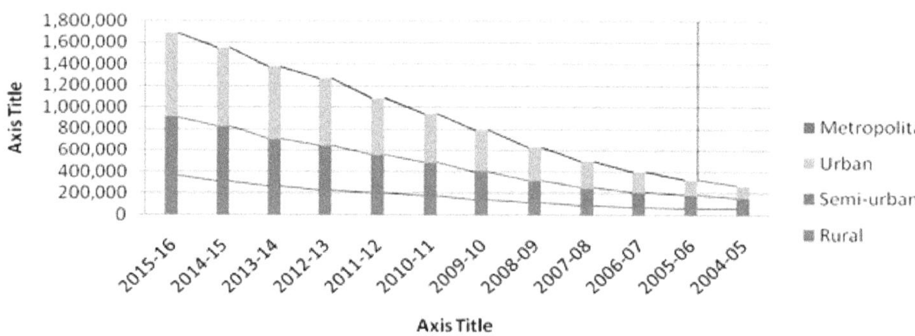

Figure 17. Percent change of bank deposit in commercial banks of Northern Eastern region during 2005-16
(Source: Author's Compilation from RBI data Bank)

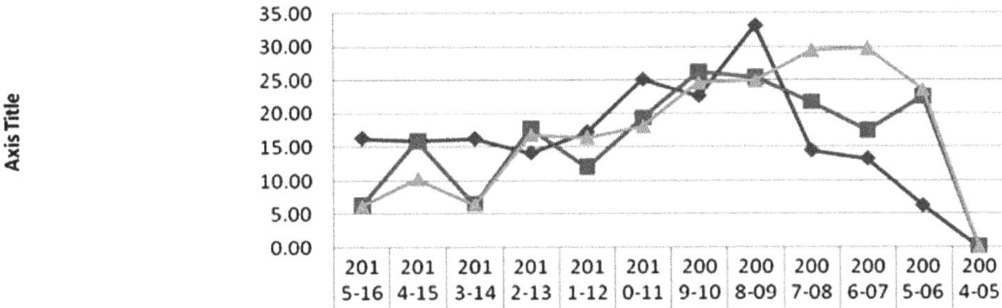

	2015-16	2014-15	2013-14	2012-13	2011-12	2010-11	2009-10	2008-09	2007-08	2006-07	2005-06	2004-05
% Change in Rural Deposits	16.32	15.98	16.23	14.13	17.23	25.10	22.59	33.11	14.43	13.21	6.21	0
% Change in Semi-urban Deposits	6.29	15.84	6.50	17.68	11.97	19.29	26.17	25.33	21.60	17.38	22.49	0
% Change in Urban Deposits	6.23	10.30	6.47	16.93	16.47	18.11	24.62	24.92	29.42	29.73	23.54	0.00

Figure 18. Trend of banks deposit in commercial banks of eastern region during 2005-16

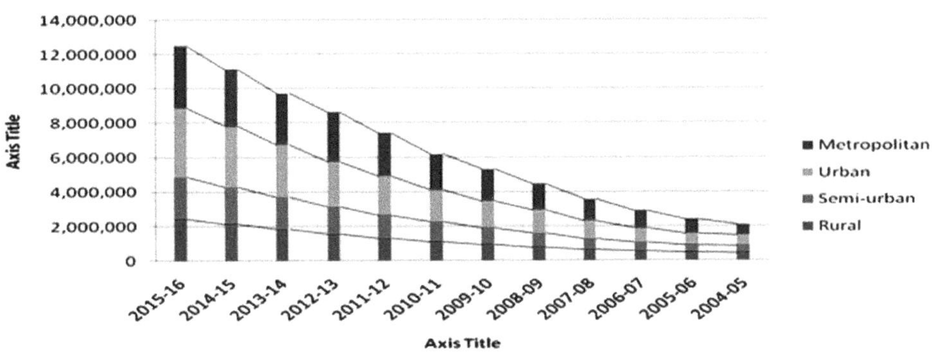

Trend of Banks Deposit in Commercial Banks of Eastern Region During 2005-16

Interpretation: Figure 18 demonstrates trend of Banks Deposit in commercial banks of Eastern Region during 2005-16. It is very clear from the above graph that in Eastern region, urban areas received highest deposits followed by metropolitan areas whereas bank deposits in rural areas are still a concern.

Later on Figure 19 demonstrates % change of Banks Deposit in commercial banks of Eastern Region During 2005-16. It is very clear from the above graph that

Figure 19. Percent change of banks deposit in commercial banks of eastern region during 2005-16
(Source: Author'sCompilation from RBI data Bank)

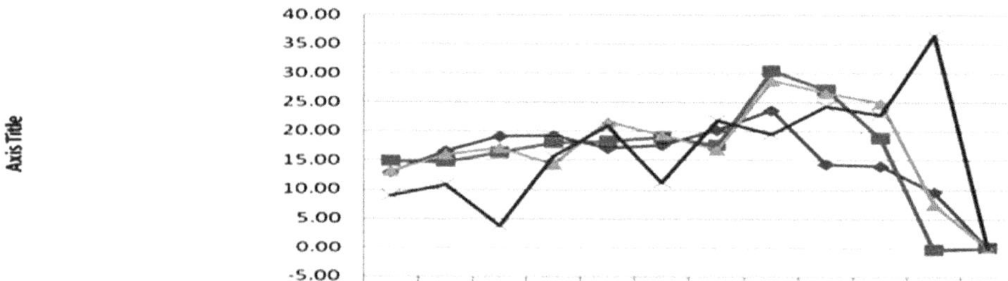

	2015-16	2014-15	2013-14	2012-13	2011-12	2010-11	2009-10	2008-09	2007-08	2006-07	2005-06	2004-05
% Change in Rural Deposits	12.8	16.5	19.0	19.2	17.0	17.6	20.2	23.6	14.3	14.0	9.55	0
% Change in Semi-urban Deposits	14.8	14.7	16.3	18.0	18.2	18.9	17.6	30.4	27.1	18.7	-0.3	0
% Change in Urban Deposits	13.1	15.9	17.0	14.3	21.5	19.3	16.8	28.7	26.6	24.8	7.38	0.00
% Change in Metropolitan Deposits	8.92	10.8	3.76	15.7	20.8	11.2	21.8	19.4	24.2	22.8	36.5	0

in Eastern region, metropolitan deposits had the highest variation whereas variance was found everywhere for the bank deposits.

Trend of Banks Deposit in Commercial Banks of Central Region During 2005-16

Interpretation: Figure 20 demonstrates Trend of Banks Deposit in commercial banks of Central region during 2005-16. It is clear from the above graph that urban areas have got the maximum bank deposits in central region whereas rural areas are now

Figure 20. Trend of Banks Deposit in Commercial Banks of Central Region During 2005-16

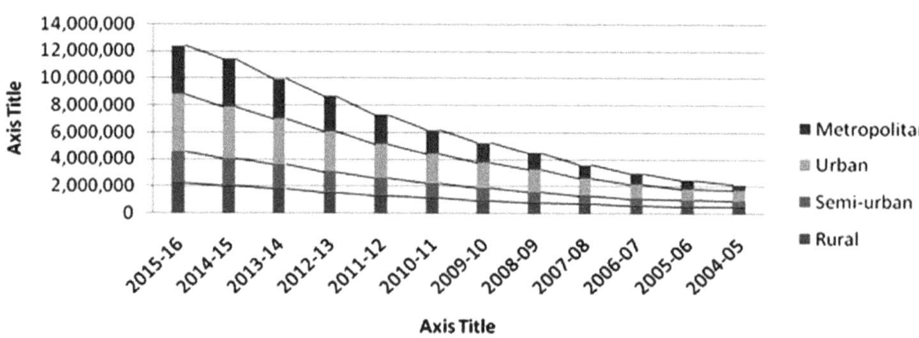

showing some corrections in this region however they are still receiving less bank deposits in comparison to other areas.

Later on Figure 21 demonstrates % change of Banks Deposit in commercial banks of central Region during 2005-16. It is very clear from the above graph that in central region, metropolitan deposits had the highest variation whereas variance was found everywhere for the bank deposits.

Trend of Banks Deposit in Commercial Banks of Western Region During 2005-16

Interpretation: Figure 22 demonstrates Trend of Banks Deposit in commercial banks of western region during 2005-16. It is clear from the above graph that metropolitan areas have got the maximum bank deposits in western region whereas rural areas were at the worst outcomes.

Later on Figure 23 demonstrates % change of Banks Deposit in commercial banks of western Region during 2005-16. It is very clear from the above graph that in Western region, urban deposits had the highest variation followed by rural deposits whereas variance was found everywhere for the bank deposits.

Trend of Banks Deposit in Commercial Banks of Southern Region During 2005-16

Interpretation: Figure 24 demonstrates Trend of Banks Deposit in commercial banks of Southern region during 2005-16. It is clear from the above graph that metropolitan areas have got the maximum bank deposits in southern region whereas urban areas

Figure 21. Percent change of banks deposit in commercial banks of central region during 2005-16
(Source: Author's Compilation from RBI data Bank)

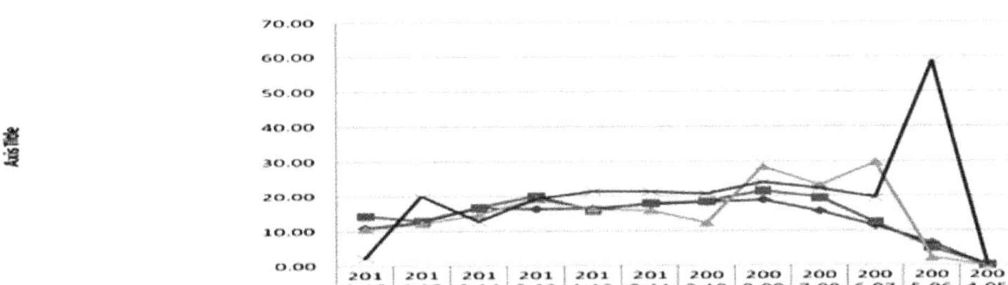

	2015-16	2014-15	2013-14	2012-13	2011-12	2010-11	2009-10	2008-09	2007-08	2006-07	2005-06	2004-05
% Change in Rural Deposits	10.87	12.53	16.54	16.26	16.37	17.56	18.16	18.80	15.57	11.38	6.44	0
% Change in Semi-urban Deposits	14.34	12.78	16.63	20.01	15.90	17.89	18.37	21.57	19.49	12.31	5.03	0
% Change in Urban Deposits	10.55	12.05	14.62	19.11	16.21	15.89	12.25	28.40	23.06	29.62	2.15	0.00
% Change in Metropolitan Deposits	2.19	19.95	12.66	19.12	21.50	21.28	20.71	23.94	22.20	19.48	58.58	0

Figure 22. Trend of banks deposit in commercial banks of western region during 2005-16

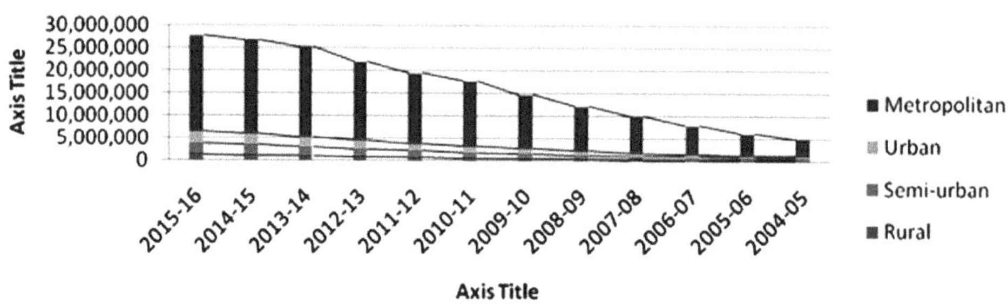

Figure 23. Percent change of banks deposit in commercial banks of western region during 2005-16
(Source: Author's Compilation from RBI data Bank)

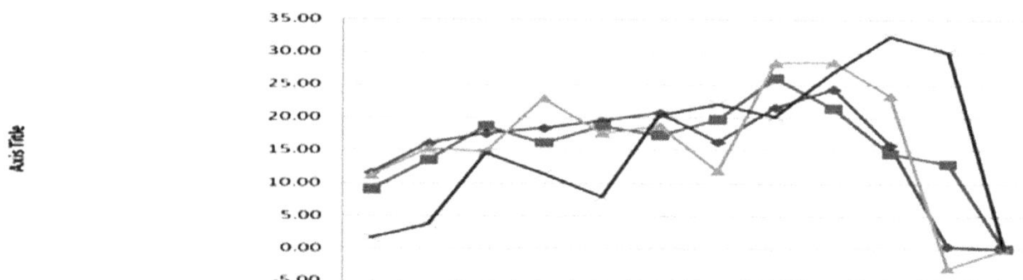

	2015-16	2014-15	2013-14	2012-13	2011-12	2010-11	2009-10	2008-09	2007-08	2006-07	2005-06	2004-05
% Change in Rural Deposits	11.53	16.03	17.52	18.36	19.45	20.69	16.25	21.55	24.32	15.84	0.39	0
% Change in Semi-urban Deposits	9.02	13.49	18.72	16.11	18.71	17.29	19.68	26.02	21.39	14.55	12.98	0
% Change in Urban Deposits	11.17	15.24	14.83	22.89	17.62	18.68	11.88	28.39	28.53	23.37	-2.89	0.00
% Change in Metropolitan Deposits	1.58	3.67	14.57	11.41	7.88	20.39	22.01	20.16	27.06	32.45	30.04	0

Figure 24. Trend of Banks Deposit in commercial banks of Southern Region during 2005-16

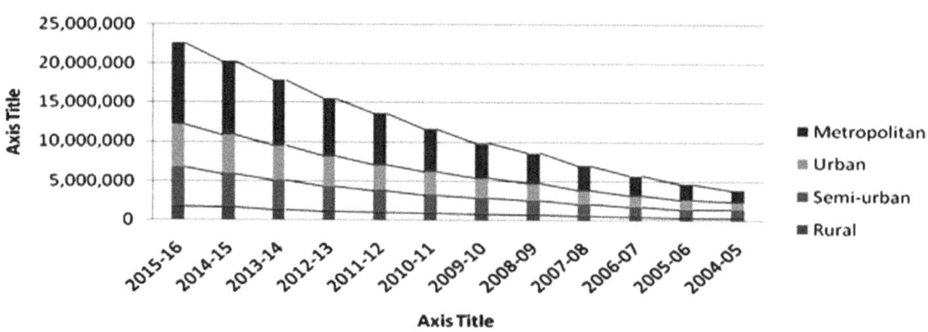

have shown increasing trend. Same as other regions, rural areas in these regions show poor show in receiving bank deposits.

Figure 25 demonstrates % change of Banks Deposit in commercial banks of southern region during 2005-16. It is very clear from the above graph that in Western region, metropolitan deposits had the highest variation followed by rural deposits and semi-urban deposits.

Trend of Bank Deposits in All Population Groups During FY 2005-16

Interpretation: Figure 26 demonstrates Trend of Banks Deposit in all population groups during 2005-16. It is clear from the above graph that western region has got the maximum bank deposits whereas North Eastern region was at the bottom with very poor performance in this regard.

Growth of Bank Credit in All Population Groups in India During 2005-16

Interpretation: Figure 27 demonstrates the Annual Growth Rates (in %) of Gross Bank Credit (Area wise) during 2005-16. Down size of gross bank credit has been realized after year 2012-13 in rural, semi-urban, urban and metropolitan areas. However metropolitan areas have shown the worst result in this regard.

Figure 25. Percent change of banks deposit in commercial banks of Southern Region during 2005-16
(Source: Author's Compilation from RBI data Bank)

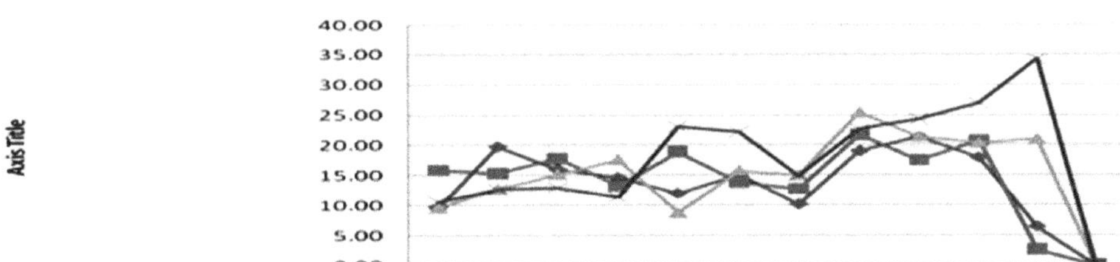

	2015-16	2014-15	2013-14	2012-13	2011-12	2010-11	2009-10	2008-09	2007-08	2006-07	2005-06	2004-05
% Change in Rural Deposits	9.60	19.7	15.9	14.6	11.9	15.1	10.1	18.9	21.3	17.9	6.38	0
% Change in Semi-urban Deposits	15.8	15.3	17.7	13.2	18.8	13.8	12.7	21.7	17.4	20.7	2.58	0
% Change in Urban Deposits	9.61	12.7	15.1	17.6	8.74	15.8	15.0	25.4	21.4	20.4	20.9	0.00
% Change in Metropolitan Deposits	10.6	12.6	12.9	11.3	23.0	22.2	14.8	22.6	24.2	26.8	34.2	0

Figure 26. Trend of Bank Deposits in All Population Groups during FY 2005-16
(Source: Author's Compilation from RBI data Bank)

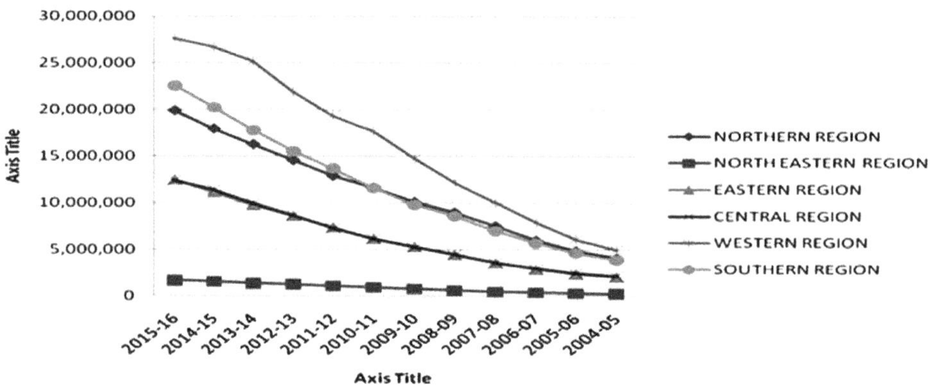

Figure 27. Growth of Bank Credit in all Population Groups in India During 2005-16
(Source: Author's Compilation from RBI data Bank)

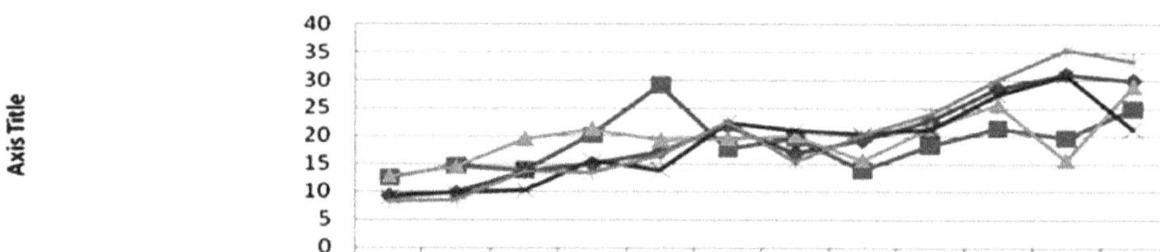

	2015-16	2014-15	2013-14	2012-13	2011-12	2010-11	2009-10	2008-09	2007-08	2006-07	2005-06	2004-05
All Scheduled Commercial Gross Bank Credit	9.3	9.8	13.8	15.1	17.3	21.9	17.1	19.3	22.8	28.5	31.1	30
Rural	12.6	14.7	14	20.2	29.1	17.7	19.7	14	18.3	21.5	19.7	24.9
Semi-urban	12.8	14.5	19.5	21.3	19.3	19.6	20.1	15.7	21.5	25.6	15.7	28.9
Urban	9.1	9.8	10.3	15.6	14	22.5	21.1	20.4	21.3	27.4	30.9	21.2
Metropolitan	8.3	8.5	13.7	13.5	16.6	22.5	15.4	20.2	23.9	30.1	35.5	33.4

Growth of Bank Credit in All Bank Groups in India During 2005-16

Interpretation: Figure 28 demonstrates annual Growth Rates (in %) of Gross Bank Credit (Bank Group wise) during 2005-16. Down size of gross bank credit has been realized after year 2012-13 for each bank group. Nationalized banks have shown a steep downward slope; however private sector banks have shown somewhat recovery from year 2014-15 in this regard.

Figure 28. Annual growth rates (%) of gross Bank Credit (Bank group wise) in India During 2005-16
(Source: Author's Compilation from RBI data Bank)

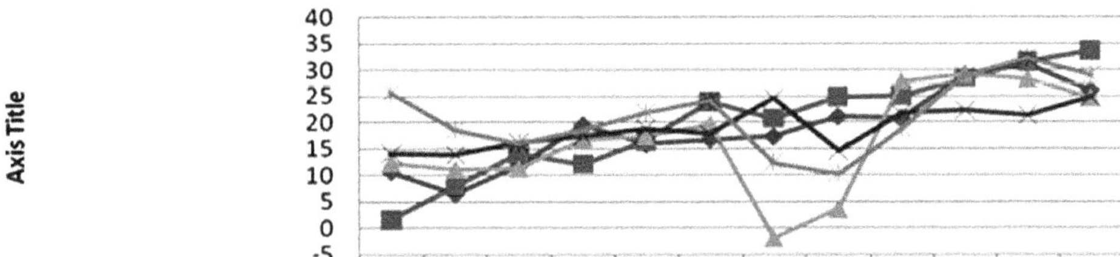

	2015-16	2014-15	2013-14	2012-13	2011-12	2010-11	2009-10	2008-09	2007-08	2006-07	2005-06	2004-05
SBI AND ITS ASSOCIATES	10.6	6.3	11.7	19.4	15.8	16.7	17.2	21	20.7	28.9	31.1	26
NATIONALISED BANKS	1.4	7.8	13.9	12	16.4	23.8	20.6	24.7	25	28.3	31.5	33.6
FOREIGN BANKS	12.3	11	11.3	16.6	17.3	19.5	-2	3.5	27.8	29.2	28.2	24.6
REGIONAL RURAL BANKS	14.2	13.9	16.3	17.3	18.7	17.7	24.4	14.6	21.6	22.1	21.2	24.7
PRIVATE SECTOR BANKS	25.7	18.6	16.1	18.5	21.8	24.2	12.4	10.2	18.8	29	32.3	29

Trend of Credit-Deposit Ratio (In Percent) During FY-2005-16

Interpretation: Figure 29 demonstrates trend of Credit-deposit Ratio (Percent) during FY-2005-16. Increasing trend is revealed from the above graph as far as credit-deposit ratio is concerned. In year 2015-16, the credit-deposit ratio for the banking sector as a whole is 77.9 percent. In the case of Indian banks, a credit-deposit ratio of over 70 percent designates burden on resources as they have to set separate funds to keep a cash reserve ratio of 4.5 percent and a statutory liquidity ratio of 23 percent.

Figure 29. Trend of credit-deposit ratio (%) during FY-2005-2016
(Source: Author's Compilation from RBI data Bank)

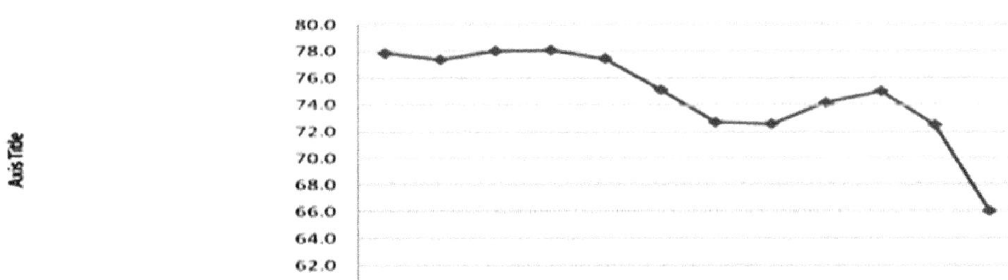

	2015-16	2014-15	2013-14	2012-13	2011-12	2010-11	2009-10	2008-09	2007-08	2006-07	2005-06	2004-05
Credit-deposit Ratio (Per Cent)	77.9	77.4	78.0	78.1	77.5	75.1	72.7	72.6	74.2	75.0	72.5	66.0

Trend of Average Monetary Aggregates During FY-2005-16

Interpretation: Figure 30 demonstrates Average Monetary Aggregates. It is revealed that Time Deposits, Demand Deposits, Currency with public and bank credit to commercial sector all have increasing trend. Time deposits stood at top while demand deposits stood at last position out of these. It is interesting to note here that bank credit to commercial sector is also growing at a good pace which shows a growing path for the economy.

Position of Number of Self Help Groups Financed by Banks During the Year During FY-2005-16

Interpretation: From Figure 31, it is revealed that SHGs were financed by banks at an increasing trend from year 2005-06 to year 2009-10 but for next two consecutive years downward trend was realized. However, this situation got turn around and once again it has got increasing trend which was on till year 2015-16. This shows a great support to SHGs by Banking Industry to run their operations.

Figure 32 demonstrates percentage change in the number of SHGs financed by Banks during the period of 2005-16. It can be clearly stated from the above graph that for continuous three years 2009-10, 2010-11 and year 2011-12 there was a negative percentage change in financing the SHGs by banks however the situation changed afterwards and for next three consecutive years, the trend was found positive in this regard. In year 2015-16 it was positive though it was dipped down to 12.67%.

Figure 30. Average monetary aggregates during FY-2005-16
(Source: Author's Compilation from RBI data Bank)

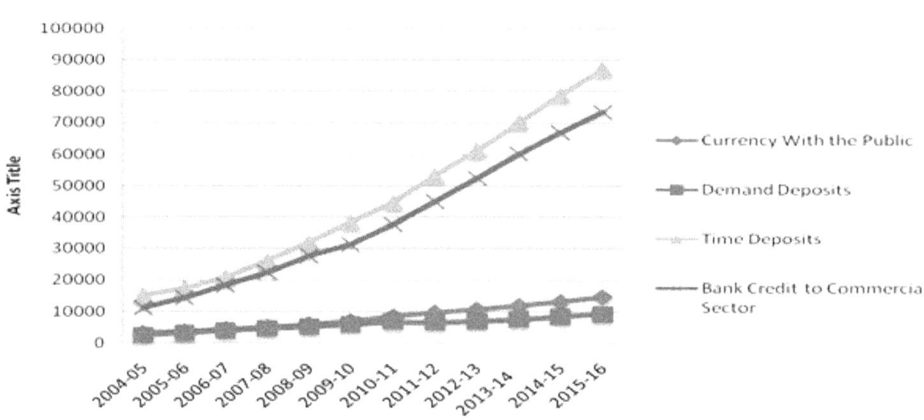

Figure 31. Number of SHGs financed by banks during the year

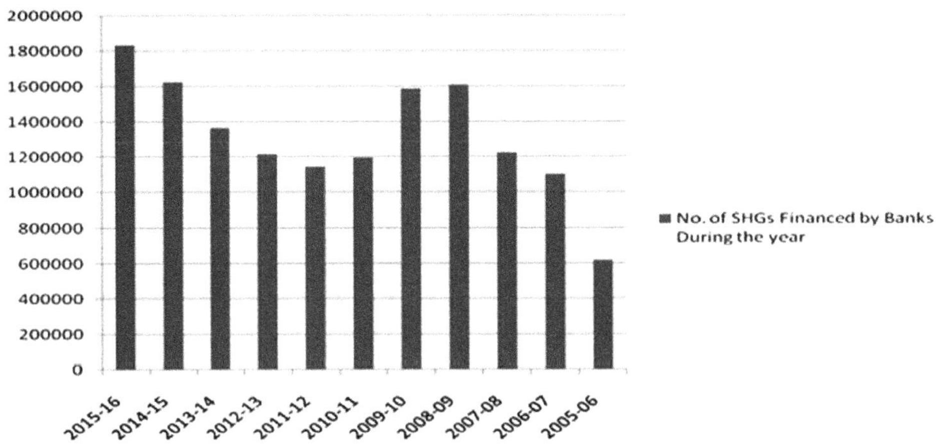

Figure 32. Percent change in number of SHGs financed by banks during the years
(Source: Author's Compilation from RBI data Bank)

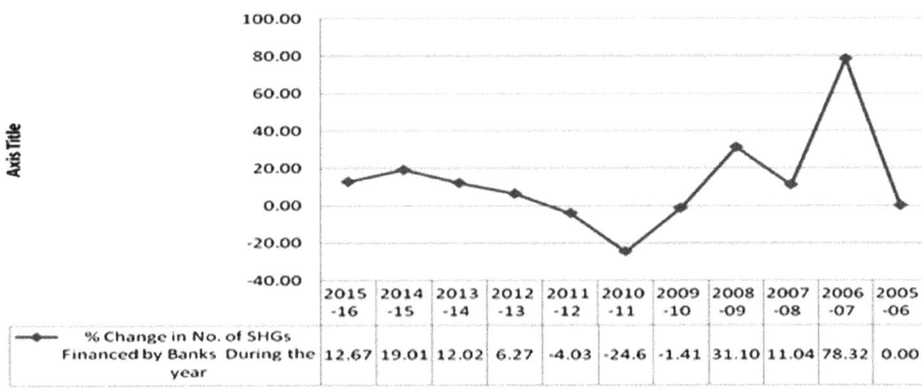

Bank Loan to Self Help Groups (SHGs) During the FY-2005-16

Interpretation: Figure 33 demonstrates the amount of Bank Loan distributed to SHGs during period 2005-16. It is revealed from the above graph that Banks were found positive in their approach while providing loan to SHGs during the period 2005-16. However, variations have been realized in the dispersal of loans to SHGs.

Figure 33. Bank loan to SHGs (Rupees Billion) during FY-2005-16
(Source: Author's Compilation from RBI data Bank)

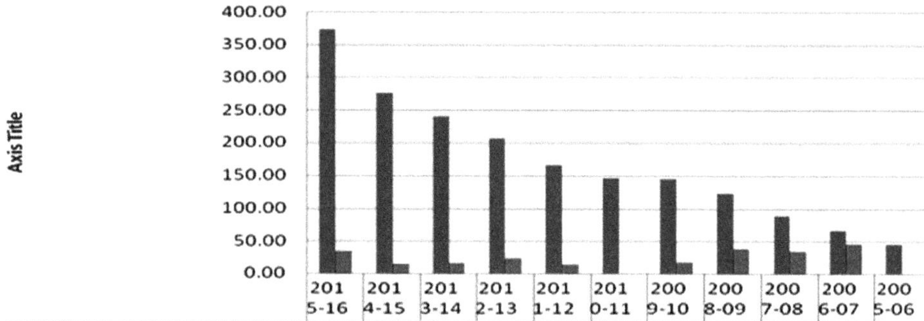

	2015-16	2014-15	2013-14	2012-13	2011-12	2010-11	2009-10	2008-09	2007-08	2006-07	2005-06
Bank Loan During the year	372.8	275.8	240.1	205.8	165.3	145.4	144.5	122.5	88.49	65.70	44.99
% Change Bank Loan During the year	35.19	14.84	16.67	24.49	13.66	0.66	17.95	38.48	34.69	46.03	0.00

Refinance to Self Help Groups (SHGs) by Banks During FY-2005-16

Interpretation: Figure 34 demonstrates the status of refinance to SHGs during FY-2005-16. Year 2011-12 and year 2013-14 were the two years where refinance to the SHGs was found with diminishing rate in comparison to their preceding years otherwise for the rest period of time refinance to SHGs maintained increasing trend. Year 2008-09 was the time when highest percentage change in refinance to SHGs was observed whereas year 2011-12 and year 2013-14 were the years which recorded negative percentage change in refinancing the SHGs.

Growth of Banking by Pradhan Mantri Jan Dhan Yojana in Various States of India

Interpretation: Table 4 demonstrates the current status of Pradhan Mantri Jan - Dhan Yojana. It is revealed from the above chart that contribution of public sector banks in the success of PMJDY is incomparable. Private Banks need to gear start in opening PMJDY accounts. Importantly public-sector banks have tried their level best to balance between urban and rural areas where more accounts under this scheme have been opened in rural or semi-urban areas. This implies that mission of public sector banks along with government efforts is to reach the unbanked and under-served population so as to objectives of financial inclusion and equitable growth can be achieved.

Figure 34. Refinance to SHGs (Rupees Billion) during FY-2005-16
(Source: Author's Compilation from RBI data Bank)

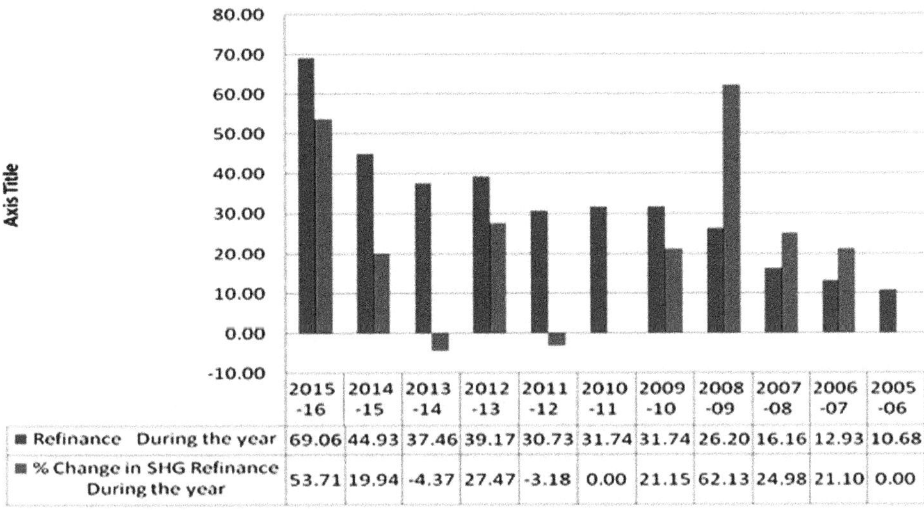

Table 4. Progress of Pradhan Mantri Jan Dhan Yojana (all figures in crore) As i 12/7/2017

Bank Category	Total Beneficiaries	Beneficiaries at Rural/ Semi-Urban Centre Bank Branches	Beneficiaries at Urban/ Metro Centre Bank Branches	No. of RuPay Cards Issued to Beneficiaries	Balance in Beneficiary Accounts
Public Sector Bank	23.42	12.80	10.62	18.07	51210.21
Regional Rural Bank	4.73	4.02	0.71	3.56	11646.20
Private Banks	0.94	0.57	0.37	0.87	2066.03
Total	29.09	17.39	11.70	22.50	64922.44

(All figures in crore)
As on 12/07/2017

Statewise Account Opening Progress of PMJDY as on 12.07.2017

Interpretation: Figure 35 demonstrates state wise account opening Report of PMJDY as on July,2017. It is revealed from the above graph that more beneficiaries were found under PMJDY at bank branches in rural/semi-urban areas in majority of the states except Delhi, Chandigarh and Mizoram were the states where beneficiaries were found under PMJDY at bank branches in Urban/Metro areas.

Figure 35. Statewise account opening report of PMJDY on 12.07.2017
(Source: Author's Compilation PMJDY data Bank)

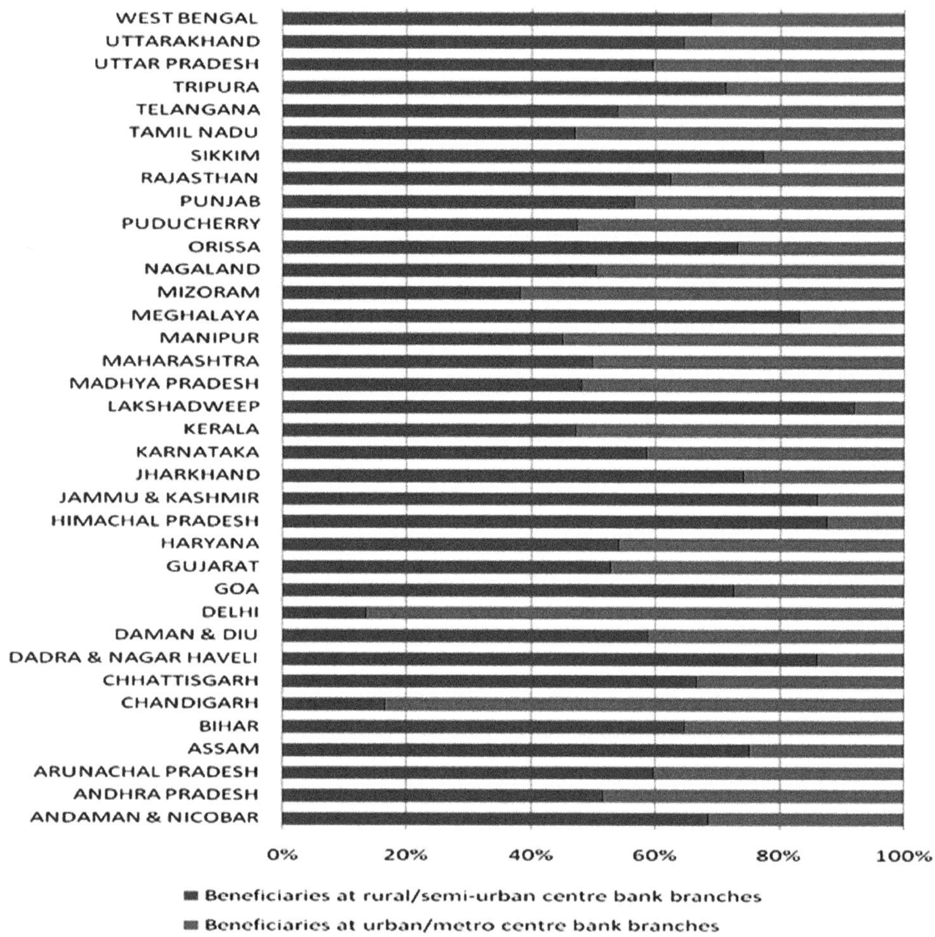

Table 5 revealed the status of top 10 states as far as accounts opened under PMJDY in India. The statistics stated that Uttar Pradesh is the state where maximum number of PMJDY accounts was opened followed by Bihar, West Bangal, Madhya Pradesh and Maharashtra. It is also evident from the table that accept Madhya Pradesh and Maharashtra all top three states have focused more in their rural or semi urban areas for such Bank accounts. For further investigation coefficient of correlation was calculated between number of PMJDY accounts (Rural, Urban & total) and Average balance per PMJDY for all the states and union territories of India. Researcher found high degree of positive correlation in this regard. Earlier researches till year 2014

Table 5. Top ten states in PMJDY

Row Labels	Sum of Beneficiaries at Rural/Semi-Urban Centre Bank Branches	Sum of Beneficiaries at Urban/Metro Centre Bank Branches	Sum of Total Beneficiaries	Rank In Total
ASSAM	9095005	2999918	12094923	8
BIHAR	19603768	10702191	30305959	2
CHHATTISGARH	8358428	4166412	12524840	7
GUJARAT	5887021	5292557	11179578	10
MADHYA PRADESH	12374510	13344473	25718983	4
MAHARASHTRA	10066527	10158285	20224812	5
ORISSA	8509434	3112761	11622195	9
RAJASTHAN	12273802	7373459	19647261	6
UTTAR PRADESH	26823003	18312654	45135657	1
WEST BENGAL	19289246	8649505	27938751	3
Grand Total	**132280744**	**84112215**	**216392959**	

Table 6. Results of correlation analysis

	Beneficiaries at Rural/ Semi-Urban Centre Bank Branches	Beneficiaries at Urban/ Metro Centre Bank Branches	Total Beneficiaries	Balance in Beneficiary Accounts (in Crore)	No. of RuPay Cards Issued to Beneficiaries
Beneficiaries at rural/semi-urban centre bank branches	1				
Beneficiaries at urban/metro centre bank branches	0.9207277	1			
Total Beneficiaries	0.987316027	0.971001132	1		
Balance in beneficiary accounts (in crore)	0.956934911	0.877388337	0.943296539	1	
No. of RuPay cards issued to beneficiaries	0.984343287	0.967801326	0.996876693	0.953377481	1

demonstrated negative correlation between the above mentioned variables. At present due to post effect of Demonetization and digitalization of banking and economy, situation got reversed. Positive correlation results imply that as the number of PMJDY accounts increased the balance in these accounts has also increased. This situation stimulates a transformation in the banking behavior of rural and urban beneficiaries.

Growth of Banking by Other Recent Initiatives

RuPay Card Distribution Statistics by Banks

Interpretation: Figure 36 reveals the top five Bank RuPay Card Statistics in India as on July 2017. There is a huge potential for cards penetration in India. In the light of this situation, RuPay Cards has addressed the needs of Indian consumers, merchants and banks very effectively since it is committed towards development of customized product and service offerings in India. National Payments Corporation of India (NPCI) initiated the launch of RuPay card in India. It was done with the intention of integration of payment systems in the country. One can access them in the 1.45 lakh ATMs and 8.75 lakh POS terminals across the country. It is also accepted on 10,000 e-commerce websites. All major public sector banks have started issuing these cards and SBI, BOI, PNB, Central bank of India and Canara Bank were found as top five banks in this regard as on July 2017. However, the number of active cards is still a challenge for the banking industry in India.

Penetration of IMPS and M-Wallet in India During FY 2012-16

Interpretation: Figure 37 shows the status of IMPS and m-Wallet penetration in India for the period 2012-2016. Growing trend of IMPS and m-Wallet usage has been revealed from the above graph. It implies that the level of modern banking literacy and awareness has been improved at a great extent with the introduction of digital economy and imitative of Govt. and RBI.

Figure 36. Statistics of RuPay Card
(Source: Author's Compilation PMJDY data Bank)

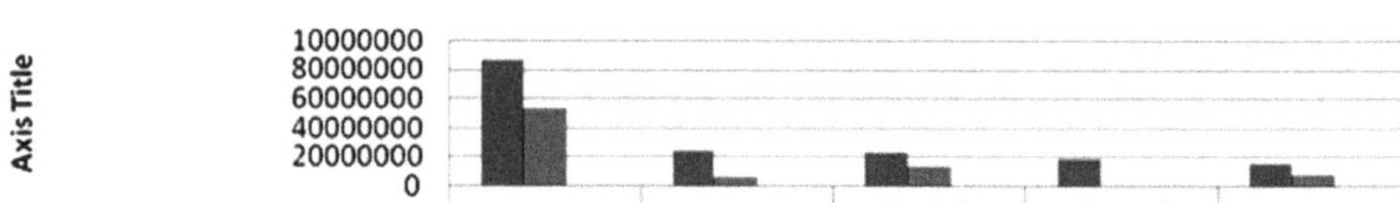

	State Bank Of India	Bank Of India	Punjab National Bank	Central Bank Of India	Canara Bank
Sum of Rupay Card Issued	86902688	24767019	24173701	19237825	15932831
Sum of Active Rupay Card	53561405	6425041	13544709	1539261	8497170
Sum of % of Rupay Card Active	61.63	25.94	56.03	8	53.33

Figure 37. Penetration of IMPS and m-Wallet in India during FY-2012-16
(Source: Author's Compilation from RBI data Bank)

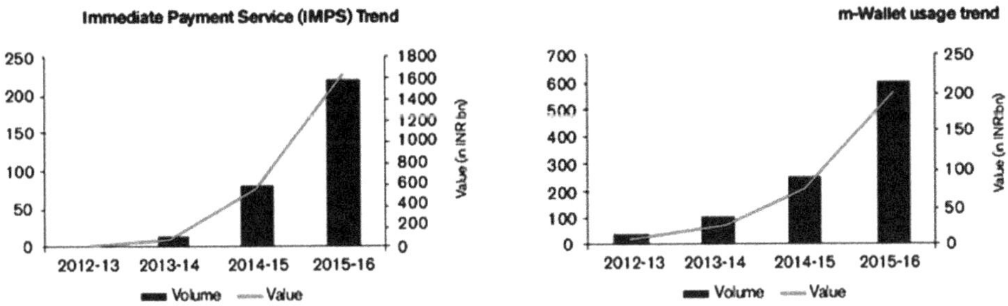

Penetration of Banking Correspondent in India

To better utilize the services of intermediaries in order to provide banking services effectively, the RBI had adopted Business Correspondents (BCs) model which permits banks to use business facilitators. This model allows banking operations by the branches of all domestic Scheduled Commercial Banks (SCBs) in rural areas with an objective to provide banking and finance facility at the doorstep of the rural population. Business Correspondent is an authorized center to offer services such as cash transactions where the bank does not have a branch. Though statistics or RBI reveals that Banking penetration has increased with a great pace since few years and there is no doubt in quoting that business correspondent have played a vital role in this direction. The growth in the numbers of business correspondent with CAGR is presented as below for the period 2010-16.

Interpretation: It can be easily observed from Figure 38 and data that in last six years' establishment of business correspondent centers has seen a tremendous growth with a 61% of CAGR. Banks have deployed 3.57 lakh business correspondents

Figure 38. Number of business correspondent

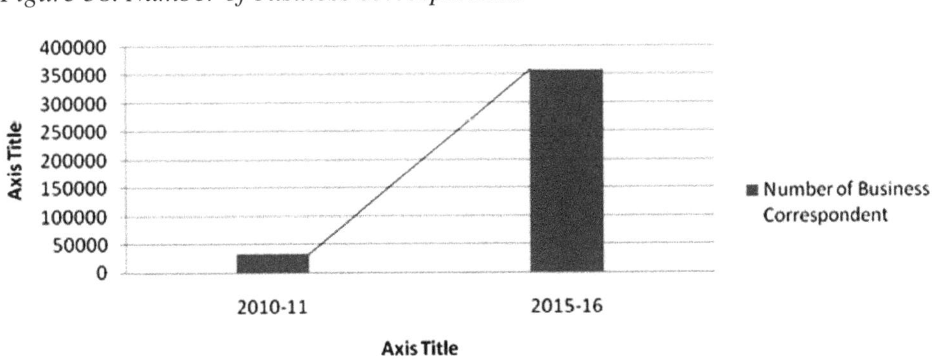

Table 7. Number of business correspondents and percent growth/CAGR

	Number of Business Correspondent	% Growth	CAGR
2010-11	33042	-	-
2015-16	357856	983.03	61%

(Source: Author's Compilation from RBI data Bank)

(BCs) across the country as of March 31, 2016 so that the rural population can access banking services at their doorsteps. Major contribution of such centers can be easily realized in financial inclusion in India.

Trend of Financial Inclusion in India Based on CRISIL Financial Inclusion Index (CRISIL-Inclusix)

CRISIL Financial Inclusion index (Inclusix) measures the extent of financial inclusion at a geographical level, starting from the district level in India. Following is the Trend of overall financial inclusion in India and region wise growth of financial inclusion (see Figure 39).

Interpretation: Figure 40 demonstrates Trend of financial inclusion index (CRISIL-Inclusix) in India for the period 2009- 2013 which shows the continued progress of banking services along the three dimensions of financial inclusion i.e. penetration of Bank branches, Total deposits and total credit by banks across India. This index shows increasing trend with 41.52% of growth since year 2009. It was found that southern region was at the top in achieving financial inclusion at a great extent followed by western region whereas north eastern part of the country has shown very less progress in this regard.

Figure 39. Trends in CRISIL-Inclusix score for India
(Source: Report published by CRISIL- Inclusix Report, Volume – III, June 2015)

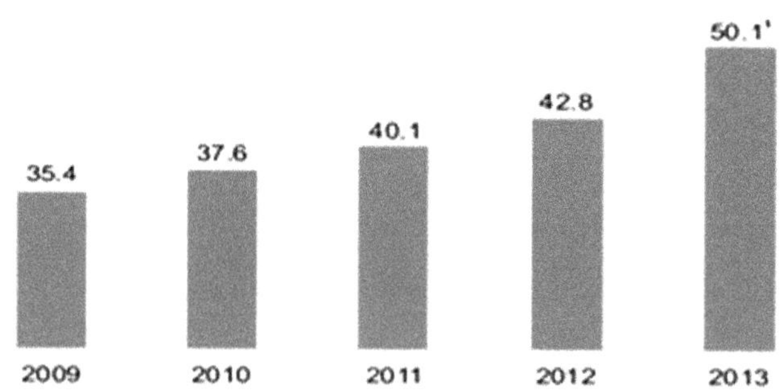

Figure 40. Region-wise CRISIL Inclusix scores for fiscal 2013
(Source: Report published by CRISIL- Inclusix Report, Volume – III, June 2015)

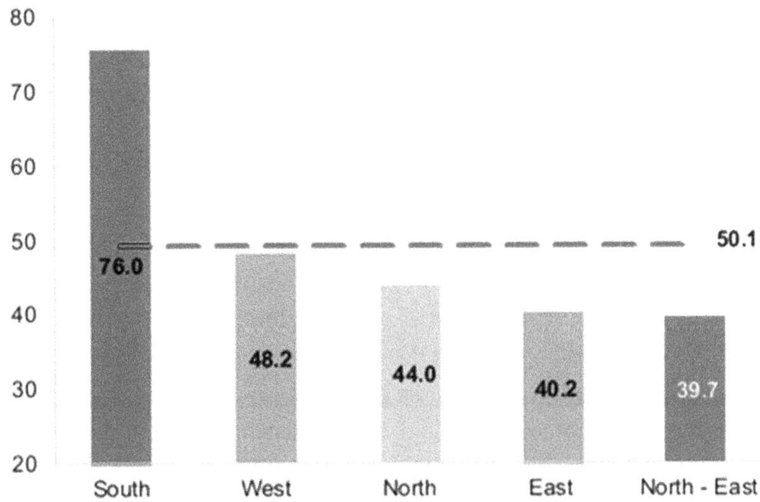

CONCLUSION

It is evident from the above discussion and statistics that banking industry is definitely a backbone for Indian economy. As a matter of fact is realized that Financial Inclusion has become an important priority of the Government especially after year 2005. To achieve the objective of Financial Inclusion in order to extend financial services to the large unbanked and underserved population of the country, strong network of banks has a vital role to play in this regard. As far as position of households availing banking services is concerned, it can be easily recognized that there were only 30.1% rural population had access to the banking as stated in the statistics of year 2001 census. In comparison to this situation 54.4% of the rural population have access to banking as per the census year 2011 which is almost 25% more access to the banking services at present. Same growth pattern has been realized for the urban population as well where researcher identified 67.8% access in year 2011 in comparison to 49.5% in year 2001 census. In total, access to the banking services in India has increased to 58.7% banking access at present in comparison to 35.5% as census year 2001.

India has seen this much awaited growth in banking access at a great pace from year 2011 and many of the wonderful initiatives like expansion of Banking Business Correspondents Agents (BCA), Swabhimaan Scheme, Direct Benefit Transfer (DBT) and Direct Benefit Transfer for LPG (DBTL), USSD Based Mobile Banking, Pradhan Mantri Jan-Dhan Yojana (PMJDY), RuPay Card by government of India and RBI have contributed towards this great success.

At the same time researcher also observed that Scheduled commercial Bank Branch and ATM network has got the expansion in real means after year 2011. Approx 38.46% growth has been identified in branch network expansion and ATM network has been elevated by 2.5 times in year 2015 in comparison to year 2011. Very importantly 29.18 crore beneficiaries have been recorded under PMJDY schemes so far with 64,776.62 cr balance in PMJDY accounts. As stated in the above sections, deposit and credit penetration across India have seen heights however since year 2013 this pace was observed a bit low. Through microfinance programmes and SHGBLP initiatives, services to small borrower from rural population have got the benefits of Indian banking. Researcher observed while analyzing the available statistics that India's per capita income has nearly doubled, with the last five years accounting for an 8 per cent GDP growth rate over the last ten years. The banking sector has also grown rapidly during the same period. The total deposits in banking industry have increased more than five times and outstanding credit in form of non-performing assets by over seven times in the last ten years.

At the same time, the nation is facing challenges in ensuring inclusive and equitable growth across the country. Financial literacy and low awareness and access to technology are again among big challenges in this sector. Less level of faith on digital transaction and weak cyber security is also a matter of concern. Data revealed that around 38% of the bank branches of scheduled commercial banks are in the rural areas and only 40% of the country's population has access to banking services. Henceforth it can be stated that there is an urgent need to fast-track the financial inclusion initiatives especially for the rural people with improved and advanced banking. Journey of financial inclusion on the wheels of Indian banking industry has still in search of the ultimate destination and it will take miles to achieve full financial inclusion.

REFERENCES

Agarwal, P. K., & Sinha, S. K. (2010). *Financial Performance of Microfinance Institutions of India. Delhi Business Review.*

Agarwal Amol. (2008). *The Need for Financial Inclusion with an Indian Perspective.* IDBI Gitlts Limited.

Agarwal Reena. (2007). *100% Finance Inclusion: A Challenging Task Ahead.* Indian Institute of Management Kozhikode.

Aghion, P., & Bolton, P. (1997). A theory of trickle-down growth and development. *The Review of Economic Studies, 64*(2), 151–172. doi:10.2307/2971707

Alimullah Miyan. (2011). Challenges of Financing Higher Education from Inclusion Perspectives. *International Conference on Innovation and Inclusion in Banking: Issues, Strategies and Options.* Kannur University.

Arunchalam, S. R. (2008). *Financial Inclusion, Considerations and Re commendations for UNDP.* United Nations Development Programme (UNDP).

Badajena, N., & Gundimeda, H. (2008). *Self Help Group Bank linkage model and financial inclusion in India.* Academic Press.

Banerjee, A. V., & Newman, A. F. (1993). Occupational choice and the process of development. *Journal of Political Economy, 101*(2), 274–298. doi:10.1086/261876

Bharati, D. B. (2016). A Comparative Study of Inclusive Growth: Economic Policy Reforms a Financial Inclusion in India. *We'Ken-International Journal of Basic and Applied Sciences, 1*(2), 39–44. doi:10.21904/weken/2016/v1/i2/98418

Bhatia, N., & Chattterjee, A. (2010). Financial Inclusion in the Slums of Mumbai. *Economic and Political Weekly, XLV*(42), 16.

Bhuvana, M., & Vasantha, S. (2016). Dimensions for measuring financial inclusion in the rural areas of Tamil Nadu. *Indian Journal of Science and Technology, 9*(32).

C. (n.d.). *CRISIL Inclusix Volume III.* Retrieved June 24, 2017, from https://www.scribd.com/document/321861143/CRISIL-Inclusix-Volume-III

Chakravarty, S., & Pal, R. (2010). *Measuring Financial Inclusion: An Axiomatic Approach.* Indra Gandhi Institute of Development Research.

Chatterjee Shankar. (2004). Networking: SGSY, Banks and SHGs: Initiative in Uttar Pradesh. *Kurukshetra, 51*(4), 27-29.

Chima, O. R. (2010). *The Democratisation of Finance? Financial Inclusion and Subprime in the UK and US*. University of Northumbria.

Clarke, G. R., Xu, L. C., & Zou, H. F. (2006). Finance and income inequality: What do the data tell us? *Southern Economic Journal*, *72*(3), 578–596. doi:10.2307/20111834

Conroy, J. (2008). *Financial Inclusion: A New Micro Finance Initiative for APEC*. The Foundation for Development Cooperation (FDC), Microfinance Workshop.

D. (2017, January 01). *Department of Financial Services | Ministry of Finance Government of India*. Retrieved June 17, 2017, from http://financialservices.gov.in

Gangadharan, K. (2012). *Financial inclusion and inclusive growth through banking lessons from India*. Reference Press.

IBEF. (2017, May 16). ibef.org/Ebook/IBEF. Retrieved from https://www.ibef.org/Ebook/IBEF-Dec-2016-Jan-2017.pdf)

Ibrahim Muhammad. (2010). *Sustainable Finance Inclusion*. Alliance for Financial Inclusion (AFI), Data Workshop Kualaumpur.

India Brand Equity Foundation. (2016, December). Financial Inclusion- Steering Growth and Empowerment. *India Now-. Business Economics (Cleveland, Ohio)*, *3*(4). https://www.ibef.org/Ebook/IBEF-Dec-2016-Jan-2017.pdf Retrieved July 11, 2017

Jalan, A. (2009). *Microfinance: does it affect rural poverty reduction? the case of two villages in southern India*. Academic Press.

Kessy, S. A., & Urio, F. M. (2010). *The Contribution of Microfinance Institutions to Poverty Reduction in Tanzania*. MkukinaNyota.

Kumar, B. P., & Philip, P. J. (2011). Financial Exclusion A Theoretical Approach. *International Conference on Innovation and Inclusion in Banking: Issues, Strategies and Options*. Kannur University.

Lathey, P. (2012). *Microfinance – As a Instrument for Poverty Reduction in Rural India*. New Delhi: Financial Inclusion and Poverty Alleviation in India, Kunal Books.

NABARD. (2017, May 16). *Status of micro finance in India*. Retrieved from https://www.nabard.org

P. (n.d.). *Pradhan Mantri Jan-Dhan Yojana | Department of Financial Services | Ministry of Finance*. Retrieved July 20, 2017, from https://pmjdy.gov.in

R. (n.d.). *Statistical Tables Relating to Banks in India*. Retrieved June 05, 2017, from https://rbi.org.in/Scripts/Statistics.aspx

Rangarajan, C. (2009). *Report of the Committee on Financial Inclusion*. New Delhi: Ministry of Finance, Government of India.

RBI. (2017, June 17). *Database on Indian Economy*. Retrieved from https://dbie.rbi.org.in/DBIE/dbie.rbi?site=home

Sarma, M. (2008). *Index of financial inclusion*. New Delhi: Indian Council for Research on International Economics Relations.

Subbarao. (2009). *Financial Inclusion: Challenges and Opportunities*. Remarks by Dr. D. Subbarao, Governor, Reserve Bank of India at the Bankers' Club in Kolkata.

Thorat, U. (2007). *Financial Inclusion-the Indian experience*. London, UK: Speech at HMT- DFID Financial Inclusion Conference.

Chapter 11
Leveraging Tax as a Tool for Financial Inclusion of MSMEs:
Micro, Small, and Medium Enterprises (MSMEs) and Financial Exclusion

Richa Sawhney
Richa Sawhney & Associates, India

ABSTRACT

Studies suggest that dealing with financial exclusion requires a multi-pronged strategy. Apart from the government policies and initiatives, tax policies have also been recognized as a potent tool that furthers the cause of financial inclusion, both directly and indirectly. As in case of other policies, a one-size-fits-all approach cannot be followed in tax policy as well, so one can see a broad spectrum of initiatives trying to tackle the different root causes of this problem. By using a carrot-and-stick approach, the tax policy is maneuvering the informal sector businesses towards the formal economy, where formal sources of finance and credit become a reality.

INTRODUCTION

MSMEs are the engine of growth and development of our country. They contribute significantly to output, export and employment generation in the economy. Their role is particularly important in providing employment to semi- skilled and unskilled workers. They act as ancillary units to the large industries and compliment them in the socio-economic growth of the country. As per the Annual Report 2016-17 of the Ministry of Micro, Small and Medium Enterprises (Annual Report), there are an estimated 512.99 lakh units in the country providing employment to around

DOI: 10.4018/978-1-5225-4035-9.ch011

1112.28 lakh persons. MSMEs contribute around 33% of manufacturing output and around 45% of the overall exports from India. They are hence, considered the best vehicle for inclusive growth, job creation and poverty alleviation.

The Committee on Medium-term Path on Financial Inclusion (CMPFI), which was set up by the Reserve Bank of India (RBI) to devise a measurable and monitorable action plan for financial inclusion of both households and small businesses, had set the vision of financial inclusion for MSMEs which includes increasing the access of MSMEs to formal finance with a greater reliance on technology that can cut costs and improve service delivery. In the process it had identified several challenges faced by the MSMEs. The key ones being:

1. MSMEs are often credit-starved, access to timely credit at a reasonable cost is one of the most difficult challenges being faced by this sector. Banks often do not have the requisite skills and time to assess their credit-worthiness.
2. MSMEs are often less inclined to access bank finance owing to onerous and complicated documentation procedures.
3. There is also voluntary exclusion, with some MSMEs not forthcoming with their detailed financing requirements owing to fear of tax complications and harassment by bureaucracy.
4. Technology does not appear to have been harnessed to the fullest extent in order to further the cause of financial inclusion.
5. In the absence of funding from mainstream financial institutions, most MSMEs have to rely on the informal sources and internal accruals. Though the informal sector may issue loans quickly and with little or no collateral, the issue is that such loans often carry high rates of interest. Internal accruals may often not be sufficient to cater to the fund requirements of the MSME.

The Annual Report points out that 87% of MSMEs are proprietorship concerns as against 0.91% set up as partnerships. Only 0.42% operates as private companies, 0.51% as self help groups and 0.22% as private co-operatives. Due to their inherent characteristics, ownership structures such as companies, partnerships and co-operatives provide greater access to financial resources as compared to operating as a proprietorship. Thus, operating as a proprietorship is also a reason of financial ill health.

Studies suggest that dealing with financial exclusion requires a multi pronged strategy. Apart from the other government policies and initiatives, tax policy has also been recognised as a potent tool which furthers the cause of financial inclusion; both directly and indirectly. As in case of other policies, "a one size fits all" approach cannot be followed in tax policy as well, so one can see a broad spectrum of initiatives trying to tackle the different root causes of this problem.

TOOL 1: INDIRECT TAX

Goods and Services Tax (GST): Forcing the Informal to Be Formal

GST was introduced in India on July 1, 2017. It is the biggest indirect tax reform in India since independence. Registration and compliances under GST are totally technology driven. The returns required to be filed envisage that all invoices and certain other prescribed data is required to be uploaded in the GST system. This is required to be done within prescribed time lines. There is a concept of matching of data provided by the seller with the data provided by the buyer. This in –fact, is an integral part of the return filing process. This matching indirectly leads to an audit trail of all transactions and is a deterrent to fudging of accounts by any entity. Though, it can still be argued that if there is collusion at each stage of the supply chain, data can still escape the system, but it is surely difficult. In the process, all transactions of any business are expected to get recorded, depicting the correct turnover. It will also ensure some sort of financial discipline, as the amount of details required by the GST database for return filing will involve some attention to be paid to accounting and financial records by small businesses as well.

Lack of reliable financial information is one of the major impediments why banks refrain from lending to MSMEs. GST database will provide the MSMEs with reliable data to furnish to banks to meet their financial needs. Even under the composition scheme applicable for small businesses a sizeable amount of data does gets captured.

Further, GST system will have detailed data about businesses and their ownerships in one place. These are all tied to Permanent Account Number (PAN). The activity carried out by each business is also captured in detail. This will make the data furnished to financial institutions more credible.

It is also felt that demonetisation and GST together will make cash transactions a lot more difficult, lead to greater compliance, expansion of tax base and indirectly will lead to enhanced financial inclusion. Finance Minister Arun Jaitley has also reiterated this understanding.

Hidden Benefits of GST

Ever since GST was introduced MSMEs have been strongly opposing it. One of the reasons being that earlier a sizeable number of them were operating in informal economy and so far have managed to stay away from the tax net. Now the MSMEs are forced to register themselves, particularly those MSMEs that are suppliers to large companies. These large companies now prefer dealing with GST registered entities to ensure getting seamless input credit.

The Economic Survey (August 2017, Volume II) specifically points out, what it terms the "hidden benefits of GST" as follows:

- The textile and clothing sector is now fully part of the tax net. Previously, some parts of the value chain, especially fabrics, were outside the tax net, leading to in formalisation and evasion. Some anomalies favoring imports of fabrics over domestic production will need to be rectified but overall the tax base has expanded.
- Similarly, one segment of land and real estate transactions has been brought into the tax net: "work contracts", referring to housing that is being built. This in turn would allow for greater transparency and formalization of cement, steel, and other sales, which tended to be outside the tax net. The formalization will occur because builders will need documentation of these input purchases to claim tax credits
- There are early signs of tax base expansion. Between June and July 2017, 6.6 lakh new agents previously outside the tax net have sought GST registration. This is expected to rise consistently as the incentives for formalization increase. Preliminary estimates point to potentially large increases in the tax base as a consequence.

The Survey points out that the longer-term benefits include the GST's impact on financial inclusion. Small businesses can build up a real-time track record of tax payments digitally, and this can be used by lending institutions for credit rating and lending purposes. Currently, small businesses are credit-constrained because they cannot credibly demonstrate their financial capability. Thus, GST would help create financial history which can be used by the lending agencies while granting credit.

GST would also help ease doing business in India as it subsumes within itself several state and central taxes, reduces cascading effect of taxes, provides increased input credit utilization. It makes "one nation, one market and one tax" true in the country by removing inter-state trade hurdles, so it can help remove voluntary financial exclusion because of fear of multiple taxes and compliances. The registration, returns, and assessment are automated hence the fear of unnecessary harassment by tax department is settled. There is composition scheme available for small businesses with lower rates of levy to ease out their compliance burden. No doubt there are teething problems and issues specific to several sectors but these being addressed by the government. All these are leading to formalisation of this sector in a big way. Hence, protests apart, MSMEs need to recognise that formalisation also opens doors for formal credit and finance

The Finance Ministry is also considering more incentives for MSMEs which comply with GST including access to loans at a discounted rate.

TOOL 2: DIRECT TAX

There are several provisions of the Income-tax Act, 1961 (the Act) which aid in financial inclusion. Union Budget 2016 (Budget, 2016) and Union Budget 2017 (Budget, 2017) gave a special thrust to this area. Few of such key provisions are listed below:

Increased Thrust on Digital Transactions

Digital transactions lead of formalisation of the economy and aid in financial inclusion. The Ministry of MSMEs is encouraging MSMEs to move towards a less cash economy. As per the Annual Report more than 15000 programs have been conducted covering more than 25000 enterprises for this purpose. To further augment this initiative, the Act contains several provisions which discourage cash transactions and promote digital economy. In some cases added benefits have been provided for digital transactions.

Disallowance of Cash Expenditure

Revenue expenditure, in respect of which payment to a person in cash exceeds INR 10,000, in a day, is not allowed as a deductible expense while computing the taxable income (section 40A(3) of the Act). The term cash here implies payment made otherwise than through an account payee cheque/ bank draft and via electronic clearing system through a bank account. Certain exceptions are however provided in specified circumstances (Rule 6DD of the Income-tax Rules, 1962).

Cash Payment Deemed to Be Income

The Act also provides for deeming a payment as profits (section 40A(3A)) if the expenditure is incurred in a particular year, but the payment is made in any subsequent year, of a sum exceeding INR 10,000, otherwise than by an account payee cheque/ account payee bank draft or via electronic clearing.

Cash Expense Not Part of Cost of the Asset

Where a taxpayer incurs any expenditure for acquisition of any asset in respect which payments made to a person in a day, otherwise than by an account payee cheque /account payee bank draft/ use of electronic clearing system, exceeds INR 10,000 (section 43), such expenditure is required to be ignored for the purposes of determination of actual cost of such asset. This advesrly impacts the depreciation claim.

Investment Linked Deduction Not Available

The Act (section 35AD) provides for investment linked deduction for specified businesses on the amount of capital expenditure (except capital expenditure incurred for acquisition of any land or goodwill or financial instrument) incurred, for the purposes of business. However, any expenditure in respect of which payment made to a person in a day, otherwise than by an account payee cheque/account payee bank draft/ use of electronic clearing system, exceeds INR 10,000, no benefit is provided.

Lower Rate for Presumptive Income

Under the presumptive income scheme (section 44AD) in case of eligible assesses carrying out eligible businesses, if the total turnover does not exceed INR two crore in a financial year, a sum equal to 8% of the total turnover, is deemed to be the profits of such business and is charged to tax. In order to encourage small unorganized business to accept digital payments, this rate of 8% has been reduced to 6% in respect of the total turnover received by an account payee cheque / account payee bank draft/ use of electronic clearing system.

Restriction on Cash Transactions

The Act provides that no person shall receive an amount of INR two lakh rupees or more,— (a) in aggregate from a person in a day; (b) in respect of a single transaction; or (c) in respect of transactions relating to one event or occasion from a person, otherwise than by an account payee cheque/ account payee bank draft or use of electronic clearing system (section 269ST).However, the said restriction does not apply to Government, any banking company, post office savings bank or co-operative bank. Penalty, amounting to a sum equal to the amount of such receipt is leviable on the person who receives a sum in contravention of these provisions (section 271DA).

Restriction on Loan or Deposit in Cash

No person can take, any loan or deposit, otherwise than by an account payee cheque/ account payee bank draft or use of electronic clearing system (Section 269SS), if, the amount of such loan or deposit is INR 20,000 or more. However, this restriction does not apply to any loan or deposit taken from or taken by the Government, banking company, post office savings bank or co-operative bank. To provide relief to agriculturists, this provision does not apply, if the lender and the borrower are both having agricultural income and neither of them has any income chargeable to tax under the Act. There are similar provisions regulating repayment of loans and deposits (Section 269T).

Thus, it is evident that an attempt has been made to discourage usage of cash in all categories of business transactions, be it revenue expenditure, capital expenditure or loans and advances.

Tackling Voluntary Exclusion

An attempt to tackle voluntary exclusion is reflected in the following provisions:

Lower Rate of Tax

High rates of tax are often considered a reason of development of parallel economy. High rate of tax induces businesses not report their financial transactions or report them partially. The Finance Minister in his Budget Speech, 2015 had indicated that the rate of corporate tax will be reduced from 30% to 25% over the next four years along with corresponding phasing out of exemptions and deductions. The Government proposed to implement this decision in a phased manner. The recent changes in this sphere have been:

- **Lower rate of corporate tax for manufacturing companies:** A domestic company is liable to pay income tax @ 25% (section 115BA) provided, if,: (i) the company has been setup and registered on or after March 1, 2016; (ii) it is engaged in the business of manufacture or production of any article and research related to distribution of such article (iii) it does not claim any profit linked or investment linked incentives.
- **Lower rate of corporate tax for small companies:** The domestic companies who have a turnover less than INR 50 crore in financial year 2015-16 will be liable to pay corporate tax @ 29% tax, plus surcharge and cess.

Studies reveal that the worldwide average statutory corporate tax rate has consistently decreased since 1980, with the largest decline occurring in the early 2000s. In 2017, the worldwide average statutory corporate income tax rate, measured across 202 tax jurisdictions, was 22.96%. Europe had the lowest regional average rate, at 18.35%.The general corporate tax rate for domestic companies in India is still 30%. It is evident that much needs to be done this sphere.

Presumptive Taxation

The rationale behind presumptive taxation schemes is to reduce the compliance burden on small businesses. The Act contains a presumptive taxation scheme for certain eligible business (section 44AD), discussed in the earlier section. Any person who opts for this scheme is not required to maintain books of accounts and supporting documents for taxation purposes. There is no tax audit by a Chartered Accountant in this case and provisions of tax deduction at source (TDS) are not applicable. The tax department does not question the profit margin as long as it is at the prescribed percent or more. In the Budget speech of the Finance Minister during Budget 2016, he mentioned that at present about 33 lakh small business people avail of this benefit. The government has recently increased the threshold limit, with intent to extend the benefit to more businesses.

Presumptive taxation regime has also been introduced for specified professionals (section 44ADA) and whose total gross receipts do not exceed fifty lakh rupees in a financial year. In this case, a sum equal to 50% of the total gross receipts is considered to be their taxable income. The taxpayer is also not required to maintain books of account (section 44AA) and get the accounts audited (section 44AB)

These schemes bring in simplicity and clarity in the taxation system while leaving minimum room of discretion with the tax department. They give a thrust to ease of doing business. So far these schemes are available for limited sectors and taxpayers, makings these available to all MSMEs would give a big boost to financial inclusion.

Paperless Return Filing, Communication and Assessment

In order to reduce compliance burden, income tax return filing has been made paperless and online (Section 139D). Government is trying to progressively simplify the tax return forms so that taxpayers can fill them on their own, without seeking help from tax experts.

Adequate legal framework for paperless assessment has also been provided. Notices and documents required to be issued by income-tax department can now issued either in paper form or in electronic form (Section 282A). Also, “hearing” before the tax office now includes communication of data and documents through electronic mode (Section 2(23C)).

Steps to Reduce Litigation

Litigation is a bane for a tax friendly regime. It creates an environment of distrust and increases compliance costs for the taxpayers and administrative costs for the Government. The Finance Minister, in the Budget Speech for 2016, mentioned that more than three lakh income tax cases are pending before the first level appellate authority with a disputed amount worth 5.5 lakh crore. Similarly there is a huge backlog with the Income-tax tribunal, the High Courts and the Apex Court. It can take up to 12 years for the matter to reach the Apex Court for final resolution of the issue.

This shows that the there is an urgent need to improve the current tax litigation process; alternate remedies need to be considered. The entire system needs to work at a higer speed to ensure that disputes get resolved in a reasonable time.

Levy of penalty for concealment of income has also resulted in large number of disputes. Budget 2017 modified the entire scheme of penalty by substantially reducing the discretionary power of the tax officers. The penalty rates were reduced to 50% of tax in case of underreporting of income and 200% of tax in case of misreporting from the earlier band of 100% - 300%. The new regulations also permit the taxpayer to buy peace. There is no penalty if taxes are paid and appeal is not filed.

The government has also formed a task force to draft a new direct tax law to replace the existing Act, which has been in force since 1961. The government should also consider providing more stable tax laws, the annual exercise of changing the tax laws through the budget should be done away with. Whenever a need arises for a change it should be carried out after stakeholder's consultation

Encouraging Innovation

Various committees have pointed out that technology has not been harnessed fully to further the cause of financial inclusion. Also there is need to encourage technological developments in this field. The following steps taken in the recent past can help tackle this issue:

Concessional Tax Regime for Income From Patents

A concessional taxation regime for income from patents has been put in place. The objective is to encourage indigenous research & development activities. This scheme provides additional incentive for companies to retain and commercialise existing patents and to develop new innovative patented products. Under this regime (section 115BBF) where the total income of the eligible taxpayer includes any income by way of royalty in respect of a patent developed and registered in India, then such royalty income is liable to be taxed at a concessional rate of 10% (plus applicable surcharge and cess) on gross amount.

Tax Benefits to Start- Ups

- **Three year tax holiday:** 100% deduction of profits of start-ups is available for three consecutive years out of seven years, beginning from the year in which the start-up is incorporated (section 80-IAC). The eligible businesses in this case are business which involves innovation, development, deployment or commercialisation of new products, processes or services driven by technology or intellectual property. To avail this benefit the start-up should be incorporated before 1 April 2019. Further the annual turnover must not exceed Rs. 25 crores in any financial year upto 31 March 2021. The start-up is also required to take an approved from Inter-Ministerial Board of Certification. This benefit is available to a start -up if it is set up either as a company or as a Limited liability partnership. MAT (18.5% along with the applicable surcharge and cess) is however required to be paid.
- **Prevention of incidence of tax on investors investing in approved start-ups:** Start-ups have the liberty to issue shares to investors at rates higher than fair value without any taxation hassles (under section 56(2)(viib)), subject to certain conditions.
- **Exemption from capital gains tax if the long term capital gains invested in specified fund**- 'Start-up India Action Plan' envisaged establishment of a Fund of Funds to promote the start-up ecosystem in the country, with the intent to raise Rs 2500 crores annually for four years to finance the start-ups. With this objective in mind, an exemption has been provided from capital gains tax if the long term capital gains proceeds are invested by an taxpayer in units of such notified fund (Section 54EE). This is subject to the condition that investment is upto 50 lakh and the amount remains invested for three years.
- **Relief from capital gains invested in start-ups:** The Act provides (section 54GB) exemption from tax on long term capital gains on transfer of a residential property, if such capital gains are invested in shares of a MSME, subject certain other conditions. This benefit has been extended to investment made in the shares of an eligible start-up. This is subject to the condition that the concerned individual or HUF should hold more than 50% shares of the company. The objective is to provide relief to an individual or HUF willing to setup a start-up company by selling residential property.
- **Relaxed norms for carry forward of losses**: It has been provided (section 79) that in the case of a company being an eligible start-up, loss can be carried forward and set off, even if change in shareholding has taken place. The pre-condition being that all the shareholders of such company on the last

day of the year in which the loss was incurred, continue to hold shares on the last day of such financial year in which set off is done. The loss should have been incurred during seven years beginning from the year of incorporation. In case of other companies 51% of shareholding of company needs to remain unchanged to avail this benefit.

It is expected that these provisions would provide a much needed fillip to start-ups in India and also help address their funding requirements. It would encourage seed-capital investment; help meet the working capital requirements particularly during the initial years. In addition it would also encourage investment in start-ups from sale of capital assets.

However, there are some areas, which still need attention. These relate to the issues pointed out by various committees on financial inclusion. Though some of these issues could be addressed by the new patent and start-up regime, some of them may be required to be specifically included in the start-up list of eligible businesses. Separate tax incentives could also be considered targeting these specific issues. Encouraging use of CSR funds may also yield positive results. These issues are:

- The CMPFI had pointed out that although a quantum jump in banking access has taken place, there is still a significant element of regional exclusion due to various reasons. This needs to be addressed by stepping up the inclusion drive in the north-eastern, eastern and central states to achieve near-universal access. This may entail a change in the banks' traditional business model through greater reliance on mobile technology for 'last mile' service delivery, given the challenges of topography and security issues in some areas. In some of the areas, mobile connectivity may not be commercially viable to start with. In that case telecom service providers may be encouraged to use their CSR funds for this purpose. Area specific tax exemptions could also be provided.
- It has been observed that despite improved financial access, usage remains low. To address this issue, specific tax incentives should be provided to entities which encourage leveraging technology to facilitate usage.
- Tax incentives should be provided to entities which carry out research, and collect information on customer preferences to increase the usage.
- India is a country with linguistic diversity, tax incentives should be considered for development of a multi-lingual mobile applications for customers who use non-smart phones. This will help popularise usage and facilitate quick adoption of technology based usage of financial services.

- Tax incentives should be provided to entities for encouraging investment in digital infrastructure.
- Pressing need has been felt for technological innovation in field of financial inclusion, Tax incentives should be provided for developing and marketing innovative financing structures and instruments for MSME financing. Special incentives could be considered to encourage fintech companies
- It has been observed that Banking Correspondent networks in India require encouragement. Their rapid expansion has been mainly spurred by government policy, rather than business incentives. This can be addressed to some extent by providing tax exemptions.
- Tax incentives could be provided to entities providing advanced training to Banking Correspondents.
- Tax incentives should be provided to entities that encourage financial literacy.
- Provide tax incentives to entities which handhold MSMEs for financial inclusion. This could imply encouraging Small Business Advisors who may (a) offer help in preparing business proposals; (b) help to prepare financial documents and financial statements and can improve record-keeping; (c) sharing information on suitable credit instruments available in the market and (d) supporting with non–financial or semi-financial business decisions such as business expansion plans. They can also (i) recommend to the banks the business proposals of entrepreneurs; (ii) perform preliminary credit appraisal on behalf of the banks and (iii) collate additional supporting information required by the banks/ credit institutions.

In nutshell, there is need to harness the strengths of private sector for furtherance of the financial inclusion in India. Tax incentives can make venturing into this sector a viable and lucrative business proposition for the private sector while augmenting the government agencies already involved in this sphere.

Encouraging Other Lenders

The CMPFI had pointed out that to ensure greater credit flow to MSMEs, apart from scheduled banks there is need for other specialised institutions, such as NBFCs and MFIs that focus on the provision of credit for different types of MSMEs. They should be encouraged by providing direct and indirect tax benefits to ensure that such institutions expand and multiply. Some of the existing tax benefits and demands of co-operative banks, NBFCs and securitisation have been discussed below:

Tax Benefits for Co-Operative Banks

Interest income in relation to certain categories of bad or doubtful debts received by certain institutions or banks, is chargeable to tax in the financial year in which it is credited to the profit and loss account or is actually received, whichever is earlier (section 43D). This provision is an exception to the accrual system of accounting which is regularly followed by such taxpayers for computation of taxable income. The benefit of this provision is available to scheduled banks, public financial institutions, state financial corporations, state industrial investment corporations and certain public companies. Recently, co-operative banks have also been added to this list. This has been done to meet their long standing demand of a level playing field.

Further, interest payable by a taxpayer on any loan taken from a co-operative bank is allowed as deduction if it is actually paid by the taxpayer before the due date of filing his tax return for the relevant year (section 43B). This ensures that the taxpayers pay interest to the co-operative bank in a timely manner. This positively impacts the cash flows the co-operative banks.

Co-operative banks can claim deduction in respect of provision for bad and doubtful debts (Section 36(1)(viia)(a)). The amount of such deduction is limited to 8.5% (recently increased from 7.5%) of the total income (computed in a specified manner) and an amount not exceeding 10% of the aggregate average advances made, (computed in the prescribed manner at the end of the previous year). This is a very significant incentive which affects their financial well being.

Looking Into Demands of the NBFC Sector

Moody's report on securitization in Indian and China, "Securitization - India and China: Securitization Funds NBFCs' Lending to Promote Spread of Financial Inclusion" mentions that NBFCs are key providers of credit to individuals and small businesses that would otherwise have limited access to bank loans or would incur high interest costs for such loans. The report mentions that NBFCs specialise in offering more tailored and flexible loan products to the under-served. Further, NBFCs turnaround time from loan application to disbursement is faster than those of banks. The report points out NBFCs knowledge of local industries and sub-markets and their ability to understand the credit profiles of their borrowers, despite a lack of information, help them underwrite credit to borrowers otherwise ineligible for bank loans.

Recognising the importance of this sector, some benefits have been extended to this sector in the recent past. Provision for bad and doubtful debts of the banks is tax deductible (section 36(1)(viia)) subject to certain conditions and certain limits .NBFCs are also required to make provisions of NPAs. Accepting the long standing demand of NBFCs, Budget 2016, has extended this benefit to NBFCs as well where they can claim an amount not exceeding 5% of the total income (computed in specified manner)

The NBFC sector has also been demanding certain other tax benefits listed below:

- In case of amalgamation of banking companies, the accumulated losses are allowed to be carried forward and claimed by the amalgamated entity (Section 72A). However, similar benefit is not specifically available to NBFCs resulting in lapse of accumulated losses upon amalgamation. Providing this benefit to NBFC will help in setting up larger NBFCs by amalgamation.
- At present tax is required to be withheld @10% (section 194A) on the interest component of the instalment paid to a NBFC However, banks are exempted from this provision. As NBFCs operate on a thin margin this tax withholding of 10% adversely impacts their cash flow. The NBFC sector has hence been demanding parity with banks in this case.
- The Act recognises the principle of taxing income on NPA on receipt basis. In accordance with the directions issued by the RBI, similar to the other financial institutions, NBFCs also follow prudential norms and are required to defer income in respect of their non-performing accounts. In the absence of specific coverage of this section for NBFCs, the current tax framework requires NBFCs to recognise income on such NPAs on an accrual basis, resulting in levy of tax on income which may not be realised at all. This impacts their cash flow pay-outs, profitability and also has a consequent impact on their cost of operations.

Addressing these issues would provide a huge boost to NBFC sector in India and in turn help the MSMEs who bank on NBFCs for their financial needs.

Encouraging Securitisation

Moody's Report says that a developed securitisation market will help the country achieve its goal of financial inclusion by providing cheap credit to under-served segments of the society. While there are various funding avenues open to NBFCs in the country, securitisation has proven to be reliable and competitively priced, and is therefore an important source of funds the NBFCs use for lending.

For reviving and strengthening the securitisation market in India, Budget 2016 introduced a new regime for taxation of securitisation trusts which has the following key elements. The income of securitisation trust is exempt. However, any income from securitisation trust would be taxable in the hands of investors. The income accrued or received from the securitisation trust shall be taxable in the hands of investor in the same manner and to the same extent as it would have happened had investor made investment directly in the underlying assets and not through the trust. Tax deduction at source shall be effected by the securitisation trust at prescribed rates. There is no distribution tax.

It evident that steps have been taken in the right direction, however based on the recommendations of the committees who have examined the issue of financial exclusion in detail the following areas require attention and should be examined by the government:

1. Tax incentives for entities that are involved in development of customer centric financial products which also take into account religious and cultural issues.
2. Tax incentives to encourage partnerships between traditional players like banks and new non bank financial service providers.
3. There is a need for new institutions or intermediaries who can help bridge the information gaps that plague these entities or even innovative ways of providing finance to this sector. Tax incentives may be used to provide level playing field for new entrants in this field.
4. Companies can be encouraged to nurture Self Help Groups as part of their CSR initiatives. Specific tax incentive should be provided for that.

We have seen that a financial exclusion of MSMEs needs a multi dimensional approach. Apart from all the other government initiatives, tax laws are also playing a significant role in this direction. By using "a carrot and a stick approach" they are manoeuvring the informal sector businesses towards the formal economy, where formal sources of finance and credit become a reality.

REFERENCES

MSME Annual Report 2016-17. (n.d.). Ministry of Micro, Small and Medium Enterprises, Government of India.

Budget Speech for 2015 by Hon'ble Finance Minister

Budget Speech for 2016 by Hon'ble Finance Minister

Business Today Online. (2017, November 1). Ease of Doing Business rankings: India makes highest-ever jump to rank 100 out of 190 countries. *Business Today Online*.

Chakrabarty. (n.d.). *Empowering MSMEs for financial inclusion and growth – Issues and Strategies*. Academic Press.

Developing securitisation market key to drive financial inclusion, PTI, 21 January 2016

Economic Survey (2017). (Vol. 2). Department of Economic Affairs, Ministry of Finance.

Financial Inclusion in digital Economy, ADB Briefs, January 2017

Hindustan Times. (2017, November 24). More incentives for MSMEs complying with GST norms. *Hindustan Times*.

Income-tax Act, 1961 as amended by Finance Act 2017

Memorandum explaining provisions of Finance Bill 2016

Memorandum explaining provisions of Finance Bill 2017

Micro, Medium & Small Scale. (n.d.). Retrieved from www.cii.in/Sectors

Notification, No. 45/2016, Dated: June 14, 2016, Ministry Of Finance, Department of Revenue, Central Board of Direct Taxes, New Delhi

PM says ease of doing business ranking will improve further, rebuts criticism from opposition. (2017). Retrieved from www.moneycontrol.com

Report of the Committee on Medium-term Path on Financial Inclusion (CMPFI), Chairman Mr. Deepak Mohanty, December 2015

Chapter 12
The Case of the Missing Customer!

Pooja Sharma
Independent Researcher, India

ABSTRACT

India's financial inclusion journey started more than a decade ago. While several technological and access-related challenges have been overcome against the backdrop of a favorable policy-making and governmental climate, the adoption issues still remain largely unaddressed. This chapter discusses these issues and provides an alternate approach to customer adoption at the bottom of the pyramid while using time-tested consumer behavior frameworks. It puts the onus on implementing agencies such as banks to adopt this customer segment in an unbiased manner to bring in the benefits of financial inclusion for all stakeholders including the unbanked customer.

THE PURSUIT OF FINANCIAL INCLUSION IN INDIA

After all, should we not give everyone access to the (banking) services we all in this room enjoy? (Dr Raghuram Rajan, 2016) (While speaking at the National Seminar on Equity, Access and Inclusion organised by National Institute of Rural Development and Panchayat Raj in Hyderabad July 18, 2016)

Indian banking system has always had a social side to it, subscribed in part due to its legacy, RBI guidelines and government initiatives. Hence, it is no surprise that Financial Inclusion (FI) as a term has gained traction over the last decade or so started by the UPA government and continued by the NDA government. India has witnessed multiple waves of FI each stronger than the previous one in its zeal and

DOI: 10.4018/978-1-5225-4035-9.ch012

rigor, while building upon the technological advancements in the Fintech space. Each of these waves or phases have attained success in enrolling more and more beneficiaries in the banking system.

UPA government led 'Swabhiman' launched in 2011 garnered more than 25crore 'no frills accounts', while the more recent Pradhan Mantri Jan Dhan Yojna (PMJDY) has managed to open a staggering 30.26 crore accounts as of September 30th, 2017 (estimates may vary based on reporting agencies, but will broadly be of this magnitude).

The initial pillars of the program were related to bringing to focus this overlooked segment and in overcoming infrastructural and access related challenges. These pillars largely defined the smart-card based approach, offline POS devices used for enrolment and transactions, introduction of business correspondent model to address lack of physical branches as the key drivers of the program. Subsequently with the advent of AADHAR, development in mobile connectivity and devices, launch of NPCI's RuPay card and other past learnings, the model was tweaked and PMJDY was evolved. This AADHAR enabled scheme created a bouquet of products and tools for the unbanked customer comprising a basic banking account, a RuPay debit card, a built-in overdraft facility and an insurance product. It further incentivised the customer to transact via freebies and touted easy access for operations via 8-lac POS devices, 1.8 lac merchant terminals and all ATMs in India subscribing to the RuPay network.

Data from RBI Annual report 14-15 (Table 1), and the World Bank Findex data 2014 (Table 2), measuring various parameters of inclusion in terms of progress in number of accounts opened, number of cards, number of villages with some form of access to financial services shows an impressive achievement on the dimension of 'coverage'. Banking outlets in villages have grown more than 7 times from 67,694 to 553,713 from 2010 to 2015. Even urban outlets covered by BCs has increased to a staggering 96,847 in 2015 from a meagre 447 in 2010. The number of basic banking accounts (BSBDAs) have increased 4 times from 73 million in 2010 to 398 million in 2015. Other statistics related to enrolment and coverage also show similar growth trajectories (RBI,2015; Demirguc-Kunt, Klappper, Singer, & Oudheusd, 2015).

This progress has been possible mainly due to the concerted efforts of multiple stakeholders:

- RBI and NPCI in creating an enabling policy making environment and setting up governance with banks towards its execution.
- Government - Irrespective of the political affiliations, this initiative has had the required continuity and thrust from UPA to NDA. The recent decision of Government of India (GoI) to enable Direct Benefit Transfer (DBT)

Table 1. Financial Inclusion Plan-Summary Progress of All Banks Including RRBs

Particulars	Year ended March 2010	Year ended March 2014	Year ended Mar 2015	Progress April 2014 - Mar 2015
1	2	3	4	5
Banking Outlets in Villages - Branches	33,378	46,126	49,571	3,445
Banking Outlets in Villages – Branchless mode	34,316	337,678	504,142	166,464
Banking Outlets in Villages -Total	67,694	383,804	553,713	169,909
Urban Locations covered through BCs	447	60,730	96,847	36,117
Basic Savings Bank Deposit A/c through branches (No. in million)	60.2	126.0	210.3	84.3
Basic Savings Bank Deposit A/c through branches (Amt. in ₹ billion)	44.3	273.3	365.0	91.7
Basic Savings Bank Deposit A/c through BCs (No. in million)	13.3	116.9	187.8	70.9
Basic Savings Bank Deposit A/c through BCs (Amt. in ₹ billion)	10.7	39.0	74.6	35.6
BSBDAs Total(No. in million)	73.5	243.0	398.1	155.1
BSBDAs Total (Amt. in ₹ billion)	55	312.3	439.5	127.3
OD facility availed in BSBDAs (No. in million)	0.2	5.9	7.6	1.7
OD facility availed in BSBDAs (Amt. in ₹ billion)	0.1	16.0	19.9	3.9
KCCs (No. in million)	24.3	39.9	42.5	2.6
KCCs (Amt. in ₹ billion)	1,240.1	3,684.5	4,382.3	697.8
GCC (No. in million)	1.4	7.4	9.2	1.8
GCC (Amt. in ₹ billion)	35.1	1,096.9	1,301.6	204.7
ICT A/Cs BC Transaction (No. in million)*	26.5	328.6	477.0	477.0
ICT A/Cs BC Transactions (Amt. in ₹ billion)*	6.9	524.4	859.8	859.8

*: During the financial year.

(source: RBI Annual Report 14-15)

framework mandatorily via the banking system provides that extra push in the right direction.

- Banks by being the execution arms of the national FI program, despite this segment not being a profitable segment for them.
- Private sector players like technology companies, card companies, mobile wallets in creating 'frugal innovations' for this market.
- NGOs at the grassroot level ensuring delivery of last mile services in not so enabling environments.

The National Financial Inclusion program has truly been a hotbed of technological innovation pursued relentlessly by the regulator and the government with a mission-like zeal.

And yet, many of the accounts opened remain dormant. The Government of India's Economic Survey Report 2016-17 finds that active use of PMJDY accounts is only 40% (active defined as at least one transaction completed in the last 90 days). Mr. Modi himself in a recent address has expressed anguish over 7 crore accounts with no transactions and no balances!

The rating agency CRISIL, a Standard and Poor's company, has a financial inclusion index called the Inclusix. The all-India Inclusix score for 2013 was 50.1 (which means that only about 50% of the country has access to formal banking services) with wide variations within various regions of the country, highest being

Table 2.

India

South Asia			Lower middle income
Population, age 15+ (millions)	887.9	GNI per capita ($)	1,570

	Country data	South Asia	Lower middle income
Account (% age 15+)			
All adults	53.1	46.4	42.7
Women	43.1	37.4	36.3
Adults belonging to the poorest 40%	43.9	38.1	33.2
Young adults (% ages 15–24)	43.2	36.7	34.7
Adults living in rural areas	50.1	43.5	40.0
Financial Institution Account (% age 15+)			
All adults	52.8	45.5	41.8
All adults, 2011	35.2	32.3	28.7
Mobile Account (% age 15+)			
All adults	2.4	2.6	2.5
Access to Financial Institution Account (% age 15+)			
Has debit card	22.1	18.0	21.2
Has debit card, 2011	8.4	7.2	10.1
ATM is the main mode of withdrawal (% with an account)	33.1	31.1	42.4
ATM is the main mode of withdrawal (% with an account), 2011	18.4	16.9	28.1
Use of Account in the Past Year (% age 15+)			
Used an account to receive wages	4.0	3.5	5.6
Used an account to receive government transfers	3.6	3.1	3.3
Used a financial institution account to pay utility bills	3.4	2.7	3.1
Other Digital Payments in the Past Year (% age 15+)			
Used a debit card to make payments	10.7	8.5	9.6
Used a credit card to make payments	3.4	2.6	2.9
Used the Internet to pay bills or make purchases	1.2	1.2	2.6
Domestic Remittances in the Past Year (% age 15+)			
Sent remittances	9.9	10.7	14.2
Sent remittances via a financial institution (% senders)	..	20.1	30.9
Sent remittances via a mobile phone (% senders)	..	7.7	7.7
Sent remittances via a money transfer operator (% senders)	..	13.7	18.3
Received remittances	9.8	12.2	17.8
Received remittances via a financial institution (% recipients)	..	15.8	26.0
Received remittances via a mobile phone (% recipients)	..	4.7	5.7
Received remittances via a money transfer operator (% recipients)	..	9.8	16.6
Savings in the Past Year (% age 15+)			
Saved at a financial institution	14.4	12.7	14.8
Saved at a financial institution, 2011	11.6	11.1	11.1
Saved using a savings club or person outside the family	8.8	8.8	12.4
Saved any money	38.3	36.2	45.6
Saved for old age	9.9	9.1	12.6
Saved for a farm or business	7.0	7.3	11.8
Saved for education or school fees	16.0	14.6	20.0
Credit in the Past Year (% age 15+)			
Borrowed from a financial institution	6.4	6.4	7.5
Borrowed from a financial institution, 2011	7.7	8.7	7.3
Borrowed from family or friends	32.3	31.4	33.1
Borrowed from a private informal lender	12.6	10.9	8.5
Borrowed any money	46.3	46.7	47.4
Borrowed for a farm or business	9.0	8.6	9.2
Borrowed for education or school fees	9.7	8.9	10.1
Outstanding mortgage at a financial institution	3.7	3.8	4.7

(Source: Global Findex Database, World Bank, 2014)

in southern region (62%) and lowest in the eastern region (28%). Even according to the Mor committee report 90% of small businesses in India still have no links with a formal financial institution and 60% of the rural and urban population do not have a 'functional' bank account. While the program scores well when viewed for 'coverage', it does not do too well from the perspective of 'usage'. The World Bank's Global Findex 2015 pegs India's unbanked at 65 percent, and of that only 4 percent use formal bank accounts to receive welfare payments. Usage of debit cards to make payments stands at a measly 10.7% while remittances stand at 9.9% as of 2014 (Demirguc-Kunt, Klapper, Singer, & Oudheusd, 2015).

Despite tremendous success achieved in coverage of financial inclusion, there is still a long way towards ensuring it in spirit!

WHERE IS THE PROBLEM?

The issue of dormant, inoperative accounts has been researched by quite a few interested agencies. The foremost among them is the Mor Committee report which seeks to address the issue of Financial Inclusion at a structural, policy and governance level. The report recommends that there can be no single model for FI in the country, each bank and financial institution needs to derive its own Financial Inclusion Plan. It also recommends certain checks and balances in terms of governance and grievance redressal for customer complaints (RBI Committee, 2013).

At another level, Microsave's research (an international financial inclusion consulting firm) indicates some of the following key deficiencies in the current FI model:

- **Business Correspondents (BCs):** Inadequacies in their incentive structure, training and capacity building
- **Design of Products and Services:** Lack of appropriate products, services and tools for this segment of population
- **Poor Marketing and Promotion Initiatives:** Lack of awareness of financial products
- **Large Number of Dormant BCs:** Despite impressive numbers of over 5 lacs BCs said to be operating in the rural and urban areas, smaller numbers are actually active on the field
- **Limited Trust of the Customer in BCs and Banking in General:** This is coupled by 'perception of disrespect' and inadequate service at the branches led in part by past experiences with the banking sector
- No real interest of banks in viewing unbanked as a viable customer segment for banking services (Dhawan, 2014).

Each research analysis provides insights to the FI program implementation in parts, but still lacks critical elements. It is the author's view that the challenge of ensuring 'effective' financial inclusion is but a multi-dimensional one with the customer at the centre of it all. The dimensions can be broadly classified in the following 3 categories:

1. **Environmental Factors:** In the initial stage of the FI program, the challenges were primarily related to inadequate rural infrastructure such as road, power, connectivity etc. and the vast geographical spread of sparsely populated villages. Tremendous progress has been and is being made in augmenting the overall infrastructure availability in terms of accessibility, communication and power. These infrastructural challenges are improving day-by-day with improved telecom penetration, physical access and power availability.

Access of the unbanked to banking outlets via branch, mobile ATMs and business correspondents is also improving every day. The Reserve Bank of India has also continued with its efforts to ensure extension of banking facilities to all unbanked villages. For this, about 490,000 unbanked villages with population less than 2,000 were identified and allotted to banks for coverage By March 2015, 3.9 lac villages were covered by 14000+ branches, 3.5 lacs (BCs) and 18000+ other modes, such as automated teller machines (ATMs) and mobile vans (RBI, 2015). The introduction of the business correspondent model has been a major driver in improving access to banking outlets and service delivery points.

The PMJDY scheme as discussed earlier looked at further easing KYC norms via AADHAR-enablement and designing and providing to every Indian a basic bouquet of products and services (comprising a basic savings a/c, a RuPay debit card and an insurance). This provides a suitable launch pad where the financially excluded individual gets empowered at a fundamental level. There is no doubt about the pace of reforms on these fronts evident by the impressive 'coverage' numbers.

However, as noted by RBI in its 2008 report, another key environmental factor is socio-economic status of individuals. The population that desires to access financial services must have the economic capacity to avail it. This roughly translates into the low-income levels prevalent in majority of the excluded population. Hence, the large population that falls below the poverty line is deprived of the financial services both in availability and capability. As a result, the extent of financial exclusion tends to be higher due to lack of demand from this segment of population (Shetty & Pinto, 2015).

There is still weakness in this fundamental aspect of enhancing the financial capability of the excluded segment ridden with low- income, seasonal employability and unemployment. The financial roller-coaster which a majority of the unbanked segment are subjected to, limits their capacity to avail of both savings and credit schemes in the formal financial sector.

2. **Demand Side:** The approach for FI till date has been that of 'carpet bombing' of the unbanked customers with accounts and cards, followed by luring them with freebies and government benefits with the hope that behavior change will happen automatically. The post-demonetization experience, of a surge in digital transactions followed by drop in electronic transactions to pre-demonetization levels should be evidence enough of the flaws in this approach.

Inadequate understanding of this deeply complex target market from the demand side is a gap in the current regulator-led approach and some of these aspects will be examined in detail in the subsequent sections of the chapter. The point to remember here is that the target market is not the village or the slum but the individual residing in that village or slum who is not availing 'formal' banking services due to various reasons. These reasons have to be investigated and addressed in the solution design.

3. **Supply Side:** Providers of the financial products and services, the banks and other formal channels of financial services, chose to keep this set of excluded customers separate from the mainstream customers. This is an exclusion of the excluded practiced in varied forms such as:
    a. **Having Distinct IT Systems for Service Delivery:** Many banks used to keep FI customer data and transactions in different databases serviced by a different set of applications aside from their mainstream core banking systems.
    b. **Having Different Distribution Channels viz. BCs (Till a Much-Needed RBI Intervention):** A FI customer could not be serviced at his or her own bank's branch. The FI program was run in parallel by corporate offices of banks with little branch involvement. Hence the branch staff was largely unaware of this customer type and most times did not have access to his account details in the bank's systems.
    c. **'Anything Will Do' Approach:** Due to the small-ticket size and high operational cost, this segment was looked upon as an unprofitable, regulator thrusted segment. Thus, everyone in the value chain adopted the charity approach, wherein the recipient should take whatever is being provided to him or her.

Lofty ideals backed by lack of real intent. Can one blame the 'for-profit' institutions in treating FI as a charity case rather than a business case? All other 'for-profit' stakeholders in the system viz. technology companies, card companies,

POS manufacturers and business correspondents, seem to have made it a profitable business case with the exclusion of banks. They still need to find the excluded as a viable customer segment warranting due respect as other banking customer segments.

Studies conducted in other markets have indicated other causes of financial exclusion which are also very relevant in the Indian context such as:

- **Exclusion Due to High Risk Perception and Wrong Product/Service Design:** Risk perception of high bad loans (NPAs) and higher operational risk causes firms to be cautious in their business with the excluded segment. This gives rise to lengthy customer documentation requirements and/or rigid conditions for product eligibility, thus making the products and services unreachable to this segment.
- **Cost-Benefit Mismatch Giving Rise to Exclusion:** This is especially true in the Indian scenario where the cost of rendering the financial service is way higher than the ticket size of the customers and their transactions, thus making it an unprofitable initiative ab initio. Cost efficiencies have been brought in by technological innovations to a large extent. Innovations in product design and service delivery could turnaround this equation towards profitability.
- **Bottom of the Marketing Pyramid:** Every marketer and every firm follows a cherry-picking approach. People at the bottom of the pyramid are clearly the last in that pecking order. Even other industries such as telecom and FMCG took to the rural markets after exhausting the potential of the easy access profitable urban markets. Financial institutions clearly seem to be in no hurry to tap this segment on a commercially sustainable basis.
- **Self-Exclusion:** A segment of population voluntarily believe that they will be denied the access of financial products or services, or customers may take a passive approach, instead of getting themselves involved with banking services offered by the financial institutions. As discussed earlier past experiences have a bearing on this behaviour of the unbanked segment.

Other studies have reported these similar causes of financial inclusion, under varied terminologies such as access exclusion, marketing exclusion, condition exclusion and price exclusion. In essence, it means that other than self-exclusion, the rest of the causes are related to market dynamics and market players. Thus, a careful evaluation of the Financial Inclusion program along these parameters, points us towards a missing common thread – CUSTOMER–CENTRICITY!

FINANCIALLY EXCLUDED: 'SEGMENT OF SEGMENTS'

Having established that a customer-centric approach is the need of the hour, let us try and understand this financially excluded customer segment. Financial inclusion is not a homogenous customer segment which can be targeted with a uniform set of tools, techniques, products and positioning. It is in fact, a condition or symptom exhibited by pockets of population within multiple customer segments rich and poor, urban and rural, male and female, literate and illiterate, young and old. Global studies of World Bank and other international institutions have shown that financial exclusion exists in a majority number of countries in the world whether high income or low income. Closer home in India it is observed that many people from all walks of life prefer the anonymity and simplicity of cash as a mode of receipt and payment as against a financial instrument like cheque, electronic fund transfer, card etc. These are the kind of behavioural and socio-cultural aspects in every customer segment which are often overlooked in formulating nation-wide programs such as financial inclusion.

In the current competitive financial services market, banks have dedicated marketing departments which engage market research companies and expert consultants to study and segment, sub-segment, sub-sub segment the target customer population based on newer and newer parameters. Significant time and effort is invested in then designing products and services addressing the segment's specific requirements. The question therefore is, how many formal financial institutions have conducted a similar exercise for the financially excluded segment to identify and understand the various sub-segments therein? Do they have a customer segment say, the excluded landless labourer who migrates to the city during non-sowing months, enrols in MGNREGA schemes in between and returns to the village during the sowing months? Who is this customer, what are his behavioural characteristics, what is the decision-making process he follows, what are his needs and aspirations? These questions and others are the starting point of understanding the financial inclusion market in its true spirit. As an example, the segment thus identified will exhibit certain characteristics such as:

- Male in age group 20-40 years
- Illiterate (though number and symbol literate)
- Higher level of awareness of modern living via city trips
- Low level of financial literacy yet can compute operations like interest in Rs. Per '000 per mth
- No/little collateral
- No credit history
- Owns a mobile device

- Has family in village comprising - older parents, wife, children, unmarried siblings
- Holds aspirations for family while bound by social/community level customs and traditions
- Income cycle
- Expense cycle

Throw in illiteracy, caste and location and you have a distinct customer segment with its unique reasons for staying out of the formal banking system. Once this detailing is understood then there is only the task of creating the tools, products and services, pricing and positioning aligned towards this particular customer segment. The service delivery mechanism and distribution systems are largely already in place

An important pre-requisite for this to happen is that the key stakeholders viz. industry, government and regulator have to climb down from the pedestal of a 'messiah' for the down-trodden and move towards treating this segment as a viable commercial segment. It is strange that other industries like FMCG, telecom and now e-commerce have already forged ahead and embraced this segment as crucial to their growth. HUL's – Shakti program, Amazon's Udaan, ITC's e-choupal, Tata Chemicals – Kisan Vikas Kendras are just some of the programs conceptualised by the individual companies and designed specifically for their respective target rural markets. These programs have also gone through their share of successes and failures, yet the moot point here is that only when the industry takes ownership of developing these segments of population collectively called financially excluded will there be any significant impact on the ground.

The term 'formal' financial services has been used judiciously because it is the banks, the insurance companies etc. which fall in this category. There are numerous financial entities in the 'informal space' viz. chit funds, micro lenders (though these are also getting slowly covered under regulatory framework), small finance companies who are already catering to this financially excluded market.

As per GoI census 2011 given in Chart 1, over 58.7% (67.8% urban + 54.4% rural) households are availing banking services, this given the design of the PMJDY scheme can translate into one savings account and 1 debit RuPay card per account. It is a good starting level empowerment for the prospective customer who hereto had problem of access, to start his journey into the formal banking system.

There is a confusion in the definition of rural as seen by government and industry. The term 'rural' is defined differently by different people. Government has defined a rural area as that which is not urban and an urban area is defined as:

- All locations within a municipality, corporation, cantonment board or a notified town area committee

Figure 1. Availing of banking services
(source: Ministry of Finance, GoI, 2017)

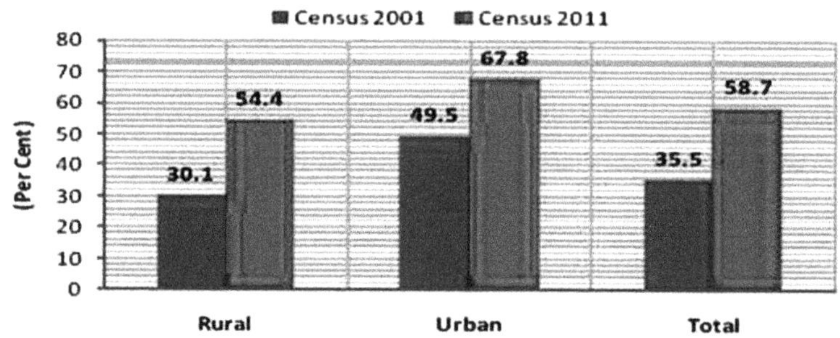

- All other locations satisfying all the following criteria:
    - Minimum population of 5,000
    - At least 75% of male workforce engaged in non-agricultural activities
    - A population density of over 400 persons per sq.km

However, this definition of rural is different from that followed by the marketing departments in various industries. According to a study, companies, depending on the products they sell, classify villages ranging from below 20,000 to 50,000 population as rural. There is yet another emerging classification between rural and urban, that of Rurban – a rural area with urban amenities. These are typically villages closer to larger cities and towns which have been influenced by the urban proximity, but remain rural from a cultural and behavioral aspect. It might have more people involved in non-agricultural activities. In a marketing sense, they neither behave like a rural market or an urban market (ISME, 2012).

Thus, financial services providers first need to define the target markets in order to understand the complexity and heterogeneity of the Indian landscape in which these financially excluded segments reside to design and create strategies to address them.

THE MISSING CUSTOMER!

Most poor people I know are proud and really want not a handout but a hand up. They do have an inherent pride and dignity, and we should treat them as those who have fallen on bad days. (Desmond Tutu)

Inspired by the above quote from Reverend Desmond Tutu, the aim of this section is to explore answers to the fundamental marketing questions such as:

- Who are the target customers? How is it decided that they should be the target customers? Were they co-opted into the FI program after being identified as target customers?
- What do these customers want from financial services? What are their needs, expectations, aspirations and constraints?
- In what form would they want to consume financial services?
- What is their view of the FI program in its current state? Do they see fundamental challenges such trust and reliability in the current model? For example, are they comfortable conducting money transactions in an open, less secure area as against a brick and mortar place? Do they find an agent not from their village trustworthy enough to deposit their hard-earned cash with him?
- How do they view the push of standard products and services to them, by the incentive-driven BC?
- Do they need to publicly stand in a line in front of the BC to withdraw their own money from accounts? How does this play out with their 'dignity and respect'?

Answers to these and several other questions will provide a high-level framework for marketers to understand, integrate and apply consumer behaviour to the financially excluded segments. Of course, detailed social and marketing research studies need to be conducted for each segment of the target population as defined by the financial institution.

One possible way of categorizing the financially vulnerable groups can be as under:

1. **Squeezed Middle:** This group is characterised by uncertain futures, being underprovided, following a lifecycle model of debt-assets breaking down.
2. **The '*Invisibles*' or 'Working Poor':** These are asset poor, low income people characterised by insecure employment or self-employment, supported by government doles or heavily in debt to maintain basic living standards and having no or low future income mobility.
3. **Lowest Income, Chronically Excluded:** These would typically be those 'below poverty line' (BPL) segment of people.
4. Other specifically disadvantaged groups like low caste, women, senior citizens, disabled people, other minorities etc. (McAteer, 2014).

Another way is to look at the influence of disposable income on financial behaviour following 4 typical zones phases.

1. Comfort zone when money inflow is enough to meet household expenses

2. Fluid zone when the household money has almost run out
3. Stress zone when small loans are needed to smoothen consumption
4. Blast zone when credit is not enough, or simply unavailable, and liquidating household assets is the only way to sustain basic household financial needs.

The mass-market keeps moving through these four zones and a closer look will provide a deeper understanding of the financial choices and consumption patterns adopted by them (Tiwari & Poddar, 2017).

Income-consumption phases of the target population are an important input while designing relevant tools, products and services for the target segment. For example, urban financial exclusion may be more sensitive to income-consumption phases as compared to physical access and financial literacy issues. While in the rural areas where income is largely agricultural the crop cycles would be a significant input for the appropriate product design and positioning.

Every buying and consumption process relies on the 3 pillars of access, buying behaviour and consumption characteristics. Specifically, for the financial services the issues of access have been addressed in the earlier sections of this chapter.

Delving more specifically into consumer behaviour and consumption characteristics, the available literature on consumer behaviour of the rural customers reveal the following characteristics. Though many of these could be more relevant to a FMCG product, it provides equal insight into the basic buying and consumption behaviour of this market.

1. While the rural literacy level is only 68.9% compared to 85% in urban area, a rural customer is as intelligent if not more and sharper in many ways than his urban counterpart. In fact, illiteracy does not translate into number and symbol illiteracy. These are important factors for the financial services case.
2. A rural customer is very conscious of "value for money" and has a functional approach towards consumption. This is a significant deviation from the current 'freebies' oriented approach to FI. Studies have shown that there are segments in the excluded population who are willing to pay for services, provided they see value in procuring them. This can be an important turning point into moving FI from the CSR bucket to a commercially viable business bucket for the financial services providers.
3. Mistrust is a deep-rooted challenge in the rural market. It could stem from their personal or their community's past experiences. Adoption of new products and services and/or modification of existing consumption patterns is a difficult task in these markets. Financial services providers would do well to incorporate this soft aspect in their service tool and service delivery design. Further behavioural studies are required to understand and breakdown this dimension

into addressable areas. Studies in the digital context are also seeking to answer the basic question of 'establishing trust' in a digital environment. Traditionally the design of the brick and mortar branches was meant to instil a feeling of security and confidence in the customer. How can this be translated in the mobile / BC -enabled delivery model remains to be seen.

4. Rural customers are more brand loyal than urban customers. This is a unique quality of this market which is quite contrary to the fickle-mindedness seen in the more affluent segments of banking customers. Where barriers to exit are high, it makes more sense to have the 'first mover' advantage and invest time and effort into sustaining it.
5. The rural customer's involvement in purchase of any product is high. Thus, the decision-making process is longer and involves not only the individual but also the family and the village community at large. Very few bankers understand this complexity. They simply run after target numbers, and in a hurry to open accounts and dole out cards, fail to include the key decision makers and influencers in the process.
6. The rural income mostly depends on the agriculture and hence income and purchase reach greater heights after harvest time. Hence, the disposable income varies across the nation depending on the area, crop, weather etc. This has been dealt with earlier in the discussion on phases of disposable income of households.
7. Traditional values, customs and perceptions have a stronger hold on the rural customers than urban customers. Improved economic status could be misconstrued in many such customer segments. It could mean that they will no longer be eligible for government benefits to start with. In the social setting they could be targets of bullying and extortion of money by friends and relatives. Many subscribe to the deep-rooted superstition of "nazar lagna" and hence would like to stay below the radar so to say. This could be one of the reasons people would rather be excluded from a formal financial system where transparency could be counter-productive.

A word of caution here, unlike a FMCG product, financial services are not point activities where consumption is event-based. Banking and financial services is more complex in its direct relationship with income and consumption and it follows a longer duration lifecycle model. Hence suitable financial services models must be used for analysis and interpretation.

Other studies of consumer behaviour identify characteristics like socio-economic environment of the consumer, his cultural environment, geographic location, occupation, media and urban exposure, occupation and literacy levels, access points of products and services, consumption patterns, decision-making processes etc. affecting buying behaviour in the rural markets.

Thus, one can conclude that buying and consumption behaviour of rural consumers are quite different from their urban counterparts. Experience of adoption of financial inclusion is varied between states with southern states recording higher adoption rates as compared to the eastern states. This leads one to add the heterogeneity with regard to location as a factor impacting buying behaviour to the rural/urban divide. e.g. a farmer in rural Haryana is much more prosperous than his counterpart in West Bengal.

While there is an urgent need to properly sub-segment the financial inclusion segment and understand the buying behaviour and consumption patterns of each of the identified segments. There is a social element of the financial inclusion, which needs to be put in context to this discussion. This is the inter-twining of social and financial inclusion where social exclusion becomes the cause for financial exclusion. One way to identify social exclusion is based on:

- Below par employment status of people marked by fewer job opportunities, temporary or seasonal work and unemployment
- Limited access to basic needs health care, education and basic infrastructure (more relevant in case of rural exclusion) and
- Unsatisfactory environmental conditions such as deprived neighbourhoods, poor housing, hard family life (especially true in case of the urban exclusion)

In such cases, addressing the demand and supply aspects of financial inclusion in isolation will not serve the purpose. It is here that the government must step up to create an ecosystem devoid of social exclusion and work in tandem with the financial services providers to make financial inclusion socially inclusive as well (Shetty & Pinto, 2015).

Looking at the above diversity in what is generically called the financial inclusion segment, it is no surprise that the current 'one size fit all' approach to FI by relying on a bank account, a card, a loan/insurance product and free payments infrastructure falls flat when measured on effectiveness and customer adoption parameters.

These excluded segments prefer products and services that provide them with a simple, trustworthy, and easily understandable approach which matches their requirements to manage their money. They don't want a long term visionary approach, but are looking at transparency with regard to where and how their money is being managed. They are looking for loans which will help them tide over liquidity phases rather than long-term repayment commitments which will push them towards a debt trap.

Empowering forces of data analytics and ultra-personalisation should make it possible to create hundreds and thousands of product combination strategies to address each segment most uniquely and with maximum fitment.

CONCLUSION

Though, the Mor Committee report on Financial Inclusion, has analysed the issue of financial inclusion from a structural and policy making aspect, it best summarises the arguments made in this chapter, quoted as follows:

As one examines the financial inclusion landscape in India, the sheer energy that has been put behind the effort and the seriousness with which providers and regulators have pursued this goal is impressive. However, it is possible that it is this very energy that has been its key weakness as well, because it has propelled highly engaged regulators and policy makers to move from one big idea to another, each time convinced that they have finally found the key to financial inclusion. While there is no question that there is a continuing need to explore new ideas; and benefit from new technologies; perhaps it is not the best regulatory strategy to centrally pick one approach and to push the entire system in that particular direction. A better approach may instead be to articulate a clear vision; establish a set of design principles; and then to permit all strategies, to flourish or to die out based on their inherent strengths and weaknesses. India is a very large and a very diverse country and no one strategy, however well designed, can ever hope to serve the entire country. (RBI Committee, 2013)

Till now the financial inclusion program of India was centred around building a scalable and cost-efficient business model that was agile and efficient to function effectively across the country's size and diversity. The challenge was to reach into interior locations, where no brick and mortar establishments are available and address the needs of the rural citizen in a holistic manner by providing them access to formal financial products. To the extent of this brief, all the participants deserve accolades in achieving impressive penetration numbers. Technology is a powerful tool, which cuts across class, caste, gender, and infrastructure outreach. This has been leveraged to provide the initial results. Technology is agnostic to size of transaction and can be used to disseminate small ticket financial services in a cost-effective, risk-controlled manner.

However, as one starts to look at the objective of FI, one realises that it is lacking in its most fundamental objective, that of effectiveness. No amount of government or RBI push will achieve the desired results. While they no doubt have to continue in removing the systemic and environmental hurdles coming in the way, it is time that market dynamics takes over. The other key stakeholders namely the financial services providers and customers need to do a handshake and agree on the terms of reference of the services. Each business viz. Banks / Financial Institutions / Micro-finance Institutions / FinTechs need to choose that particular excluded segment which makes business sense fitting in the overall strategy of the organisation. They need to respect the customers and address the market as they would address say the HNI segment, the millennials, Emerging HNIs; with right products, pricing, positioning, packaging, distribution and delivery.

One possible approach can be for banks to move customers towards goal-oriented financial planning. It may be worthwhile for banks to extend this approach to the excluded customer. The pre-requisite for this or any other approach to work is for the banks to define, segment and understand the target customer segment and map the requirements to financial needs. The fundamental principles of marketing apply equally to products and services including financial services.

Even as this is evaluated there are some crucial learnings:

- Financial Inclusion is a manifested outcome and not a customer segment
- It is spread across multiple customer segments, with one common thread that of exclusion
- Financial exclusion studies should be undertaken in the context of social exclusion. For if the underlying social exclusion issues are not sorted out, financial exclusion is not going away.
- Service providers must conduct internal studies to segment the market and identify the appropriate segment aligning with the organisation's overall strategy, culture and ethos.
- The excluded segment is not synonymous with poor and deprived, as there is tremendous potential in this untapped market.
- The excluded population deserves and aspires for quality products and services. There is a need for a customer-centric product, services and tool design
- Establishing trust, respect and dependability are other critical aspects of strategy formulation

It's time financially inclusion came out of the shadow of charity to become a viable and sustainable business case for banks and financial institutions. Only then will it be viewed with a marketer's lens and made customer-centric!

REFERENCES

Bhuvana, M., & Vasantha, D. (2016). Drivers of Financial Inclusion to Reach Out Poor. *Arabian Journal of Business and Management Review*, *6*(4). doi:10.4172/2223-5833.1000235

CRISIL. (2015). *CRISIL Inclusix*. CRISIL. Retrieved October 10, 2017, from https://crisil.com/pdf/corporate/CRISIL-Inclusix-Volume-III.pdf

Demirguc-Kunt, A., Klapper, L., Singer, D., & Oudheusd, P. V. (2015, April). *Global Findex Database 2014*. Policy Research Working Paper, WPS7255. World Bank.

Dhawan, R. (2014, April). *Why Is Financial Inclusion in India Not Improving? New Numbers, New Approaches*. Retrieved October 9, 2017, from www.microsave.net: http://blog.microsave.net/why-is-financial-inclusion-in-india-not-improving-new-numbers-new-approaches/

ISME. (2012, November). *Consumer Behaviour: Rural Vs Urban Customer.* Retrieved October 1, 2017, from www.isme.com: http://www.isme.in/consumer-behaviour-rural-vs-urban-customer/

McAteer, M. (2014). *Developing Financial Resilience*. Retrieved from www.preston.gov.uk

Ministry of Finance. GOI. (2017). *Economic Survey 2016-17, Volume 2*. Government of India. Retrieved October 11, 2017, from http://indiabudget.nic.in/es2016-17/echapter_vol2.pdf

N, A., & Joseph, J. (2014). A Study on Consumer Behaviour towards FMCG Products among the Rural-Suburban HHs of Ernakulam. *International Journal of Economics & Management Sciences, 3*(5). doi:10.4172/2162-6359.1000208

RBI. (2015). *RBI Annual Report 2014-15*. Reserve Bank of India.

RBI Committee. (2013). *Committee on Comprehensive Financial Services for Small Businesses and Low Income Households*. Reserve Bank of India. Retrieved October 11, 2017, from https://rbidocs.rbi.org.in/rdocs/PublicationReport/Pdfs/CFS070114RFL.pdf

Shetty, N., & Pinto, D. (2015). Financial Exclusion: Concept, Causes & Consequences, A Tri-Dimensional Literature Analysis. *International Journal of Applied Financial Management Perspectives*, *4*(1), 1605–1613.

Srivastava, D. P., & Kumar, M. (2011). Consumer Behavior In Rural Marketing-A New Paradigm. *Asian Journal of Technology & Management Research, 1*(1). Retrieved from www.ajtmr.com/papers/vol1issue1/consumer-behaviorin-rural-marketing.pdf

Swamy, V. (2014). Financial Inclusion, Gender Dimension, and Economic Impact on Poor Households. *World Development, 20*, 1–15. doi:10.1016/j.worlddev.2013.10.019

Tiwari, A., & Poddar, S. (2017, May). *The Four Zones: A Missing Chapter in the Financial Inclusion Guidebook*. Retrieved October 3, 2017, from www.microsave.net: http://blog.microsave.net/the-four-zones-a-missing-chapter-in-the-financial-inclusion-guidebook/

Tiwari, A., Srivastava, B., Chandra, R., Poddar, S., & Parmar, N. (2017). *Understanding the Financial Behaviour of the Mass Market: The Key to Financial Inclusion.* Microsave. Retrieved October 4, 2017, from http://www.microsave.net/resource/understanding_the_financial_behaviour_of_the_mass_market_the_key_to_financial_inclusion

Wharton. (2014, September 18). *Financial Inclusion in India: Moving Beyond Bank Accounts*. Retrieved October 3, 2017, from knowledge.wharton.upenn.edu: http://knowledge.wharton.upenn.edu/article/financial-inclusion-india-aims-move-beyond-bank-accounts/

Chapter 13
The Study of the Relationship Between the Slum Customers and the Factors Affecting Bank Account Opening Under Pradhan Mantri Jan Dhan Yojna in Lucknow

Vaibhav Misra
Symbiosis International University, India

Anubha Vashisht
Symbiosis International University, India

Parul Tolani
Babasaheb Bhimrao Ambedkar Univerisity, India

Kushendra Mishra
Babasaheb Bhimrao Ambedkar University, India

ABSTRACT

The study is conducted over 113 respondents from the slum area of Lucknow city with the objective of exploring the relationship between the slum customers and the factors affecting bank account opening under Pradhan Mantri Jan Dhan Yojna in Lucknow city. The data is collected using structured questionnaire consisting of both open-ended and close-ended questions. The area of sampling is selected on judgement basis and the data is collected using convenience sampling. It is found that there is a positive relationship between slum customers and the factors affecting bank account opening under Pradhan Mantri Jan Dhan Yojna.

DOI: 10.4018/978-1-5225-4035-9.ch013

INTRODUCTION

To benefit the weaker section and to empower the Indian economy Pradhan Mantri Jan Dhan Yojna introduced by Prime Minister "Mr. Narendra Modi" on 15 August 2014. This is considered to be a National Mission on Financial Inclusion. It is a consolidated approach to bring together the financial perspective of all households in the country. Priya Sharma designed the logo of this scheme. The name was chosen through some online sources. "Mera Khata - Bhagya Vidhata" is the slogan of the scheme. The purpose of this scheme is providing access to assorted financial services such as saving bank account, facility of remittances, pension and insurance to the excluded sections i.e. weaker section of the society (www.pmjdy.gov.in, 2016a).

Under this scheme, 1.5 crores bank account were opened on the inauguration day. 26.20 crores account were opened till 28th December 2016. 15.96 crores account were opened only in rural India which contributes to 60.92% of total account opened under this scheme (http://pmjdy.gov.in, 2016a). Further. The total amount deposited under this scheme till 28th December 2016 was 71036.59 rupees (http://pmjdy.gov.in, 2016a). 24.13% of the accounts opened in this scheme had zero balance (http://pmjdy.gov.in, 2016a). This scheme has the option of opening an account with zero balance. It also provides the facility of accidental insurance of Rs. 1 lakhs and regular life insurance of amount 30000. The overdrawn facility of Rs. 5000 is also one of the benefits ensured by government under this scheme.

NEED FOR THE STUDY

This study may help us to find out whether the scheme is properly implemented at the ground level by the banks. What were the problems faced by the slum people in opening their bank account under this scheme. This study may help government to identify the major problems faced by the people for whom this scheme was started as the scheme itself says "Mera Khata- Bhagya Vidhata".

The study will benefit the government and banks in analysing the reason why the slum people are not attracted towards the bank account opening under this scheme.

LITERATURE REVIEW

Joshi and Rajpurohit (2016) focussed on the failure of government for creating the awareness to rural customers about the scheme. They also found that demographic factors are not significantly related to the level of awareness of rural consumers about the financial inclusion scheme. They also considered the level of awareness about the financial inclusion was due to lack of understanding about the banking services in financial betterment.

Kumar and Kaushik (2016) conducted the study to examine the major steps towards the financial inclusion i.e. Pardhan Mantri Jan-Dhan Yojana (PMJDY). They collected data using structured questionnaire on five point likert scale. They found risk as an important factor affecting the view point of the bankers regarding Pradhan Mantri Jan Dhan Yojna using factor analysis on twenty five variables.

Pillai (2016) conducted the study on 62 farmers Marunji, Hinjiwadi, and Punawale villages of Mulshi Taluka of Pune with the objective to examine the knowledge level of Jan Dhan Yojana schemes and usage / adoption of scheme benefits by the Farmers. They used descriptive statistics and chi-square test for data analysis and found that people in rural areas do not have the knowledge about the scheme. They lack in financial literacy. Further he suggests that awareness about the scheme should be considered necessary for the success of the scheme.

Tripathi et al. (2016) conducted the study to explore the efforts taken by banks for spreading financial literacy about the scheme. They used regression analysis and found that there was an increase in credit disbursement and deposits in bank. They also found that banks made low efforts in creating financial literacy among the people. They considered financial literacy as threat for Pradhan Mantri Jan Dhan Yojana scheme.

Verma and Garg (2016) carried out a study on the workers of Central University of Rajasthan and the villagers of Bandrasindri village in Ajmer district of Rajasthan to study the effectiveness of Pradhan Mantri Jan Dhan Yojana (PMJDY) by analysing the effectiveness of the financial literacy programme and awareness towards the scheme. They gathered the primary data through discussions with the respondents. They found that the government and banks need to do more efforts to eliminate the financial untouchability and create financial literacy among the population.

Barhate and Jagtap (2014) focused on financial inclusion, strategy of Pradhan Mantri Jan-Dhan Yojna and issues related to the success of the scheme. They concluded that every new thing requires determination and attitude towards success path. They also concluded that to withstand the heat of economic down surge and fight poverty, the Jan Dhan Yojana is good mechanism.

Chowhan and Pande (2014) focused on the importance of financial inclusion and the impact of Pradhan Mantri Jan-Dhan Yojna on all the stakeholders in our country. This study concluded that the Pradhan Mantri Jan-Dhan Yojna protects the financial wealth and other resources of rural population in exigent circumstances. It also mitigates the exploitation of vulnerable sections by the usurious money lenders by facilitating easy access to formal credit (Kumar, 2014).

Khuntia (2014) analyzed the recent trends, key areas and the barriers in the process of financial inclusion in India with special reference to Pradhan Mantri Jan-Dhan Yojna. The study suggested the strategies to ensure maximum financial inclusion for the under privileged and unbanked areas.

Kumar (2014) offered some unique and innovative solution which can be augmented with the existing solutions to boost financial inclusion. The study concluded that financial inclusion is not standalone effort. Financial literacy, branch expansion, innovative services, e- governance, infrastructure, and various other integrated approaches should be implemented simultaneously.

Pathak et al. (2014) made a study to find out number of accounts to be opened in Pradhan Mantri Jan-Dhan Yojna and how the weaker section will be benefited from this scheme. This study suggested that the banks should be instructed of economic changes to maximize social good and to serve as a platform to raise the level of economic activity.

A study on, “An Analytical Study: Relevance of Financial Inclusion for Developing Nations” by Sharma and Kukreja (2013), emphasizes on the impact of financial inclusion in building up the India’s position in comparison with the other countries economy.

A study by Ranparia (2013) on Financial Inclusion in Gujarat: A Study on Banker’s Initiatives depicts about the various financial inclusion and concludes about the progress and present status of financial inclusion of the state (Kumar and Venkatesha, 2014).

OBJECTIVE OF THE STUDY

The objective of the study is:

To explore the relationship between the slum customers and the factors affecting bank account opening under Prandhan Mantri Jan Dhan Yojna in Lucknow city.

RESEARCH METHODOLOGY

Study Area

The area selected for the study is slum area of Lucknow city. The selection of study area is made on the personal judgement and convenience.

Sample Size and Sampling Method

The determined sample size for the study is 150 respondents from the slum area of Vikas Nagar, Lucknow. The population was equally distributed for collecting the data on the basis of gender. The area of the sampling is determined on our personal judgement. Convenience Sampling is used for collecting the data from the respondents.

Data Collection

The study is based on both primary and secondary data. The data was collected using structured questionnaire from the 113 respondents from the slum area of Vikas Nagar, Lucknow. Rest of the respondents did not answer to the questionnaire. The educational background of the respondents were below the average, therefore, the data also was collected through scheduling technique. The sufficient time was given to respondents in order to understand the questions and give their responses. Further, the questions included in the questionnaire were translated to them in Hindi so that they can understand the questions are the error can be minimized. The opinion of the respondents is given high consideration as much of the secondary is not available. Secondary data is collected through the reputed and respective journals in the field of management, economics, commerce, etc. The newspaper and websites are also used to collect the information related to the study.

Statistical Tools and Techniques Employed

The major statistical tests used in the study are: Shapiro-Wilk test to test the normality of the data and Spearman's correlations statistical tools used in the study are:

- The question related to the factors affecting respondents in opening bank account under Pradhan Mantri Jan Dhan Yojna is analyzed using likert scale.
- The Normality of data of the variances analysed using Levene Statistic Test.
- Correlation Analysis is used to find out the relationship between the respondent's responses about the acceptance of the scheme and their gender.

Statistical Software Used

The statistical software used for data analysis during the study is SPSS 21.0.

FINDINGS AND DISCUSSIONS

The factors have been identified using the personal opinion and our experience from the field and from Parthrose et al. (2015). The total sample population for the study is determined to 150 but only 113 respondents responded against the questionnaire. The following factors have been identified for the study and are represented in Table 1:

The analysis is conducted considering the monthly income of the respondents as an independent variable. While conducting the analysis economical background of the respondents is also studied. Furthermore, the minimum age of the respondents who are considered for the study is 18 years.

Table 2 represents the gender of the respondents, it is found that the number of male respondents is 50 which contributes to 44.2% of the responded population; whereas, the number of female respondents is 63 which contributes to 55.8% of the responded population.

Table 3 shows the different age group in which the respondent falls in. It is found that majority falls in the age group of 28 years to 38 years with 34 respondents which are 30.1% of the responded population. This is followed by 18 years to 28 years of age with 31 respondents which contribute to 27.4% of the responded population. Therefore, visualizing the table it can be said that the maximum respondents considered in the study are young, as the cumulative percentage of the young respondents is 57.5.

Table 1. Factors affecting the opening bank account under Pradhan Mantri Jan Dhan Yojna

S.N	Factors
1	Lack of Enough Money to Save
2	Lack of Financial Literacy
3	Distance to Bank
4	Improper or Incomplete Documents
5	Behaviour of Bank Employees
6	Past Experiences of the Peer Group

Table 2. Gender

		Frequency	Percent	Valid Percent	Cumulative Percent
Valid	Male	50	44.2	44.2	44.2
	Female	63	55.8	55.8	100.0
	Total	113	100.0	100.0	

Table 3. Respondent's age

		Frequency	Percent	Valid Percent	Cumulative Percent
Valid	18 years-28 years	31	27.4	27.4	27.4
	28 years-38 years	34	30.1	30.1	57.5
	38 years-48 years	26	23.0	23.0	80.5
	48 years-58 years	17	15.0	15.0	95.6
	58 years or over	5	4.4	4.4	100.0
	Total	113	100.0	100.0	

Table 4 focuses on the monthly income of the respondents. The table demonstrates that the respondents belong to various income categories starting from below Rs.2000 to Rs.8000-Rs.10000 with the class interval of 2000. It can be found that the 25 respondents' falls in the income category of Rs.8000 to Rs.10000 as their monthly household income which is the highest among the entire category, followed by the category of Rs.4000- Rs.6000 and Rs.6000- Rs.8000 having each with 24 respondents.

The normality of the data was checked using Shapiro-Wilk Test. We used Shapiro-Wilk test because it is considered to be the most powerful test to check the normality of data (Razali & Wah, 2011). It is found that all the responses received towards the factors are with the p value of .000. As the value of $p < .05$ it can be said that data is not normally distributed.

It is found that the data was not normally distributed; therefore, non parametric correlation (Spearman's Rank Correlation) technique is used for analysis.

Table 6 demonstrates the relationship between the respondents' age and the factors that affect them to open bank account under Pradhan Mantri Jan Dhan Yojna. We used Spearman correlation because our data was not normally distributed. In the Spearman's Correlation the respondents' age is considered as independent variable and the factors affecting the opening of account under the scheme are considered as dependent variables. It is found that all the factors are having positive correlation

Table 4. Monthly income

		Frequency	Percent	Valid Percent	Cumulative Percent
Valid	Below 2000	9	8.0	8.0	8.0
	2000-4000	31	27.4	27.4	35.4
	4000-6000	24	21.2	21.2	56.6
	6000-8000	24	21.2	21.2	77.9
	8000-Above	25	22.1	22.1	100.0
	Total	113	100.0	100.0	

Table 5. Tests of normality

	Kolmogorov-Smirnov[a]			Shapiro-Wilk		
	Statistic	df	Sig.	Statistic	df	Sig.
Lack of Enough Money to Save	.255	113	.000	.863	113	.000
Lack of Financial Literacy	.254	113	.000	.871	113	.000
Distance to Bank	.280	113	.000	.851	113	.000
Improper or Incomplete Documents	.285	113	.000	.850	113	.000
Behaviour of Bank Employee	.301	113	.000	.851	113	.000
Past Experiences of Peer Group	.257	113	.000	.869	113	.000
a. Lilliefors Significance Correction						

Table 6. Correlation table

S.N	Factors	Correlation Coefficient (r_s)	Significance
1	Lack of Enough Money to Save	.883	.000
2	Lack of Financial Literacy	.740	.000
3	Location of the Bank	.283	.002
4	Improper or Incomplete Documents	.833	.000
5	Behaviour of Bank Employees	.919	.000
6	Past Experiences of the Peer Group	.927	.000

and are significant at .01 level or 1%. Therefore, considering at the responses from the respondents it can be concluded that there is positive relationship between the factors affecting opening account in bank under Pradhan Mantri Jan Dhan Yojna and respondents' age group.

CONCLUSION

Based on the study and the data collection we can conclude that the slum customers and the factors affecting the bank account opening under Pradhan Mantri Jan Dhan Yojna is having positive relationship.

It has been observed that the slum customers are highly influenced by the past experiences of the peer group while opening the bank account under the scheme. It may be that the peer group might have faced some good or bad experience in the past, the same might have been discussed with the customers. But based on the data it can be concluded that it has created high influence on slum customer for opening a bank account under Pradhan Mantri Jan Dhan Yojna.

It is concluded on the basis of the data collected from the slum area of Lucknow city that the behaviour of the bank employee has high impact over the customers while opening a bank account under Pradhan Mantri Jan Dhan Yojna. It could be because the literacy level of the customers in slum area is very low; therefor it becomes hard to make them understand the basics of the procedure. This may result the change in the behaviour of the bank employee.

However, rest of the factors also have low affect on the slum customers in opening bank account under Pradhan Mantri Jan Dhan Yojna as compared to the past experiences of the peer group and behaviour of the bank employees, except location of the bank. Location of the bank has minimum affect on the slum customers in opening bank account under Pradhan Mantri Jan Dhan Yojna.

REFERENCES

Barhate, G. H., & Jagtap, V. R. (2014). Pradhan Mantri Jan-Dhan Yojana: National Mission on Financial Inclusion. *International Journal of Applied Research.*, *4*(12), 340–342.

Chowhan, S. S., & Pande, J. C. (2014). Pradhan Mantri Jan Dhan Yojana: A Giant Leap Towards Financial Inclusion. *International Journal of Research in Management and Business Studies.*, *1*(4), 19–22.

Joshi, M. C., & Rajpurohit, V. P. (2016). Awareness of Financial Inclusion: An Empirical Study. *Research Review International Journal of Multidisciplinary, 1*(6), 1-6.

Khuntia, R. (2014). Pradhan Mantri Jan Dhan Yojana: A New Drive Towards Financial Inclusion in India. ZENITH. *International Journal of Business Economics and Management Research.*, *4*(11), 10–20.

Kumar, D., & Venkatesha, H. R. (2014). Financial Inclusion using Pradhan Mantri Jan- Dhan Yojna- A Conceptual Study. *Asia Pacific Journal of Research.*, *1*(20), 37–42.

Kumar, P. G. (2014). *Bank Accounts for All: PM Modi That's Not Financial Inclusion.* Accessed from http://www.firstpost.com/politics/bank-accounts-for-all-pm-modi-thats-not-financial-inclusion-1610443.html

Kumar, P. G. (2014). *Bank Accounts for All: PM Modi That's Not Financial Inclusion.* Accessed from http://www.firstpost.com/politics/bank-accounts-for-all-pm-modi-thats-not-financial-inclusion-1610443.html

Kumar,, S., & Kaushik. (2016). A Study of Bankers' Viewpoint Toward Factors Affecting the Pradhan Mantri Jan-Dhan Yojana in Selected Public Sector Banks. *RIJBFA Radix International Journal of Banking. Finance and Accounting*, *5*(2), 1–10.

Kumar, V. (2014). Financial Inclusion in India: Unique Solutions. *Indian Streams Research Journal.*, *4*(8), 1–3.

Parthrose, E. P., Baby, A., & Maheshwari, U. M. (2015). A Study on Challenges Faced by Customers in Financial Inclusion. *International Journal of Scientific Research and Management.*, *3*(1), 1989–1995.

Pathak, A., Soni, A., & Agarwal, B. P. (2014). Pradhan Mantri Jan Dhan Yojana for Weaker Section- An Evaluation. Shabd Braham. *International Research Journal of Indian Languages.*, *2*(12), 69–74.

Pillai, T. J. (2016). Financial Inclusion and Pradhan Mantri Jan Dhan Yojana: An Empirical Study Conducted in the villages of Mulshi Taluka in Pune District. *Indian Journal of Science and Technology*, *8*(1).

Pradhan Mantri Jan Dhan Yojana (PMJDY). (2016a). *Scheme Details*. Retrieved on January 20, 2015 from https://www.pmjdy.gov.in/scheme

Pradhan Mantri Jan Dhan Yojana (PMJDY). (2016b). *Progress Report*. Retrieved on December 30, 2016 from http://pmjdy.gov.in/account

Ranparia, N. D. (2013). Financial Inclusion in Gujarat: A Study on Banker's Initiatives. *International Journal of Scientific Research.*, *2*(February), 32–34.

Razali, N. M., & Wah, Y. B. (2011). Power comparisons of shapiro-wilk, kolmogorov-smirnov, lilliefors and anderson-darling tests. *Journal of Statistical Modeling and Analytics*, *2*(1), 21-33.

Sharma, A., & Kukereja, S. (2013). An Analytical Study: Relevance of Financial Inclusion for Developing Nations. Research Inventy. *International Journal of Engineering Science*, *2*(6), 15–20.

Tripathi, R., Yadav, N., & Shastri, R. K. (2016). Financial inclusion in India through Pradhan Mantri Jan Dhan Yojana: An empirical analysis of statistical evidence. *Indian Journal of Finance*, *10*(10), 42–55. doi:10.17010/ijf/2016/v10i10/103014

Verma, Y., & Garg, P. (2016). Pradhan Mantri Jan Dhan Yojana (PMJDY): A step towards eradicating financial untouchability. *Indian Journal of Finance*, *10*(1), 56–64. doi:10.17010/ijf/2016/v10i1/85845

Chapter 14
Financial Inclusion Through Microenterprises of Rural SHGs:
An Empirical Study in South Rajasthan

Rahul Vyas
Pacific Business School, India

Nidhi Nalwaya
PIM India, India

ABSTRACT

The elementary aim of microenterprises and Self Help Groups (SHGs) is to empower the impoverished populace, particularly of the rural areas, and furthermore provide financial sustainability so as to improve livelihoods. The pervasive twin threats of unemployment and exclusion from the financial framework in the rural areas are the major challenges to the economic and social development of India. A self-help group is a potent means to remove poverty in the same vein microenterprises contribute significantly to economic development and social stability by affording employment opportunities, thereby emerging as a vehicle through which low-income people can escape poverty. SHGs and microenterprises are a significant means for socio-economic transformation through financial inclusion. The objective of the chapter is to study and analyze the impact of microenterprises and SHGs on the financial inclusion of people in rural areas of Tribal South Rajasthan.

INTRODUCTION

The growing Commercialization of Indian Rural Economy in the context of increasing dependence of agriculture on external inputs, mobilization of savings towards consumerism and an progressively literate population have opened up altogether unknown vistas for the Micro-Enterprise development in the rural areas.

DOI: 10.4018/978-1-5225-4035-9.ch014

Micro Enterprises in the study area, as elsewhere, are undergoing a significant transformation. While certain traditional industries are being carried out with low technology, using low quality raw material and catering to the low-income groups of the customers, many others are facing urgent need to enhance their capital base for productivity improvement, cost reduction and innovating for effective marketing.

A Self Help group (SHG) is a self-governed, peer-controlled small and informal association of the people, usually from socio-economically homogeneous families who are organized around savings and credit activities. Funds for credit activities are collected through regular savings deposited by all of its members on a weekly or fortnightly basis. In the meetings generally the discussion is focused on common village problems and planning for solution, sharing information to make efforts to improve health and literacy skills.

Narasiah (2004) opined that SHGs play a crucial role in empowering women. Manimekalai (2004) also remarked that the SHGs have the enough potential for establishing capacity building and self-efficiency among women. Sinha (2005) in his work observed that micro-finance contributed significantly to saving and borrowing of the poorer section of the country. Suguna (2006) also remarked that the emergence of SHGs as silent revolution in the spread of rural credit for rural development. Lolheihzovi (2007) considered SHGs as best engine of growth of human resource. In addition, remarkable studies have been done by Ali-Akpajiak&Pyke (2000), Krishna (2003), Panda (2005), Jerinabi (2006) and Chen, Jhabvala, Kanbur and Richard (2007).

Vijayalakshmi, D., Gowda, K. N., Jamuna, K. V., Ray, B. R., &Sajjan, J. T(2012) concluded that SHGs were improving the standard of living of all families who came in the project area. Appropriate strategies for empowerment of SHG women were addressed through organizing appropriate trainings both on and off-campus, including higher level trainings, follow-up activities, providing relevant leaflets and folders, exposures besides recognizing and encouraging women to come forward and take up processing and of linger millet products value addition and income generating activities. The SHG project has made a successful impact in improving the livelihood security for rural women. Nalwaya N, Vyas R.(2012) concluded that Retail capacity is today the single most important constraint when it comes to increased outreach. Singh S. Dilan,(2010) considered the Manipur SHG model superior. Subrahmanyam N.,(2009) studied the regional perspectives and analysis. Singh N. Tejmani, (2009) explained the various SHG practices in the country. Tangirala, H.S.K.,(2008) concluded that co operatives can be developed through economic development, Verma Renu, (2008) suggested rural women development measures. Tanya Jakimow, P. K. (2006) studied gender inequality. Tracey L. Moyle, M. D. (2006).concluded about women development. Akinsanmi, A. (2005). Studied working Poverty and Productivity of women.

OBJECTIVES OF THE STUDY:

- To study Micro Entrepreneurship activities of Rural SHG members and the ensuing financial inclusion thereof.
- To analyze the impact of SHGs on Micro Entrepreneurship Development in South Rajasthan.

RESEARCH METHODOLOGY

Research Design

The research paper is descriptive in its approach to the stated Research Objectives.

Data Collection

- **Primary data:** Collected by administering Questionnaire to the selected sample.
- **Secondary data:** Obtained from various published records, books et al.

Methods of Data Collection

For collection of data the following instruments have been used: Questionnaire prepared in view of objectives of the study.

Sample Size

Stratified Purposive sampling was applied for the Sample Selection, 100 SHGs(25 each from Banswara, Sirohi, Kherwara, Dungarpur) in tribal south Rajasthan were selected. Two members from each SHG ie (200) SHG members were selected for the study.

The Districts of Banswara, Sirohi, Kherwara, Dungarpur were chosen for the present study .

Sample Area

The study was carried out in South Rajasthan.

Measurement and Data Analysis

SPSS was used for analysis purpose of the collected data and analyzed by using percentage and various statistic tools viz., Mean, Median, Standard deviation et al.

ANALYSIS AND INTERPRETATION

9 members are male and 191 are female out of selected sample, On the basis of caste of SHG-members 68 percent of total member are General, 29 percent of SHG members are Scheduled Tribe, 2 percent of them are OBC and only 1 percent members are from Scheduled Caste.The majority of SHG members are in the age group ranging from 25 to 44 years. Range of Income is also one of the factors for joining SHG

The distribution of SHG-members according to their organizational grade is shown in table 2. An increasing trend is observed since 2004 up to 2008 but there is a downtrend from 2009,similarly, in case of year of membership taken.

It is revealed that Sewing is the main economic activities of Micro Enterpriseby SHG members with 52 percent and followed Pappad makingwith 24 percent, embroidery with 8 percent, Incense stick manufacturing and grocery items with 4 percent each

The primary form of financing in SHG micro enterprises is from bank loans as 37% SHGs are financed by bank micro-credit. Second source of finance is both self financing of SHG members as well as bank loan with 28% and it is followed by self financing

The data reveals thatthe minimum and maximum amount of internal loan received by SHG members is Rs.500 and Rs.15, 000 respectively. The average internal loan amount received by SHG members is Rs.2705. The average amount of bank loan received by SHG members

It is observed that the highest number of SHG members i.e. 72 (36%) members received loan amount below Rs. 2,000 and minimum number of SHG members i.e. 4 (2%) members received loan amount Rs.14,001-16,000. The prevalent method of loan recovery is both principal amount as also interest repayment in installments. Frequency of collection of loan for 98 percent of SHG members' is monthly payment and only 2 percent is weekly. So, the credit performance of SHG members is quite satisfactory.

The majority of SHGs (45%) sell goods by both retail and wholesale price and next method is wholesale price (30%) then retail price (25%).Frequency of manufacturing, Total Number of employees, Selling Price of products, Place,

Table 1. Distinctiveness of respondents

Characteristics		No. of Respondents	% Respondents
Gender	Male	9	4.5
	Female	191	95.5
Marital status	Married	131	65.5
	Unmarried	60	30
	Widowed	8	4
	Divorced	1	0.5
Educational Qualification	Illiterate	33	16.5
	Educated	167	83.5
Caste	General	136	68
	OBC	4	2
	Scheduled Caste	2	01
	Scheduled Tribe	58	29
Age	20-24	18	9
	25-29	39	19.5
	30-34	60	30
	35-39	30	15
	40-44	31	15.5
	45-49	16	8
	50-54	6	3
Range of Income	Below 2000	6	3
	2001-4000	85	42.5
	4001-6000	73	36.5
	6001-8000	20	10
	8001-10000	4	2
	10001-20000	7	3.5
	Above 20000	5	2.5

Median Age= 32, Average Monthly Income = Rs. 5037/-
Source: Field survey

Frequency of Remuneration and Monthly Profit of the business are the main parameters to measure the performance of a micro-enterprise. If the frequency of production is high and there is good market for product then the profit of the enterprises will be maximum.

Table 2. Respondents' distribution according to organizational grade

Organization of SHGs		No. of Respondents	% Respondents
SHGs in nearby Locality	No	64	32
	Yes	136	68
	Total	**200**	**100**
Year of Establishment	2004	8	4
	2005	8	4
	2006	14	7
	2007	28	14
	2008	22	11
	2009	52	26
	2010	26	13
	2011	10	5
	2012	14	7
	2013	18	9
	Total	**200**	**100**
Year of Membership Taken	2004	8	4
	2005	8	4
	2006	16	8
	2007	28	14
	2008	20	10
	2009	48	24
	2010	26	13
	2011	10	5
	2012	16	8
	2013	20	10
	Total	**200**	**100**
Total No. of Members	10-15	64	32
	15-20	112	56
	20-above	24	12
	Total	**200**	**100**

Source: Field survey

Table 3. Economic activities of Micro Enterprise

	Activity	Frequency	Percent
Micro-Enterprise Activities	Sewing	104	52
	Embroidery	16	8
	Incense stick manufacturing	8	4
	Beauticians	2	1
	Grocery	8	4
	Pottery	6	3
	Handicrafts	6	3
	others	2	1
	Pappad making	48	24
	Total	**200**	**100**

Source: Field survey

Figure 1. Economic activities of Micro Enterprise

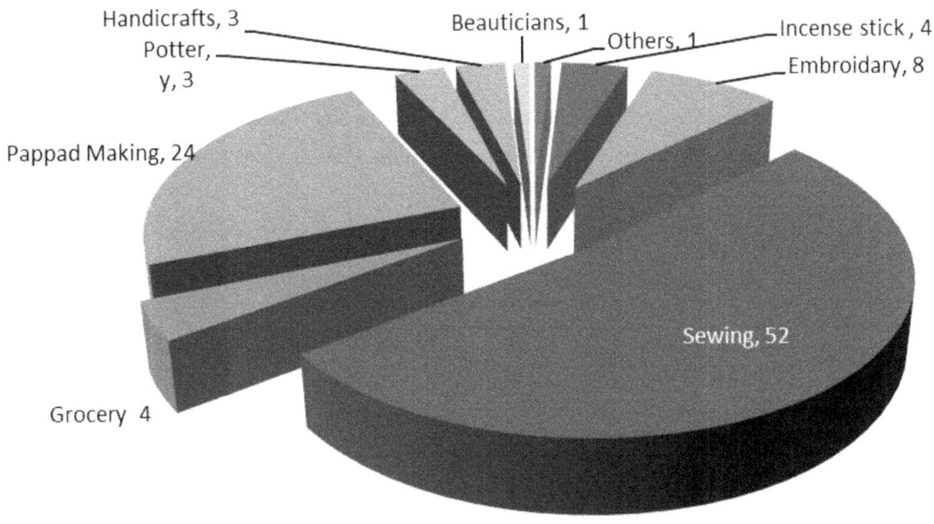

Sewing and Pappad Making are most profitable economic activity practiced by SHG members since the members achieved a profit of Rs 1,000 & above. Next in line is Incense stick manufacturingas 87.5 percent of SHG members got monthly profit of Rs.1, 000 & above the rest 12.5 percent of them earn monthly profit in the range Rs. 500-1,000. Similarly, other activities like pottery, handicrafts etc. also provide monthly profit at par withIncense stick manufacturing. But, Pappad Makingwhich is one of the widespread trades practiced by SHG also provides monthly profit of

Table 4. Form of financing

	Source	Frequency	Percent
Form of Financing	Bank loan	72	36
	Borrowed from money lender	2	1
	Bank loan as well as own money	56	28
	Bank loan, borrowed from money lender	8	4
	Selffinancing	34	17
	Others	12	6
	Sub-Total	184	92
	No Response	16	8
Total		**200**	**100**

Source: Field survey

Table 5. Frequency distribution of number of members in the group / internal and external loan amount received per member

	No. of Members in Group	Frequency	Percent
Total No. of MEMBERS	0-5	3	1.5
	6-10	32	16
	11-15	57	28.5
	16-20	100	50
	21-25	4	2
	Above 25	4	2
	Total	**200**	**100**
Internal Amount Received per Member	Below2000	58	72.5
	2001-4000	8	10
	4001-6000	6	7.5
	8001-10000	6	7.5
	14001-16000	2	2.5
	Total	**80**	100
Bank Loan Amount Received per Member(Rs.)	Below2000	54	35.1
	2001-4000	46	29.9
	4001-6000	30	19.5
	6001-8000	8	5.2
	8001-10000	8	5.2
	10001-12000	2	1.3
	12001-14000	4	2.6
	14001-16000	2	1.3
	Total	**154**	**100**

Source: Field survey

Table 6. Means of distribution and collection of loans granted

	Amount of Loan	Frequency	Percent
Total Amount Disbursed	Below2000	72	36
	2001-4000	54	27
	4001-6000	32	16
	6001-8000	10	5
	8001-10000	10	5
	10001-12000	4	2
	12001-14000	4	2
	14001-16000	8	4
	No Response	6	3
	Total	**200**	**100**
Total Amount Realized	0-1000	30	15
	1001-2000	54	27
	2001-4000	56	28
	4001-6000	28	14
	6001-8000	8	4
	8001-10000	10	5
	Above 10000	14	7
	Total	**200**	**100**
Principal Amount Disbursed	0-50	20	10
	51-100	70	35
	101-150	34	17
	151-200	20	10
	201-250	16	8
	251-300	14	7
	301-600	8	4
	601-800	2	1
	801-1000	14	7
	Above 1000	2	1
	Total	**200**	**100**
Frequency of Collection	Weekly	4	2
	Monthly	196	98
	Total	**200**	**100**

Source: Field survey

Table 7. Metrics of performance based on production and sales

		Frequency	Percent
Frequency of Manufacturing	Daily	26	13
	Weekly	88	44
	Monthly	86	43
	Total	**200**	**100**
Total Number of Employees	Less than 5	30	15
	5 to 10	96	48
	10 & above	74	37
	Total	**200**	**100**
Selling Price of Products	Maximum Retail Price	50	25
	Whole Sale Rate	60	30
	Both	90	45
	Total	**200**	**100**
Place	Local market	196	98
	Home visit	2	1
	Other States	2	1
	Total	**200**	**100**
Frequency of Remuneration/ Wages/ Salary	Daily	10	5
	Weekly	64	32
	Monthly	126	63
	Total	**200**	**100**
Monthly Profit (Rs.)	Below 500	6	3
	500-1,000	58	29
	1000 & above	136	68
	Total	**200**	**100**

Source: Field survey

Rs. 1,000 and above among 71.15 percent of the entrepreneurs, monthly profit Rs.500-1,000 in 20.8 percent of entrepreneurs and monthly profit Rs. below 500 in 8.3 percent of the entrepreneurs.

Most of the women members of SHG's started receiving one or the other benefit from the group. These benefits so received are given in table 9. A large majority of benefits of obtained by SHG members were after joining the group.

Table 8. Distribution of SHG members based on the monthly profit generated by the selected economic activity

Economic Activity	Profit per Month(Rs.)			Total
	Below 500	500-1,000	1000 & Above	
Sewing	-	-	2(100)	2(1)
Beautician	-	4(50)	4(50)	8(4)
Incense stick manufacturing	-	2(12.5)	14(87.5)	16(8)
Pappad Making	2(1.93)	28(26.92)	74(71.15)	104(52)
Grocery	-	8(100)	-	8(4)
others	4(8.3)	10(20.8)	34(70.8)	48(24)
Pottery	-	2(33.3)	4(66.7)	6(3)
Handicrafts	-	2(33.3)	4(66.7)	6(3)
Embroidery	-	2(100)	-	2(1)
Total	**6(3)**	**58(29)**	**136(68)**	**200(100)**

$\chi^2 = 45.373$, d.f.=18, P-value <0.001
Source: Field survey

Table 9. Benefits of SHG MEMBERS

	Benefits					
	Incremental Savings	Bank Accounts Opened	Financial Independence	Upgradation of Technology	Superior Decision Making Power	Others(Social/ Literacy Improvement)
Yes	190(80)	166(83)	144(72)	140(70)	108(54)	184(92)
No	10(20)	34(17)	56(28)	60(30)	92(46)	16(8)
Total	**200(100)**	**200(100)**	**200(100)**	**200(100)**	**200(100)**	**200(100)**

Source: Field survey Multiple response

CONCLUSION

The SHG is prospective mechanism for self-employment which leads to growth of micro enterprises in any region and the micro credit system works as an integral part thereof, Micro enterprises contribute significantly to economic growth, social stability and the resultant financial inclusion of the members. SHG can help in the growth of micro enterprises, income from micro enterprise provides better amenities: be it in the perspective of food, housing, health care or education for families. Micro Enterprises and SHGs are the key means for Rural socio-economic transformation and expansion of micro enterprises through SHG and micro credit system has led to financial inclusion of a vast rural population which in turn is helping in eradicating poverty.

REFERENCES

Akinsanmi, A. (2005). Working Under Constraint: Women, Poverty and Productivity. *Women and Environments International, 66/67*, 17–18.

Ali-Akpajiak, C. A., & Pyke, T. (2003). *Measuring Poverty in Nigeria*. UK Oxfam.

Chen, M., Jhabvala, R., Kanbur, R., & Richards, C. (2007). *Membership Based Organizations of the Poor: Concepts, Experience and Policy*. London: Routledge.

Frances. (2005). The Maturing Of Indian Micro Finance. *Guragaon.Eda Rural Systems*, 6-24.

Jerinabi, U. (2006). *Micro Credit Management by Women's Self Help Groups*. New Delhi: Discovery Publishing House.

Krishna, M. (2003). *Poverty Alleviation and Rural Poor*. New Delhi: Mittal Publication.

Lolheihzovi. (2007). *Women's Development in India*. New Delhi: Mittal Publication.

(submitted to). Manimekalai. (2004). *Impact of various forms of micro financing on women*. [Department of Women and Child Development, Ministry of Sinha.]. *Report*.

Moyle, T. L., Dollard, M., & Biswas, S. N. (2006, October). Personal and Economic Empowerment in Rural Indian Women. *International Journal of Rural Management, 2*(2), 245–266. doi:10.1177/097300520600200207

Nalwaya, N., & Vyas, R. (2012). MFI-a study of socio economic indicators of women SHG,sin south rajasthanwith perspective of financial sustainability. *Abhinav International Monthly Refreed Journal of Research in Management and Technology, 2*(6).

Narasaiah, M. L. (2004). *Women and Microcredit*. Sonali Publications.

Panda, R. K. (2005). *Emerging Issues on Rural Credit*. New Delhi: APH Publishing Corporation.

Renu, V. (2008). Microfinance and Empowerment of Rural Women. *Kurukshetra. Journal of Rural Development, 56*(11), 3–5.

Singh S. D. (2010). Saving approaches of Self-Help Group Members- a study with reference to Manipur. *Prajnan, Journal of Social and Management Sciences, 39*(1), 29-39.

Subrahmanyam, N. (2009). Microfinance and SHG-Bank Linkage: Regional analysis and perspectives. *Prajnan. Journal of Social and Management Sciences*, *38*(3), 183–202.

Tangirala, H. S. K. (2008). SHG is a tool of Economic Development of Co-operatives and its members. *Kurukshetra. Journal of Rural Development*, *57*(2), 22–24.

Tanya Jakimow, P. K. (2006). A Critique of the Blueprint for Self-help Groups in India. *Indian Journal of Gender Studies*, *13*(3), 375–400.

Tejmani, S. N. (2009). Microfinance practices in India: An overview. *International Review of Business Research Papers*, *5*(5), 131–146.

Tracey, L., & Moyle, M. D. (2006). *Personal and Economic Empowerment in Rural Indian Women*. Academic Press.

Vijayalakshmi, D., Gowda, K. N., Jamuna, K. V., Ray, B. R., & Sajjan, J. T. (2012). Empowerment of self help group women through value addition of finger millet. *Journal of Dairying, Foods and Home Sciences, 31*(3), 223-226.

Compilation of References

Agarwal Amol. (2008). *The Need for Financial Inclusion with an Indian Perspective.* IDBI Gitlts Limited.

Agarwal Reena. (2007). *100% Finance Inclusion: A Challenging Task Ahead.* Indian Institute of Management Kozhikode.

Agarwal, P. K., & Sinha, S. K. (2010). *Financial Performance of Microfinance Institutions of India. Delhi Business Review.*

Aghion, P., & Bolton, P. (1997). A theory of trickle-down growth and development. *The Review of Economic Studies, 64*(2), 151–172. doi:10.2307/2971707

Akinsanmi, A. (2005). Working Under Constraint: Women, Poverty and Productivity. *Women and Environments International, 66/67*, 17–18.

Albinsson, P. A., & Yasanthi Perera, B. (2012). Alternative marketplaces in the 21st century: Building community through sharing events. *Journal of Consumer Behaviour, 11*(4), 303–315. doi:10.1002/cb.1389

Ali-Akpajiak, C. A., & Pyke, T. (2003). *Measuring Poverty in Nigeria.* UK Oxfam.

Alimullah Miyan. (2011). Challenges of Financing Higher Education from Inclusion Perspectives. *International Conference on Innovation and Inclusion in Banking: Issues, Strategies and Options.* Kannur University.

Allen, F., Demirguc-Kunt, A.,; & Klapper, L. (2012). *The Foundations of Financial Inclusion: Understanding Ownership and Use of Formal Accounts.* World Bank Policy Research Working Paper 6290.

Allen, F., Demirgüç-Kunt, A., Klapper, L. F., & Martinez Peria, M. S. (2012). The foundations of financial inclusion: Understanding ownership and use of formal accounts. *Policy Research Working Paper*, 6290.

Amezcua, E. L., Arroyo M. G., & Espinosa F. (2015). Contexto de la educación financiera en México. *Ciencia Administrativa*, (1), 21-30.

Analytics India Magazine. (2017). *Analytics India Industry Study*. Retrieved from https://analyticsindiamag.com/wp-content/uploads/2017/07/Analytics-India-Industry-Study-2017.pdf

Andrianaivo, M. a. (2012). Mobile phones, financial inclusion and growth. *Review of Economics and Institutions*, 30.

Annamalai, C., & Vijayarani, K. (2014). Awareness of financial inclusion on tribal people in Dharmapuri district. *Asia Pacific Journal of Research*, *1*(17), 56–62.

Arunchalam, S. R. (2008). *Financial Inclusion, Considerations and Re commendations for UNDP*. United Nations Development Programme (UNDP).

Atkinson, A., & Messy, F. A. (2012). Measuring financial literacy. *OCDE Working Papers on Finance, Insurance, and Private Pensions,* (15). OECD Publishing. doi:10.1787/5k9csfs90fr4-en

ATM Market Place. (2010, June 28). *ATM Market Place: Articles*. Retrieved from ATM Market Place: https://www.atmmarketplace.com/articles/changing-atm-strategies-to-increase-revenue-opportunities/

Aviva. (2017). *UK: Generation regret: Over a third of millennials who went to university regret doing so as they struggle with debts and squeezed finances*. Retrieved May 5, 2017, from http://www.aviva.com/media/news/item/uk-generation-regret-over-a-third-of-millennials-who-went-to-university-regret-doing-so-as-they-struggle-with-debts-and-squeezed-finances-17653/

Badajena, N., & Gundimeda, H. (2008). *Self Help Group Bank linkage model and financial inclusion in India*. Academic Press.

Bagli, S., & Dutta, P. (2012). A study of financial inclusion in India. *Radix International Journal of Economics & Business Management, 1*(8).

Banco Base. (2016, September 8). *¿Cómo administran los millennials sus finanzas personales?* Retrieved May 7, 2017, from http://blog.bancobase.com/como-administran-los-millennials-sus-finanzas-personales

Bandyopadhyay, T. (2016, April 11). *Why banking in India will never be the same again*. Retrieved from http://www.livemint.com/Opinion/VXJOMNx2O5xbi2nXIr8nPJ /Why-banking-in-India-will-never-be-the-same-again.html

Banerjee, A. V., & Newman, A. F. (1993). Occupational choice and the process of development. *Journal of Political Economy*, *101*(2), 274–298. doi:10.1086/261876

Banking Association South Africa. (2015). *South Africa Annual Review*. Retrieved on May 3, 2017 from http://www.banking.org.za/news-media/publications/reports

Bardhi, F., & Eckhardt, G. M. (2012). Access-based consumption: The case of car sharing. *The Journal of Consumer Research*, *39*(4), 881–898. doi:10.1086/666376

Barhate, G. H., & Jagtap, V. R. (2014). Pradhan Mantri Jan-Dhan Yojana: National Mission on Financial Inclusion. *International Journal of Applied Research.*, *4*(12), 340–342.

Barton, C., Koslow, L., & Beauchamp, C. (2014). *The reciprocity principle: How millennials are changing the face of marketing forever.* Boston Consulting Group. Retrieved May 6, 2017, from https://www.bcgperspectives.com/content/articles/marketing_center_consumer_customer_insight_how_millennials_changing_marketing_forever/?chapter=5#chapter5

Basu. (2013). Policy Reforms in Foreign Investment. *FSI*, 5.

BBVA Innovation Center. (2015, June 25). *Los millenials un desafio para la banca*. Retrieved May 7, 2017, from http://www.centrodeinnovacionbbva.com/noticias/los-millennials-un-desafio-para-la-banca

Beck, T., Demirguc-Kunt, A., & Levine, R. (2004). *Finance, Inequality and Poverty: Cross-Country Evidence, World Bank Policy Research.* Working Paper 3338, The World Bank. Retrieved from http://documents.worldbank.org/curated/en/824991468778185410/Finance-inequality-and-poverty-cross-country-evidence

Behl, A. (2016). Analyzing the Barriers towards. *Indian Journal of Science and Technology*, 15.

Belk, R. (2014). You are what you can access: Sharing and collaborative consumption online. *Journal of Business Research*, *67*(8), 1595–1600. doi:10.1016/j.jbusres.2013.10.001

Better Money Habits. (n.d.). Retrieved May 2017 from https://bettermoneyhabits.bankofamerica.com/en/saving-budgeting/spending-tool

Bharati, D. B. (2016). A Comparative Study of Inclusive Growth: Economic Policy Reforms a Financial Inclusion in India. *We'Ken-International Journal of Basic and Applied Sciences*, *1*(2), 39–44. doi:10.21904/weken/2016/v1/i2/98418

Bhatia, N., & Chattterjee, A. (2010). Financial Inclusion in the Slums of Mumbai. *Economic and Political Weekly*, *XLV*(42), 16.

Bhuvana, M., & Vasantha, S. (2016). Drivers of Financial Inclusion to Reach Out Poor. *Arabian Journal of Business and Management Review*, *6*(235).

Bhuvana, M., & Vasantha, D. (2016). Drivers of Financial Inclusion to Reach Out Poor. *Arabian Journal of Business and Management Review*, *6*(4). doi:10.4172/2223-5833.1000235

Bhuvana, M., & Vasantha, S. (2016). Dimensions for measuring financial inclusion in the rural areas of Tamil Nadu. *Indian Journal of Science and Technology*, *9*(32).

Biroch, R., & Pozzebon, M. (2016). Improving financial inclusion: Towards a critical financial education framework. *Rev. adm. empres.*, *56*(3).

Bokman, A., Fiedler, L., Perrey, J., & Pickersgill, A. (2014). *Five Facts how customer analytics boost corporate performance*. Retrieved from http://www.mckinsey.com/business-functions/marketing-and-sales/our-insights/five-facts-how-customer-analytics-boosts-corporate-performance

Bolton, R. N., Kannan, P. K., & Bramlett, M. D. (2000). Implications of Loyalty Program Membership and Service Experiences for Customer Retention and Value. *Journal of the Academy of Marketing Science*, *28*(1), 95–108. doi:10.1177/0092070300281009

Bourlier, A., & Gomez, G. (2017). Strategies for Expanding into Emerging Markets with e-commerce. *Euromonitor International*. Retrieved on November 09 2017 from http://unctad.org/meetings/en/Contribution/dtl-eWeek2017c08-euromonitor_en.pdf

Brandenburger, A. M., & Stuart, J. H. Jr. (1996). Value-based business strategy. *Journal of Economics & Management Strategy*, *5*(1), 5–24. doi:10.1111/j.1430-9134.1996.00005.x

Briefing, I. (2014, June 17). *Reserve Bank of India to Offer Differentiated Banking Licenses*. Delhi: National Capital Region.

Brown, M., Grigsby, J., van der Klaauw, W., Wen, J., & Zafar, B. (2016). Financial education and the debt behavior of the young. *Review of Financial Studies*, *29*(9), 2490–2522. doi:10.1093/rfs/hhw006

Bruhn, M., Lara Ibarra, G., & McKenzie, D. J. (2013). *Why is voluntary financial education so unpopular? Experimental evidence from Mexico*. World Bank. doi: 10.1596/1813-9450-6439

Budget Speech for 2015 by Hon'ble Finance Minister

Budget Speech for 2016 by Hon'ble Finance Minister

Bumeran. (2017). *Los Millennials y sus hábitos financieros*. Retrieved May 5, 2017, from http://www.bumeran.com.mx/

Business Today Online. (2017, November 1). Ease of Doing Business rankings: India makes highest-ever jump to rank 100 out of 190 countries. *Business Today Online*.

C. (n.d.). *CRISIL Inclusix Volume III*. Retrieved June 24, 2017, from https://www.scribd.com/document/321861143/CRISIL-Inclusix-Volume-III

Carrie, G. (2017). *Customer analytics and its importance*. Retrieved from https://www.sas.com/en_us/insights/marketing/customer-analytics.html

Catalyst. (2015). *Catalyst quick take: Generations in the workplace*. New York: Catalyst. Retrieved May 6, 2017, from http://www.catalyst.org/knowledge/generations-demographic-trends-population-and-workforce

Cazal, D. (2011). RSE et théorie des parties prenantes: les impasses du contrat. *Revue de la Régulation,* (9). Retrieved from http://regulation.revues.org

CFI. (2009). *Financial Inclusion: What's the Vision?* Retrieved from http://www.centerforfinancialinclusion.org/publications-a-resources/browse-publications/216-financial-inclusion-whats-the-vision

CGAP. (2010). *Update on Branchless Banking Policy and Regulation in Mexico.* Retrieved from https://www.cgap.org/sites/default/files/CGAP-Regulation-of-Branchless-Banking-in-Mexico-Jan-2010.pdf

Chaiken, S. (1980). Heuristic versus systematic information processing and the use of source versus message cues in persuasion. *Journal of Personality and Social Psychology, 39*(5), 752–766. doi:10.1037/0022-3514.39.5.752

Chakrabarty. (n.d.). *Empowering MSMEs for financial inclusion and growth – Issues and Strategies.* Academic Press.

Chakraborty, K. C. (2006). Financial Inclusion: Concepts, Issues, And Roadmap. Institute for Development and Research in Banking Technology.

Chakravarty, S., & Pal, R. (2010). *Measuring Financial Inclusion: An Axiomatic Approach.* Indra Gandhi Institute of Development Research.

Charreaux, G., & Desbrières, P. (1998). Gouvernance des entreprises: Valeur partenariale contre valeur actionnariale. *Finance Contrôle Stratégie, 1*(2), 57–88.

Chatterjee Shankar. (2004). Networking: SGSY, Banks and SHGs: Initiative in Uttar Pradesh. *Kurukshetra, 51*(4), 27-29.

Chen, M., Jhabvala, R., Kanbur, R., & Richards, C. (2007). *Membership Based Organizations of the Poor: Concepts, Experience and Policy.* London: Routledge.

Chima, O. R. (2010). *The Democratisation of Finance? Financial Inclusion and Subprime in the UK and US.* University of Northumbria.

Chowhan, S. S., & Pande, J. C. (2014). Pradhan Mantri Jan Dhan Yojana: A Giant Leap Towards Financial Inclusion. *International Journal of Research in Management and Business Studies., 1*(4), 19–22.

CIBC. (n.d.). *CIBC Advice Centre.* Retrieved from CIBCC: https://www.cibc.com/ca/student-life/banking-101/intro-to-banking/benefit-online-bnkng.html

Claessens, S. (2006). Access to Financial Services: A Review of the Issues and Public Policy Objectives. *The World Bank Research Observer, 21*(2), 1–34. doi:10.1093/wbro/lkl004

Clarke, G. R., Xu, L. C., & Zou, H. F. (2006). Finance and income inequality: What do the data tell us? *Southern Economic Journal, 72*(3), 578–596. doi:10.2307/20111834

Cognizant report. (2015). *Digital Banking: Enhancing Customer Experience; Generating Long-Term Loyalty*. Retrieved from https://www.cognizant.com/InsightsWhitepapers/Digital-Banking-Enhancing-Customer-Experience-Generating-Long-Term-Loyalty.pdf

Comparaguru.com. (2016, September 8). *5 tipos ideales de crédito para millennials*. Retrieved May 7, 2017, from https://www.comparaguru.com/blog/5-tipos-ideales-de-credito-para-millennials

Conroy, J. (2008). *Financial Inclusion: A New Micro Finance Initiative for APEC*. The Foundation for Development Cooperation (FDC), Microfinance Workshop.

Contreras, L. (2014, July 17). *Créditos, una opción costosa para estudiar*. Retrieved from http://www.forbes.com.mx/creditos-una-opcion-costosa-para-estudiar/#gs.gWKiLME

Corrigan, G., & Battista, A. (2015). *19 charts that explain India's economic challenge*. Retrieved from https://www.weforum.org/agenda/2015/11/19-charts-that-explain-indias-economic-challenge/

Coulter, R. H., & Zaltman, G. (1995). Seeing the voice of the customer: Metaphor-based advertising research. *Journal of Advertising Research*, *35*(4), 35–51.

Couteret, P. (1997). L'impact de la confiance interpersonnelle sur l'implication organisationnelle: le cas de l'adjoint au dirigeant de petite entreprise. *Actes du 8ème congrès de l'AGRH*, 163-177.

Couteret, P. (1999). La pertinence du concept de confiance Dans la transition entre contrôle du manager et autonomie du subordonné: le cas des petites entreprises. *Actes du 10ème congrès de l'AGRH*, Lyon, France.

Cova, B. (2008). *CONSUMER MADE quand le consommateur devient producteur. In Décisions Marketing n°50* (pp. 19–27). Avril-juin.

Crédito Joven. (2017). *Para iniciar tu negocio*. Retrieved April 25, 2017, from http://www.creditojoven.gob.mx/portalcj/content/iniciar-tu-negocio.html

CRISIL. (2015). *Crisil Inclusix, An index to measure India's progress on financial inclusion*. Retrieved on March 16, 2017 from https://www.crisil.com/about-crisil/crisil-inclusix-report.html

CRISIL. (2015). *CRISIL Inclusix*. CRISIL. Retrieved October 10, 2017, from https://crisil.com/pdf/corporate/CRISIL-Inclusix-Volume-III.pdf

Cudmore, B. A., Patton, J., Ng, K., & McClure, C. (2010). The millennials and money management. *Journal of Management and Marketing Research*, *4*(1), 1–28.

D. (2017, January 01). *Department of Financial Services | Ministry of Finance Government of India*. Retrieved June 17, 2017, from http://financialservices.gov.in

Deb, A. (2014). *It's Time to Listen to the Voice of the Consumer*. Retrieved from http://www.cgap.org/blog/its-time-listen-voice-consumer

Debord, G. (1992). *La société du spectacle (1967)* (p. 83). Paris: Gallimard.

Defourny, J., Laville, J.-L., & Cattani, A.-D. (2005). *Dictionnaire de l'autre économie*. Paris: Desclee de Brouwer.

Deloitte. (2017). *The Deloitte Millennial Survey 2017*. Retrieved May 6, 2017, from https://www2.deloitte.com/global/en/pages/about-deloitte/articles/millennialsurvey.html

Demirgüç-Kunt, A., & Klapper, L. F. (2012). Measuring financial inclusion: The global findex database. *Policy Research Working Paper*, 6025.

Demirguc-Kunt, A., Klapper, L., Singer, D., & Oudheusd, P. V. (2015, April). *Global Findex Database 2014*. Policy Research Working Paper, WPS7255. World Bank.

Demirguc-Kunt, Klapper, Singer, & Van Oudheusden. (2015). *The Global Findex Database 2014: Measuring Financial Inclusion around the World*. Policy Research Working Paper 7255, World Bank.

DEPR. (2013). *Banking Structure in India - The Way Forward (Discussion Paper)*. Reserve Bank of India, Department of Banking Operations and Development (DBOD) and Department of Economic and Policy Research (DEPR). Mumbai: Reserve Bank of India. Retrieved from https://rbidocs.rbi.org.in/rdocs/PublicationReport/Pdfs/DPBS27082013_F.pdf

DeVaney, S. A. (2015). Understanding the Millennial generation. *Journal of Financial Service Professionals*, *69*(6), 11–14.

Developing securitisation market key to drive financial inclusion, PTI, 21 January 2016

Dhanani, S. (2015, March 5). How prepaid and mobile are driving commerce in emerging markets. *Digital Transactional Processing Industry Solutions Insights*. Retrieved May 7, 2017, from http://cartaworldwide.com/news-insights/how-prepaid-and-mobile-are-driving-commerce-in-emerging-markets/

Dhawan, R. (2014, April). *Why Is Financial Inclusion in India Not Improving? New Numbers, New Approaches*. Retrieved October 9, 2017, from www.microsave.net: http://blog.microsave.net/why-is-financial-inclusion-in-india-not-improving-new-numbers-new-approaches/

Dixit, R., & Ghosh, M. (2013). Financial Inclusion For Inclusive Growth Of India - A Study. *International Journal Of Business Management & Research*, *3*(1), 147–156.

Dovall, A. (2016). *Digital payments soar by up to 300% after demonetisation*. Retrieved from http://timesofindia.indiatimes.com/business/india-business/Digital-payments-soar-by-up-to-300-after-demonetisation/articleshow/55902284.cms

Dun and Bradstreet Report. (2008). *Deutche Bank Distribution Going to the Next Level*. Retrieved on May 21, 2017 from http://www.dnb.co.in/FESConfTool/Uploads/Agenda/Distribution%20 Agenda.pdf

Duran, N. (2012). *L'actionnaire individuel client: étude du cas français*. Toulon: Université de Toulon.

Economic Survey (2017). (Vol. 2). Department of Economic Affairs, Ministry of Finance.

Elouadi, S. (2014). *Analyse des effets induits par l'actionnariat salarié sur la création de valeur partenariale des entreprises du SBF 250*. Thèse de doctorat. Université du Sud.

Elouadi, S. (2015). Les effets attitudinaux de l'actionnariat salarié: une étude empirique dans le contexte des entreprises françaises du SBF 250. *Question (s) de management*, (3), 11-24.

Elouadi, S. (2016). To increase the development of human capital through employee ownership: an empirical analysis in the context of French companies in the SBF 250. *Memorias, 14*(26).

Eventbrite. (2016). *Millennials: Fueling the experience economy*. Retrieved May 6, 2017, from https://www.eventbrite.com/blog/academy/millennials-fueling-experience- economy/?Email=&InferredCountry=United+States&UTM_Source__c=&UTM_campaign__c=&Ref_Code__c=&UTM_Content__c=&UTM_Medium__c=&UTM_Term__c=&FirstName=&LastName=&Company=&Phone=&avg_ticket_price__c=&formid=1044&munchkinId=269-CEG-133

Express, F. (2012, March). Rupee Exchange Depreciation: Impact Analysis. *Financial Express*, p. 3.

EY. (2015). *Mobile money: The next wave of growth*. EY.

Fernandes, D., Lynch, J. G. Jr, & Netemeyer, R. G. (2014). Financial literacy, financial education, and downstream financial behaviors. *Management Science, 60*(8), 1861–1883. doi:10.1287/mnsc.2013.1849

Fernbach, P. M., Kan, C., & Lynch, J. G. Jr. (2015). Squeezed: Coping with constraint through efficiency and prioritization. *The Journal of Consumer Research, 41*(5), 1204–1227. doi:10.1086/679118

Financial Inclusion in digital Economy, ADB Briefs, January 2017

Financial Inclusion Labs. (2016, April). *Financial Inclusion Labs*. Retrieved from Financial Inclusion Labs: http://www.fisfilab.com/2016/04/atms-as-access-enablers-to-financial-inclusion/

Financial Inclusion Summit. (2016). Retrieved from http://cashlesscatalyst.org/wp-content/uploads/2017/01/Financial-Inclusion-Summit.pdf>. /

Finlayson, A. (2011). Financialisation, Financial Literacy and Asset-Based Welfare. *British Journal of Politics and International Relations, 11*(3), 400–421. doi:10.1111/j.1467-856X.2009.00378.x

Frances. (2005). The Maturing Of Indian Micro Finance. *Guragaon.Eda Rural Systems*, 6-24.

Fundamo. (n.d.). *MTN Uganda Achieves One of The Most Remarkable Mobile Money Growth Rates Working With Fundamo*. Fundamo. Retrieved from http://docplayer.net/7800095-Mtn-uganda-achieves-one-of-the-most-remarkable-mobile-money-growth-rates-working-with-fundamo-case-study-mtn-uganda.html

Gambetta, N., García-Benau, M. A., & Zorio-Grima, A. (2016). Data analytics in banks' audit: The case of loan loss provisions in Uruguay. *Journal of Business Research*, *69*(11), 4793–4797. doi:10.1016/j.jbusres.2016.04.032

Gandhi, R. (2015). Dy. Governor, RBI in the V. Narayan Memorial Lecture. *Differentiated banks: Design Challenges*. Retrieved from https://www.rbi.org.in/Scripts/BS_SpeechesView.aspx?Id=954

Gandhi, R. (2015, April 20). Differentiated Banks: Design Challenges. *Differentiated Banks: Design Challenges*. Kumbakonam, Tamil Nadu, India: Reserve Bank of India. Retrieved from https://rbi.org.in/scripts/BS_SpeechesView.aspx?Id=954

Gangadharan, K. (2012). *Financial inclusion and inclusive growth through banking lessons from India*. Reference Press.

García, N., Grifoni, A., López, J. C., & Mejía, D. (2013). *N° 12. La educación financiera en América Latina y el Caribe*. Situación actual y perspectivas.

GFK. (2016). *Enjoy life today, worry about savings and investments later*. Retrieved May 31, 2016, from http://www.gfk.com/global-studies/global-studies-enjoy-life/

Gibson, K. (2000). The Moral Basis of Stakeholder Theory. *Journal of Business Ethics*, *26*(3), 245–257. doi:10.1023/A:1006110106408

Goldman-Sachs. (2017). *Millennials coming of age*. Retrieved from http://www.goldmansachs.com/our-thinking/pages/millennials/

Goyal, M. A. (2016). Pradhan Mantri Jan Dhan Yojana: A Step Towards Financial Inclusion. *Pacific Business Review International, 8*(9).

Gupta, N. (2014). *How Analytics Drive Innovative Financial Services for the Poor*. Retrieved from http://www.cgap.org/blog/how-analytics-drive-innovative-financial-services-poor

Gupte, M. (2011). *Articles: Business Standard.* Retrieved from Business Standard: http://www.business-standard.com/article/pf/what-are-neft-and-rtgs-111053100076_1.html

Gwalani, H. A., & Parkhi, S. (2014). Financial Inclusion–Building A Success Model In The Indian Context. *Procedia: Social and Behavioral Sciences*, *133*, 372–378. doi:10.1016/j.sbspro.2014.04.203

Handoo, J. (2010). *Financial inclusion in India: Integration of technology, policy and market at the bottom of the pyramid*. Retrieved on April 20, 2017 from http://skoch.in/fir/role%20%financial%20%inclusion%20

Harris. (2017). *Harris Poll: Millennials increasingly dictating health of America's top brands*. Retrieved May 6, 2017, from http://www.theharrispoll.com/business/Millennials-Dictating-Health-of-Brands.html

Hastings, J. S., Madrian, B. C., & Skimmyhorn, W. L. (2013). Financial literacy, financial education, and economic outcomes. *Annual Review of Economics*, *5*(1), 347–373. doi:10.1146/annurev-economics-082312-125807 PMID:23991248

Hastings, J. S., & Tejeda-Ashton, L. (2008). *Financial literacy, information, and demand elasticity: Survey and experimental evidence from Mexico (No. w14538)*. National Bureau of Economic Research. doi:10.3386/w14538

Helfer, J.-P. (2005). Et si le marketing était éthique par définition? In La responsabilité sociale de l'entreprise. Mélanges en l'honneur du Professeur Roland Pérez. EMS.

Hershfield, H. E., Goldstein, D. G., Sharpe, W. F., Fox, J., Yeykelis, L., Carstensen, L. L., & Bailenson, J. N. (2011). Increasing saving behavior through age-progressed renderings of the future self. *Journal of Marketing Research*, *48*(SPL), S23-S37.

Hindustan Times. (2017, November 24). More incentives for MSMEs complying with GST norms. *Hindustan Times*.

Hota, J. (2013). *Publications: Researchgate*. Retrieved from Researchgate: http://www.researchgate.net/publication/235436177_Growth_of_ATM_Industry_in_India

IBEF. (2017, May 16). ibef.org/Ebook/IBEF. Retrieved from https://www.ibef.org/Ebook/IBEF-Dec-2016-Jan-2017.pdf)

IBM Executive Report. (2012). *Analytics: The real-world use of big data in financial services*. Retrieved from https://www-935.ibm.com/services/multimedia/Analytics_The_real_world_use_of_big_data_in_Financial_services_Mai_2013.pdf

Ibrahim Muhammad. (2010). *Sustainable Finance Inclusion*. Alliance for Financial Inclusion (AFI), Data Workshop Kualaumpur.

Income-tax Act, 1961 as amended by Finance Act 2017

India Brand Equity Foundation. (2016, December). Financial Inclusion- Steering Growth and Empowerment. *India Now-. Business Economics (Cleveland, Ohio)*, *3*(4). https://www.ibef.org/Ebook/IBEF-Dec-2016-Jan-2017.pdf Retrieved July 11, 2017

Indian Brand Equity Foundation report. (2016). *Indian Banking Industry Analysis*. Retrieved from https://www.ibef.org/industry/banking-presentation

Infosys. (2012). *Why banks are turning to analytics?* Retrieved from https://www.edgeverve.com/wp-content/uploads/2017/03/why-banks-are-turning-analytics.pdf

International Monetary Fund. (2012). *World Economic Outlook Report: Growth Resuming, Dangers Remain*. International Monetary Fund. Retrieved from http://www.imf.org/external/pubs/ft/weo/2012/01/

International Monetary Fund. (2016). *IMF Releases the 2016 Financial Access Survey, A Key Tool to Foster Financial Inclusion*. Retrieved on April 12, 2017 from https://www.imf.org/en/News/Articles/2016/10/03/PR16441-IMF-Releases-the-2016-Financial-Access-Survey

Irving Fisher Committee on Central Bank Statistics. (2016). *Measures of Financial Inclusion – A Central Bank Perspective*. Survey conducted by the Irving Fisher Committee on Central Bank Statistics (IFC). Retrieved from https://www.bis.org/ifc/publ/ifc_finan_inclu.pdf

ISME. (2012, November). *Consumer Behaviour: Rural Vs Urban Customer.* Retrieved October 1, 2017, from www.isme.com: http://www.isme.in/consumer-behaviour-rural-vs-urban-customer/

Jabbour, A. (2016, July 6). *Banks need to adapt to millennials, not vice versa*. Retrieved from https://www.americanbanker.com/opinion/banks-need-to-adapt-to-millennials-not-vice-versa

Jain, D. (2014a). Differentiated banking - Is India really prepared? *Journal of Indian Institute of Banking and Finance*, *85*(4), 27–32.

Jain, D. D. (2014b). Differentiated Bank Licences: Emergence of a New Bank Structure. *Pacific Business Review International*, *6*(12), 144–145.

Jain, M. R. (2016). A Study of Financial Inclusion of Household Workers in Jaipur. *Sumedha Journal of Management*, *5*(2), 94.

Jalan, A. (2009). *Microfinance: does it affect rural poverty reduction? the case of two villages in southern India*. Academic Press.

Jerinabi, U. (2006). *Micro Credit Management by Women's Self Help Groups*. New Delhi: Discovery Publishing House.

Joseph, D. (2014). A study on Financial Inclsuion and Financial Literacy. *International Journal of Business and Administration Research Review*, *2*(4), 126–134.

Joshi, M. C., & Rajpurohit, V. P. (2016). Awareness of Financial Inclusion: An Empirical Study. *Research Review International Journal of Multidisciplinary, 1*(6), 1-6.

Kainth, G. S. (2014). *Differentiated Banking in India: A Long Way to Go.* Amritsar: Guru Arjan Dev Institute of Development Studies. Retrieved from http://www.academia.edu/8126893/differentiated_banking_in_india_a_long_way_to_go

Kannan, R. (n.d.). *E-Banking: Kannan Personal*. Retrieved from Kannan Personal: http://kannanpersonal.com/inbank2/e-banking/rbi-role.html

Kapoor, R. (2016). *7 Reasons Why Demonetization Is A Masterstroke By Modi*. Retrieved from http://www.huffingtonpost.in/rana-kapoor/7-reasons-why-demonetization-is-a-masterstroke-by-modi/

Kapoor, A. (2014, February). Financial inclusion and the future of the Indian economy. *Futures*, *56*, 35–42. doi:10.1016/j.futures.2013.10.007

Kardes, F. R., Posavac, S. S., & Cronley, M. L. (2004). Consumer inference: A review of processes, bases, and judgment contexts. *Journal of Consumer Psychology*, *14*(3), 230–256. doi:10.120715327663jcp1403_6

Kathuria, R. M. (2009). *An econometric analysis of the impact of mobile*. Vodafone Policy Paper.

Kefela, G. T. (2010). Promoting access to finance by empowering consumers: Financial literacy in developing countries. *Educational Research Review*, *5*(5), 205.

Kessy, S. A., & Urio, F. M. (2010). *The Contribution of Microfinance Institutions to Poverty Reduction in Tanzania*. MkukinaNyota.

Khan, S. H. R. (2012). Issues and challenges in financial inclusion – policies, partnerships, processes & products. Deputy Governor of the Reserve Bank of India, at the symposium on "Financial inclusion in Indian Economy", organized by the Indian Institute of Public Administration, Bhubaneswar, India.

Khokhar, A. S. (2016). *Digital Literacy: How Prepared Is India to Embrace It?* Academic Press.

Khuntia, R. (2014). Pradhan Mantri Jan Dhan Yojana: A New Drive Towards Financial Inclusion in India. ZENITH. *International Journal of Business Economics and Management Research.*, *4*(11), 10–20.

Klapper, L., Lusardi, A., & van Oudheusden, P. (n.d.). *Financial Literacy around the World: Insights from the S&P Global Finlit Survey*. Retrieved from http://gflec.org/wp-content/uploads/2015/11/Finlit_paper_16_F2_singles.pdf

KPMG. (2015). Digital India. *KPMG*, 36.

KPMG. (2015). *Financial Services: Role of Digital Banking in Furthering Financial Inclusion*. Retrieved from https://www.researchgate.net/profile/.../Digital+banking+in+india4.pdf

KPMG. (2016). *Customer Adoption of Digital Initiatives*. KPMG.

Krause, S. (2016). *How can we leverage digital technology for financial inclusion?* Retrieved from https://blogs.worldbank.org/psd/psd/how-can-we-leverage-digital-technology-financial-inclusion

Krishna, M. (2003). *Poverty Alleviation and Rural Poor*. New Delhi: Mittal Publication.

Krishnan, D. R. (2014). Differentiated banks and Financial Inlcusion. *20th Thinkers and Writers Forum.*

Kumar, B. P., & Philip, P. J. (2011). Financial Exclusion A Theoretical Approach. *International Conference on Innovation and Inclusion in Banking: Issues, Strategies and Options*. Kannur University.

Kumar, P. G. (2014). *Bank Accounts for All: PM Modi That's Not Financial Inclusion*. Accessed from http://www.firstpost.com/politics/bank-accounts-for-all-pm-modi-thats-not-financial-inclusion-1610443.html

Kumar,, S., & Kaushik. (2016). A Study of Bankers' Viewpoint Toward Factors Affecting the Pradhan Mantri Jan-Dhan Yojana in Selected Public Sector Banks. *RIJBFA Radix International Journal of Banking. Finance and Accounting*, *5*(2), 1–10.

Kumar, D., & Venkatesha, H. R. (2014). Financial Inclusion using Pradhan Mantri Jan- Dhan Yojna- A Conceptual Study. *Asia Pacific Journal of Research.*, *1*(20), 37–42.

Kumar, N. D. (2013). Current Situation of Financial Inclusion in India and Its future vision. *International Journal of Management and Social Sciences Research*, *2*(8).

Kumar, V. (2014). Financial Inclusion in India: Unique Solutions. *Indian Streams Research Journal.*, *4*(8), 1–3.

Kumbhar, V. (2011). *Financial Inclusion Through M-Banking Services: Scope And Problems In India*. Academic Press.

La Vanguardia. (2017, April). *Santander lanza '1, 2, 3 Smart', la cuenta para millennials.* Retrieved May 7, 2017, from http://www.lavanguardia.com/economia/20170417/421773258411/santander-1-2-3-smart-cuenta-millennial-jovenes.html

Lathey, P. (2012). *Microfinance – As a Instrument for Poverty Reduction in Rural India.* New Delhi: Financial Inclusion and Poverty Alleviation in India, Kunal Books.

Laureti, C. (2009). *Role of Savings in Competitive Microfinance Markets and Feasibility of the Business Correspondent Model in India*. European Microfinance Program.

Lavin, M. (2014, October 28). *Los millenials y la nueva banca*. Retrieved May 7, 2017, from https://www.forbes.com.mx/los-millenials-y-la-nueva-banca/

Lee, J., & Kwon, K. N. (2002). Consumers' use of credit cards: Store credit card usage as an alternative payment and financing medium. *The Journal of Consumer Affairs*, *36*(2), 239–262. doi:10.1111/j.1745-6606.2002.tb00432.x

Léger, J. H. (2008). *La communication financière (2nd ed.).* Paris: Dunod.

Lemoine, J. F., & Onnée, S. (2003). Vers une analyse des enjeux et des pratiques de la gestion de la relation avec l'actionnaire individuel. Décisions Marketing, 31, 25-37.

Lemoine, J. F., & Onnée, S. (2000), Le statut d'actionnaire-client: faisons le point, *5ème congrès mondial de l'ASAC-IFSAM*, Canada, Montréal: juillet.

Levin, P. (2013). *Big ambition meets effective execution: How EcoCash is Altering Zimbabwe's Financial Landscape.* London: GSMA. Retrieved from https://www.gsma.com / mobilefordevelopment/wp-content/uploads/2013/07/EcoCash-Zimbabwe.pdf

Liew, L. H., & Wu, H. X. (2008). *The Making of China's Exchange Rate Policy: from plan to WTO entry*. Edward Elgar Publishing.

Live Mint. (2015, September 21). *Live Mint: Money*. Retrieved from Live MINT: http://www.livemint.com/Money/5f8BrGcfJG8mO6Iwdz6TCN/Newage-banking-increases-the-ambit-of-financial-inclusion.html

Logsdon, B. (2016). *Little-known millennial loyalty trends: Marketing insights*. Retrieved May 6, 2017, from https://www.ama.org/publications/MarketingInsights/Pages/millenials-driven-by-loyalty-rewards.aspx

Lolheihzovi. (2007). *Women's Development in India*. New Delhi: Mittal Publication.

Lusardi, A., & Mitchell, O. S. (2014). The economic importance of financial literacy: Theory and evidence. *Journal of Economic Literature*, *52*(1), 5–44. doi:10.1257/jel.52.1.5 PMID:28579637

Lynch, J. G. Jr, Netemeyer, R. G., Spiller, S. A., & Zammit, A. (2010). A generalizable scale of propensity to plan: The long and the short of planning for time and for money. *The Journal of Consumer Research*, *37*(1), 108–128. doi:10.1086/649907

Maccaro, C. (2015). *Why finance brands need to inspire & empower millennials now*. Retrieved April 16, 2017, from https://www.ama.org/resources/Best-Practices/Pages/-Empower-Millennials.aspx

Magni, M., Martínez, A., & Motiwala, R. (2016). *Saving, scrimping, and... splurging?* McKinsey & Company Report. Retrieved March 8, 2017, from http://www.mckinsey.com/industries/consumer-packaged-goods/our-insights/saving-scrimping-and-splurging-new-insights-into-consumer-behavior?cid=other-eml-ttn-mip-mck-oth-1612

Majumdar, C. A. (2013). Financial Inclusion In Hooghly. *Economic and Political Weekly*, *48*(21), 55–60.

Malcolm, H. (2012). Millennials struggle with financial literacy. *USA Today*.

Mallya, A. (2014). *Finacle: Infosys*. Retrieved from Infosys: http://www.infosysblogs.com/finacle/2014/10/the_evolution_of_banking_chann.html

Manimekalai. (2004). *Impact of various forms of micro financing on women*. [Department of Women and Child Development, Ministry of Sinha.]. *Report*.

Martinet, A.-C. (1984). *Management Stratégique, Organisation et Politique*. Paris: Mc Graw Hill.

Mauléon, F., & Saulquin, J. (2009). Une approche comparative de la RSE par le statut juridique. Le cas des banques coopératives et des actions solidaires en France. *Management & Avenir*, *23*(3), 105–122. doi:10.3917/mav.023.0105

Mazer, R., & Kaffenberger, M. (2014). *Simple Messages Help Consumers Understand Big Data*. Retrieved from http://www.cgap.org/blog/simple-messages-help-consumers-understand-big-data

McAteer, M. (2014). *Developing Financial Resilience*. Retrieved from www.preston.gov.uk

McCormick, M. H. (2009). The effectiveness of youth financial education: A review of the literature. *Journal of Financial Counseling and Planning*, *20*(1), 70–83.

McGrath, C. P. (2013). *Innovative Inclusion: How Telesom ZAAD Brought Mobile Money to Somaliland.* London: GSMA. Retrieved from https://www.gsma.com/mobilefordevelopment / wp-content/uploads/2013/07/Telesom-Somaliland.pdf

McNally, P. (2014). *Case study: Zoona.* London: GSMA. Retrieved from https://www.gsma.com/mobilefordevelopment/wp-content/uploads/2016/02/Case_Study_-Zoona.pdf

MDI. (2014). *Millennial Disruption Index*. Retrieved April 20, 2017, from: http://www.millennialdisruptionindex.com/

Mehra, P. (2016, March 29). *All you need to know about payment banks*. Retrieved from http://www.thehindu.com/business/all-you-need-to-know-about-payment-banks/article 7561353.ece

Memorandum explaining provisions of Finance Bill 2016

Memorandum explaining provisions of Finance Bill 2017

Merkle Inc. (2017). *Merkle Inc: Industry Solutions: Financial Services*. Retrieved from Merkle Inc: https://www.merkleinc.com/industry-solutions/financial-services/payments-and-credit-card-marketing

Meshram, P., & Randad, A. (2015). A Survey and Study of an Awareness of Financial Inclusion in an around Pune City, Pune. *International Journal of Engineering Technology, Management and Applied Sciences*, *3*(5), 327–333.

Michie, J. (2012). *Mutual advantage? The future implications of mutualism for employment relations*. University of Oxford.

Micro, Medium & Small Scale. (n.d.). Retrieved from www.cii.in/Sectors

Miller, Reichelstein, Salas, & Zia. (2014). *Can You Help Someone Become Financially Capable? A Meta-Analysis of the Literature.* World Bank Policy Research Working Paper 6745.

Ministry of Finance. GOI. (2017). *Economic Survey 2016-17, Volume 2*. Government of India. Retrieved October 11, 2017, from http://indiabudget.nic.in/es2016-17/echapter_vol2.pdf

Mir, S. B. (2014). A Study On The Effectiveness Of The Financial Inclusion Program In Jammu And Kashmir: Initiatives By The Major Banks. *Global Journal Of Finance And Management*, *6*(3), 281–286.

Mohan, R. (2006). *Financial Sector Reforms and Monetary Policy: The Indian Experience*. RBI.

Mohanty, D., Gulati, A., Demirguk-Kunt, A., Hota, A. P., Sukthankar, P., & Udgata, A. (2015). *Report of the Committee on Medium-term Path on Financial Inclusion*. Reserve Bank of India. Retrieved from https://rbidocs.rbi.org.in/rdocs/PublicationReport/Pdfs/FFIRA27F4530706A41A0BC394D01CB4892CC.PDF

Mohanty, D. (2015). *Report Of Thethe Committee on Medium-term Path on Financial Inclusion*. RBI.

Molina, D. I. (2016). *Fintech: Lo que la tecnología hace por las finanzas*. Profit Editorial.

Morgan, P. A. (2014). *Financial Stability And Financial Inclusion*. Academic Press.

Moyle, T. L., Dollard, M., & Biswas, S. N. (2006, October). Personal and Economic Empowerment in Rural Indian Women. *International Journal of Rural Management*, *2*(2), 245–266. doi:10.1177/097300520600200207

MSME Annual Report 2016-17. (n.d.). Ministry of Micro, Small and Medium Enterprises, Government of India.

Muhia, p. G. (2014). *Factors influencing microfinance customer retention: The case of bright enriched empowerment programme in Nairobi county, Kenya*. University of Nairobi Research Archive.

Mukherjee, A. A. (2012). *Financial Inclusion Of The Poor And Marginalised In Jharkhand: Analysis Of The Existing Model*. Academic Press.

Music Biz/LOOP. (2016, July 12). *Millennials turn from radio to embrace streaming*. Retrieved May 7, 2017, from https://musicbiz.org/news/music-bizloop-study-millennials-turn-radio-embrace-streaming/

N, A., & Joseph, J. (2014). A Study on Consumer Behaviour towards FMCG Products among the Rural-Suburban HHs of Ernakulam. *International Journal of Economics & Management Sciences*, *3*(5). doi:10.4172/2162-6359.1000208

NABARD. (2017, May 16). *Status of microfinance in India*. Retrieved from https://www.nabard.org

Nalwaya, N., & Vyas, R. (2012). MFI-a study of socio economic indicators of women SHG,sin south rajasthanwith perspective of financial sustainability. *Abhinav International Monthly Refreed Journal of Research in Management and Technology*, *2*(6).

Nandru, P., Anand, B., & Rentala, S. (2016). Exploring the factors impacting financial inclusion: Evidence from South India. *Annual Research Journal of SCMS, Pune*, *4*, 1–15.

Narasaiah, M. L. (2004). *Women and Microcredit*. Sonali Publications.

Narasimhan, C. R. (2014, July 27). *Differentiated banks: Has their time come?* Retrieved from http://www.thehindu.com/opinion/columns/C_R_L__Narasimhan/differentiated-banks-has-their-time-come/article6252844.ece

National Bank for Agriculture and Rural Development (NABARD). (2012). *Status of Micro Finance in India 2011–12*. National Bank for Agriculture and Rural Development NABARD. Retrieved from http://indiamicrofinance.com/wp-content/uploads/2012/11/Status-of-Microfinance-2011-12.pdf

Neha Sharma, R. G. (2017). Financial Inclusion Initiatives In Rajasthan: An Overview. *Inspira-Journal of Commerce, Economics & Computer Science*, *3*(1), 156–160.

Norman, A. S. (2010). Importance of financial education in making informed decision on spending. *Journal of Economics and International Finance*, *2*(10), 199–207.

Notification, No. 45/2016, Dated: June 14, 2016, Ministry Of Finance, Department of Revenue, Central Board of Direct Taxes, New Delhi

OECD. (2005). *Recommendation on principles and good practices for financial education and awareness*. Directorate for Financial and Enterprise Affairs. Retrieved from http://www.oecd.org/finance/financial-education/35108560.pdf

Office of the Registrar General & Census Commissioner. (2011). *2011 Census Data*. Retrieved from http://www.censusindia.gov.in/2011-Common/CensusData2011.html

Onnée, S. (2004). *L'intégration des actionnaires individuels lors d'une fusion transeuropéenne: enjeux socioculturels et pratiques de gestion*. Congrès CIDEGEF.

Ory, J. N., Jaeger, M., & Gurtner, E. (2006). La banque à forme coopérative peut-elle soutenir durablement la compétition avec la banque SA? *Finance-Contrôle-Stratégie*, *9*(2), 121–157.

P. (n.d.). *Pradhan Mantri Jan-Dhan Yojana | Department of Financial Services | Ministry of Finance*. Retrieved July 20, 2017, from https://pmjdy.gov.in

Padmashantini, P., Gengeswari, K., & Sharmeela-Banu, S. A. (2013). Investigation on the Customer retention practices at a major retailer in Malaysia. *Interdisciplinary Journal of Research in Business.*, *2*(Issue. 10), 40–50.

Panda, R. K. (2005). *Emerging Issues on Rural Credit*. New Delhi: APH Publishing Corporation.

Park, C. A. (2015). *Financial Inclusion*. Poverty, And Income Inequality In Developing Asia.

Parthrose, E. P., Baby, A., & Maheshwari, U. M. (2015). A Study on Challenges Faced by Customers in Financial Inclusion. *International Journal of Scientific Research and Management.*, *3*(1), 1989–1995.

Pathak, A., Soni, A., & Agarwal, B. P. (2014). Pradhan Mantri Jan Dhan Yojana for Weaker Section- An Evaluation. Shabd Braham. *International Research Journal of Indian Languages.*, *2*(12), 69–74.

Pénicaud, C. (2014). *Mobile Money in Côte d'Ivoire: A Turnaround Story*. London: GSMA. Retrieved from https://www.gsma.com/mobilefordevelopment/wp-content/uploads/2014/05/MMU_Cote_dIvoire_Turnaround_Story.pdf

Peppers, D., & Rogers, M. (2016). *Managing Customer Experience and Relationships: A Strategic Framework*. John Wiley & Sons. doi:10.1002/9781119239833

Perez, R. (2002). L'actionnaire socialement responsable. *Revue Française de Gestion*, *141*, 131-151.

Pew Research Center. (2010). *Millennials, a portrait of generation next: Confident. Connected. Open to change.* Retrieved April 25, 2017, from http://www.pewsocialtrends.org/files/2010/10/millennials-confident-connected-open-to-change.pdf

Philip, H. E., Ozanne, L. K., & Ballantine, P. W. (2015). Examining temporary disposition and acquisition in peer-to-peer renting. *Journal of Marketing Management*, *31*(11-12), 1310–1332. doi:10.1080/0267257X.2015.1013490

Pillai, T. J. (2016). Financial Inclusion and Pradhan Mantri Jan Dhan Yojana: An Empirical Study Conducted in the villages of Mulshi Taluka in Pune District. *Indian Journal of Science and Technology*, *8*(1).

Planning Commission. (2011). *Economic Survey 2010-11: Statistical Appendix*. Government of India. Retrieved from http://www.indiabudget.gov.in/es2010-11/estat1.pdf

PM says ease of doing business ranking will improve further, rebuts criticism from opposition. (2017). Retrieved from www.moneycontrol.com

PMJDY. (2018, January 3). *Pradhan Mantri Jan Dhan Yojana (PMJDY)*. Retrieved from PMJDY - Progress Report: https://pmjdy.gov.in/account

Pokhriyal, A., & Ghildiyal, V. (2011). Progress of Microfinance and Financial Inclusion "A Critical Analysis of SHG-Bank Linkage Program in India". *International Journal of Economics and Finance*, *3*(2), 255. doi:10.5539/ijef.v3n2p255

Pradhan Mantri Jan Dhan Yojana (PMJDY). (2016a). *Scheme Details*. Retrieved on January 20, 2015 from https://www.pmjdy.gov.in/scheme

Pradhan Mantri Jan Dhan Yojana (PMJDY). (2016b). *Progress Report*. Retrieved on December 30, 2016 from http://pmjdy.gov.in/account

Pradhan Mantri Jan Dhan Yojana (PMJDY). (2018). *Progress Report*. Retrieved from https://www.pmjdy.gov.in/statewise-statistics

Prahalad, C. K., & Ramaswamy, V. (2004). Co-creation experiences: The next practice in value creation. *Journal of Interactive Marketing*, *18*(3), 5–14. doi:10.1002/dir.20015

PWC. (2014). *Connecting the dots: Wiring business, technology and operations*. Retrieved from https://www.pwc.in/assets/pdfs/publications/2014/8th-cii-banking-tech-summit-connecting-the-dots.pdf

PwC. (2017). *Los mercados emergentes siguen carentes de sistemas financieros aptos para el propósito*. PwC. Retrieved November 9, 2017 from https://www.pwc.com/ia/es/prensa/pdfs/pwc-project-blue.pdf

R. (n.d.). *Statistical Tables Relating to Banks in India*. Retrieved June 05, 2017, from https://rbi.org.in/Scripts/Statistics.aspx

Radcliffe, I. M. (2010). *Mobile Payments go Viral: M-PESA in Kenya*. World Bank. Retrieved from http://siteresources.worldbank.org/AFRICAEXT/Resources/258643-1271798012256/M-PESA_Kenya.pdf

Rajan, P. (2008). Payments in India Going the E-way. Bangalore: Celent.com.

Rajan. (1984). *Publications: Reserve Bank of India*. Retrieved from Reserve Bank of India: http://www.rbi.org.in/scripts/PublicationsView.aspx?id=162

Rajan, R. e. (2007). *A Hundred Small Steps: Report of the Committee on Financial Sector Reforms*. SAGE Publications.

Ramesh, S., & Sahai, P. (2007). *Universal financial inclusion in India: the way forward*. CAB Calling. Retrieved on April 15, 2017 from: http://cab.org.in/CAB%20Calling%20Content/Financial%20Inclusion%

Rangarajan, C. (2008). *Report of the Committee on financial inclusion*. Academic Press.

Rangarajan. (1989). *Publications: Reserve Bank of India*. Retrieved from Reserve Bank of India: http://www.rbi.org.in/scripts/PublicationsView.aspx?id=162

Rangarajan, C. (2009). *Report of the Committee on Financial Inclusion*. New Delhi: Ministry of Finance, Government of India.

Ranparia, N. D. (2013). Financial Inclusion in Gujarat: A Study on Banker's Initiatives. *International Journal of Scientific Research.*, *2*(February), 32–34.

Rao, Y. V., & Budde, S. R. (2015). Banking technology innovations in India: Enhancing customer value and satisfaction. *Indian Journal of Science and Technology*, *8*(33). doi:10.17485/ijst/2015/v8i33/78280

Razali, N. M., & Wah, Y. B. (2011). Power comparisons of shapiro-wilk, kolmogorov-smirnov, lilliefors and anderson-darling tests. *Journal of Statistical Modeling and Analytics, 2*(1), 21-33.

RBI Committee. (2013). *Committee on Comprehensive Financial Services for Small Businesses and Low Income Households*. Reserve Bank of India. Retrieved October 11, 2017, from https://rbidocs.rbi.org.in/rdocs/PublicationReport/Pdfs/CFS070114RFL.pdf

RBI. (2012). *FAQS: RBI*. Retrieved from Reserve Bank of India: http://www.rbi.org.in/commonman/english/scripts/FAQs.aspx?Id=205

RBI. (2015). *RBI Annual Report 2014-15*. Reserve Bank of India.

RBI. (2016). *Role of Financial Education*. RBI.

RBI. (2017). *Bank-wise volumes in mobile transactions*. RBI.

RBI. (2017, June 17). *Database on Indian Economy*. Retrieved from https://dbie.rbi.org.in/DBIE/dbie.rbi?site=home

RBI. (2018). *Payment systems in India: Vision 2018*. RBI.

RBI: Scripts: Annual Report Publications. (2014, August 21). Retrieved from Rbi: https://www.rbi.org.in/Scripts/AnnualReportPublications.aspx?Id=1127

Reddy, D. Y. (2006). *The Role of Financial Education: The Indian Case*. OECD.

Reddy, J. R. (2016). Financial inclusion: Issues and challenges in India. *Anveshana's Inernational Journal Research in Regional, Law, Social Sciences Journal of Management*, *1*(5), 1–12.

Renu, V. (2008). Microfinance and Empowerment of Rural Women. *Kurukshetra. Journal of Rural Development*, *56*(11), 3–5.

Report of the Committee on Medium-term Path on Financial Inclusion (CMPFI), Chairman Mr. Deepak Mohanty, December 2015

Reserve Bank of India. (2015-16). *Report on Trends and Progress of Banking in India 2015-2016*. Retrieved on May 20, 2017 from https://rbidocs.rbi.org.in/rdocs/Publications/PDFs/0FRTP16A120A29D260148E58B484D4A60E381BB.PDF

Reserve Bank of India. (n.d.). *RBI: Scripts*. Retrieved from RBI.ORD: https://rbi.org.in/scripts/bs_viewcontent.aspx?Id=2598

Resurgent India. (2016). *Financial inclusion summit 2016*. Retrieved from http://cashlesscatalyst.org/wp-content/uploads/2017/01/Financial-Inclusion-Summit.pdf

Richez-Battesti, N. (2006). Gouvernance coopérative et reconquête du sociétariat: une aventure inachevée? Le cas des banques coopératives en France. *XXIIème Conférence Internationale de recherche coopérative*.

Sandeen, C. (2008). Boomers, Xers, and Millennials: Who are they and what do they really want from continuing higher education? *Continuing Higher Education Review*, *72*, 11–31.

Sarma, M. (2008). *Index of Financial Inclusion*. Indian Council for Research on International Economic, Relations Working Paper No. 215, ICRIER.

Sarma, M. (2008). *Index of financial inclusion*. New Delhi: Indian Council for Research on International Economics Relations.

Sarma, M., & Pais, J. (2011). Financial Inclusion and Development. *Journal of International Development*, *23*(5), 613–628. doi:10.1002/jid.1698

Scaraboto, D. (2015). Selling, sharing, and everything in between: The hybrid economies of collaborative networks. *The Journal of Consumer Research*, *42*(1), 152–176. doi:10.1093/jcr/ucv004

Schaus, P. (2016). *What millennials want from their bank.* ABA Bank Marketing. Retrieved May 2017 from http://ababankmarketing.com/insights/what-millennials-want-from-their-bank/

Sendhilvelan, M., & Karthikeyan, K. (2006). No Frills Account: A Basic Drive for Financial Inclusion. Southern Economist, 45, 13 – 14.

Senthikumar, Iyyappan, & Subramaniam. (2012). *Customer awareness on electronic banking in Thanjavur town — An empirical study*. Academic Press.

Servon, L. J., & Kaestner, R. (2008). Consumer financial literacy and the impact of online banking on the financial behavior of lower-income bank customers. *The Journal of Consumer Affairs*, *42*(2), 271–305. doi:10.1111/j.1745-6606.2008.00108.x

Shah, P., & Dubhashi, M. (2015). Review Paper on Financial Inclusion-The Means of Inclusive Growth. *Chanakya International Journal of Business Research*, *1*(1), 37–48. doi:10.15410/cijbr/2015/v1i1/61403

Sharma, A., & Kukereja, S. (2013). An Analytical Study: Relevance of Financial Inclusion for Developing Nations. Research Inventy. *International Journal of Engineering Science*, *2*(6), 15–20.

Sharma, P., & Sachdeva, S. (2014). Financial Inclusion in India - Issues and Challenges. *International Journal of Management and Social Sciences Research*, *3*(6), 41–44.

Shetty, N., & Pinto, D. (2015). Financial Exclusion: Concept, Causes & Consequences, A Tri-Dimensional Literature Analysis. *International Journal of Applied Financial Management Perspectives*, *4*(1), 1605–1613.

Shodhganga. (n.d.). *Inflibnet: Shodhganga.* Retrieved from Shodhganga: http://shodhganga.inflibnet.ac.in/bitstream/10603/2031/13/13_chapter%204.pdf

Shubhashis. (2009). How Can Technology Facilitate Financial Inclusion in India? *Review of Market Integration*, 23.

Shukla, T., & Singh, A. (2015). Financial Inclusion: An Empirical Study of Banking Products. *International Conference on Management and Information Systems*, 17-27.

Shyam, M. (2013). *Finacle: Solutions: Thought Papers: Documents: Infosys.* Retrieved from Infosys: http://www.infosys.com/finacle/solutions/thought-papers/Documents/Evolution-of-cheques-and-paper-based-clearing-in-India.pdf

Simplydecoded. (2012, 11 3). *Business and Economics: SimplyDecoded.* Retrieved from Simply Decoded: http://www.simplydecoded.com/2012/11/03/what-is-micr/

Singh S. D. (2010). Saving approaches of Self-Help Group Members- a study with reference to Manipur. *Prajnan, Journal of Social and Management Sciences, 39*(1), 29-39.

Singh, A. (2016). Digital Literacy: How Prepared Is India to Embrace It? *International Journal of Digital Literacy*, 7.

Singh, C. (2016). *Challenges to financial inclusion.* Retrieved on May 1, 2017 from http://www.thehindubusinessline.com/opinion/jan-dhan-yojana-fraud-should-be-curbed/article9169214.ece

Singh, H., & Sekhon, M. K. (2005). Cash-in Benefits of the Kisan Credit Card Scheme: Onus is Upon the Farmer. *Indian Journal of Agricultural Economics, 60*(3), 319–334.

Singh, S. (2016). A study on financial inclusion awareness among selected working women of Satna (M.P.). *International Journal of Science Techology and Management, 5*(4), 122–128.

Sohn, S. H., Joo, S. H., Grable, J. E., Lee, S., & Kim, M. (2012). Adolescents' financial literacy: The role of financial socialization agents, financial experiences, and money attitudes in shaping financial literacy among South Korean youth. *Journal of Adolescence, 35*(4), 969–980. doi:10.1016/j.adolescence.2012.02.002 PMID:22418452

Srinivasan. (2007). Policy Issues and Role of Banking System in Financial Inclusion. *Economic and Political Weekly, 42*(30), 3091-3093+3095.

Sriram, D. N. (2016). Financial Inclusion in India: A Review. *Review of Management*, 17.

Srivastava, D. P., & Kumar, M. (2011). Consumer Behavior In Rural Marketing-A New Paradigm. *Asian Journal of Technology & Management Research, 1*(1). Retrieved from www.ajtmr.com/papers/vol1issue1/consumer-behaviorin-rural-marketing.pdf

Srivastava, U., & Gopalkrishnan, S. (2015). Impact of Big Data Analytics on Banking Sector: Learning for Indian Banks. *Procedia Computer Science, 50*, 643–652. doi:10.1016/j.procs.2015.04.098

Stanley, M. (n.d.). *Get ready for India's internet boom. Morgan Stanley.*

Strauss, W., & Howe, N. (1991). Generations: The history of America's future, 1584 to 2069. New York: Academic Press.

Subbarao, D. (2009). *Duvvuri Subbarao: Financial Inclusion - Challenges and Opportunities.* Reserve Bank of India. Retrieved from https://www.bis.org/review/r091215b.pdf

Subbarao. (2009). *Financial Inclusion: Challenges and Opportunities.* Remarks by Dr. D. Subbarao, Governor, Reserve Bank of India at the Bankers' Club in Kolkata.

Subrahmanyam, N. (2009). Microfinance and SHG-Bank Linkage: Regional analysis and perspectives. *Prajnan. Journal of Social and Management Sciences, 38*(3), 183–202.

Subrashanka. (2014, February 4). *slideshare.* Retrieved from https://www.slideshare.net/bobsubhrasankha/marketing-credit-card

Sukaram, K. (2015). Financial Access: Inclusion and Literacy. Symbiosis Centre for Management Studies, 3(1), 188-207.

Swamy, V. (2014). Financial Inclusion, Gender Dimension, and Economic Impact on Poor Households. *World Development, 20*, 1–15. doi:10.1016/j.worlddev.2013.10.019

Tangirala, H. S. K. (2008). SHG is a tool of Economic Development of Co-operatives and its members. *Kurukshetra. Journal of Rural Development*, *57*(2), 22–24.

Tanya Jakimow, P. K. (2006). A Critique of the Blueprint for Self-help Groups in India. *Indian Journal of Gender Studies*, *13*(3), 375–400.

Tejmani, S. N. (2009). Microfinance practices in India: An overview. *International Review of Business Research Papers*, *5*(5), 131–146.

Thaler, R., & Sunstein, C. (2009). *Nudge: Improving decisions about health, wealth, and happiness*. New York, NY: Penguin.

The World Bank. (2014). *Global Findex*. Retrieved from http://www.worldbank.org/globalfindex

The World Bank. (2018). *Overview*. Retrieved on May 1, 2017 from http://www.worldbank.org/en/topic/financialinclusion/overview

Thorat, U. (2007). *Usha Thorat: Financial Inclusion - the Indian Experience*. Financial Inclusion Conference 2007. London. BIS Review. Retrieved from https://www.bis.org/review/r070626f.pdf

Thorat, U. (2007). *Financial Inclusion-the Indian experience*. London, UK: Speech at HMT-DFID Financial Inclusion Conference.

Tiwari, A., & Poddar, S. (2017, May). *The Four Zones: A Missing Chapter in the Financial Inclusion Guidebook*. Retrieved October 3, 2017, from www.microsave.net: http://blog.microsave.net/the-four-zones-a-missing-chapter-in-the-financial-inclusion-guidebook/

Tiwari, A., Srivastava, B., Chandra, R., Poddar, S., & Parmar, N. (2017). *Understanding the Financial Behaviour of the Mass Market: The Key to Financial Inclusion*. Microsave. Retrieved October 4, 2017, from http://www.microsave.net/resource/understanding_the_financial_behaviour_of_the_mass_market_the_key_to_financial_inclusion

Torreblanca, E. (2016, July 22). *Créditos blandos a jóvenes mexicanos*. Retrieved April 25, 2017, from http://www.elfinanciero.com.mx/opinion/creditos-blandos-a-jovenes-mexicanos.html

Tracey, L., & Moyle, M. D. (2006). *Personal and Economic Empowerment in Rural Indian Women*. Academic Press.

Tripathi, R., Yadav, N., & Shastri, R. K. (2016). Financial inclusion in India through Pradhan Mantri Jan Dhan Yojana: An empirical analysis of statistical evidence. *Indian Journal of Finance*, *10*(10), 42–55. doi:10.17010/ijf/2016/v10i10/103014

Vasantha, S., Varadharaj, V., & Varadharajan, R. (2013). Self Help Group Bank Linkage Model As Catalyst For Financial Inclusion In An Unbanked Rural Area. *Indian Journal of Commerce & Management Studies*, *4*(1).

Verdone, M. (2015). How to be hip: Big banks can market to millennials. *Advertising Age*. Retrieved May 2017 from http://adage.com/article/cmo-strategy/hip-ways-banks-market-millennials/299176/

Verma, Y., & Garg, P. (2016). Pradhan Mantri Jan Dhan Yojana (PMJDY): A step towards eradicating financial untouchability. *Indian Journal of Finance, 10*(1), 56–64. doi:10.17010/ijf/2016/v10i1/85845

Vijayalakshmi, D., Gowda, K. N., Jamuna, K. V., Ray, B. R., & Sajjan, J. T. (2012). Empowerment of self help group women through value addition of finger millet. *Journal of Dairying, Foods and Home Sciences, 31*(3), 223-226.

VISA. (2016). *Accelerating The Growth of Digital Payments in India' Department of Payment and Settlement System*. Visa.

Wansink, B. (2015). Change their choice! Changing behavior using the CAN approach and activism research. *Psychology and Marketing, 32*(5), 486–500. doi:10.1002/mar.20794

Wharton. (2014, September 18). *Financial Inclusion in India: Moving Beyond Bank Accounts*. Retrieved October 3, 2017, from knowledge.wharton.upenn.edu: http://knowledge.wharton.upenn.edu/article/financial-inclusion-india-aims-move-beyond-bank-accounts/

Wizbowski, R. (2014, March 21). *Articles: Datacardedge*. Retrieved from Datacardedge: http://datacardedge.com/articles/debit-cards-emerging-growth-opportunities-banks-india/

Wright, G. A. N., Chhopra, P., Mehta, S., & Shukla, V. (2013). *Financial Inclusion Through Digital Financial Services*. Retrieved from http://www.microsave.net/files/pdf/1367585756_Financial_Inclusion_Through_E_M_Banking.pdf

About the Contributors

Juan Amezcua is a PhD in Business Management specialized in responsible consumer behavior. 20 years of teaching experience in marketing strategies with undergraduate and graduate students. Business Consultant.

Arturo Briseño is a PhD in Business Management specialized in Corporate Social Responsibility and firm performance. Professor in management at both graduate and undergraduate levels

Alicia De la Pena is a PhD in Business Administration under the responsible consumer behavior research track. 25 years teaching experience to undergraduate and graduate students. Business consultant.

Rachid Elotmani is a Researcher Professor at ISCAE of Casablanca, teaching Marketing and Sales.

Sara Elouadi is a Professor Researcher at Hassan II University and author of several articles on employee ownership. She teaches accounting and finance.

Kushendra Mishra is an Associate Professor, Department of Rural Management, Babasaheb Bhimrao Ambedkar University (A Central University), Lucknow.

Vaibhav Misra is currently associated with Faculty of Management, Symbiosis International University, Pune as Research Scholar. The authors is also Member of International Board with European Center for Business, Education and Science, Bulgaria and also included in Editorial Board with some of the journals of international repute.

Vijay Prakash Misra is an Assistant Professor, Symbiosis Centre for Management Studies, Pune, Symbiosis International University.

Smriti Pathak completed PhD in economics and Management from Bhopal University in 2013. Have an academic experience of 12 years and corporate experience of 2 years. Have written more than 15 research papers, book chapters.

Deepa Pillai is an Associate Professor at Symbiosis School of Banking and Finance, Pune and is also an Associate member of the Institute of Cost and Management Accountants of India.

Alfredo Sánchez-Aldape is a PhD in business management. Experience in Balanced Scored Card and Hospital Administration. Professor with 15 years of experience.

Juana Saucedo-Soto is a PhD in Business Management. 30 years of experience teaching business management to undergraduate students.

Richa Sawhney is a practising chartered accountant with over 20 years of experience in tax and regulatory matters. Core area of specialisation is international tax. Also, a member of the Institute of Cost and Management Accountants of India. She has a Bachelor's degree in Commence from prestigious Shri Ram College of Commerce, Delhi. She has been associated with organisations such as PwC and Deloitte for about 16 years. She leads the L& E division in PwC. As part of Knowledge Management, Centre of Excellence and L&E initiatives she has been actively involved in monitoring, analysing key tax policy developments and making representations to the concerned authorities. She was part of lobbying initiatives on Direct Taxes Code, LLPs and Withholding Tax matters. Developed position papers on emerging tax issues, thought leadership publications on policy developments such as GAAR, and several other publications such as the PwC Master Guides, Annual Budget Reports and Doing Business in India Reports. Regular contributor of articles on emerging tax issues in International tax journals and portals. She has been closely associated with the Direct Tax Committees of Assocham and Amcham. Also associated as faculty member with Institute of Chartered Accountants of India for their e-learning program for Direct Taxation.

Abhineet Saxena is a post-doctoral fellow-ICSSR, Deptt. of Economic Administration and Financial Management, University of Rajasthan, Jaipur.

Ashish Sharma is an astute professional with 16 years of academic and administrative experience with major contribution in Training and development. Development of capability and competency matrix across all work areas Academic Institutions, Corporate Expertise in managing overall operations with focus on profitability and student-parent satisfaction keeping in view the organization's mission with proven ability in enhancing production process operations. Deft at setting the academic tone, hire, evaluate, and help improve the skills of teachers and other staff. Adept at educating students and parents about colleges, admission process, walk-ins, trends, procedures & testing. Extensive experience in general administrative activities, personnel management, corporate policy implementation and facilities management across assignments. Worked on Setting up of new facility of training and development including the content development and continuous up gradation. Worked on various modules on Communication, Grooming, Selling Skills, Customer Service and complaint Handling etc.

Pooja Sharma has spent 22 years being a technologist for the banking industry. She holds an MBA from Indian Institute of Management, Bangalore in Finance & International Business. She is currently pursuing her Doctoral degree and is also a senior consultant at a leading Indian IT company in their Banking and Financial Services unit. During her 2 decades of experience, she has played an instrumental part of the transformation journey of the Indian banking system from the days of core banking systems to the current wave of digital and analytics. In 2007, she successfully incubated the financial inclusion business for one of the largest technology players in the market. Her work and expertise lie in understanding and designing financial services solutions for the 'bottom of the pyramid' with special focus on rural & community banking. She has written a few research papers on varied topics, and writes a blog under heading of 'poojanomics.com'. Besides work, she actively supports the causes of education and women empowerment.

Yuvraj Sharma is working as an analyst at SLK Global Solutions Pvt. Ltd., Bangalore. He has worked for the industry for 4 years and has been into analytics since the past 2.5 years. His area of interest is exploring knowledge through writing research papers, case studies and articles on emerging technologies. He has completed his Master's in IT and B-tech in computer science from Rajasthan Technical University.

Parul Tolani works as freelance, completed M.Phil from Babasaheb Bhimrao Ambedkar University, Lucknow.

Ravi Kumar V. V. is an Associate Professor with Symbiosis Institute of Business Management, Pune and an Ex banker.

Anubha Vashisht is Dy Director and Associate Professor with Symbiosis Centre for Management Studies, Symbiosis International University, Noida.

Rahul Vyas is an Assistant Professor and Coordinator at Pacific Business School. He is a Ph D in Management. His areas of research interest include Financial inclusion, Public Policy and Managerial Economics.

Index

www.ingramcontent.com/pod-product-compliance
Lightning Source LLC
LaVergne TN
LVHW081337300926
849161LV00008B/1993